Pages listed are first occurrences. ☑ P9-CQW-548

Topography of a bird

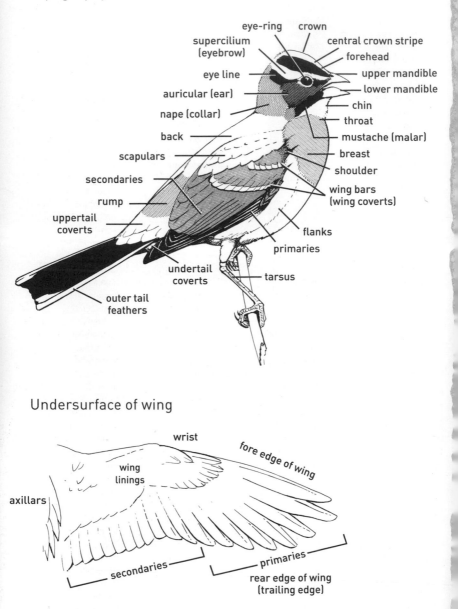

eye-ring crown
supercilium (eyebrow) central crown stripe
forehead
eye line upper mandible
lower mandible
auricular (ear) chin
nape (collar) throat
back mustache (malar)
scapulars breast
secondaries shoulder
rump wing bars (wing coverts)
uppertail coverts flanks
primaries
undertail coverts tarsus
outer tail feathers

Undersurface of wing

wrist
fore edge of wing
wing linings
axillars
secondaries
primaries
rear edge of wing (trailing edge)

On the upper surface of the secondaries, some waterfowl have a bright-colored patch, called a *speculum.*

PETERSON FIELD GUIDE

TO

BIRDS

of Western North America

Area Covered
by This Book

PETERSON FIELD GUIDE TO

BIRDS

of Western North America

FOURTH EDITION

ROGER TORY PETERSON

HOUGHTON MIFFLIN HARCOURT

BOSTON NEW YORK

WITH CONTRIBUTIONS FROM

Michael DiGiorgio
Paul Lehman
Michael O'Brien

AND

Jeffrey A. Gordon
Larry Rosche
Bill Thompson III

Photographs by Jeffrey A. Gordon

Key to photographs: i: Hermit Warbler; ii–iii: Trumpeter Swans; vi: Pinyon Jay;
vii: Wilson's Phalarope; ix: Calliope Hummingbird; xii: Heermann's Gull; xiii: Black-
throated Sparrow; xv: Williamson's Sapsucker; xvi: Eared Grebe; 1: Green-tailed
Towhee; 14–15: Spotted Owl; 368–369: Wrentit; 370: Western Meadowlark;
470: Lazuli Bunting; 480: Black-crowned Night-Heron

For information about permission to reproduce selections from this book, write to
trade.permissions@hmhco.com or to Permissions, Houghton Mifflin Harcourt
Publishing Company, 3 Park Avenue, 19th Floor, New York, New York 10016.

www.hmhco.com

PETERSON FIELD GUIDES and PETERSON FIELD GUIDE SERIES are registered
trademarks of Houghton Mifflin Harcourt Publishing Company.

Library of Congress Cataloging-in-Publication Data

Peterson, Roger Tory, 1908–1996.
Peterson field guide to birds of Western North America / Roger Tory
Peterson ; with contributions from Michael DiGiorgio ... [et al.] — 4th ed.
p. cm.
Rev. ed. of: A field guide to Western birds. 3rd ed. 1990.
Includes index.
ISBN 978-0-547-15270-7
1. Birds — West (U.S.) — Identification. 2. Birds — Canada, Western — Identification.
I. DiGiorgio, Michael. II. Peterson, Roger Tory, 1908–1996. Field guide to Western
birds. III. Title. IV. Title: Field guide to birds of Western North America.
QL683.W4P4 2009
598.0978 — dc22
2009039158

Book design by Anne Chalmers

Printed in China

SCP 10 9
4500696451

THE LEGACY OF AMERICA'S GREAT NATURALIST AND CREATOR of this field guide series, Roger Tory Peterson, is preserved through the programs and work of the Roger Tory Peterson Institute of Natural History (RTPI), located in his birthplace of Jamestown, New York. RTPI is a national nature education organization with a mission to continue the legacy of Roger Tory Peterson by promoting the teaching and study of nature and to thereby create knowledge of and appreciation and responsibility for the natural world. RTPI also preserves and exhibits Dr. Peterson's extraordinary collection of artwork, photography, and writing.

You can become a part of this worthy effort by joining RTPI. Simply call RTPI's membership department at 800-758-6841 ext. 226, fax 716-665-3794, or e-mail members@rtpi.org for a free one-year membership with the purchase of this book. Check out our award-winning website at www.enaturalist.org. You can link to all our programs and activities from there.

CONTENTS

FOREWORD

Sometime in my early teens I became intensely interested in bird watching. True, I had already spent a significant amount of time watching and learning about birds—not surprising, given the household in which I was raised—but it grew into an extremely focused pursuit. I spent countless hours wandering woods and slogging through salt marshes near our home in Old Lyme, Connecticut, searching for new birds. In the process, I managed to wear out several copies of the Peterson Field Guide—and I had a great time. I also acquired a much deeper understanding of my surroundings. I think most people get their start in natural history this way. In fact, I can remember someone assuring me that, at one time, virtually all the heads of the top environmental organizations in this country got their starts with a Peterson Field Guide in hand.

Being able to recognize and identify birds is crucial to our awareness of the world around us. My father used the comings and goings of birds as both a biological clock and a litmus test for the condition of the environment. The arrival and departure of migrating birds signaled to him changes in both weather and climatic conditions. The increase or decrease in the population of certain species gave him insight into the overall health of the environment—changes for either good or ill. As his friend Bob Lewin once noted, "Roger was always interested in numbers." Whether it was counting the number of moths on our screen door or the number of flamingos on a lake in Africa, the results were equally significant.

Dad always likened the process of writing a field guide to serving a prison sentence. The projects are always lengthy, and the spatial and visual constraints pronounced. Unlike stream of consciousness, field guide writing seems more akin to composing a telegram—fitting the maximum amount of information into a minimal amount of space. Likewise, the illustration can never be free and loose; it must always be tightly controlled, showing the essence of the bird in question. In both these endeavors, Dad excelled. Someone once confided to me that Dad's rendition of a robin was not only a robin, but the perfect robin. Somehow he was able to convey a bird outside of a specific moment in time and place: the robin idealized, with feathers neatly patterned and plump. His results were all the more remarkable when one watched how they were achieved. He worked mostly from memory, using only a dry, beat-up specimen of the bird for details of anatomy and occasionally a photograph or two. Somehow he was able to piece together an image of the bird as it should have been. Not just any robin, but all robins.

Dad's innovative approach was the product of a rich variety of influences. He was born in Jamestown, a small town in upstate New York known primarily for farming and light manufacture. His first foray into art was encouraged by his seventh-grade schoolteacher, and much of what he learned about birds was either self-taught or picked up from those around him. His family could not afford to send him to college, so he put himself through art school in New York City instead. This was fortuitous, as his time in New York shaped much of what was to come. There he found inspiration from such luminaries in the birding world as Louis Agassiz Fuertes and Ludlow Griscom, and he fell in with a group of avid young birders who called themselves the Bronx County Bird Club, many of whom went on to prominent careers in the biological sciences.

In 1929, Bill Vogt, Bronx County Bird Club member and editor of *Audubon* magazine's precursor, *Bird-Lore*, suggested that Dad combine his expertise in art and bird identification to create a field guide. This was at a time when definitive identification was more often made with a shotgun and dissecting knife than a pair of binoculars. The Peterson system of identification, relying on arrows to point out differences in similar-looking species, seems both simple and obvious in hindsight. At the time, however, it was an enormous innovation. Suddenly the average person could confidently identify the birds around him with just a pair of binoculars and one small book. Birding went from being the slightly odd pursuit of an eccentric few to being one of the largest spectator sports in America today. The repercussions have been enormous.

Each of Dad's many skills and talents was noteworthy in and of itself, but pieced together, they made him truly unique. His skills as an artist were unquestioned. His early artistic training caused him to emphasize the visual rather than the technical—an especially useful trait when trying to design an identification guide for the uninitiated. At the same time, he was a lifelong student of birds and had a tremendous reservoir of technical information. Many consider him to have been one of the finest field naturalists of his era. His writing style was simple, direct, and entertaining, reducing complex information to the essential bones without losing a certain lyrical quality, synthesizing scattered information into original observation.

Less frequently mentioned, but well known to his peers, was his extraordinarily acute sense of hearing. Yale University School of Medicine tested his hearing late in his life and found it to be exceptional—well into the 99th percentile of human capability—allowing him to register frequencies far above the norm. Bird walks with him were always a source of wonder. He was forever hearing and identifying distant birds that the rest of us could barely discern. I am still amazed by his uncanny ability to render bird calls into written English so that they're immediately recognizable. Overlaying all this was his incredible focus. For 70 or more years, his single overriding pleasure was the pursuit and identification of birds, to which he brought inspirational energy, skill, and enthusiasm.

In the foreword to the fifth edition of *A Field Guide to the Birds of Eastern and Central North America,* Robert Bateman referred to Dad's lifework as causing ever-expanding "ripples on a pond." This is apt. More than anything else, Dad thought of himself as a teacher. His greatest wish was to pass along his love of birds and the outdoors, to imbue the rest of us with the same sense of wonder and environmental responsibility that he himself derived from watching birds. His childhood interest, like mine, had morphed into something larger. While birds always remained his focus, they were the most visible aspect of a much greater ecological system. For him, they acted as the early warning system for the overall condition of the environment. By opening up the world of birds through his field guides, he hoped our relationship with nature would shift from one of exploitation to one of stewardship. In this, he has had more than a little success. With each new field guide owner, our world becomes a little richer, a little more full of promise. It may indeed be as Bateman says: "Roger Tory Peterson's life has been one of the most important lives of the last 100 years."

—Lee Allen Peterson

EDITOR'S NOTE

In the past 75 years, ever since Roger Tory Peterson's pioneering *Field Guide to the Birds* changed the way we look at birds and jump-started the environmental movement, many birders have grown up using their Peterson Field Guide, and the book holds a special place in their hearts. Today, however, there are more field guides than ever, and more on the way. The Peterson guide is still set apart by its original concept. The Peterson Identification System is a powerful tool, just as useful and easy to understand today as it was when the first Peterson Field Guide was published. In 2008, we honored the centennial of Roger Peterson's birth with a new edition combining eastern and western North America. It was not simply a commemoration but a useful, up-to-date resource. This new edition for western North America is based on the considerable updating that was done for the North American guide and additionally incorporates changes introduced in the Fiftieth Supplement to the American Ornithologists' Union *Check-List of North American Birds,* released in 2009.

Revisions include an update of the taxonomy (to include, for example, splits, such as Canada and Cackling geese, and name changes, such as Oldsquaw to Long-tailed Duck). Birds newly recorded in North America, such as Black-tailed Gull, Long-billed Murrelet, and Eurasian Collared-Dove, are included. The text has been revised to accurately reflect our current knowledge of birds. The range maps are all new. The art has been updated where necessary. New paintings were done for birds that didn't previously occur in North America and for figures that Peterson painted over or discarded as he adapted the plates from one book to another. For some birds, the information we have about them is better than what was available when Peterson was painting, so a few of his paintings have been replaced with new ones; others have been digitally enhanced.

Peterson was an innovator. If he were a young bird watcher today, there's a good chance he would be at the forefront of new birding technology. To accompany this book, we've created a set of videos that are easy to use, educational, and fun. These supplements to the book cover key individual species, popular groupings of birds, and such topics as how to use range maps, identification basics, and bird topography. Jeffrey Gordon and Bill Thompson III created the videos, which we hope will enhance your enjoyment of birds and bird watching. The videos can be found on the Peterson Field Guides channel on YouTube.

When Roger Tory Peterson died, we lost a uniquely talented artist and naturalist. He had a profound influence on a vast number of young naturalists, however, who have devoted their lives to birds and other animals, the environment, education, art, and other vocations and avocations. The team of expert birders who brought a wealth of knowledge to the creation of the *Peterson Field Guide to Birds of North America* worked diligently to enhance Peterson's legacy while ensuring that all of the content was current and highly useful for today's birder. Paul Lehman and Bill Thompson III revised all the text. Michael O'Brien painted the new species, laid out the plates, directed the digital work, and consulted editorially. Paul Lehman supplied the information for the new range maps, graphic artist Larry Rosche created the maps digitally, and Marshall Iliff reviewed them all. Michael DiGiorgio did the digital enhancements of the art and executed the layout of the plates digitally. Kimball Garrett reviewed and revised some of the voice descriptions.

For this fourth edition of the *Peterson Field Guide to Birds of Western North America,* Paul Lehman and Michael O'Brien completely overhauled the text. Michael also reviewed the plates, and Paul updated the range maps. Michael DiGiorgio painstakingly executed the digital layout of the plates. At Houghton Mifflin Harcourt, Anne Chalmers, Teresa Elsey, Katrina Kruse, Jill Lazer, Sara Shaffer, and Taryn Roeder all played critical roles in producing this book.

At a time when environmental concerns are paramount, it's essential that we as readers revisit the sources that inspired and deepened our appreciation of the natural world. Roger Tory Peterson's voice is for the generations, and it's with tremendous pride that we present it to you, revitalized and as relevant as always.

—LISA A. WHITE

PETERSON FIELD GUIDE

TO

BIRDS

of Western
North America

INTRODUCTION

How to Identify Birds

Veteran birders will know how to use this book. Beginners, however, should spend some time becoming familiar in a general way with the illustrations. The plates, for the most part, have been grouped in taxonomic sequence. However, in cases where there is a great similarity of shape and action, similar-appearing birds may be grouped outside their strict taxonomic order. This should aid in field identification and not frustrate the true taxonomist to any great degree.

Birds that could be confused are grouped together when possible and are arranged in identical profile for direct comparison. The arrows point to outstanding field marks, which are explained opposite. The text also gives aids such as voice, actions, and habitat, not visually portrayable, and under a separate heading discusses species that might be confused. The general range is not described for most species in the text. The annotated three-color range maps in the back of the book (pp. 372–369) provide detailed range information. Thumbnail versions of the maps also appear next to the species accounts for quick reference.

In addition to the plates of birds normally found in the region covered in this field guide, there are also plates depicting accidentals from Eurasia, the sea, and the Tropics, as well as some of the exotic escapes that are sometimes seen.

What Is the Bird's Size?

Acquire the habit of comparing a new bird with some familiar "yardstick"—a House Sparrow, robin, pigeon, etc.—so that you can say to yourself, "Smaller than a robin, a little larger than a House Sparrow." The measurements in this book represent lengths in inches (with centimeters in parentheses) from bill tip to tail tip of specimens on their backs as in museum trays. For species that show considerable size variation, a range of measurements is given. For less variable species, only one measurement is given.

What Is Its Shape?
Is it plump like a starling (left) or slender like a cuckoo (right)?

What Shape Are Its Wings?
Are they rounded like a bobwhite's (left) or sharply pointed like a Barn Swallow's (right)?

What Shape Is Its Bill?
Is it small and fine like a warbler's (1), stout and short like a seed-cracking sparrow's (2), dagger-shaped like a tern's (3), or hook-tipped like a bird of prey's (4)?

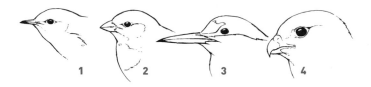

1   2   3   4

What Shape Is Its Tail?

Is it deeply forked like a Barn Swallow's (1), square-tipped like a Cliff Swallow's (2), notched like a Tree Swallow's (3), rounded like a Western Scrub-Jay's (4), or pointed like a Mourning Dove's (5)?

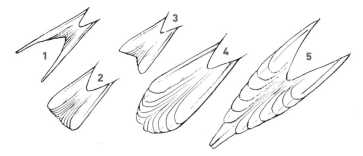

How Does It Behave?

Does it cock its tail like a wren or hold it down like a flycatcher? Does it wag its tail? Does it sit erect on an open perch, dart after an insect, and return as a flycatcher does?

Does It Climb Trees?

If so, does it climb upward in spirals like a creeper (left), in jerks like a woodpecker (center) using its tail as a brace, or go down headfirst like a nuthatch (right)?

How Does It Fly?

Does it undulate (dip up and down) like a flicker (1)? Does it fly straight and fast like a dove (2)? Does it hover like a kingfisher (3)? Does it glide or soar?

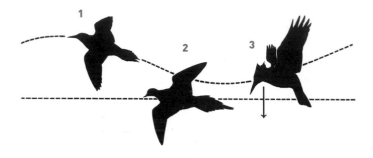

Does It Swim?

Does it sit low in the water like a loon (1) or high like a gallinule (2)? If a duck, does it dive like a scaup or a scoter (3) or dabble and upend like a Mallard (4)?

Does It Wade?

Is it large and long-legged like a heron or small like a sandpiper? If one of the latter, does it probe the mud or pick at things? Does it teeter or bob?

What Are Its Field Marks?

Some birds can be identified by color alone, but most birds are not that easy. The most important aids are what we call field marks, which are, in effect, the "trademarks of nature." Note whether the breast is spotted as in a thrush (1), streaked as in a thrasher (2), or plain as in a cuckoo (3).

Tail Pattern

Does the tail have a "flash pattern"—a white tip as in the Eastern Kingbird (1), white patches in the outer corners as in the Spotted Towhee (2), or white sides as in the juncos (3)?

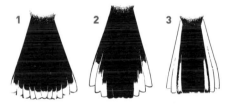

Rump Patch

Does it have a light rump like a Cliff Swallow (1) or flicker (2)? Northern Harrier, Yellow-rumped Warbler, and several shorebirds also have distinctive rump patches.

Eye Stripes and Eye-ring

Does the bird have a stripe above, through, or below the eye, or a combination of these stripes? Does it have a striped crown? A ring around the eye, or "spectacles"? A "mustache" stripe? These details are important in many small songbirds.

Wing Bars

Do the wings have light wing bars or not? Their presence or absence is important in recognizing many warblers, vireos, and flycatchers. Wing bars may be single or double, bold or obscure.

Wing Pattern

The basic wing pattern of ducks (shown below), shorebirds, and other water birds is very important. Notice whether the wings have patches (1) or stripes (2), are solidly colored (3), or have contrasting black tips.

Bird Songs and Calls

Using sounds to identify birds can be just as useful as using visual clues. In fact, in many situations, birds are much more readily identified by sound than by sight. The species accounts here include a brief entry on voice, with interpretations of these songs and calls, in an attempt to give birders some handle on the vocalizations they hear. Authors of bird books have attempted, with varying success, to fit songs and calls into syllables, words, and phrases. Musical notations, comparative descriptions, and even ingenious systems of symbols have also been employed. To supplement this verbal interpretation, there are recording collections available for nearly every region of the world and for individual groups of birds. The *Peterson Birding by Ear* CDs provide a step-by-step method for learning how to develop your listening and identification skills. Preparation in advance for particular species or groups greatly enhances your ability to identify them. Some birders do a majority of their birding by ear, and there is no substitute for actual sounds—for getting out into the field and tracking down the songster and committing the song to memory. However, an audio library is a wonderful resource to return home to when attempting to identify a bird heard in the field. Many such collections can now be taken into the field on digital audio devices. *Caution:* If using recordings to attract birds, limit the number of playbacks, and do not use them on threatened species or in heavily birded areas.

Bird Nests

The more time you spend in the field becoming familiar with bird behavior, the more skilled you'll become at finding bird nests. It is as exciting to keep a bird nest list as it is to keep a life list. Remember, if you happen to find a nest during the breeding season, leave the site as undisturbed as possible. Back away, and do not touch the nest, eggs, or young birds. Often squirrels, raccoons, and several other mammals, grackles, and cowbirds are more than happy to have you "point out" a nest and will raid it if you disrupt the site or call attention to it. Many people find young birds that have just left the nest and may appear to be alone. Usually they are not lost but are under the watchful eye of a parent bird and are best left in place rather than scooped up and taken to a foreign environment. In the winter, nest hunting can be great fun and has little impact, as most nests will never be used again. They are easy to see once the foliage is gone, and it can be a challenge to attempt to identify the maker. Books such as *A Field Guide to Birds' Nests* and *A Field Guide to Western Birds' Nests,* both in the Peterson Field Guide series, will expand your ornithological expertise.

Conservation

Birds undeniably contribute to our pleasure and quality of life. But they also are sensitive indicators of the environment, a sort of "ecological litmus paper," and hence more meaningful than just chickadees and cardinals that brighten the suburban garden, grouse and ducks that fill the sportsman's bag, or rare warblers and shorebirds that excite the field birder. The observation and recording of bird populations over time lead inevitably to environmental awareness and can signal impending changes.

To this end, please help the cause of wildlife conservation and education by contributing to or taking part in the work of the following organizations: **The Nature Conservancy** (4245 North Fairfax Drive, Suite 100, Arlington, VA 22203; www.nature.org), **National Audubon Society** (700 Broadway, New York, NY 10003; www.audubon.org), **Defenders of Wildlife** (1130 17th Street NW, Washington, DC 20036; www.defenders.org), **Roger Tory Peterson Institute of Natural History** (311 Curtis Street, Jamestown, NY 14701; www.rtpi.org), **National Wildlife Federation** (11100 Wildlife Center Drive, Reston, VA 20190; www.nwf.org), **World Wildlife Fund** (1250 24th Street NW, PO Box 97180, Washington, DC 20090; www.wwf.org), **Cornell Laboratory of Ornithology** (159 Sapsucker Woods Road, Ithaca, NY 14850; www.birds.cornell.edu), **Ducks Unlimited** (One Waterfowl Way, Memphis, TN 38120; www.ducks.org), **Bird-Life International** (Wellbrook Court, Girton Road, Cambridge CB3 0NA, U.K.; www.birdlife.org), **Partners in Flight** (www.partnersinflight.org), **American Bird Conservancy** (PO Box 249, The Plains, VA 20198; abcbirds.org), as well as your local land trust and natural heritage program and your local Audubon and ornithological societies and bird clubs. These and so many other groups that have come into the forefront of bird conservation in the last 20 years merit your support.

The Maps and Ranges of Birds

The ranges of many species have changed markedly over the past 50 or more years. Some species are expanding because of protection given them, changing habitats, bird feeding, or other factors. Some "increases" may simply be the result of more field-guide-educated birders being in the field, helping to more thoroughly document bird populations and distributions. Other avian species have diminished alarmingly and may have been extirpated from major parts of their range. The primary culprit here has been habitat loss, although other factors such as increased competition or predation from other species may sometimes be involved. Species that are in serious decline in North America run the gamut, from Ivory Gull to Lesser Prairie-Chicken and Loggerhead Shrike to Bewick's Wren, Rusty Blackbird, and Red Knot.

Successful introductions of some species, such as Trumpeter Swan and Eurasian Collared-Dove, have resulted in self-sustaining, growing populations (the latter was introduced to the Bahamas, then arrived in the U.S. on its own). And a good number of additional vagrant species — out-of-range visitors from faraway lands — continue to be found (such as a Brown-backed Solitaire in Arizona). Some species that were formerly thought to occur only exceptionally have, over the past several decades, become much more regular visitors (such as Lesser Black-backed Gull) and sometimes even local breeders (such as Ruddy Ground-Dove). It is not always certain if such changes in status are the result of actual population increases or if they merely reflect better observer coverage and advances in field identification skills.

Range maps need to be of sufficient size to denote adequate detail and to include written information on such topics as population trends and extralimital occurrences. Thus, the range maps in this guide have been purposely placed near the back of the book where they can be reproduced in a large size not possible in the main body of the text. The maps are organized taxonomically, following the order published by the American Ornithologists' Union. In addition, thumbnail versions of the same maps are placed in the main text next to the species accounts to provide a quick overview of a species' range without needing to turn the page. The key to the range maps is located on page 371 and also on the inside of the front cover, for quick reference.

Range maps don't depict how abundant a particular species is within its range. The following list defines terms of abundance used throughout the book. The definitions presume you're in the habitat and season in which a species would occur.

Common: Always or almost always encountered daily, usually in moderate to large numbers.

Fairly common: Usually encountered daily, generally not in large numbers.

Uncommon: Occurs in small numbers and may be missed on a substantial number of days.

Scarce: Present only in small numbers or difficult to find within its normal range.

Rare or very rare: Annual or probably annual in small numbers but still largely within its normal range.

Casual: Beyond its normal range; occurs at somewhat regular intervals but usually less frequently than annually.

Accidental: Beyond its normal range; one record or a very few records.

Vagrant: Beyond its normal range.

Local: Limited geographic range within the U.S. and Canada.

Introduced: Not native; deliberately released.

Exotic: Not native; either released or escaped. A term used especially for species that are present in limited numbers and may or may not be breeding. Other species, such as House Sparrow and European Starling, were also introduced but are so well established that, in the sense used here, they are no longer considered exotic.

Unestablished exotic: Nonnative releasee or escapee that does not have a naturalized breeding population, though some may be breeding in very localized areas.

Habitats

Gaining a familiarity with a wide range of habitats will greatly enhance your overall knowledge of the birds in a specific region, increase your skills, and add to your enjoyment of birding. It is unlikely you will ever see a meadowlark in an oak woodland or an Oak Titmouse in a meadow. Birders know this, and if they want to go out to run up a large day list, they do not remain in one habitat but shift from site to site based on time and species diversity for a given type of habitat.

A few birds do invade habitats other than their own at times, especially on migration. A warbler that spends the summer in Montana might be seen, on its journey through California, in a palm. In cities, migrating birds often have to make the best of it, like a Marsh Wren hiding in a weedy lot in downtown Los Angeles. Strong weather patterns can also alter where a bird happens to appear. Tropical storms, for example, can be a disaster for many species. As these violent storms sweep over the ocean, the eye can often "vacuum" up oceanic species that seek shelter in its calmness. Upon reaching land, these normally offshore species are faced with an entirely strange habitat and account for sightings such as a Laysan Albatross flying over Death Valley or numbers of storm-petrels on an inland reservoir in the desert Southwest.

Most species, however, are quite predictable for the major portion of their lives, and for the birder who has learned where to look, the rewards are great.

To start, familiarize yourself with individual habitat types. Become familiar with the dominant plant types that are indicators—for example, pinyon-juniper woods, grass-shrub meadows, salt- or freshwater wetlands—and keep accurate records of what species you find in each. In a short time you will have a working knowledge of the predominant species in each habitat, and this will help you with identification by allowing you to anticipate what might be found there.

The seasonal movements of birds at your sites will provide an overview of migrant species that come through at a given time and will be a reference point for future visits during these migration periods. A forest dotted with migrant warblers in spring may revert to relative quiet accented by the burry call of a Western Wood-Pewee in midsummer.

Be sure not to overlook cities and towns, where well-adapted species can be found. Peregrine Falcons have shown remarkable adaptability, nesting on strategic ledges in the walled canyons of many cities. The fertile grounds for hunting Rock Pigeons and European Starlings seem to suit this raptor quite well.

Ecotones are edges where two habitat types interface—a forest and a shrub meadow, for example. As this is not a gradual change, ecotones offer habitat for species from both of the adjoining areas and are therefore rich in bird life.

The changes in habitat over the years will also affect your favorite birding areas. Fields turn to shrubby lots and then woodlands. Savannah Sparrow and meadowlarks may move on, but Lazuli Buntings and Lincoln's Sparrows establish themselves. This dynamic is normal in the natural world. However, humankind's alterations to this process have had a great impact. Forest fragmentation is an example. As land development continues, it is affecting numerous species. A sudden disruption has a more drastic effect than a slow change, which allows for adaptation. As we divide up habitat with roadways, we have created a greater edge effect, and this allows Brown-headed Cowbirds to penetrate into forest areas where they would not have ventured in the past. They now parasitize many more species than before, and such parasitization is leading to marked declines in total numbers of many species. This forest fragmentation is also affecting the success rate of nestling fledging by increasing the numbers of some predators and by altering prime habitat requirements for obtaining food to raise the young.

Some species are obligates to a specific habitat type, and searching these areas greatly improves your chances of finding such birds. These include Golden-crowned Kinglet nesting in coniferous woodlands or American Dipper nesting exclusively along rushing mountain streams. Even in migration, many species remain faithful to selected habitats, such as waterthrushes along watercourses. Running or dripping water has proven to be an important attractant for migrating land birds, and in areas where fresh water is scarce, a water drip can be a gold mine for migrant warblers and other passerines.

Subspecies and Geographic Variation

Many species of birds inhabit wide geographic areas. The Song Sparrow *(Melospiza melodia),* for example, breeds throughout North America, from Mexico north into Alaska. In such a wide-ranging species, there are geographic subsets within the population that show distinct local plumage patterns and song variants. When the distinct geographic forms of a species reach a point when the population is dominated by individuals that are recognizably different from typical individuals of the "parent" species, the local group is formally designated a subspecies of the parent species. The subspecies is named by attaching a third, subspecific name to the scientific name of the species. Thus, the pale Song Sparrow of the southwestern United States is called *Melospiza melodia saltonis,* to distinguish that form from another subspecies. With at least 31 recognizable subspecies, the Song Sparrow ranks among the highest of North American birds in the number of its geographic varieties.

Often a subspecific group is so distinct from the parent species that several members can be easily recognized in the field by bird watchers. A good example of this is the Dark-eyed Junco *(Junco hyemalis)*. With 12 subspecies, at least 5 are easily discerned: the "Oregon," "Pink-sided," "White-winged," "Slate-colored," and "Gray-headed." For the birder, identification of subspecies can add greater challenges to birding and, when documented, valuable information, especially when subspecies are reclassified to full species status. Such has been the case, for example, with the splitting of Western Flycatcher *(Empidonax difficilis)* into Pacific-slope Flycatcher *(E. difficilis)* and Cordilleran Flycatcher *(E. occidentalis)*. Field studies of Sage Grouse *(Centrocercus urophasianus)* leading to the separation of Greater Sage-Grouse *(C. urophasianus)* and Gunnison Sage-Grouse *(C. minimus)* prove how valuable these studies of subspecific populations can be. The shifting of this line between subspecies and species is ongoing. Recording data on location and numbers can prove helpful in completing a picture of a species' distribution or even a new species that has been overlooked.

In this edition, species that have distinct subspecies that are easily recognized, such as Yellow-rumped Warbler *(Dendroica coronata)* and Dark-eyed Junco have been represented. When in the field, challenge yourself to discern the subspecies. It will increase your visual and listening skills and add a new level of understanding and enjoyment of birds.

PLATES

Geese, Swans, and Ducks Family Anatidae

Web-footed waterfowl. RANGE: Worldwide.

Geese

Large, gregarious waterfowl; heavier bodied, longer necked than ducks; bills thick at base. Noisy in flight; some fly in lines or V formations. Sexes alike. Geese are more terrestrial than ducks, often grazing. FOOD: Grasses, seeds, waste grain, aquatic plants; eelgrass (Brant); shellfish (Emperor Goose).

GREATER WHITE-FRONTED GOOSE · Fairly common · M3
Anser albifrons (see also p. 22)
28 in. (71 cm). Gray-brown with *pink* bill; adult with *white patch on front of face* and variable *black bars* on belly. Only other N. American goose with yellow or orange feet is Emperor Goose. *Immature:* Dusky with pinkish bill, yellow or orange feet. May be confused with domestic barnyard geese. VOICE: High-pitched tootling, *kah-lah-a-luk,* in chorus. HABITAT: Marshes, fields, lakes, bays; in summer, tundra.

EMPEROR GOOSE · Scarce, local · M4
Chen canagica (see also p. 22)
26 in. (66 cm). Alaskan. *Adult:* A small blue-gray goose, *scaled* with black and white; identified by its *white head and hindneck.* Throat *black* (not white as in dark-morph Snow and Ross's geese). Golden or *orange legs. Juvenile:* Has dark head and bill. SIMILAR SPECIES: Blue-morph Snow Goose. HABITAT: In summer, tundra; in winter, rocky shores, mudflats, seaweed.

SNOW GOOSE · Locally common · M5
Chen caerulescens (see also p. 22)
White morph: 25–33 in. (64–84 cm). *White* with *black primaries.* Head often rust-stained from feeding in muddy or iron-rich waters. Bill pink with black "lips." Feet pink. Base of bill curves back slightly toward eye. *Immature:* Pale gray; dark bill and legs. Dark morph ("Blue" Goose): 25–30 in. (64–76 cm): Dark with a *white head.* Suggests Emperor Goose, but has *white throat, dark "lips," and lacks scaly pattern.* Intermediates with white morph of Snow are frequent. *Immature:* Similar to young Greater White-fronted Goose, but feet and bill *dark.* VOICE: Loud, nasal, double-noted *houck-houck,* in chorus. SIMILAR SPECIES: Ross's Goose. HABITAT: Marshes, grain fields, ponds, bays; in summer, tundra.

ROSS'S GOOSE *Chen rossii* (see also p. 22) · Uncommon · M6
23 in. (58 cm). Like a small Snow Goose, but neck shorter, head rounder (steeper forehead). Bill with *gray-blue or purple-blue base,* stubbier (with *vertical border* between base and facial feathering), *lacking distinctive "grinning black lips";* warts at bill base difficult to see. Hybrids with Snow Goose occur. *Immature:* Whiter than young Snow Goose. Rare "Blue" morph shows more extensively dark neck, whiter wing patches than "Blue" Snow Goose. VOICE: Higher than Snow, suggesting Cackling Goose. SIMILAR SPECIES: Snow Goose. HABITAT: Same as Snow Goose.

GEESE

GREATER WHITE-FRONTED GOOSE

immature

adult

adult

Immature

EMPEROR
GOOSE

adult

adult

immature

adult

SNOW GOOSE dark morph
("Blue" Goose)

adult

adult
ROSS'S GOOSE

immature

adult

Snow

intergrade
between dark
and white
morphs

SNOW
GOOSE
white morph

Ross's

Snow

17

BRANT *Branta bernicla* (see also p. 22)   Locally fairly common M7
24–26 in. (59–66 cm). A small black-necked goose. Has white stern, conspicuous when it upends, whitish flanks, and band of white on neck (absent in immature). Travels in large irregular flocks. Pacific Coast subspecies, "Black" Brant *(B. b. nigricans)*, has dark belly and complete white band across foreneck. Eastern subspecies, "Pale-bellied" Brant *(B. b. hrota)*, a casual visitor to the West Coast, has *light belly, less contrasty flanks, and two separated neck patches.* A small population of intermediate birds breeds at Melville I., Canada, and winters at Puget Sound. **VOICE:** Throaty *cr-r-r-ruk* or *krr-onk, krrr-onk.* **SIMILAR SPECIES:** Foreparts of Canada and Cackling geese not black to waterline, and those species have large white face patch. Brant is more strictly coastal. **HABITAT:** Salt bays, estuaries; in summer, tundra.

CACKLING GOOSE *Branta hutchinsii*   Uncommon M8
23–32 in. (58–81 cm). Recently elevated to full-species rank separate from Canada Goose, this species includes the variably sized subspecies *hutchinsii* ("Richardson's"), *taverneri* ("Taverner's"), *minima* ("Ridgway's"), and *leucopareia* ("Aleutian"). Like Canada Goose, shows variable breast color and neck collar. **VOICE:** High, cackling *yel-lik.* **SIMILAR SPECIES:** Told from Canada by smaller size, shorter neck, smaller, rounder head, stubbier bill, and higher-pitched voice. Distinction between larger Cacklings and smaller Canadas subtle. **HABITAT:** Lakes, marshes, fields; in summer, tundra. Seen as often with flocks of Snow and Greater White-fronted Geese as with Canadas.

CANADA GOOSE *Branta canadensis* (see also p. 22)   Common M9
30–43 in. (76–109 cm). The most widespread goose in N. America. Note black head and neck, or "stocking," that contrasts with pale breast and *white chin strap.* Flocks travel in strings or in Vs, "honking" loudly. Substantial variation in size and neck length exists among populations. **VOICE:** Deep, musical honking or barking, *ka-ronk* or *ka-lunk.* Small subspecies (and Cackling Goose) have higher-pitched calls. **SIMILAR SPECIES:** Cackling Goose. **HABITAT:** Lakes, ponds, bays, marshes, fields. Resident in many areas, frequenting parks, lawns, golf courses.

"Pale-bellied"
(Atlantic)

immature

adult

BRANT

"Black"
(Pacific)

"Richardson's"

"Aleutian"

CACKLING GOOSE

"Lesser"

"Dusky"

CANADA GOOSE

Swans

Long-necked all-white swimmers. Young are pale gray-brown. Sexes alike. Feed by immersing head and neck or by "tipping up." FOOD: Aquatic plants, seeds.

TUNDRA SWAN　　　　　　　　Uncommon to locally common M11
Cygnus columbianus (see also p. 22)
52–53 in. (132–135 cm). Our most widespread native swan. Often heard long before a high-flying flock can be spotted. Bill *black,* usually with *small yellow basal spot.* Eurasian form ("Bewick's" Swan), casual from AK to CA, has *much yellow on bill* above nostrils. *Immature:* Dingy, with mostly pinkish bill. VOICE: Mellow, high-pitched cooing: *woo-ho, woo-woo, woo-ho.* SIMILAR SPECIES: Trumpeter and Mute swans. HABITAT: Lakes, large rivers, bays, estuaries, grain fields; in summer, tundra.

TRUMPETER SWAN *Cygnus buccinator*　　　　　　Uncommon M10
58–60 in. (147–152 cm). Larger than Tundra Swan, with longer, heavier, *all-black bill,* which has *straight ridge* recalling Canvasback. Black on lores wider, *embracing eyes* and lacking yellow spot (some Tundras also lack this spot). Bill base forms *V* shape (rather than U shape) on forehead. *Immature:* Keeps dusky body color later into first spring and summer than does Tundra. VOICE: *Deeper, more nasal calls* than Tundra Swan. HABITAT: Lakes, ponds, large rivers; in winter, also bays, grain fields, marshes.

MUTE SWAN *Cygnus olor*　　　　　　　　　Uncommon, local
60 in. (152 cm). Introduced from Europe. Often swims with S curve in neck; wings arched over back. Black-knobbed orange bill tilts down. Wingbeats make a "whooshing" sound. *Immature:* Dingy, with pinkish bill. VOICE: Not mute but makes hissing sounds, weak bugling. RANGE: Introduced population around Victoria, BC, and scattered records elsewhere. HABITAT: Ponds; coastal lagoons, salt bays.

Whistling-Ducks

Long-necked, long-legged waterfowl closely related to geese. Named for their high-pitched calls. Gregarious. FOOD: Seeds of aquatic plants and grasses.

FULVOUS WHISTLING-DUCK　　　　　　　　Very rare M2
Dendrocygna bicolor (see also p. 44)
20 in. (51 cm). Note *tawny* body, dark back, *pale side stripes. Black underwings, white band* on rump. VOICE: Squealing slurred whistle, *ka-whee-oo.* SIMILAR SPECIES: Black-bellied Whistling-Duck, female Northern Pintail. HABITAT: Freshwater marshes, ponds, irrigated land. Seldom perches in trees.

BLACK-BELLIED WHISTLING-DUCK　　　　　Uncommon, local M1
Dendrocygna autumnalis
21 in. (53 cm). Rusty with *black belly,* bright *coral red* bill, pink legs. Broad *white wing patch. Immature:* Has gray bill and legs. VOICE: Four- or five-part high-pitched squealing whistle. HABITAT: Ponds, freshwater marshes; frequently perches in trees.

SWANS AND
WHISTLING-
DUCKS

immature
adult
immature
adult

TUNDRA
SWAN

MUTE
SWAN

adult

adult

MUTE SWAN

adult

immature

TUNDRA SWAN

TRUMPETER
SWAN

adult

Fulvous
Whistling-
Duck

FULVOUS
WHISTLING-
DUCK

Black-bellied
Whistling-Duck

BLACK-BELLIED
WHISTLING-DUCK

21

Geese and Swans in Flight

CANADA GOOSE *Branta canadensis* p. 18

BRANT *Branta bernicla* p. 18
Small; black head and neck, white stern.

GREATER WHITE-FRONTED GOOSE *Anser albifrons* p. 16
Adult: Gray-brown neck, black bars or splotches on belly.
Immature: Dusky, with light bill and feet.

EMPEROR GOOSE *Chen canagica* p. 16
Gray with white head, black throat, white tail.

TUNDRA SWAN *Cygnus columbianus* p. 20
Very long neck. *Adult:* Plumage entirely white.

SNOW GOOSE (WHITE MORPH) *Chen caerulescens* p. 16
Adult: White with black primaries.

SNOW GOOSE (DARK MORPH, "BLUE" GOOSE) p. 16
Chen caerulescens
Adult: Dark body, white head.
Immature: Dusky, with dark bill and feet.

ROSS'S GOOSE *Chen rossii* p. 16
Smaller, slightly shorter necked and shorter billed than Snow Goose.

Many geese and swans fly in line or V formation.

"Pale-bellied"

BRANT

CANADA GOOSE

"Black"

adult

EMPEROR GOOSE

immature

GREATER WHITE-FRONTED GOOSE

immature

TUNDRA SWAN

adult

SNOW GOOSE dark morph ("Blue" Goose)

adult

SNOW GOOSE white morph

ROSS'S GOOSE

Dabbling Ducks

Feed by dabbling and upending; sometimes feed on land. Take flight directly into air. Most species have an iridescent speculum on secondaries above. Sexes not alike; in midsummer, males molt into drab "eclipse" plumage, usually resembling females. FOOD: Aquatic plants, seeds, grass, waste grain, small aquatic life, insects.

NORTHERN PINTAIL
Fairly common M20
Anas acuta (see also p. 42)

Male 25–26 in. (63–66 cm); female 20–21 in. (51–54 cm). *Male:* Slender, slim-necked, with long, *needle-pointed tail.* A conspicuous *white point* runs onto side of dark head. *Female:* Mottled brown; note slender neck, *gray bill.* In flight both sexes show a *single light border* on rear edge of speculum. VOICE: Male, a double-toned whistle: *prrip, prrip;* wheezy notes. Female, a low quack. SIMILAR SPECIES: Compare female's overall shape and bill with those of other dabbling ducks. HABITAT: Marshes, prairies, ponds, lakes, salt bays.

AMERICAN WIGEON
Fairly common M15
Anas americana (see also p. 42)

19–20 in. (48–51 cm). In flight, recognized by *large white patch on forewing.* (Similarly placed blue patch of Northern Shoveler and Blue-winged Teal often appears whitish.) When swimming, rides high, picking at water like a coot. *Male:* Warm brownish; head pale gray with green eye patch. Note *white crown* (nicknamed "Baldpate"). *Female:* Brown; gray head and neck; whitish belly and forewing. VOICE: Male, a three-part whistled *whooa whee-whew.* Female, *quaack.* SIMILAR SPECIES: Told from female Gadwall and Northern Pintail by whitish patch on forewing, small bluish bill. See Eurasian Wigeon. HABITAT: Marshes, lakes, bays, fields, grass.

EURASIAN WIGEON *Anas penelope*
Rare M14

19–20 in. (48–51 cm). *Male:* Note *red-brown* head, *buff* crown. A *gray-sided* wigeon with rufous-pinkish breast. *Female:* Very similar to female American Wigeon, but in many Eurasians head is tinged with *rust* or *orange-buff;* in others it is not. Surest point is dusky (not white) axillars, or "wingpits." VOICE: Male, a long whistle, *wheeee-oo.* Female, a purr or quack. HABITAT: Same as American Wigeon, with which it is usually found.

WOOD DUCK *Aix sponsa* (see also p. 42)
Uncommon M12

18–19 in. (45–49 cm). Highly colored; often perches in trees. In flight, white belly contrasts with dark breast and wings. Note also the long, almost square, dark tail; short neck; and angle at which bill points downward in flight. *Male:* Bizarre face pattern, sweptback crest, and rainbow iridescence unique. In eclipse, more like female but with brighter bill and suggestion of breeding head pattern. *Female:* Dull-colored; note dark crested head and *white eye patch.* VOICE: Male, hissing *jeeeeeb,* with rising inflection. Female, a loud, rising squeal, *oo-eek,* and sharp *crrek, crrek.* HABITAT: Wooded swamps, rivers, ponds, marshes.

DABBLING DUCKS

♀
♂

NORTHERN PINTAIL

♀
♂

AMERICAN WIGEON

♀
♂

EURASIAN WIGEON

♀

♂ in eclipse (summer)

♂

WOOD DUCK

SILHOUETTES OF DUCKS ON LAND

dabbling ducks (dabblers)

sea and bay ducks (divers)

mergansers (divers)

Ruddy Duck (diver)

whistling-ducks (dabblers)

GADWALL *Anas strepera* (see also p. 42)   **Fairly common M13**
19–20 in. (48–51 cm). *Male: Gray* body with brown head and *black rump, white speculum* on rear edge of wing, and dull ruddy patch on forewing (may be difficult to see). When swimming, wing patches may be concealed. Belly white, feet yellow, bill dark. *Female:* Brown, mottled, with *white speculum,* yellow feet, orange sides on dark bill. **VOICE:** Male, a low, reedy *bek;* a whistling call. Female, a nasal quack. **SIMILAR SPECIES:** Female told from female Mallard by steeper forehead, wing pattern, more nasal call. **HABITAT:** Lakes, ponds, marshes.

"MEXICAN" MALLARD *Anas platyrhynchos diazi*   **Uncommon, local**
20–21 in. (51–54 cm). This subspecies of Mallard was formerly regarded as a distinct species called Mexican Duck. Intergrades with Mallard are frequent. Both sexes very similar to female Mallard but with *grayish brown* instead of whitish tail. Bill of male like bill of male Mallard (unmarked yellowish green). Yellow-orange bill of female has a dark ridge. Has white border *on both sides* of wing patch, thinner than in female Mallard. **VOICE:** Same as Mallard's. **SIMILAR SPECIES:** Mallard. **RANGE:** Resident from se. AZ to sw. TX. **HABITAT:** Ponds.

MALLARD *Anas platyrhynchos* (see also p. 44)   **Common M16**
22–23 in. (55–59 cm). *Male:* Note uncrested *glossy green head* and *white neck ring,* grayish body, chestnut chest, white tail, yellowish bill, orange feet, blue speculum. *Female:* Mottled brown with *whitish tail.* Dark bill patched with orange, feet orange. In flight, shows white bar *on both sides* of blue speculum. **VOICE:** Male, *yeeb;* a low *kwek.* Female, boisterous quacking. **SIMILAR SPECIES:** Female Gadwall. **HABITAT:** Marshes, wooded swamps, grain fields, ponds, rivers, lakes, bays, city parks.

DABBLING DUCKS

dabbling ducks tip up

dabbling ducks spring directly from the water

♂ ♀

GADWALL

♂ (female similar)

"MEXICAN" MALLARD

♀

♂

MALLARD

27

BLUE-WINGED TEAL
Uncommon M17

Anas discors (see also p. 42)

15–16 in. (38–41 cm). A half-sized dabbling duck. *Male:* Note *white facial crescent* and large *chalky blue* patch on *forewing.* Molting males hold eclipse plumage late in year, resemble females. *Female:* Brown, mottled; dark eye line; partial eye-ring; pale loral spot; blue on forewing. **VOICE:** Male, quiet whistled peeping notes. Female, a high quack. **SIMILAR SPECIES:** Cinnamon and Green-winged teal. **HABITAT:** Ponds, marshes, mudflats, flooded fields.

CINNAMON TEAL *Anas cyanoptera*
Fairly common M18

16–17 in. (41–43 cm). *Male:* A small, *dark chestnut* duck with large chalky blue patch on forewing. Adult has *red eye,* which it retains in eclipse plumage. In flight suggests Blue-winged Teal. *Female:* Very similar to female Blue-winged but tawnier; bill slightly larger (more shoveler-like), face pattern duller. *Juvenile:* Even more similar to female Blue-winged, with slightly smaller bill, somewhat bolder face pattern than adult female Cinnamon. **VOICE:** Like Blue-winged. **HABITAT:** Marshes, freshwater ponds, mudflats, flooded fields.

NORTHERN SHOVELER
Fairly common M19

Anas clypeata (see also p. 42)

18–19 in. (46–49 cm). The long *spoon-shaped bill* gives this duck a front-heavy look. When swimming, sits low, with bill angled, straining water. *Male:* Rufous belly and sides; *white breast;* pale blue patch on forewing. *Female:* Note large spatulate bill, blue-gray forewing patch, white tail, orange feet. Bill color variable. **VOICE:** Male, a soft *thup-thup.* Female, short quacks. **SIMILAR SPECIES:** Cinnamon Teal, Mallard. **HABITAT:** Marshes, ponds, sloughs; in winter, also salt bays.

GREEN-WINGED TEAL
Common M21

Anas crecca carolinensis (see also p. 42)

14–15 in. (36–39 cm). Teal are small, fly in tight flocks. Green-wingeds lack light wing patches (speculum *deep green*). *Male:* Small, compact, gray; head rusty with green cheek patch. On swimming birds, note *vertical white mark* near shoulder, butter-colored streak near tail. *Female:* A small speckled duck with *green* speculum, *pale sides of undertail coverts.* **VOICE:** Male, a high, froglike *dreep.* Female, a sharp *quack.* **SIMILAR SPECIES:** Female Blue-winged and Cinnamon teal slightly larger and larger-billed, have light blue wing patches; in flight, males show dark belly. Green-winged has white belly, broader dark border to underwing. **HABITAT:** Marshes, rivers, bays, mudflats, flooded fields.

GREEN-WINGED ("COMMON") TEAL (Eurasian subspecies)

Anas crecca crecca
Rare

15–15½ in. (38–40 cm). Considered conspecific with "American" Green-winged Teal by most N. American taxonomists but as a separate species by Europeans. *Male:* Longitudinal (not vertical) white stripe above wing, bolder buffy borders to eye patch. *Female:* Like American race. Intergrades known. **RANGE:** Regular visitor to w. AK; rare but regular along Pacific Coast; casual inland.

TEAL

BLUE-WINGED TEAL

♂ ♀

CINNAMON TEAL

♂ ♀

NORTHERN SHOVELER

♂ ♀

GREEN-WINGED TEAL

♂ Eurasian

♂ ♀ American

DIVING DUCKS

Often grouped into "sea ducks" and "bay ducks," but many are found on lakes and rivers and breed in marshes. All dive; dabbling ducks rarely do. Legs close to tail; hind toe with a paddlelike flap (lacking in dabblers). Must patter across surface of water while getting airborne. Sexes not alike. FOOD: Small aquatic animals and plants. Seagoing species eat mostly mollusks and crustaceans.

EIDERS

Eiders are seagoing ducks, seldom seen ashore except when breeding. They usually mass in flocks off rocky coasts and often fly in line formations. In flight, males show white shoulders. FOOD: Mostly mollusks, crustaceans.

SPECTACLED EIDER *Somateria fischeri* Rare, local M28
21–22 in. (53–56 cm). *Male:* Suggests male Common Eider, but head largely pale green, with large *white "goggles"*; breast black. *Female:* Note *ghost image of goggles.* Feathering at base of bill extends far down upper mandible. VOICE: Similar to Common Eider, but softer. SIMILAR SPECIES: Female Common Eider larger and often shows broad pale eyebrow, not goggles. See King Eider. HABITAT: In summer, Arctic coasts, tundra ponds; in winter, leads in pack ice.

KING EIDER Rare to uncommon M29
Somateria spectabilis (see also p. 46)
22 in. (56 cm). *Male:* A stocky sea duck; on water, foreparts appear white, rear parts black. Note protruding *orange bill-shield.* In flight, wings show large white patches. *Female:* Stocky; warm brown, weak pale eye-ring and thin stripe curving behind and down from eye, flanks barred with crescent-shaped marks. Note facial profile and dark bill. *Immature male:* Dusky, with light breast, *orangey* bill. VOICE: Courting male, a low crooning phrase. Female, grunting croaks. SIMILAR SPECIES: Common Eider larger, with flatter head profile, longer bill-lobe before eye; male Common has *white* back, female has evenly barred flanks, grayer bill. Immature male Common has grayish bill, often some white on back. Compare eclipse male in flight with White-winged Scoter. HABITAT: Rocky coasts, ocean. Nests on tundra.

COMMON EIDER Fairly common, local M30
Somateria mollissima (see also p. 46)
24–25 in. (61–64 cm). This bulky, long-necked duck is oceanic. *Male:* This and Spectacled Eider are only ducks in N. America with *black belly and white back.* Forewing and back white; head white with black crown, greenish nape. *Female:* Large, brown, *closely barred, with pale eyebrow;* long, flat facial profile. *Immature male:* At first brownish; later dusky with white breast and collar; may develop chocolate head or breast; white areas come in irregularly. VOICE: Male, a moaning *ow-ooo-urr.* Female, a grating *kor-r-r.* SIMILAR SPECIES: King Eider. Female scoters smaller, lack heavy dark barring of female eiders. HABITAT: Rocky coasts, shoals; in summer, also tundra.

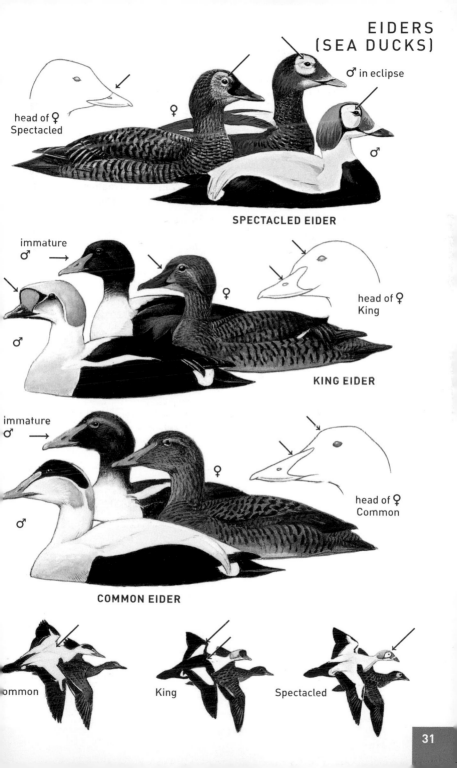

EIDERS
(SEA DUCKS)

head of ♀
Spectacled

♀

♂ in eclipse

♂

SPECTACLED EIDER

immature
♂ →

♀

head of ♀
King

♂

KING EIDER

immature
♂ →

♀

head of ♀
Common

♂

COMMON EIDER

ommon

King

Spectacled

STELLER'S EIDER *Polysticta stelleri*   Scarce, local   M27

17 in. (43 cm). Unlike other eiders in shape, bill. *Male:* Black and white, with *yellow-buff underparts, white head,* black throat, and green bump on back of head. Note *round black spot* on side of breast. As in other eiders, white forewing is conspicuous in flight. *Female:* Dark brown, mottled, with pale eye-ring; distinguished from other eiders by much smaller size and *shape of its small head and blue-gray bill.* Purple speculum bordered in white, visible at short range, suggests a female Mallard. **VOICE:** Usually silent. Male's crooning note resembles Common Eider's but is quieter. Female has a low growl. **SIMILAR SPECIES:** Other eiders, Long-tailed Duck. **HABITAT:** Coasts, ocean; in summer, also tundra ponds.

HARLEQUIN DUCK   Uncommon   M31
Histrionicus histrionicus (see also p. 46)

16–17 in. (41–44 cm). A smallish, dark sea duck with a long tail. *Male:* Spectacularly patterned: slaty with chestnut sides and odd white patches and spots. In flight, has stubby shape of a goldeneye but appears uniformly dark. *Female:* A small dusky duck with three round white spots on each side of head; no wing patch. **VOICE:** Usually silent. Male, a squeak; also *gwa gwa gwa.* Female, *ek-ek-ek-ek.* **SIMILAR SPECIES:** Female Bufflehead has white wing patch and only one face spot. Female scoters larger, with larger bills. **HABITAT:** Turbulent mountain streams in summer; rocky coastal waters and harbors in winter.

LONG-TAILED DUCK (OLDSQUAW)   Uncommon, local   M35
Clangula hyemalis (see also p. 46)

Male 21–22 in. (53–56 cm); female 16 in. (41 cm). The only sea duck combining much *white on body and unpatterned dark wings.* It flies in bunched, irregular flocks, rocking side to side as it flies. Male has pink on bill. *Nonbreeding male:* Note needlelike tail, pied pattern, dark cheek. *Breeding male:* Dark with white flanks and belly. Note white eye patch, pink on bill. *Nonbreeding female:* Dark unpatterned wings, white face with dark cheek spot. *Breeding female:* Similar but darker. *Immature:* Lacks long tail feathers. **VOICE:** Talkative; a musical *ow-owdle-ow* or *owl-omelet.* **SIMILAR SPECIES:** Bufflehead. In flight, sometimes confused with alcids because of white body, dark wings, and rapid wingbeats. **HABITAT:** Coastal waters, harbors, large lakes; in summer, tundra pools and lakes.

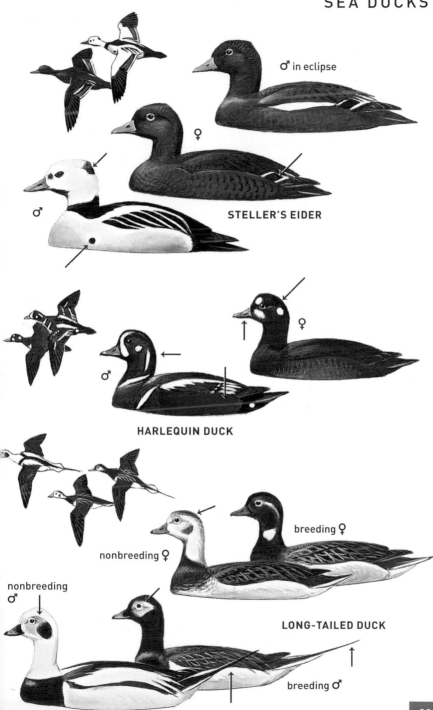

♂ in eclipse

♀

♂

STELLER'S EIDER

♀

♂

HARLEQUIN DUCK

breeding ♀

nonbreeding ♀

nonbreeding ♂

LONG-TAILED DUCK

breeding ♂

SCOTERS

Scoters are heavy, blackish sea ducks seen in large flocks along ocean coasts. They often fly in thin line formation. They are usually in flocks, either single species or mixed, so look them over carefully. Scoters are usually silent but during courtship and mating may utter low whistles, croaks, or grunting noises; wings whistle in flight. **FOOD:** Mainly mollusks, crustaceans.

WHITE-WINGED SCOTER
Uncommon to fairly common M33

Melanitta fusca (see also p. 46)

21 in. (53 cm). White-winged, largest of the three scoters, has a bill feathered to nostril. On water, white wing patch is often barely visible or fully concealed (wait for bird to flap or fly). *Male:* Black, with a "teardrop" of white near eye; bill orange with black basal knob. *Female:* Sooty brown, with white wing patch and two light oval patches on face (sometimes obscure; patches more pronounced on young birds). Asian subspecies *stejnegeri,* very rare in w. AK, has hornlike knob at base of bill. **VOICE:** Usually silent. **SIMILAR SPECIES:** Other scoters. **HABITAT:** Salt bays, coastal waters; in summer, lakes.

SURF SCOTER
Fairly common to common M32

Melanitta perspicillata (see also p. 46)

19–20 in. (48–51 cm). The "skunkhead-duck." *Male:* Black, with one or two *white patches* on crown and nape. Heavy, sloping bill patterned with orange, black, and white. *Female:* Dusky brown; dark crown; two light spots on each side of head (sometimes obscure; more evident on young birds), one mostly vertical, the other more horizontal. **VOICE:** Usually silent. A low croak; grunting sounds. **SIMILAR SPECIES:** Female White-winged Scoter slightly larger overall, has more extensive feathering on bill, more horizontal, oval face patches, and white wing patch (may not show until bird flaps). Black Scoter has rounder head profile (more like Redhead, whereas Surf Scoter more like Canvasback) and has silvery underside to flight feathers; female and immature have entirely pale cheeks. **HABITAT:** Coastal waters, salt bays; in summer, lakes.

BLACK SCOTER
Rare to uncommon M34

Melanitta nigra (see also p. 46)

18½–19 in. (47–48 cm). *Male:* An all-black sea duck. Bright *orange-yellow knob* on bill ("butter nose") is diagnostic. In flight, underwing shows two-toned effect (silvery gray and black), more pronounced than in other two scoters. *Female:* Sooty; *entirely light cheeks* contrast with dark cap. **VOICE:** Usually silent. Male, melodious cooing notes. Female, growls. **SIMILAR SPECIES:** Some young male Surf Scoters may lack head patches and appear all black, but they have round black spot at base of higher-sloping bill. Female and immature scoters of other two species have smaller light spots on side of head, not entirely pale cheeks. Female Black Scoter may suggest nonbreeding adult male Ruddy Duck. **HABITAT:** Coastal waters, bays; in summer, tundra and taiga ponds.

SCOTERS (SEA DUCKS)

scoters fly in line or V formation

White-winged

Surf

Black

immature

♀

♂

WHITE-WINGED SCOTER

♂

♀

immature ♂

SURF SCOTER

immature ♂

♂

♀

BLACK SCOTER

diving ducks (sea ducks and bay ducks) raft on water, skitter when taking wing

CANVASBACK   Uncommon M22
Aythya valisineria (see also p. 48)
21–22 in. (53–56 cm). *Male:* Very white looking, with black chest and *chestnut red* head sloping into *long blackish* bill. *Female:* Pale grayish brown, with *long, sloping head profile.* In winter often form mixed flocks with Redheads, scaup. **VOICE:** Male, in courtship, cooing notes. Female, raspy *krrrr*, etc. **SIMILAR SPECIES:** Redhead. **HABITAT:** Lakes, salt bays, estuaries; in summer, freshwater marshes and lakes.

REDHEAD *Aythya americana* (see also p. 48)   Uncommon M23
19–20 in. (48–51 cm). *Male:* Gray; black chest and *round rufous head;* bill bluish with black tip. *Female:* Brown overall with round head, black-tipped bill. Both sexes have *gray wing stripe.* **VOICE:** Male, in courtship, a harsh catlike *meow;* a deep purr. Female, soft *krrr* notes. **SIMILAR SPECIES:** Canvasback has sloping forehead; male much whiter. See female Ring-necked Duck, scaup. **HABITAT:** Lakes, salt bays, estuaries; in summer, freshwater marshes and ponds.

RING-NECKED DUCK   Fairly common M24
Aythya collaris (see also p. 48)
17–17½ in. (43–46 cm). *Male:* Note *black back, vertical white mark* before wing. *Female:* Very dark with peaked crown, indistinct light face patch, light eye-ring, light ring on bill. Both sexes with *gray* (not white) wing stripe. **VOICE:** Female a quacking growl: *arrp-arrp-arrp.* Male in courtship gives a low-pitched whistle. **SIMILAR SPECIES:** Female Redhead paler with rounder crown. Male Tufted Duck, rare winter visitor along Pacific Coast and regular migrant in w. AK, has wispy crest, white sides, white wing stripe. Female scaup have distinct white face and wing patches. **HABITAT:** Wooded lakes, ponds; in winter, also rivers, bays.

GREATER SCAUP *Aythya marila* (see also p. 48)   Common M25
18–18½ in. (46–48 cm). Very similar to Lesser Scaup. Slightly larger, with more gently rounded — sometimes almost flat-topped — head, bill slightly wider with larger black tip (nail), and *white wing stripe longer.* *Male:* Whiter on sides than Lesser. *Female* (not shown): Averages slightly paler brown than Lesser, averages a larger white patch at base of bill, and may show pale ear patch in fall and winter. Best identified by size, shape, and wing stripe. **VOICE:** Male, in display, soft, wheezy whistles. Female, raspy *scaup-scaup.* **SIMILAR SPECIES:** Lesser Scaup, Ring-necked Duck, Redhead. **HABITAT:** Lakes, rivers, bays, estuaries, nearshore ocean waters; in summer, tundra and taiga ponds.

LESSER SCAUP *Aythya affinis* (see also p. 48)   Common M26
16½–17 in. (42–44 cm). Both sexes with *peaked rear crown* (in relaxed pose only, e.g., while sleeping — flatter crown when active); white wing stripe *restricted to secondaries* (extends to inner primaries on Greater). *Male:* Head glossed with purple. Flanks finely barred. *Female:* Dark brown, with clean-cut white patch near bill. **VOICE:** Male, in display, a soft whistle. Female, a loud *scaup.* **SIMILAR SPECIES:** Greater Scaup, Ring-necked Duck, Redhead. **HABITAT:** Lakes, bays, nearshore ocean waters; in summer, marsh and taiga ponds.

CANVASBACK

♂

♀

diving ducks run
and patter

REDHEAD

♂

♀

RING-NECKED DUCK

♂

♀

Lesser

Greater

ater

Lesser

♂

♀

GREATER SCAUP

♂

LESSER SCAUP

♂

♀

COMMON GOLDENEYE
Fairly common M37
Bucephala clangula (see also p. 48)
18½–19 in. (47–49 cm). *Male:* Note large, *round white spot* before eye. White looking, with black back and puffy, green-glossed head that appears black at a distance. In flight, short-necked; wings show large white patches. *Female:* Gray, with white collar and dark brown or rusty-brown head; wings with large square white patches that may show on closed wing. **VOICE:** Wings "whistle" in flight. Courting male has harsh nasal double note, suggesting *pee-ik* of Common Nighthawk. Female, a harsh *gaak*. **SIMILAR SPECIES:** Barrow's Goldeneye. Male scaup have black chest. Male Common Merganser long, low, with different bill. **HABITAT:** Forested lakes, rivers; in winter, also lakes, salt bays, protected seacoasts.

BARROW'S GOLDENEYE
Scarce to uncommon M38
Bucephala islandica
18 in. (46 cm). *Male:* Note *white facial crescent*. Similar to Common Goldeneye, but blacker above; head glossed with *purple* (not green); nape puffier; shows *dark "spur"* on shoulder toward waterline. *Female:* Similar to female Common; head slightly darker, with steeper forehead and suggestion of puffy nape, bill shorter and more triangular, less white in wing. Bill may become all *orangey yellow*, often a good field mark but subject to seasonal change. Female Common Goldeneye often has band of yellow on bill. **VOICE:** Usually silent. Courting male, a grunting *kuk, kuk*. Female near nest, a soft *coo-coo-coo*. Wings of both species whistle in flight. **SIMILAR SPECIES:** Common Goldeneye, Bufflehead. **HABITAT:** Wooded lakes, ponds; in winter, lakes and rivers, protected coastal waters.

BUFFLEHEAD *Bucephala albeola* (see also p. 48)
Common M36
13½–14 in. (34–36 cm). Small. *Male:* Mostly white with black back; puffy head with *large, bonnetlike white patch*. In flight, shows large white wing patch. *Female:* Dark and compact, with *white cheek spot*, small bill, smaller wing patch. **VOICE:** Male, in display, a hoarse rolling note. Female, a harsh *ec-ec-ec*. **SIMILAR SPECIES:** Male Hooded Merganser has spikelike bill, dark sides. See female Black Scoter and nonbreeding adult male Ruddy Duck. See also Long-tailed Duck. **HABITAT:** Lakes, ponds, rivers; in winter, also salt bays.

RUDDY DUCK
Fairly common M42
Oxyura jamaicensis (see also p. 48)
15 in. (38 cm). Small, chubby; note *white cheek* and dark cap. Often cocks long tail upward. Flight "buzzy." Can barely walk on land. *Breeding male:* Rusty red with white cheek, black cap, large, strikingly *blue* bill. *Nonbreeding male:* Gray with *white cheek*, gray bill. *Female:* Similar to nonbreeding male, but duskier cheek crossed by dark line. **VOICE:** Courting male, a sputtering *chick-ik-ik-ik-k-k-k-kurrrr*, accompanied by head bobbing. **SIMILAR SPECIES:** Female Bufflehead, Black Scoter. **HABITAT:** Freshwater marshes, ponds, lakes; in winter, also salt bays, harbors.

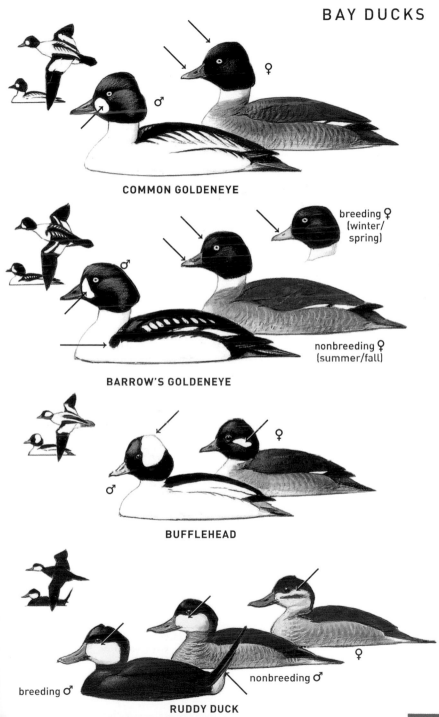

♂

♀

COMMON GOLDENEYE

breeding ♀
(winter/
spring)

♂

nonbreeding ♀
(summer/fall)

BARROW'S GOLDENEYE

♀

♂

BUFFLEHEAD

♀

breeding ♂

nonbreeding ♂

RUDDY DUCK

MERGANSERS

Long-lined, slender-bodied diving ducks with spikelike bill, saw-edged mandibles. Most species have a crest. In flight, bill, head, neck, and body are on a horizontal axis. Sexes not alike. FOOD: Chiefly fish.

COMMON MERGANSER   Fairly common M40
Mergus merganser (see also p. 44)
24–25 in. (62–64 cm). In flight, lines of these slender ducks follow the winding courses of rivers. Whiteness of adult males and merganser shape (bill, neck, head, and body held horizontally) identify this species. *Male:* Note long whitish body, black back, green-black head. Bill and feet red; breast tinged rosy peach. *Female and immature:* Gray with crested rufous head contrasting with white chin and clean white chest; large square white wing patch. VOICE: Male, in display, low staccato croaks. Female, a guttural *karrr.* SIMILAR SPECIES: Female Red-breasted Merganser very similar to female Common. Note distinct cutoff of rusty head and neck from breast in Common; this is diffuse in Red-breasted. Female mergansers, which are rusty-headed, suggest male Canvasback or Redhead, but those have black chest, no crest, different bill. HABITAT: Lakes, ponds, rivers; in winter, open lakes, rivers, rarely coastal bays.

RED-BREASTED MERGANSER   Common M41
Mergus serrator (see also p. 44)
22½–23 in. (56–58 cm). *Male:* Rakish; black head glossed with green and *crested;* breast at waterline dark rusty, separated from head by *wide white collar;* bill and feet red. *Female and immature:* Gray, with crested, dull rusty head that *blends* into color of neck; large white wing patch; red bill and feet. VOICE: Usually silent. Male, a hoarse croak. Female, *karrr.* SIMILAR SPECIES: Male Common Merganser whiter, without collar and breast-band effect; lacks crest. In female Common, white chin and chest *sharply delineated* from brighter rufous head and pale gray body. Common's bill slightly thicker at base. HABITAT: Woodland, tundra, and coastal lakes, open water; in winter, also bays, tidal channels, nearshore ocean waters.

HOODED MERGANSER   Uncommon M39
Lophodytes cucullatus (see also p. 44)
17–18 in. (43–46 cm). *Male:* Note vertical *fan-shaped white crest,* which may be raised or lowered. Breast white, with two black bars on each side. Wing with white patch; *flanks rusty brown. Female:* Recognized as a merganser by silhouette and spikelike bill; known as this species by its small size, dusky look, and *dark head, bill, and chest.* Note loose *tawny crest.* VOICE: In display, low grunting or croaking notes. SIMILAR SPECIES: Male Bufflehead chubbier, with *white* sides. Other female mergansers larger and *grayer,* with rufous head, reddish bill. In flight, wing patch and silhouette separate female Hooded Merganser from female Wood Duck. HABITAT: Wooded lakes, ponds, rivers; in winter, also tidal channels, protected bays.

mergansers fly with bill, head, body, and tail on the same horizontal axis

saw-edged mandibles of merganser

♂

♀

COMMON MERGANSER

♂

♀

RED-BREASTED MERGANSER

♂ crest down

♂ in eclipse

♂ crest up

♀

HOODED MERGANSER

Common

Red-breasted

Hooded

Flight Patterns of Dabbling Ducks

Note: Only males are diagnosed below. Although females are unlike the males, their wing patterns are quite similar. The names in parentheses are common nicknames used by hunters.

NORTHERN PINTAIL (SPRIG) *Anas acuta*   p. 24
Underside: Needle tail, white breast, thin neck.
Topside: Needle tail, neck stripe, single thin white border on speculum.

WOOD DUCK *Aix sponsa*   p. 24
Underside: White belly, dusky wings, long square tail.
Topside: Stocky; long dark tail, white border on dark wing.

AMERICAN WIGEON (BALDPATE) *Anas americana*   p. 24
Underside: White belly, pointed dark tail.
Topside: Large white shoulder patch.

NORTHERN SHOVELER (SPOONBILL) *Anas clypeata*   p. 28
Underside: Dark belly, white breast, white tail, spoon bill.
Topside: Large pale bluish shoulder patch, spoon bill.

GADWALL *Anas strepera*   p. 26
Underside: White belly, white underwing.
Topside: White patch on rear edge of wing.

GREEN-WINGED TEAL *Anas crecca*   p. 28
Underside: Small; light belly, dark head, broad dark borders to underwing.
Topside: Small, dark-winged; green speculum.

BLUE-WINGED TEAL *Anas discors*   p. 28
Underside: Small; dark belly, narrow dark borders to underwing.
Topside: Small; large chalky blue shoulder patch.

upper wing of a dabbling duck showing the iridescent speculum (secondaries)

NORTHERN PINTAIL

WOOD DUCK

DABBLING DUCKS IN FLIGHT

Underside

♂

♀

AMERICAN WIGEON

♀

♂

♂

♀

NORTHERN SHOVELER

♂

♀

GADWALL

♀

♂

GREEN-WINGED TEAL

♂

♀

BLUE-WINGED TEAL

Topside

♂

♀

WOOD DUCK

NORTHERN PINTAIL

♀

♂

♀

AMERICAN WIGEON

♂

♀

NORTHERN SHOVELER

♂

♀

GADWALL

♂

♀

GREEN-WINGED TEAL

♂

BLUE-WINGED TEAL

♀

43

FLIGHT PATTERNS OF DABBLING DUCKS AND MERGANSERS

Note: Only males are diagnosed below. Although most females are unlike the males, their wing patterns are quite similar. Mergansers have a distinctive flight silhouette. Duck hunters often call mergansers "sheldrakes" or "sawbills."

MALLARD *Anas platyrhynchos*   p. 26
Underside: Dark chest, light belly, white neck ring, white tail.
Topside: Dark head, neck ring, two white borders on bluish speculum.

FULVOUS WHISTLING-DUCK *Dendrocygna bicolor*   p. 20
Underside: Tawny, with blackish wing linings.
Topside: Dark, unpatterned wings; white band on rump.

COMMON MERGANSER *Mergus merganser*   p. 40
Underside: Merganser shape; dark head, white body, white wing linings.
Topside: Merganser shape; white chest, large white wing patches.

RED-BREASTED MERGANSER *Mergus serrator*   p. 40
Underside: Merganser shape; dark chest band, white collar.
Topside: Merganser shape; dark chest, large white wing patches.

HOODED MERGANSER *Lophodytes cucullatus*   p. 40
Underside: Merganser shape; dusky wing linings.
Topside: Merganser shape; small white wing patches.

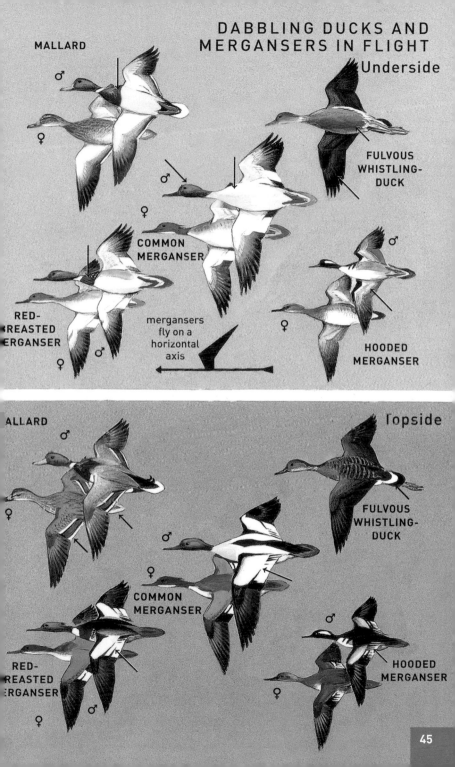

DABBLING DUCKS AND
MERGANSERS IN FLIGHT
Underside

MALLARD

♂

♀

FULVOUS
WHISTLING-
DUCK

♂

COMMON
MERGANSER

RED-
BREASTED
MERGANSER

♀

♂

mergansers
fly on a
horizontal
axis

♀

HOODED
MERGANSER

MALLARD

Topside

♂

♀

FULVOUS
WHISTLING-
DUCK

♂

♀

COMMON
MERGANSER

RED-
BREASTED
MERGANSER

♀   ♂

♂

HOODED
MERGANSER

♀

45

Flight Patterns of Diving Ducks

Note: Only males are diagnosed below.

LONG-TAILED DUCK (OLDSQUAW) *Clangula hyemalis*　　　p. 32
Underside: Dark unpatterned wings, white belly.
Topside: Dark unpatterned wings, much white on body.

HARLEQUIN DUCK *Histrionicus histrionicus*　　　p. 32
Underside: Solid dark below, white head spots, small bill.
Topside: Dark with white marks, small bill, long tail.

SURF SCOTER *Melanitta perspicillata*　　　p. 34
Underside: Black body, white head patches (not readily visible from below), sloping forehead.
Topside: Black body, white head patches, sloping forehead.

BLACK SCOTER *Melanitta nigra*　　　p. 34
Underside: Black plumage, paler flight feathers, rounded forehead.
Topside: All-dark plumage. Body slightly smaller and pudgier than Surf Scoter's, rounded forehead.

WHITE-WINGED SCOTER *Melanitta fusca*　　　p. 34
Underside: Black body, white wing patches.
Topside: Black body, white wing patches.

COMMON EIDER *Somateria mollissima*　　　p. 30
Topside: White back, white forewing, black belly.

KING EIDER *Somateria spectabilis*　　　p. 30
Topside: Whitish foreparts, black rear parts.

DIVING DUCKS IN FLIGHT

HARLEQUIN DUCK

Underside

LONG-TAILED DUCK

♂
♀
♂
♀

SURF SCOTER

BLACK SCOTER

WHITE-WINGED SCOTER

Topside

♂
♀

LONG-TAILED DUCK

♂
♀

HARLEQUIN DUCK

♂
♀

COMMON EIDER

♂

KING EIDER

♂
♀

BLACK SCOTER

♂
♀

SURF SCOTER

♂

♀

WHITE-WINGED SCOTER

47

FLIGHT PATTERNS OF DIVING DUCKS, ETC.

Note: Only males are diagnosed below. The first five all have a black chest. The names in parentheses are common nicknames used by hunters.

CANVASBACK *Aythya valisineria*　　　　　　　p. 36
Underside: Black chest, long profile.
Topside: White back, long profile. Lacks contrasty wing stripe of next four species.

REDHEAD *Aythya americana*　　　　　　　p. 36
Underside: Black chest, roundish rufous head.
Topside: Gray back, broad gray wing stripe.

RING-NECKED DUCK *Aythya collaris*　　　　　p. 36
Underside: Not safe to tell from scaup overhead; gray wing stripe sometimes evident.
Topside: Black back, broad gray wing stripe.

GREATER SCAUP (BLUEBILL) *Aythya marila*　　　p. 36
Underside: Black chest, white stripe showing through wing.
Topside: Broad white wing stripe (extending onto primaries).

LESSER SCAUP (BLUEBILL) *Aythya affinis*　　　p. 36
Topside: Wing stripe restricted to secondaries.

COMMON GOLDENEYE (WHISTLER) *Bucephala clangula*　　p. 38
Underside: Dark wing linings, white wing patches, rounded dark head.
Topside: Large white square wing patch, short neck, dark head.

RUDDY DUCK *Oxyura jamaicensis*　　　　　　p. 38
Underside: Stubby; white face, dark chest, long tail.
Topside: Small; dark with white cheeks, long tail.

BUFFLEHEAD (BUTTERBALL) *Bucephala albeola*　　　p. 38
Underside: Like a small goldeneye; note head patch.
Topside: Small; large wing patches, white head patch.

Silhouettes of Ducks on Land

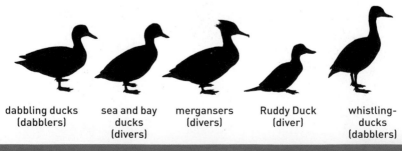

| dabbling ducks (dabblers) | sea and bay ducks (divers) | mergansers (divers) | Ruddy Duck (diver) | whistling-ducks (dabblers) |

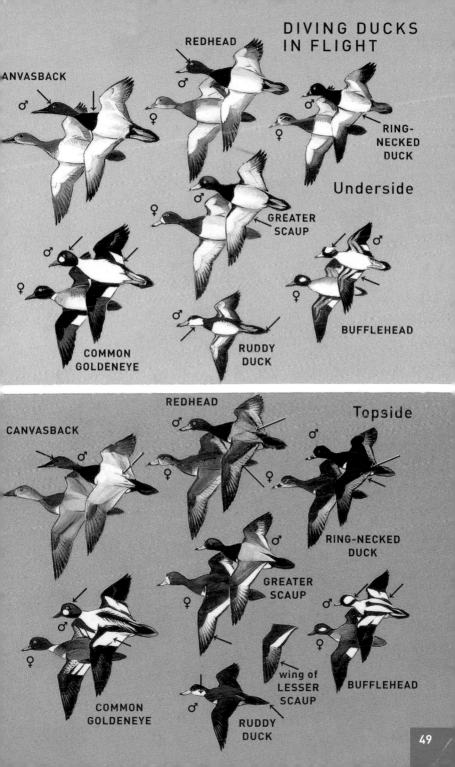

DIVING DUCKS IN FLIGHT

CANVASBACK
♂

REDHEAD
♂
♀

RING-NECKED DUCK
♂
♀

Underside

GREATER SCAUP
♂
♀

COMMON GOLDENEYE
♂
♀

RUDDY DUCK
♂

BUFFLEHEAD
♂
♀

REDHEAD
♂
♀

Topside

CANVASBACK
♂

RING-NECKED DUCK
♂
♀

GREATER SCAUP
♂
♀

COMMON GOLDENEYE
♂
♀

wing of LESSER SCAUP

RUDDY DUCK
♂

BUFFLEHEAD
♂
♀

49

Stray Waterfowl

GARGANEY *Anas querquedula*   Vagrant
15½ in. (38 cm). *Male:* Broad white eyebrow stripe, silvery shoulder patch (in flight). *Female:* Told from Blue-winged and Cinnamon teal by bolder face pattern (shared by Green-winged Teal), dark legs, paler primaries (in flight), and bold white borders on speculum. **RANGE:** Very rare visitor from Eurasia to w. Aleutians; casual elsewhere in N. America, with widespread records; many records from West Coast, fewer inland. **HABITAT:** As in other teal.

TUFTED DUCK *Aythya fuligula*   Regular vagrant
16½–17 in. (41–43 cm). *Male:* Differs from male Ring-necked Duck in having thin wispy crest, entirely *white* sides, and *white* (not gray) wing stripe; from scaup, by black back, wispy crest. *Female:* May have faint trace of tuft. Darker back, usually less white on face than female scaup; lacks eye-ring of female Ring-necked; eyes yellow. **VOICE:** Similar to Ring-necked Duck. **RANGE:** Regular visitor from Eurasia to w. AK; very rare elsewhere along Pacific coast; casual inland. **HABITAT:** Sheltered ponds, bays, reservoirs. Usually with scaup.

SMEW *Mergellus albellus*   Vagrant
16 in. (41 cm). Smaller and shorter-billed than other mergansers. *Male:* Very white, with *black eye patch* and slight drooping black-and-white crest behind eye. In flight, shows conspicuous black-and-white wings. *Female:* Small and gray, with *white cheeks, chestnut cap.* **RANGE:** Rare but regular spring visitor from Asia to w. AK; accidental elsewhere. Some birds might be escapees.

Unestablished Exotics

CHINESE GOOSE *Anser cygnoides*	Exotic
EGYPTIAN GOOSE *Alopochen aegyptiacus*	Exotic
BAR-HEADED GOOSE *Anser indicus*	Exotic
GRAYLAG GOOSE *Anser anser*	Exotic
WHITE-CHEEKED PINTAIL *Anas bahamensis*	Exotic
MANDARIN *Aix galericulata*	Exotic
COMMON SHELDUCK *Tadorna tadorna*	Exotic
RUDDY SHELDUCK *Tadorna ferruginea*	Exotic

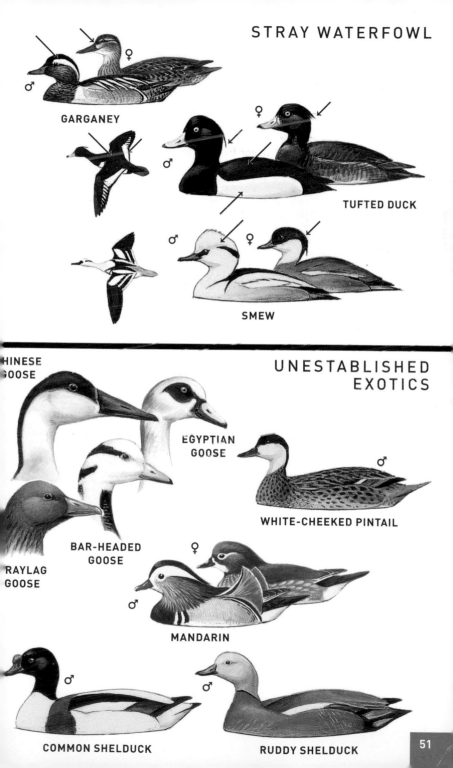

STRAY WATERFOWL

GARGANEY

♂

♀

TUFTED DUCK

♀

♂

SMEW

♂ ♀

UNESTABLISHED EXOTICS

CHINESE GOOSE

EGYPTIAN GOOSE

BAR-HEADED GOOSE

GRAYLAG GOOSE

WHITE-CHEEKED PINTAIL

♂

MANDARIN

♀

♂

COMMON SHELDUCK

♂

RUDDY SHELDUCK

♂

51

Gallinaceous, or Chickenlike, Birds (Turkeys, Pheasants, Grouse, Partridges, and Old World Quail)
Family Phasianidae

Often called "upland game birds." Turkeys are very large, with wattles and fan-like tail. Pheasants (introduced) have long pointed tail. Grouse are plump, chickenlike birds, without long tail. Partridges (of Old World origin) are intermediate in size between grouse and quail. Quail are the smallest. **FOOD:** Insects, seeds, buds, berries. **RANGE:** Nearly worldwide.

WILD TURKEY   Uncommon to fairly common M64
Meleagris gallopavo
Male 46–47 in. (117–120 cm); female 36–37 in. (91–94 cm). A stream-lined version of barnyard turkey, with rusty instead of white tail tips (southwestern birds have buff-white tail tips). *Male:* Head naked; bluish with red wattles, intensified in display. Tail erected like a fan in display. Bronzy iridescent body; barred wings (primaries and secondaries); prominent "beard" on breast. *Female and immature:* Smaller, with smaller and duller head; less iridescent; less likely to have a beard. **VOICE:** "Gobbling" of male like domestic turkey's. Alarm *pit!* or *put-put!* Flock call *keow-keow.* Hen clucks to her chicks. **HABITAT:** Woods, mountain forests, field edges, clearings. Reintroduced in many areas, and such birds are adapting well to being near people.

GREATER SAGE-GROUSE   Uncommon M53
Centrocercus urophasianus
Male 27–28 in. (69–71 cm); female 22–23 in. (56–58 cm). A large grayish grouse of open sage country, as large as a small turkey; identified by its contrasting *black belly patch* and spikelike tail feathers. Male is considerably larger than female, has black throat, and, in communal dancing display, puffs out its white chest, exposing two yellow air sacs on neck, at same time erecting and spreading its pointed tail feathers in a spiky fan. **VOICE:** Flushing call *kuk kuk kuk.* In courtship display, male makes a popping sound. **SIMILAR SPECIES:** Gunnison Sage-Grouse, but these two resident species do not overlap. See female Ring-necked Pheasant. **HABITAT:** Sagebrush plains; also foothills and mountain slopes where sagebrush grows.

GUNNISON SAGE-GROUSE   Scarce, very local M54
Centrocercus minimus
Male 21–22 in. (53–56 cm); female 18–19 in. (46–49 cm). Recently split taxonomically from Greater Sage-Grouse, this species is found only in a very geographically restricted region of sw. CO and se. UT. Differs from Greater Sage-Grouse by its slightly smaller size, longer "crest," and more distinct white barring on tail. Identification by range is most reliable.

MISCELLANEOUS CHICKENLIKE BIRDS

♂

♂ display

♀

WILD TURKEY

GUNNISON SAGE-
GROUSE

GREATER SAGE-
GROUSE

♂ display

♂ display

♀

PTARMIGANS

Hardy Arctic and alpine grouse with feathered feet. They molt three times a year; camouflaging themselves to match the seasons, they change from dark plumage in summer to white in winter. During spring and fall molts they have a patchy look. A red comb above eye may be erected or concealed. **FOOD:** Buds, leaves, seeds.

WILLOW PTARMIGAN *Lagopus lagopus*   Fairly common M56
15 in. (39 cm). Willow and Rock ptarmigans are fairly similar. In breeding season, Willows are variable, but most males are chestnut brown, redder than any Rock; females are warm buffy brown that can overlap brown of Rock. White of wings retained all year and, in flight, contrast with summer body plumage. Nonbreeding white overall with black tail, the latter retained year-round. There is much variation between various molts. **VOICE:** Deep raucous calls. Male, a staccato crow, *kwow, kwow, tobacco, tobacco,* etc., or *go-back, go-back.* **SIMILAR SPECIES:** Rock Ptarmigan always has smaller and more slender bill that lacks strong curve on ridge shown by Willow. In winter, male Rock has *black mark* between eye and bill, lacking in both sexes of Willow. Habitats overlap, but Rock tends to prefer higher, more barren hills. See White-tailed Ptarmigan. **HABITAT:** Tundra, willow scrub, muskeg; in winter, sheltered valleys at slightly lower altitudes.

ROCK PTARMIGAN *Lagopus muta*   Uncommon M57
14 in. (36 cm). Breeding male is usually browner or grayer than breeding Willow Ptarmigan, lacking rich chestnut around head and neck. Some Rocks may be even paler than shown here, or are like dark birds from w. Aleutians (shown in center). Females of the two species are similar, but Rock has smaller bill. Nonbreeding white male Rock has *black mark* between eye and bill. This is absent in most females, which may be told from female Willow by Rock's smaller bill. **VOICE:** Croaks, growls, cackles; usually silent. **SIMILAR SPECIES:** Willow and White-tailed ptarmigans. **HABITAT:** Tundra, above timberline in mountains (to lower levels in winter); also near sea level in bleak tundra of northern coasts.

WHITE-TAILED PTARMIGAN *Lagopus leucura*   Uncommon M58
12½–13 in. (31–33 cm). The only ptarmigan normally found south of Canada. Note *white tail,* particularly in flight. In breeding season, brown with white belly, wings, and tail. Nonbreeding pure white except for black eyes and bill. **VOICE:** Cackling notes, clucks, soft hoots. **SIMILAR SPECIES:** The other two ptarmigans have *black* tail. **HABITAT:** Alpine tundra, including rocky outcrops and stunted willow thickets.

PTARMIGANS

WILLOW PTARMIGAN

nonbreeding

♀

♂

nonbreeding

breeding

♂

breeding
♀

spring

♂

western
Aleutians

♀

nonbreeding
♂

-eding

♂

breeding ♀

breeding

**ROCK
PTARMIGAN**

♂

♀

nonbreeding

♂

breeding

breeding ♀

molting

breeding

WHITE-TAILED PTARMIGAN

RUFFED GROUSE *Bonasa umbellus*　　　　　Uncommon M52
17 in. (43 cm). Note short crest, barred flanks, and fan-shaped tail with black band near tip. A large chickenlike bird of brushy woodlands, usually not seen until it flushes with a startling whir. Two color morphs occur. Rusty birds more common in southern parts of range (and in Pacific Northwest), gray birds more common northward. **VOICE:** Sound of drumming male suggests a distant motor starting up. Low muffled thumping starts slowly, accelerating into a whir: *Bup . . . bup . . . bup . . . bup . . . bup bup up r-rrrr.* **SIMILAR SPECIES:** Other grouse. **HABITAT:** Low in deciduous and mixed woodlands.

SPRUCE GROUSE *Falcipennis canadensis*　　　Scarce M55
16–17 in. (41–43 cm). A *tame,* dark grouse. *Male:* Sharply defined *black breast,* with some white spots or bars on sides and *chestnut band* on tip of tail. Birds of n. Rockies and Cascades, known as "Franklin's" Grouse, lack chestnut tail tip and have large white spots on uppertail coverts. *Female:* Dark rusty or grayish brown, thickly barred breast; tail short and dark, with rusty tip (except in "Franklin's" race). **VOICE:** Female, call an accelerating, then slowing, series of *wock* notes; also cluck notes. Wing flutter from male's courtship display may sound like distant rumble of thunder. **SIMILAR SPECIES:** Sooty and Dusky grouse larger and longer-tailed, have larger bill, less boldly patterned below. **HABITAT:** Coniferous forests, muskeg.

SOOTY GROUSE　　　　　　　　　　　　Uncommon M60
Dendragapus fuliginosus [formerly Blue Grouse]
20 in. (51 cm). This is the more coastal of the two species formerly lumped as Blue Grouse. A large dark grouse with long neck and tail. Distinct gray band on tail tip. *Male:* In courtship display shows yellow eye combs and inflates bright yellow neck sacs. *Female:* Gray-brown, mottled. **VOICE:** Courting male gives a series of five to seven low, muffled booming or hooting notes, ventriloquial, usually from perch in a tree; much louder than calls of Dusky Grouse. **SIMILAR SPECIES:** See Dusky and Spruce grouse. Females of both Sooty and Dusky grouse may be confused with Ruffed Grouse, but Ruffed has slight crested look, bold flank bars, and lighter tail with *black band* near tip. **HABITAT:** In summer, all forest types, mountain meadow edges; may move to higher-elevation coniferous forests in winter.

DUSKY GROUSE　　　　　　　　　　　　Uncommon M59
Dendragapus obscurus [formerly Blue Grouse]
20 in. (51 cm). This is the more interior of the two species formerly lumped as Blue Grouse. *Male:* In courtship display, eye combs may change from yellow to red. Neck sacs *purplish red. Female:* See Sooty Grouse. **VOICE:** Courting male gives a series of five to seven low, muffled booming notes, ventriloquial, usually from ground; lower pitched and substantially softer than Sooty Grouse. **SIMILAR SPECIES:** Sooty Grouse tends to be darker overall; male has yellowish neck sacs, more obvious gray tail tip; no range overlap. See Spruce Grouse. Female Dusky Grouse may be confused with Ruffed Grouse; see under Sooty Grouse. **HABITAT:** In summer, all forest types, alpine meadow edges; may move to higher-elevation coniferous forests in winter.

FOREST GROUSE

RUFFED GROUSE

♂ display

gray morph

rusty morph

SPRUCE GROUSE

♂

♀

♂

♂ display

typical

"Franklin's"

♀

♂

♂ display

♂ display

♂

SOOTY GROUSE

DUSKY GROUSE

57

SHARP-TAILED GROUSE
Uncommon, local M61

Tympanuchus phasianellus

17 in. (43 cm). A pale, speckled-brown grouse of prairies and brushy draws. Note *short pointed tail,* which in display or flight shows *white* at sides. Slight crested look. Marked below by dark bars, spots, and chevrons. Displaying male has yellow eye combs and inflates *purplish* neck sacs. **VOICE:** Cackling *cac-cac-cac,* etc. Courting note a single low *coo-oo,* accompanied by quill-rattling, foot-shuffling. **SIMILAR SPECIES:** Prairie-chickens have *rounded, dark* tail and are more barred, rather than spotted, below. Female Ring-necked Pheasant has *long pointed* tail. Ruffed Grouse has banded, *fan-shaped* tail and black neck ruff. **HABITAT:** Prairies, agricultural fields, forest edges, clearings, coulees, open burns and clear-cuts in coniferous and mixed forests.

GREATER PRAIRIE-CHICKEN
Uncommon, local M62

Tympanuchus cupido

17 in. (43 cm). A henlike bird of prairies. Brown, heavily barred. Note *rounded dark tail* (black in male, barred in female). Courting males in communal "dance" inflate orange neck sacs, show off orangey yellow eye combs, and erect black hornlike neck feathers. **VOICE:** "Booming" male in dance makes a hollow *oo-loo-woo,* suggesting sound made by blowing across a bottle mouth. **SIMILAR SPECIES:** Lesser Prairie-Chicken. Sharp-tailed Grouse, often called "Prairie-Chicken," slightly paler overall, has more spots or chevrons on underparts, and has more pointed, white-edged tail. Female Ring-necked Pheasant slightly larger, has long pointed tail. **HABITAT:** Native tallgrass prairie, now very localized; agricultural land.

LESSER PRAIRIE-CHICKEN
Scarce, local M63

Tympanuchus pallidicinctus

16 in. (41 cm). A small, pale brown prairie-chicken; best identified by range. Male's neck sacs are dull *purplish* or *plum colored* (not yellow-orange as in Greater Prairie-Chicken). Breast barring usually paler and thinner than Greater's. **VOICE:** Male's courtship "booming" not as rolling or loud as Greater Prairie-Chicken's. Both sexes give clucking, cackling notes. **SIMILAR SPECIES:** Greater Prairie-Chicken, Sharp-tailed Grouse. **HABITAT:** Sandhill country (sage and bluestem grass, oak shrublands), agricultural land.

PRAIRIE GROUSE

SHARP-TAILED GROUSE

♂

♂ display

GREATER PRAIRIE-CHICKEN

♂

♂ display

LESSER PRAIRIE-CHICKEN

♂

♂ display

INTRODUCED GAME BIRDS

RING-NECKED PHEASANT Fairly common M51
Phasianus colchicus
Male 31–33 in. (79–84 cm); female 21–23 in. (53–59 cm). A large chickenlike bird introduced from Eurasia. Note long pointed tail. Runs swiftly; flight strong, takeoff noisy. *Male:* Highly colored and *iridescent*, with *scarlet wattles* on face and *white neck ring* (not always present). *Female:* Mottled brown, with *long pointed tail*. **VOICE:** Crowing male gives loud double squawk, *kork-kok*, followed by brief whir of wings. When flushed, harsh croaks. Roosting call a two-syllable *kutuck-kutuck*, etc. **SIMILAR SPECIES:** Female sage-grouse have black belly patch. **HABITAT:** Farms, fields, marsh edges, brush, grassy roadsides. Periodic local releases for hunting.

GRAY PARTRIDGE *Perdix perdix* Uncommon, local M50
12½–13 in. (32–34 cm). Introduced from Europe. A rotund gray-brown partridge, larger than a quail; note short *rufous* tail, *rusty face*, chestnut bars on sides. Male has dark U-shaped splotch on belly. **VOICE:** Loud, hoarse *kar-wit, kar-wit*. **SIMILAR SPECIES:** Chukar (another introduced species of West, which also has rufous tail) prefers rockier habitat, has red bill and legs, black "necklace." **HABITAT:** Cultivated land, hedgerows, bushy pastures, meadows.

CHUKAR *Alectoris chukar* Uncommon M49
13½–14 in. (34–36 cm). Introduced from Asia. Like a large quail; gray-brown with *bright red legs and bill;* light throat bordered by clean-cut black "necklace." Sides *boldly barred*. Tail *rufous*. **VOICE:** Series of raspy *chuck*s; a sharp *wheet-u*. **SIMILAR SPECIES:** Gray Partridge. Mountain Quail smaller and darker, with long head plume, dark bill, dull legs. Red-legged Partridge *(Alectoris rufa)*, an occasional escapee, is similar but has streaked breast. **HABITAT:** Rocky, grassy, or brushy slopes; arid mountains, canyons. Birds recently released for hunting may be found well out of range and habitat.

HIMALAYAN SNOWCOCK *Tetraogallus himalayensis* Very local
28 in. (71 cm). An Asian species, introduced to Ruby and Humboldt mountains of n. NV. Large, gray-brown body; paler face and neck with rusty brown stripes. Shows white in wing in flight. Flies downslope in the morning to forage and walks upslope during the day. **VOICE:** Calls include cackles and clucks; display call a loud whistle. **SIMILAR SPECIES:** Chukar. **HABITAT:** Rugged, rocky alpine slopes.

RING-NECKED PHEASANT

GRAY PARTRIDGE

CHUKAR

Red-legged Partridge
for comparison

HIMALAYAN SNOWCOCK

61

NEW WORLD QUAIL Family Odontophoridae

Quail are smaller than grouse. Sexes alike or unlike. **FOOD:** Insects, seeds, buds, berries. **RANGE:** Nearly worldwide.

CALIFORNIA QUAIL *Callipepla californica*   Common M45
10 in. (25 cm). A small, plump, grayish, chickenlike bird, with a *short black plume* curving forward from crown. Male has *black-and-white face* and throat, *scaled belly.* Female duller. **VOICE:** Three-syllable *qua-quergo,* or *Chi-cago.* Also light clucking and sharp *pit* notes. Male on territory, a loud *kurr.* **SIMILAR SPECIES:** Gambel's Quail. **HABITAT:** Broken chaparral, woodland edges, coastal scrub, parks, farms.

GAMBEL'S QUAIL *Callipepla gambelii*   Common M46
10½–11 in. (26–28 cm). Replaces California Quail in most desert habitats. Note *black patch* on *unscaled belly;* flanks and crown more russet (a local name is "Redhead"). **VOICE:** Loud *kaaaa;* also *ka-KAA-ka-ka* and sharp *ut, ut* notes. **HABITAT:** Variety of shrubby desert environments, including parks, suburbs.

MOUNTAIN QUAIL *Oreortyx pictus*   Uncommon M43
11 in. (28 cm). Distinguished from California Quail by long *straight* head plume and *chestnut* (not black) *throat.* Note chestnut-and-white side pattern. Female similar to male but duller, with shorter plume. **VOICE:** Mellow *wook?* or *to-wook?* repeated at intervals by male; loquacious *wew-wew-wew-wew* series. **HABITAT:** Open pine and mixed forests, brushy ravines, montane chaparral.

SCALED QUAIL *Callipepla squamata*   Fairly common M44
10 in. (25 cm). A pale grayish quail of arid country, with scaly markings on breast and back. Note *short bushy white crest,* or "cotton top," a common nickname for this species. Runs; often reluctant to fly. **VOICE:** Guinea hen–like *che-kar* (also interpreted as *pay-cos*). **HABITAT:** Shrub-grasslands, brush, arid country.

NORTHERN BOBWHITE   Uncommon, local, declining M47
Colinus virginianus
9½–10 in. (24–26 cm). A small, rotund fowl, with short dark tail. Male has conspicuous white throat and eyebrow; in female these are buff. A dark Mexican subspecies, "Masked" Bobwhite, with *black throat* and *rusty underparts,* was once found in s. AZ, where it has been locally introduced. **VOICE:** Clearly whistled *Bob-white!* or *poor, Bob-whoit!* Covey call *ko-loi-kee?* answered by *whoil-kee!* **SIMILAR SPECIES:** Other quail. **HABITAT:** Brushy open country, roadsides, open woodlands. Recent hunting releases fairly widespread.

MONTEZUMA QUAIL *Cyrtonyx montezumae*   Scarce, local M48
8½–9 in. (21–23 cm). A rotund quail of mountains and canyons. Note male's *clown face,* bushy nape, and *spotted sides.* Female brown, with less obvious facial striping. Tame (sometimes called "Fool's Quail"). **VOICE:** Male gives a descending whistle; a soft whinnying or quavering cry; ventriloquial. **HABITAT:** Grassy oak canyons, wooded mountain slopes with bunch grass.

QUAIL

♀
CALIFORNIA
QUAIL
♂

♀
♂
GAMBEL'S
QUAIL

♂
MOUNTAIN
QUAIL

♂
SCALED
QUAIL

♂
"Masked"
♀
♂
NORTHERN
BOBWHITE

♂
MONTEZUMA
QUAIL
♀

63

Loons Family Gaviidae

Large, long-bodied swimmers with daggerlike bill; dive from surface or sink. Thrash along water on takeoff. Airborne, loons are slow and hunch-backed; large webbed feet project beyond stubby tail. Seldom on land except at nest. Sexes alike. Immatures more scaly above than nonbreeding adults. **FOOD:** Small fish, crustaceans, other aquatic life. **RANGE:** Northern parts of N. Hemisphere.

RED-THROATED LOON *Gavia stellata*   Fairly common M65
25 in. (64 cm). Note slim snakelike head and neck, thin, slightly *upturned bill, often uptilted head. Breeding:* Plain back, gray head, *rufous throat. Nonbreeding:* Spotted upperparts; adult has extensively white neck; first winter has smudgy gray neck. **VOICE:** When flying, a repeated *kwuk.* Guttural ptarmigan-like calls and falsetto wails on breeding grounds. **SIMILAR SPECIES:** Other loons, grebes. **HABITAT:** Nearshore ocean, bays, estuaries; in summer, tundra lakes.

PACIFIC LOON *Gavia pacifica*   Fairly common M67
25–26 in. (64–66 cm). Smaller than Common Loon, with slightly thinner straight bill, often puffier look to head. Often travels in sizable flocks offshore. *Breeding: Pale gray nape.* Back with four checkered patches. *Nonbreeding:* Note sharp, straight separation of dark and white on neck. Dark feathering around eye. **VOICE:** Deep, barking *kwow;* rising falsetto wails on breeding grounds. **SIMILAR SPECIES:** Nonbreeding adult Red-throated Loon also has straight separation of dark and white on neck but shows much more white. Other loons, grebes. **HABITAT:** Ocean, bays, large lakes; in summer, tundra lakes and sloughs.

ARCTIC LOON *Gavia arctica*   Rare, local M66
27–28 in. (69–73 cm). A bit larger than Pacific Loon, with more angular head and *white rear-flank patches.* In breeding plumage has darker gray nape and bolder white streaking on neck. **SIMILAR SPECIES:** Red-throated Loon also may show white flanks. **HABITAT:** Same as Pacific Loon.

COMMON LOON *Gavia immer*   Fairly common M68
31–32 in. (78–81 cm). Large with *stout,* daggerlike bill. In flight shows large, trailing feet. *Breeding:* Black head and bill. *Checkered back,* broken white necklace. *Nonbreeding:* Note *half-collared neck pattern. Pale "eyelids."* **VOICE:** In breeding season, falsetto wails, yodeling, quavering laughter; at night, a tremulous *ha-oo-oo.* In flight, a barking *kwuk.* **SIMILAR SPECIES:** Other loons, cormorants. **HABITAT:** In summer, lakes, taiga ponds; in winter, larger lakes, bays, ocean.

YELLOW-BILLED LOON *Gavia adamsii*   Rare M69
34–35 in. (86–89 cm). Similar to Common Loon, but bill *pale ivory* (upper ridge always dark to tip in Common) and slightly uptilted: straight above, slightly angled below. In nonbreeding plumage, *paler* head and neck than Common, usually with small *dark ear patch.* **SIMILAR SPECIES:** Common Loon. **HABITAT:** In summer, tundra lakes; in winter, coastal waters. May appear on inland lakes well south of breeding range.

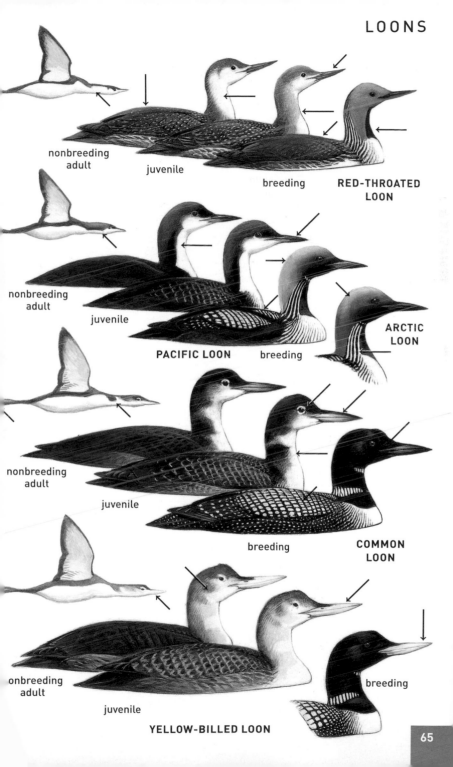

LOONS

nonbreeding
adult

juvenile

breeding

**RED-THROATED
LOON**

nonbreeding
adult

juvenile

PACIFIC LOON

breeding

**ARCTIC
LOON**

nonbreeding
adult

juvenile

breeding

**COMMON
LOON**

nonbreeding
adult

juvenile

breeding

YELLOW-BILLED LOON

GREBES Family Podicipedidae

Ducklike divers with flat, lobed toes; thin neck; tailless look. All but Pied-billed Grebe have white wing patches, pointed bills. Sexes alike. Most young have striped heads. May dive from surface or sink. Flight labored. **FOOD**: Small fish, other aquatic life. **RANGE**: Worldwide.

PIED-BILLED GREBE *Podilymbus podiceps*   Fairly common M70
13–13½ in. (33–34 cm). A small brown diver with "chicken bill," puffy white stern. *Breeding: Black throat patch* and *ring* around pale bill. *Nonbreeding:* Lacks black markings. **VOICE**: Song *kuk-kuk-cow-cow-cow-cowp-cowp-cowp;* also a sizzling whinny and sharp *kwah*. **HABITAT**: Ponds, lakes, marshes; in winter, also salt bays and estuaries.

HORNED GREBE *Podiceps auritus*   Fairly common M71
13½–14 in. (34–36 cm). *Breeding: Golden ear patch* and *chestnut neck.* *Nonbreeding:* Black cap *clean-cut to eye level;* white foreneck, thin straight bill. **VOICE**: Loud *gamp*, trills on breeding grounds. Usually silent in nonbreeding season. **SIMILAR SPECIES**: Eared Grebe. **HABITAT**: Lakes, ponds; in winter, large lakes, bays, coastal waters.

EARED GREBE *Podiceps nigricollis*   Common M73
12½–13 in. (32–33 cm). Note peaked crown, skinny neck, and slightly upturned, all-dark bill. *Breeding: Wispy golden ear tufts, black neck.* *Nonbreeding:* Dark cap extends *below eye,* neck usually dusky. **VOICE**: On breeding grounds, a musical *poo-ee-chk*. **HABITAT**: Prairie lakes, ponds; in winter, saline lakes, coastal bays and estuaries.

RED-NECKED GREBE *Podiceps grisegena*   Uncommon M72
18–19 in. (46–49 cm). A largish grebe. *Breeding:* Long *rufous neck, light cheek,* black cap. *Nonbreeding:* Grayish with white crescent on neck; *yellowish* on bill. In flight, double wing patch. **VOICE**: Loud braying on breeding grounds. **SIMILAR SPECIES**: Loons, mergansers. **HABITAT**: Lakes, ponds; in winter, large lakes, salt water.

LEAST GREBE *Tachybaptus dominicus*   Casual
9½ in. (24 cm). Smaller, darker than Pied-billed Grebe, with white wing patches (usually concealed), puffy undertail coverts, slender *black bill, golden eyes.* **VOICE**: A chattering whinny. **RANGE**: Casual visitor along Mexican border. **HABITAT**: Ponds and lake edges.

WESTERN GREBE *Aechmophorus occidentalis*   Common M74
25 in. (64 cm). A large slate-and-white grebe with long neck. Bill long, greenish yellow with dark ridge. Black of cap extends *below eye.* **VOICE**: Loud, reedy *crik-crick*. **SIMILAR SPECIES**: Clark's Grebe, loons. **HABITAT**: Rushy lakes; in winter, large lakes, bays, coasts.

CLARK'S GREBE   Uncommon to fairly common M75
Aechmophorus clarkii
25 in. (64 cm). Very similar to Western Grebe. Intermediates are known. Bill *orange-yellow.* Dark eye *surrounded by white* (may be dusky in nonbreeding plumage). Back and flanks slightly paler than Western's. Downy young are white, not gray. **VOICE**: Single-noted *creet* or *criik*. **HABITAT**: Similar to Western, but scarce in ocean.

GREBES

lobed foot of grebe

PIED-BILLED GREBE

nonbreeding adult

juvenile

downy young

breeding

nonbreeding variant

HORNED GREBE

ll of rned

nonbreeding

breeding

nonbreeding variant

non-breeding

EARED GREBE

of ed

non-breeding

breeding

immature

RED-NECKED GREBE

onbreeding

breeding

EAST GREBE

♂ display

WESTERN GREBE

CLARK'S GREBE

ALBATROSSES Family Diomedeidae

Birds of open ocean, with rigid gliding and banking flight. Much larger than gulls; wings proportionately longer. "Tube-nosed" (nostrils in two tubes); bill large, hooked, covered with horny plates. Sexes alike. Largely silent at sea. **FOOD**: Cuttlefish, fish, squid, other small marine life; some feeding at night. **RANGE**: Mainly cold oceans of S. Hemisphere; three species nest north of equator in Pacific.

LAYSAN ALBATROSS *Phoebastria immutabilis*　　　　Scarce M76
32 in. (81 cm); wingspan 6½ ft. (198 cm). White body with *dark back and wings*, suggesting a huge, dark-backed gull with extra-long wings. Whitish underwing has some *dark smudges*. Bill and feet pale pinkish gray. Immature similar.

BLACK-FOOTED ALBATROSS　　　　　　　　Uncommon M77
Phoebastria nigripes
32–33 in. (81–84 cm); wingspan 7 ft. (213 cm). Great size, *sooty color*, tremendously long saberlike wings, and rigid shearwater-like gliding identify this species, the albatross found most regularly off our Pacific Coast. Seldom seen from shore. At close range shows whitish face and pale areas toward wingtips. Bill and feet *dark*. Older adults develop more white on head and white patches at base of tail. **SIMILAR SPECIES**: Immature Short-tailed Albatross slightly larger, has *pinkish bill and feet*.

SHORT-TAILED ALBATROSS *Phoebastria albatrus*　　　Casual
36–37 in. (91–94 cm); wingspan 7½ ft. (229 cm). *Adult: White back, pink bill*, yellowish nape. Underwing white with dark edge. *Immature:* Dark brown, bill and feet *pinkish*. **SIMILAR SPECIES**: Black-footed and Laysan albatrosses. **RANGE**: Breeds on islands off Japan. Formerly near extinction, slowly recovering. Ranges from Bering Sea to CA, where almost all sightings involve young birds.

Black-footed

variant

BLACK-
FOOTED
ALBATROSS

LAYSAN
ALBATROSS

Laysan

immature
Short-
tailed

adult

Short-tailed

immature

SHORT-
TAILED
ALBATROSS

SHEARWATERS AND PETRELS
Family Procellariidae

Gull-like birds of open sea that glide low over waves (usually with wings more stiffly extended than shown here). They often bank, or arc, up and down like a roller coaster, particularly in strong winds. Typically fly with several flaps and then a glide. Wings narrower than those of gulls. Shearwaters and petrels, along with albatrosses and storm-petrels, have tubelike external nostrils on bill, so are often called "tubenoses." Largely silent at sea; most apt to call at feeding frenzies. **FOOD:** Fish, squid, crustaceans, ship refuse. **RANGE:** Oceans of world. Most species only occasionally or rarely seen from our mainland shores.

NORTHERN FULMAR
Uncommon to fairly common M78
Fulmarus glacialis
18½–19 in. (47–49 cm). A stiff-winged oceanic seabird; shearwater-like, but stockier with larger head, shorter, rounder wings; flies like shearwater but with quicker wingbeats, less gliding. Note rounded forehead; *stubby, yellowish, tubenose bill;* longish tail. Primaries may show a *pale flash or patch.* Comes in several color morphs. *Light morph:* Gull-like in plumage. *Intermediate morph:* Variable. *Dark morph* (breeds mostly from Aleutians southward): Smoky gray, wingtips darker. All morphs may be found together in winter. **VOICE:** Hoarse, grunting *ag-ag-ag-arrr* or *ek-ek-ek-ek-ek.* **SIMILAR SPECIES:** At a distance, shape and flight style distinguish light morph from gulls and dark morph from dark shearwaters. **HABITAT:** Open ocean, sometimes found in harbors during and immediately following years of high abundance; breeds colonially on sea cliffs.

MURPHY'S PETREL *Pterodroma ultima*
Very rare
15½–16 in. (40–41 cm). A dark petrel with wholly *dark underwing linings,* faint dark M across back and wings, somewhat wedge-shaped tail, and *pale face and throat.* **SIMILAR SPECIES:** Sooty Shearwater, dark-morph Northern Fulmar. Accidental Great-winged Petrel (*Pterodroma macroptera;* not illustrated) slightly larger, browner, more white on face. **RANGE:** Breeds in sw. Pacific; very rare but somewhat regular visitor far offshore from CA to s. BC, mostly in spring.

COOK'S PETREL *Pterodroma cookii*
Rare
10½–11 in. (27–28 cm). *Dark M* across gray upperside and *gleaming white* underside suggest much larger Buller's Shearwater, but note paler head with black ear patch and light sides of tail. **RANGE:** Nests off New Zealand; ranges across Pacific, rarely but perhaps regularly to waters well off West Coast from s. AK to Baja CA.

MOTTLED PETREL *Pterodroma inexpectata*
Rare
14 in. (36 cm). *Dark M* across back and upperwing suggests Buller's Shearwater or Cook's Petrel, but note contrasting *dark belly* and *heavy diagonal black bar* across underwing. **RANGE:** Nests in New Zealand; regular summer visitor to deep offshore Alaskan waters, very rare though probably somewhat regular south to well off CA, mostly in late fall and winter.

tubed bill of Fulmar, also typical of petrels

dark morph

light morph

NORTHERN FULMAR

MURPHY'S PETREL

COOK'S PETREL

MOTTLED PETREL

71

SHORT-TAILED SHEARWATER   Uncommon M83
Puffinus tenuirostris
16–17 in. (40–43 cm). Very similar to Sooty Shearwater; best distinguished by *shorter bill, rounder head, variably smoky gray* wing linings (whiter in Sooty), slightly smaller size, narrower wings, more rapid wingbeats. May have contrasty pale throat. **RANGE:** Common off AK in summer and early fall; much less common farther south, mostly between late fall and late winter.

SOOTY SHEARWATER *Puffinus griseus*   Common M82
17–18 in. (43–46 cm). Often seen in flocks in summer, sometimes close to shore. Looks all dark at a distance; arcs above waves on narrow, rigid wings. In good light, note *whitish wing linings.* **SIMILAR SPECIES:** Dark jaegers (white in primaries), Short-tailed and Flesh-footed shearwaters, dark-morph Northern Fulmar.

FLESH-FOOTED SHEARWATER *Puffinus carneipes*   Rare M80
17–17½ in. (43–45 cm). This dark-bodied shearwater is a rare but regular visitor. *Larger* than Sooty Shearwater; flight more sluggish. Distinguished by *pale pink bill* (with dark tip), *pinkish feet,* dark wing linings (and slightly paler flight feathers). **SIMILAR SPECIES:** Dark-morph Northern Fulmar, Sooty Shearwater.

PINK-FOOTED SHEARWATER   Fairly common M79
Puffinus creatopus
19½ in. (50 cm). Two fairly common shearwaters with *mostly white underparts* are regular along West Coast: Pink-footed and Black-vented. Pink-footed is much larger, has pinkish bill, slower wingbeats. Black-vented is much *smaller,* has all-dark bill and faster wingbeats with little arcing. **SIMILAR SPECIES:** See Buller's Shearwater.

BULLER'S SHEARWATER   Uncommon, irregular M81
Puffinus bulleri
16 in. (41 cm). An uncommon and beautiful white-bellied shearwater. Separated from Pink-footed and Black-vented by *gleaming white underparts, dark M* pattern on back and wings, clean-cut dark cap, intermediate size. Occurs in fall (late Aug. through Oct.) in variable numbers from year to year.

BLACK-VENTED SHEARWATER   Fairly common, local M85
Puffinus opisthomelas
13½–14 in. (34–36 cm). A small shearwater, dark brown above and whitish below with dusky breast sides, dark undertail coverts, dark cap extending below eye. Small size, *dark-and-white* pattern, and rapid wingbeats with short glides are distinctive. Often seen in flocks from shore, mostly in fall and winter. **SIMILAR SPECIES:** Manx, Pink-footed, and Buller's shearwaters.

MANX SHEARWATER *Puffinus puffinus*   Rare M84
13½ in. (34 cm). This primarily Atlantic species has been found with increasing regularity along the West Coast. Similar to Black-vented Shearwater but note blacker upperparts, *white undertail coverts*, and clean-cut face pattern. **SIMILAR SPECIES:** Black-vented Shearwater.

SHEARWATERS

SHORT-
TAILED
SHEARWATER

SOOTY
SHEARWATER

FLESH-
FOOTED
SHEARWATER

PINK-FOOTED
SHEARWATER

BLACK-
VENTED
SHEARWATER

BULLER'S
SHEARWATER

MANX
SHEARWATER

73

STORM-PETRELS Family Hydrobatidae

Dark little birds that flutter or bound over open ocean; they nest colonially on islands, returning to burrows at night. Nostrils in a fused tube over top of bill. Usually silent at sea; most apt to call at feeding frenzies. Can be "chummed in" by tossing out ground fish, suet, puffed wheat or popcorn in fish oil, etc. **FOOD:** Plankton, crustaceans, small fish. **RANGE:** All oceans except Arctic.

WILSON'S STORM-PETREL *Oceanites oceanicus*   Casual M86
7¼–7½ in. (18–19 cm). A casual visitor from the Atlantic. Smaller and shorter-winged than Leach's, with more direct flight. Note *white rump patch that wraps around sides; feet project* past *square-cut tail* in flight. Often follows ships (Leach's does not).

FORK-TAILED STORM-PETREL   Scarce M87
Oceanodroma furcata
8½ in. (22 cm). *Pale gray* overall, with contrasting *slaty underwing linings;* our other Pacific storm-petrels are blackish overall. Dark eye patch; faint dark bar across upperwing.

LEACH'S STORM-PETREL   Uncommon M88
Oceanodroma leucorhoa
8 in. (20 cm). Note obscurely divided *white rump,* slightly forked tail.

Pale bar on upperwing often reaches leading edge. In flight, bounds erratically on long angled wings, changing speed and direction — all suggesting a nighthawk. Does not follow ships. Birds nesting in Mex. and fall visitors off s. CA lack white rump. **VOICE:** At night on breeding grounds, nasal chattering notes and long crooning trills. **SIMILAR SPECIES:** See Wilson's and Black storm-petrels. **HABITAT:** Prefers deeper offshore waters than other storm-petrels.

ASHY STORM-PETREL   Uncommon M89
Oceanodroma homochroa
8 in. (20 cm). Separated from Black and dark-rumped Leach's storm-petrels by slightly smaller size, shorter wings, more fluttery, direct flight (shallower wingbeats). At close range, plumage looks more ashy colored; underwings and rump show *pale cast.*

BLACK STORM-PETREL   Fairly common M90
Oceanodroma melania
9 in. (23 cm). The largest all-black storm-petrel found off CA, primarily from late spring through early fall. Forked tail. Larger than Ashy Storm-Petrel, with longer wings and *more languid flight.* **SIMILAR SPECIES:** Dark-rumped Leach's Storm-Petrel is larger, has slower wingbeats, more direct flight; Leach's tends to be farther offshore.

LEAST STORM-PETREL *Oceanodroma microsoma*   Rare M91
5¾ in. (15 cm). A late-summer and fall visitor in variable numbers. Small. Our only regularly occurring storm-petrel with *very short rounded or wedge-shaped* tail. Flight similar to Black Storm-Petrel. **SIMILAR SPECIES:** Ashy Storm-Petrel is larger and paler with forked tail and quicker, shallower wingbeats. Also smaller, Mexican breeding dark-rumped Leach's Storm-Petrel.

ubed bill
f storm-
etrel

WILSON'S
STORM-PETREL

FORK-TAILED
STORM-PETREL

LEACH'S
STORM-
PETREL

Leach's
Storm-
petrel

dark-
rumped
form
(see p. 74)

ASHY
STORM-PETREL

LEAST
STORM-
PETREL

LACK STORM-
PETREL

75

Gannets and Boobies Family Sulidae

Seabirds with large, pointed bill and pointed tail, making them appear tapered at both ends. Larger and longer necked than most gulls. Sexes mostly alike. Boobies sit on buoys, rocks; fish by plunging from air like Brown Pelicans. Mostly silent at sea, except when at feeding frenzies. FOOD: Fish, squid. RANGE: Gannets live in cold seas (N. Atlantic, S. Africa, Australia), boobies in tropical seas. All nest colonially on islands.

BLUE-FOOTED BOOBY *Sula nebouxii*　　　　　　　　Casual M93
32–33 in. (81–83 cm). *Adult:* White body, whitish head, *light patches on upper back and rump,* dark mottled back and wings, *blue feet. Immature:* Has slightly darker head and neck. SIMILAR SPECIES: Immature Masked and Brown boobies. Adult male Brown Booby also has pale head, grayish bill.

BROWN BOOBY *Sula leucogaster*　　　　　　　　　　Rare M94
29–30 in. (74–76 cm). *Adult:* Sooty brown with *white belly in clean-cut contrast* to dark breast. White wing linings contrast with dark flight feathers. Bill and feet yellowish. Males pale around head, have grayer bill. *Immature:* Underparts mostly dark, with little contrast between breast and belly; bill grayish. SIMILAR SPECIES: Immature Red-footed Booby (which has dark tail) more buffy overall with dark underwing; has lilac color at base of bill; feet orangey pink. Immature Masked Booby resembles adult Brown Booby, but brown of head not as sharply demarcated from paler underparts. Blue-footed Booby has weaker contrast below, shows whitish patches on upper back and rump.

RED-FOOTED BOOBY *Sula sula*　　　　　　　　　　　Casual
27–28 in. (69–71 cm). The smallest booby. *Adult:* Feet *bright red,* tail *white.* Two color morphs. *White morph:* Gannetlike; white, with black tip and trailing edge of wing (as in Masked Booby), tail white. *Dark morph:* Brown back and wings, paler head; white tail and belly; in flight, *underwing dark,* thin dark trailing edge on upperwing. (Pacific Coast records are of these.) *Immature:* Tan overall with *dark underwing,* pink and lilac base of bill, dull pink or orangey pink feet. SIMILAR SPECIES: Brown Booby. RANGE: Casual along West Coast.

MASKED BOOBY *Sula dactylatra*　　　　　　　　　　Casual
31–32 in. (79–81 cm). *Adult:* White with *black tail,* black along entire *rear edge* of wing, and black in *face.* Greenish yellow bill. Mostly white underwing. *Immature:* Variably mottled with dark on upperwing and head, but shows white collar. VOICE: Usually silent. In nesting colony, a variety of whistles, grunts, bill-rattling. SIMILAR SPECIES: Other boobies. RANGE: Casual along CA coast.

adult

juvenile

adult

adult

BLUE-FOOTED BOOBY

♂

♀

♀

♂

subadult

BROWN BOOBY

RED-FOOTED BOOBY

white morph

brown morph

adults

adults

adults

juvenile

MASKED BOOBY

PELICANS Family Pelecanidae

Huge waterbirds with long flat bill and great throat pouch (flat when deflated). Neck long, body robust. Sexes alike. Flocks fly in lines or Vs or kettles, alternating several flaps with a glide. In flight, head is hunched back on shoulders, the long bill resting on breast. Pelicans swim buoyantly. **FOOD:** Mainly fish, crustaceans. **RANGE:** N. and S. America, Africa, s. Eurasia, E. Indies, Australia.

AMERICAN WHITE PELICAN   Uncommon to common M95
Pelecanus erythrorhynchos
62 in. (157 cm). Huge; wingspan 8–9½ ft. (244–290 cm). White, with black primaries and a great orange-yellow bill. Adults in breeding condition have "centerboard" on ridge of bill; reduced or lacking at other seasons. *Immature:* Dusky wash on head, neck, and wings. Does not plunge from air like Brown Pelican but scoops up fish while swimming, often working in groups. Flocks may fly in lines and broken Vs and circle high in air on thermals. **VOICE:** In colony, a low groan. Young utter whining grunts. **SIMILAR SPECIES:** Swans, Wood Stork, Whooping Crane, Snow Goose. **HABITAT:** Lakes, marshes, salt bays.

BROWN PELICAN *Pelecanus occidentalis*   Common M96
48–50 in. (122–127 cm); wingspan 6½ ft. (198 cm). A ponderous dark waterbird. *Adult:* Much white and buff on head and neck. Dark chestnut brown on neck when breeding. *Immature:* Duskier overall, with paler underparts. Size, shape, and flight (a few flaps and a glide) indicate a pelican; dark color and habit of *plunging bill-first* proclaim it as this species. Lines of pelicans glide low over water, almost touching it with wingtips. **VOICE:** Adults silent (rarely a low croak). Nestlings squeal. **HABITAT:** Salt bays, beaches, ocean; more rarely inland lakes. Perches on piers, rocks, buoys, beaches.

FRIGATEBIRDS Family Fregatidae

Dark tropical seabirds with extremely long wings (longer relative to body weight than any other bird). Bill long, hooked; tail deeply forked. Frigatebirds do not swim. **FOOD:** Fish, jellyfish, squid, young seabirds. Food snatched from water in flight, scavenged, or pirated from other seabirds. **RANGE:** Pantropical oceans.

MAGNIFICENT FRIGATEBIRD *Fregata magnificens* Very rare M102
39–40 in. (100–102 cm); wingspan 7½ ft. (230–235 cm). A large seabird with extremely long angled wings and *scissorlike* tail (often folded in a *point*). Soars with extreme ease. Most birds seen in w. U.S. are juveniles. **SIMILAR SPECIES:** Great Frigatebird *(Fregata minor)* of HI (not illustrated) is accidental off CA and elsewhere. Adult male retains light brown wing coverts, but very difficult to separate from Magnificent; female has whitish or grayish throat, red eye-ring; juvenile has rust-tinged head. Lesser Frigatebird *(Fregata ariel)* recorded in WY and CA. Adult male has white spur on axillars. Juvenile has russet head. **RANGE:** Very rare summer visitor at Salton Sea and along s. CA coast; casual farther north and inland. **HABITAT:** Tropical oceans. May follow ships.

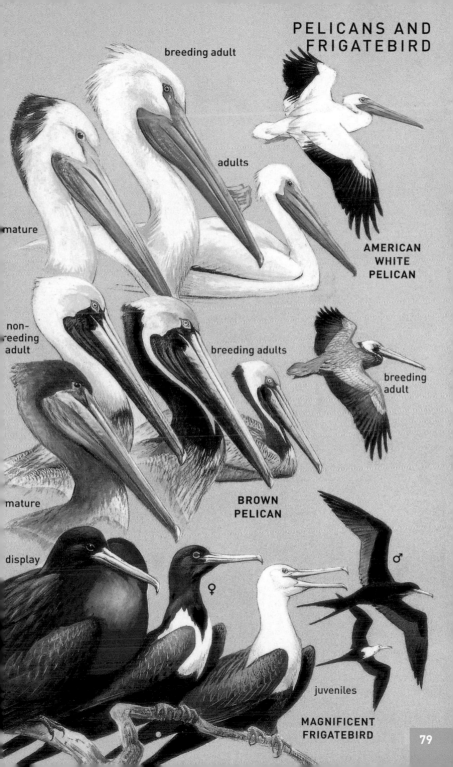

PELICANS AND FRIGATEBIRD

breeding adult

adults

mature

**AMERICAN
WHITE
PELICAN**

non-
reeding
adult

breeding adults

breeding
adult

mature

**BROWN
PELICAN**

display

♀

♂

juveniles

**MAGNIFICENT
FRIGATEBIRD**

CORMORANTS Family Phalacrocoracidae

Large blackish waterbirds that often stand erect on rocks, posts, or dead limbs with neck in an S; may rest with wings spread out to dry. Adults may have colorful facial skin, throat pouch, and eyes. Bill slender, hook-tipped. Sexes alike. Cormorants swim low like loons, but with bill tilted up at an angle. They often fly in lines or Vs, somewhat in manner of geese. Silent except for occasional low grunts at nesting colonies. FOOD: Fish, crustaceans. RANGE: Nearly worldwide.

DOUBLE-CRESTED CORMORANT   Common M99
Phalacrocorax auritus
32–33 in. (81–84 cm). Almost any cormorant found inland can be called this species except in sw. states where Neotropic occurs. Coastally, told from others by *orangey* throat pouch. In flight, shows *kink* in neck. *Adult:* All black. Crest seldom evident. *Immature:* Brownish belly, pale throat and chest. SIMILAR SPECIES: Other cormorants, loons. HABITAT: Coasts, lakes, rivers; nests colonially on rocky islands, sea cliffs, or in trees at lakes.

NEOTROPIC CORMORANT   Uncommon M98
Phalacrocorax brasilianus
25–26 in. (64–66 cm). Similar to Double-crested, but smaller, slimmer, *longer tailed;* usually lacks *orange loral stripe* and has smaller throat patch with point at rear. In breeding plumage, white filoplumes on neck and *white border* to throat pouch. *Immature:* Paler below. SIMILAR SPECIES: Other cormorants. HABITAT: Freshwater wetlands, ponds, lakes.

BRANDT'S CORMORANT   Common M97
Phalacrocorax penicillatus
34 in. (86–89 cm). *Adult:* Almost size of Double-crested Cormorant, but has dark chin (*blue* when breeding) and flies without marked kink in neck. *Buffy throat patch* behind pouch. *Immature:* If a young cormorant along Pacific Coast has whitish breast, it is Double-crested; if it appears more uniformly dark, it is most likely Brandt's (buffy or pale brown breast) or Pelagic (deep brown breast). HABITAT: Ocean, coasts, littoral; nests colonially on sea cliffs.

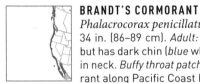

PELAGIC CORMORANT   Fairly common M101
Phalacrocorax pelagicus
26–29 in. (66–73 cm). Smaller than other Pacific cormorants; more *slender neck* (no kinks in flight), longish tail, small head, *thinner bill. Adult:* In breeding condition has double crest and *white patch* on flanks. *Immature:* Deep brown all over, darkest on back. SIMILAR SPECIES: Other cormorants, loons. HABITAT: Ocean, coasts, bays. Despite name, seldom seen far from shore.

RED-FACED CORMORANT   Uncommon, local M100
Phalacrocorax urile
30–31 in. (76–79 cm). Distinguished from Pelagic Cormorant by thicker mostly *pale bill. Adult: Bright red* face extends to *forehead and behind eye.* Throat pouch *bluish.* Has white flank patches when breeding. HABITAT: Ocean, coasts; nests on sea cliffs.

See also flight
figures on p. 83

CORMORANTS

DOUBLE-
CRESTED
CORMORANT

breeding

cormorants swim
with bill uptilted

NEOTROPIC
CORMORANT

immature

breeding

adult

breeding
adult

BRANDT'S
CORMORANT

Pelagic
immature

adult

Pelagic
adult

PELAGIC
CORMORANT

adult

immature

RED-FACED
CORMORANT

TROPICBIRDS Family Phaethontidae

These seabirds resemble (but are unrelated to) large terns with two greatly elongated central tail feathers (adults) and stouter, very slightly decurved bill. Tropicbirds dive headfirst and swim with tail held clear of water. Sexes alike. Largely silent at sea. **FOOD:** Squid, fish, crustaceans. **RANGE:** Tropical oceans.

RED-BILLED TROPICBIRD *Phaethon aethereus*   Rare M92
18 in. (45 cm), adults to 37 in. (94 cm) with tail-streamers. A ternlike seabird that flies with rapid, shallow wingbeats. *Adult:* Two *extremely long central tail feathers, heavy red bill,* black patch through cheek, black primaries, and *finely barred back. Immature:* Lacks long tail, has orange-yellow bill. **SIMILAR SPECIES:** Red-tailed Tropicbird.

RED-TAILED TROPICBIRD *Phaethon rubricauda*   Casual
18 in. (46 cm), adults to 37 in. (94 cm) with tail-streamers. Slower wingbeats than Red-billed Tropicbird. *Adult:* Whiter above than Red-billed; tail-streamers *red. Immature:* Lacks tail-streamers, thinly barred on back, bill dusky, mostly white primaries. **RANGE:** Nests in tropical and subtropical Pacific. Casual far off CA coast, perhaps rare but regular.

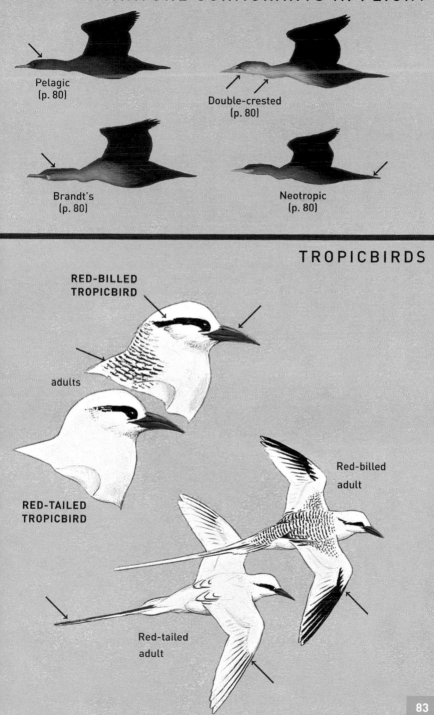

IMMATURE CORMORANTS IN FLIGHT

Pelagic
(p. 80)

Double-crested
(p. 80)

Brandt's
(p. 80)

Neotropic
(p. 80)

TROPICBIRDS

RED-BILLED
TROPICBIRD

adults

RED-TAILED
TROPICBIRD

Red-billed
adult

Red-tailed
adult

83

BITTERNS, HERONS, AND ALLIES
Family Ardeidae

Medium to large wading birds with long neck, spearlike bill. They stand with neck erect or head back on shoulders. In flight, neck is folded in an S; legs trail. Many herons have plumes when breeding. Sexes similar. FOOD: Fish, frogs, crawfish, other aquatic life; mice, gophers, small birds, insects. RANGE: Worldwide except colder regions.

GREAT BLUE HERON *Ardea herodias*   Common M105
45–47 in. (115–120 cm). A lean gray bird, often miscalled a "crane"; may stand 4 ft. (122 cm) tall. Long legs, long neck, daggerlike bill, and, in flight, folded neck indicate a heron. Great size and blue-gray color mark it as this species. VOICE: Deep harsh croaks: *frahnk, frahnk, frahnk.* SIMILAR SPECIES: Sandhill Crane. HABITAT: Marshes, swamps, shores, tidal flats, moist fields.

LITTLE BLUE HERON *Egretta caerulea*   Scarce, local M108
24 in. (61 cm). A small, slender heron. *Adult:* Bluish slate with deep maroon-brown neck; legs dark, bill pale blue with dark tip. *Immature:* All white with *grayish wingtips.* Legs *dull olive;* base of bill pale *blue-gray;* lores dull grayish or gray-green. Birds in transition are boldly pied white and dark. See p. 86. VOICE: Loud, nasal *scaaah.* SIMILAR SPECIES: Immature Little Blue like Snowy Egret except bill slightly thicker and grayer based, lores duller, and wingtips (usually) dusky. Reddish Egret. HABITAT: Marshes, ponds, mudflats, swamps, rice fields.

TRICOLORED HERON *Egretta tricolor*   Casual M109
26 in. (66 cm). A very slender, dark heron with contrasting *white belly* and white rump. *Long* slender bill. *Adult:* Mostly bluish above and on neck. White crown plumes and pale rump plumes when breeding. *Immature:* Neck rusty brown. VOICE: Series of drawn-out nasal quacks. SIMILAR SPECIES: Great Blue and Little Blue herons. RANGE: Casual visitor along s. CA coast and inland to Southwest. HABITAT: Marshes, swamps, shores.

REDDISH EGRET *Egretta rufescens*   Very rare, local M110
30–31 in. (76–79 cm). Note pinkish, black-tipped bill of adult in breeding condition. Loose-feathered; neck shaggy (adult). Pale eye. Neutral gray, with rusty head and neck (immature duller, with all-dark bill). When feeding, races about with spread wings. VOICE: Infrequently vocal; sometimes a harsh *kraaak!* SIMILAR SPECIES: Resembles adult Little Blue Heron, which is darker with bill pale bluish at base. RANGE: Very rare visitor along s. CA coast; casual inland to Southwest. HABITAT: Salt marshes, tidal flats.

DARK HERONS AND EGRET

juvenile

herons' necks may stretch or be looped in when they are standing

herons fly with neck pulled in

adult

GREAT BLUE HERON

adult

LITTLE BLUE HERON

(juvenile on p. 87)

juvenile

adult

TRICOLORED HERON

adult

REDDISH EGRET

Reddish Egret "dancing" while feeding

85

GREAT EGRET *Ardea alba*   Common M106
38–39 in. (97–100 cm). A tall, stately, slender white heron with largely *yellow bill.* Legs and feet *black.* When breeding, *straight plumes* on back extend beyond tail; bill may have dark ridge; lores greenish. When feeding, assumes an eager, forward-leaning pose, with neck extended. **VOICE:** Low, hoarse croak. Also *cuk, cuk, cuk.* **SIMILAR SPECIES:** Snowy Egret has all-black bill, yellow feet. Cattle Egret much smaller. **HABITAT:** Marshes, ponds, shores, mudflats, moist fields.

SNOWY EGRET *Egretta thula*   Common M107
24 in. (61 cm). Note the *"golden slippers."* A medium-sized heron, with *slender black bill,* black legs, and *yellow feet. Recurved plumes* on back during breeding season. Lores yellow (briefly red in high breeding condition). When feeding, rushes about, shuffling its feet to stir up food. Nonbreeding and young birds may show yellowish or greenish on much of rear side of legs, lores duller. **VOICE:** Low croak; in colony, a bubbling *wulla-wulla-wulla.* **SIMILAR SPECIES:** Great Egret larger, has largely yellow bill. Cattle Egret has yellow bill. White immature Little Blue Heron has blue-gray base to thicker bill, grayer lores, less active feeding style. **HABITAT:** Marshes, ponds, shores, tidal flats.

LITTLE BLUE HERON *Egretta caerulea* (adult on p. 84)
Immature: White with dusky wingtips. Also pied pattern with blue-gray plumage. Base of bill blue-gray, lores greenish gray, legs dull olive. May be confused with immature Snowy Egret. Little Blue has less active feeding style: tends to stand still with neck outstretched at a 45-degree angle. Snowy tends to run around more.

CATTLE EGRET *Bubulcus ibis*   Uncommon to common M111
19–20 in. (48–51 cm). Slightly smaller, stockier, and thicker necked than Snowy Egret. In breeding plumage shows *buff-orange* on crown, breast, and back (but may appear whitish at a distance); little or no buff at other times. Bill relatively short and yellow (orange-pink when nesting). Legs coral pink (nesting); immature may have yellow, greenish, or dusky legs. **VOICE:** Usually silent. Near breeding colony, a series of nasal grunts. **SIMILAR SPECIES:** Snowy Egret has black bill. Immature Little Blue Heron has blue-gray bill. Great Egret much larger. **HABITAT:** Farms, marshes, highway edges. Often associates with cattle.

WHITE HERONS AND EGRETS

GREAT EGRET

SNOWY EGRET

changing

juvenile

LITTLE BLUE HERON
(adult on p. 85)

CATTLE EGRET

breeding

nonbreeding

87

BLACK-CROWNED NIGHT-HERON
Uncommon M113
Nycticorax nycticorax
25 in. (64 cm). This stocky, thick-billed, short-legged heron is usually hunched and inactive; flies to feed at dusk. *Adult: Black back and cap* contrast with pale gray or whitish underparts. Eyes red; legs yellowish or greenish (pinkish in high breeding condition). Breeding birds have two long white head plumes. *Immature:* Brown, streaked and spotted with buff and white. Bill with greenish base; eyes small, reddish. **VOICE:** Flat *quok!* or *quark!* Most often heard at dusk. **SIMILAR SPECIES:** American Bittern, Yellow-crowned Night-Heron. **HABITAT:** Marshes, shores; roosts in trees.

YELLOW-CROWNED NIGHT-HERON
Rare to casual M114
Nyctanassa violacea
24 in. (61 cm). A chunky heron with longer neck and legs than Black-crowned. *Adult:* Gray overall; head black with buffy-white cheek patch and yellowish crown. *Immature:* Similar to young Black-crowned, but grayer, more finely streaked and spotted; wing coverts have *pale edges.* Bill thicker and lacks greenish yellow base. In flight, entire foot and some of lower leg extend beyond tail. **VOICE:** *Quark,* higher pitched than call of Black-crowned. **RANGE:** Rare along eastern border of region. Casual visitor to s. CA and Southwest. **HABITAT:** Swamps, marshes, streams.

GREEN HERON *Butorides virescens*
Fairly common M112
17–18 in. (43–46 cm). A small dark heron that looks crowlike in flight (but flies with bowed wingbeats). When alarmed, stretches neck, elevates shaggy crest, and jerks tail. *Adult:* Comparatively *short* legs are *greenish yellow* or *orange* (when breeding). Back with blue-green gloss; neck deep chestnut. *Immature:* Streaked neck and breast, browner above. **VOICE:** Loud *skyow* or *skewk;* series of *kuck* notes. **HABITAT:** Lakes, ponds, marshes, streams.

LEAST BITTERN *Ixobrychus exilis*
Uncommon, secretive M104
12–13 in. (31–33 cm). Very small, thin, furtive; straddles reeds. Note large *buff wing patch* (lacking in rails). Back black in adult male, rusty brown in female and immature. **VOICE:** Song a low, muted *coo-coo-coo;* also gives a raspy, rail-like *khak-khak-khak* series. **SIMILAR SPECIES:** Green Heron. **HABITAT:** Freshwater marshes, reedy ponds.

AMERICAN BITTERN *Botaurus lentiginosus*
Uncommon M103
28 in. (71 cm). A stocky brown heron; size of a young night-heron but warmer brown with longer yellowish bill. In flight, *entire trailing edge of wing is dark* and bill held horizontal. Wingbeats much more rapid than night-herons'. At rest or when approached, often stands rigid, bill pointing up. *Black stripe shows on neck.* **VOICE:** "Pumping" sound, a low, deep, resonant *oong-ka´ choonk,* etc. Flushing call *kok-kok-kok.* **SIMILAR SPECIES:** Immature night-herons, Green Heron, and (much smaller) Least Bittern. **HABITAT:** Marshes, reedy lakes. Unlike night-herons, seldom sits in trees.

adult

BLACK-CROWNED
NIGHT-HERON

juvenile

juvenile

adult

YELLOW-CROWNED
NIGHT-HERON

LEAST
BITTERN

juvenile

adult

GREEN HERON

AMERICAN
BITTERN

89

Ibises and Spoonbills
Family Threskiornithidae

Ibises are long-legged, heronlike waders with slender, decurved bill. Spoonbills have spatulate bill. Both fly in Vs or lines and, unlike herons, fly with neck outstretched, alternately flapping and gliding. FOOD: Small crustaceans, small fish, insects, etc. RANGE: Tropical and temperate regions.

WHITE-FACED IBIS *Plegadis chihi*　　　　Fairly common M116
23–24 in. (58–62 cm). A long-legged wader with *long decurved bill.*
Breeding adult: Note *white border* around face meets behind eye; variably red legs; pinkish to red lores; *red eye. Immature and non-breeding adult:* Lack most of white on face; body and legs duller.
VOICE: Deep gooselike quacking. SIMILAR SPECIES: Glossy Ibis. HABITAT: Freshwater marshes, pond edges, irrigated land.

GLOSSY IBIS *Plegadis falcinellus*　　　　Rare to casual M115
23–24 in. (58–62 cm). Very similar to White-faced Ibis and usually seen with them. Distinguished by dark eyes and dark facial skin with pale blue edges. Immatures not always distinguishable. Hybrids with white-faced are known. RANGE: Rare visitor to plains; casual to West Coast.

WHITE IBIS *Eudocimus albus*　　　　　　　　Casual
24–25 in. (62–64 cm). *Adult:* White. Note *red face,* long *decurved red bill,* and *restricted black in wingtips. Immature:* Dark brownish, with *white belly, white rump,* decurved *orangey pink bill.* VOICE: Low and nasal *uuhhnn!* or *quaahh!* SIMILAR SPECIES: Wood Stork, White-faced Ibis. RANGE: Casual visitor to Southwest. HABITAT: Salt, brackish, and fresh marshes, pond edges.

ROSEATE SPOONBILL *Platalea ajaja*　　　　Casual
32 in. (81 cm). A *pink* wading bird with long, flat, spoonlike bill. When feeding, sweeps its bill from side to side. Immature whiter than adult. SIMILAR SPECIES: Escaped flamingos of several species also pinkish. RANGE: Casual visitor to Southwest. HABITAT: Marshes, ponds, lagoons, mudflats.

Storks Family Ciconiidae

Large, long-legged, and heronlike, with straight, recurved, or decurved bill. Some have naked head. Sexes alike. Walk is sedate; flight deliberate, with neck and legs extended. FOOD: Frogs, crustaceans, lizards, rodents. RANGE: S. U.S. to S. America; Africa, Eurasia, E. Indies, Australia.

WOOD STORK *Mycteria americana*　　　　Rare, local M117
39–41 in. (100–105 cm). Very large; wingspan 5½ ft. (168 cm). White, with *dark naked head* and *much black in wing;* black tail. Bill long, thick, slightly decurved. *Immature:* Bill yellowish. Often soars very high on thermals. VOICE: Hoarse croak; usually silent. SIMILAR SPECIES: In flight, American White Pelican, Whooping Crane. RANGE: Rare but regular summer visitor to Salton Sea; casual elsewhere in Southwest. HABITAT: Marshes, ponds, lagoons.

WHITE-FACED IBIS

cial mparison breeding eason

Glossy Ibis

adult

GLOSSY IBIS

immature

adult

immature

adult

WHITE IBIS

adult

ROSEATE SPOONBILL

juvenile

Wood Stork

White Ibis (p. 90) or comparison

adult

immature

WOOD STORK

91

CRANES Family Gruidae

Stately birds, more robust than herons, often with red facial skin. Note tufted appearance over rump. In flight, neck extended. Migrate in Vs or lines like geese. Large herons are sometimes wrongly referred to as cranes. **FOOD:** Omnivorous. **RANGE:** Nearly worldwide except Cen. and S. America and Oceania.

WHOOPING CRANE *Grus americana*   Rare, very local M155
51–52 in. (130–132 cm); wingspan 7½ ft. (229 cm). The tallest N. American bird and one of the rarest. Large *white* crane with *red face.* Primaries *black.* Young birds washed with rust, especially on head. **VOICE:** Shrill, buglelike trumpeting, *ker-loo! ker-lee-oo!* **SIMILAR SPECIES:** Wood Stork has dark head, more black in wing. Egrets and swans lack black in wings. See also American White Pelican and Snow Goose. **HABITAT:** Prairies, fields and pastures, coastal marshes; in summer, muskeg. *Endangered* but slowly increasing.

COMMON CRANE *Grus grus*   Accidental
44–50 in. (112–127 cm). Eurasian. Note black neck, white cheek stripe. Feathers arching over rump are blacker than those of Sandhill Crane. Inasmuch as this stray (probably from Asia) has been recorded in AK, AB, NE, KS, and elsewhere to date, it should be looked for among flocks of Sandhill Cranes. (Some escapees have also occurred in East.)

SANDHILL CRANE *Grus canadensis*   Uncommon M154
36–48 in. (90–122 cm); wingspan 6–7 ft. (183–213 cm). Note *bald red crown,* bustlelike rear. A long-legged, long-necked, gray bird, often stained with rust. Immature browner. In flight, neck extended and wings flap with an upward flick. **VOICE:** Rolling, bugled *garoo-a-a-a,* repeated. Young birds also give a very different, cricketlike call. **SIMILAR SPECIES:** Great Blue Heron is sometimes wrongly called a crane. **HABITAT:** Prairies, fields, marshes, tundra. Lesser (subspecies) nests in tundra, Greater (subspecies) in grasslands and bogs.

storks, ibises, and cranes
fly with neck outstretched

CRANES

adult

**WHOOPING
CRANE**

juvenile

adult

**COMMON
CRANE**

adult

juvenile

SANDHILL CRANE

NEW WORLD VULTURES Family Cathartidae

Blackish; often seen soaring high in wide circles. Their naked heads are relatively smaller than those of hawks and eagles. Vultures are often locally called "buzzards." Silent away from nest site. **FOOD:** Carrion. **RANGE:** S. Canada to Cape Horn.

TURKEY VULTURE *Cathartes aura* (see also p. 122)   Common M119
26–27 in. (66–69 cm); wingspan 6 ft. (183 cm). Nearly eagle-sized. Overhead, note dark color with *two-toned wings* (flight feathers paler). Soars with wings in dihedral (shallow V); rocks and tilts unsteadily. At close range, small, naked *red head* of adult is evident; immatures have dark head. **SIMILAR SPECIES:** Black Vulture; Zonetailed Hawk, which "mimics" Turkey Vulture; and eagles, which have larger, feathered head, shorter tail, and soar in a steady flat plane. **HABITAT:** Wide variety of habitats. Usually seen soaring in sky or perched on dead trees, posts, or on ground feeding, or sunning with wings outstretched.

BLACK VULTURE   Uncommon, local M118
Coragyps atratus (see also p. 122)
25 in. (64 cm); wingspan less than 5 ft. (152 cm). This dark scavenger is readily identified by short, square tail that barely projects beyond rear edge of wings and by *whitish patch* toward wingtip. Legs longer and whiter than Turkey Vulture's. Note *quick, shallow flapping*, alternating with short glides. **SIMILAR SPECIES:** Turkey Vulture has longer, rounded tail; flapping is slower, less frequent; soars with noticeable dihedral. *Caution:* Young Turkey Vulture has dark head. **HABITAT:** Similar to Turkey Vulture's but avoids higher mountains.

CALIFORNIA CONDOR *Gymnogyps californianus*   Rare, local M120
46–47 in. (117–120 cm); wingspan 8½–9½ ft. (259–290 cm). Was heading toward extinction; last wild birds captured in 1987. Captive breeding program successful, and some of these birds released to wild in CA, AZ, and Baja CA. Much larger than Turkey Vulture. *Adult:* Extensive *white underwing linings* toward fore edge of wing. Head yellow-orange. *Immature:* Dusky-headed and lacks white wing linings, but almost twice the size of Turkey Vulture and has much broader proportions and shorter tail. Condor has *flatter wing-plane* when soaring; does not rock or tilt. **SIMILAR SPECIES:** Many Golden Eagles show some white under wing, but this color is placed differently; overall shape also different. **HABITAT:** Mountains, canyons, grassy foothills, chaparral. Nests on mountain ledges.

VULTURES

adult

immature

TURKEY
VULTURE

adult

BLACK
VULTURE

adult

CALIFORNIA CONDOR

95

BIRDS OF PREY

We tend to call all diurnal (day-flying) raptors with a hooked bill and hooked claws "birds of prey." Actually, they fall into two quite separate families:

1. The hawk group (Accipitridae) — kites, harriers, accipiters, buteos, and eagles
2. The falcon group (Falconidae) — falcons and caracaras

The illustrations on the following pages present the most obvious field marks. For a more in-depth treatment of variable plumages, see the various specialty guides that deal with raptors.

The many raptors can be sorted out by their basic shapes and flight styles. When not flapping, they may alternate between soaring, with wings fully extended and tail fanned, and gliding, with wings slightly pulled back and tail folded. These two pages show some basic silhouettes.

full soar

glide

BUTEOS are stocky, with broad wings and a wide, rounded tail. They soar and wheel high in the open sky.

full soar

glide

ACCIPITERS have a small head, short rounded wings, and a longish tail. They typically fly with several rapid beats and a short glide.

glide

full soar

ARRIERS are slim, with long, slim, round-tipped wings and a long tail. They fly open country and glide low, with a vulturelike dihedral.

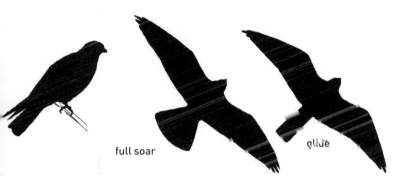

full soar

glide

TES in the western U.S. are falcon-shaped, but unlike falcons, they are buoy-t gliders, not power fliers.

full soar

glide

LCONS have long pointed wings and a long tail. Their wing strokes are strong rapid.

EAGLES, KITES, HAWKS, AND ALLIES
Family Accipitridae

Diurnal birds of prey, with hooked bill, hooked talons. Though persecuted and misunderstood by many, they are very important in the ecosystem. **RANGE:** Almost worldwide.

EAGLES

Distinguished from buteos by their greater size, proportionately longer wings, and larger bill. **FOOD:** Golden Eagle eats chiefly rabbits, large rodents, snakes, game birds; Bald Eagle eats fish, injured waterfowl, carrion.

BALD EAGLE   Uncommon to locally common M124
Haliaeetus leucocephalus (see also p. 122)
31–37 in. (79–94 cm); wingspan 7–8 ft. (213–244 cm). National bird of U.S. *Adult:* With its *white head and tail,* this bird is "all field mark." Bill yellow, massive. Wings held flat when soaring. *Immature:* Variable, depending on age; first year mostly dark with *whitish in wing linings.* Older birds mottled with white on body, underwings, tail, and head. **VOICE:** Harsh, high-pitched cackle, *kleek-kik-ik-ik-ik,* or lower *kak-kak-kak.* **SIMILAR SPECIES:** Golden Eagle, Turkey Vulture. **HABITAT:** Coasts, rivers, large lakes; in migration and winter, also mountains, open country.

GOLDEN EAGLE   Uncommon M140
Aquila chrysaetos (see also p. 122)
30–40 in. (76–102 cm); wingspan 7 ft. (213 cm). This majestic eagle glides and soars flat-winged with occasional shallow wingbeats. *Adult:* Uniformly dark or with slight lightening at base of tail. On hindneck, a *wash of buffy gold. Immature:* In flight, shows *white flash in wings* at base of primaries, and *white tail* with *broad dark terminal band.* **VOICE:** Seldom heard, a yelping bark, *kya;* also whistled notes. **SIMILAR SPECIES:** Immature Bald Eagle has larger head, usually has *extensive blotchy white in wing linings* and often on body. **HABITAT:** Open mountains, foothills, plains, deserts, open country.

OSPREYS

A large bird of prey that hovers above water and plunges feet-first for fish. **FOOD:** Fish. **RANGE:** All continents except Antarctica.

OSPREY *Pandion haliaetus* (see also p. 122)   Uncommon M121
23–24½ in. (58–62 cm); wingspan to 6 ft. (183 cm). Large. Our only raptor that hovers over water and plunges feet-first for fish. (Bald Eagle may pick up fish from surface.) *Adult:* Blackish above, *white below;* head largely white, suggesting Bald Eagle, but with *broad black mask through eyes.* Flies with gull-like kink or crook in wings, showing black "wrist" patch below. *Juvenile:* Has scaly pattern on back. **VOICE:** Series of sharp, annoyed whistles. **SIMILAR SPECIES** Large gulls. Immature Bald Eagle may show dusky "mask." **HABITAT** Rivers, lakes, marshes, coasts.

overhead flight patterns on
p. 123

EAGLES AND
OSPREY

BALD
EAGLE

juvenile

adult

GOLDEN
EAGLE

juvenile

Golden Eagle

adult

hovering

OSPREY

adult

99

KITES

Graceful birds of prey of southern distribution. Western U.S. species are falcon-shaped with pointed wings. **FOOD:** Large insects, reptiles, rodents.

MISSISSIPPI KITE
Uncommon, local M123

Ictinia mississippiensis (see also p. 116)

14–14½ in. (36–37 cm). Falcon-shaped, graceful, and gray. Gregarious; spends much time soaring. *Adult:* Dark above, lighter below; head *pale gray;* tail and underwing blackish. No other falconlike bird has *black unbarred tail.* Broad *white patch* shows on rear edge of upperwing (not visible from below on birds soaring overhead). *Immature:* Lacks pale patch on wing, has weak white bands on tail. *Juvenile:* Heavily streaked on rusty underparts. **VOICE:** Usually silent; near nest, a two-syllable *phee-phew.* **SIMILAR SPECIES:** Male Northern Harrier. **HABITAT:** Nests in riparian woodlands, residential areas, groves, shelterbelts.

WHITE-TAILED KITE
Uncommon M122

Elanus leucurus (see also p. 116)

15½–16 in. (39–41 cm). This whitish kite is falcon-shaped, with long pointed wings, *long grayish white tail,* and *black shoulders.* Overhead, shows oval black patch at carpal joint ("wrist") of underwing. Soars and glides like a small gull; *often hovers. Adult:* Pale gray above, with white head and underparts. *Juvenile:* Like adult, but has *rusty breast,* brown back, and narrow dark band near tip of tail. **VOICE:** Whistled *kew kew kew,* abrupt or drawn out. **HABITAT:** Open groves, river valleys, marshes, grasslands, roadsides. May form communal roosts at night in nonbreeding season.

HARRIERS

Slim raptors with slim wings, long tail. Flight low, languid, gliding, with wings held in shallow V (dihedral). Sexes not alike. They hunt in open country.

NORTHERN HARRIER
Uncommon to fairly common M125

Circus cyaneus (see also p. 116)

18–21 in. (46–54 cm). A slim, long-winged, long-tailed raptor of open country. Glides and flies buoyantly and unsteadily low over ground, with wings held slightly above horizontal, suggesting Turkey Vulture's dihedral. In all plumages shows *white rump patch. Adult male:* Pale gray, whitish beneath. Overhead, wingtips have "dipped-in-ink" look. *Adult female:* Brown, with heavy streaks below. *Immature:* Russet below without streaks. **VOICE:** Weak, nasal whistle, *pee, pee, pee.* **SIMILAR SPECIES:** Short-eared Owl. **HABITAT:** Marshes, fields, farms, prairies.

adult

juvenile

MISSISSIPPI KITE

adult

juvenile

adult

juvenile

adult

WHITE-TAILED KITE

juvenile

juvenile

♂

NORTHERN HARRIER

♀

ACCIPITERS (BIRD HAWKS)

Long-tailed woodland raptors with short, rounded wings, adapted for hunting among trees. Typical flight mixes quick beats and a glide. Sexes similar; females larger. Size helps distinguish species but not always reliable in the field. **FOOD:** Chiefly birds, some small mammals. Sharp-shinned and Cooper's often seen hunting birds at backyard feeders.

SHARP-SHINNED HAWK
Uncommon to fairly common M126

Accipiter striatus (see also p. 114)

10–14 in. (25–36 cm). A small, slim woodland hawk, with slim *square-tipped* tail and *short, rounded wings. Adult:* Dark back, *rusty-barred* breast. Orange eye. *Immature:* Dark brown above, *thickly streaked* with rusty brown on underparts. Yellow eye. **VOICE:** Like Cooper's Hawk, but shriller; a high *kik, kik, kik* given near nest. **SIMILAR SPECIES:** Female Cooper's obviously larger, with *larger head, rounded* tail, with thicker white tip, thicker legs; male Cooper's and female Sharp-shinned closer in size. Adult Cooper's has more defined cap. Immature Cooper's *tawnier* on head and has whiter, more *finely streaked* breast. **HABITAT:** Breeds in extensive forests; in migration and winter, open woodlands, wood edges, residential areas.

COOPER'S HAWK
Fairly common M127

Accipiter cooperii (see also p. 114)

14–20 in. (36–51 cm). Very similar to Sharp-shinned Hawk but larger, particularly female. See Sharp-shinned Hawk. **VOICE:** About nest, a rapid nasal *kek, kek, kek;* suggests a flicker. Also a sapsucker-like mewing. **SIMILAR SPECIES:** Sharp-shinned Hawk, Northern Goshawk. **HABITAT:** Like Sharp-shinned but prefers more open areas, also nests in residential areas.

NORTHERN GOSHAWK
Scarce M128

Accipiter gentilis (see also p. 114)

21–26 in. (53–66 cm). Larger, broader-winged, broader-tailed, more buteo-like than Cooper's Hawk. *Adult:* Crown and cheek blackish; *broad white stripe over eye.* Underparts *pale gray, finely barred;* back paler than in Cooper's or Sharp-shinned hawk. *Immature:* Buffier overall than immature Cooper's with bolder eyebrow, more extensive streaking below, and wavy, irregular tail banding. **VOICE:** *Kak, kak, kak* or *kuk, kuk, kuk,* heavier than Cooper's, given near nest. **SIMILAR SPECIES:** Cooper's Hawk. A soaring goshawk may be initially misidentified as a buteo. **HABITAT:** Coniferous and mixed forests, especially in mountains; forest edges; winters also in wooded lowlands.

ACCIPITERS

juvenile

accipiters have
small head,
short rounded
wings, long tail

adult

SHARP-
SHINNED
HAWK

additional
overhead
flight
patterns on
p. 115

juvenile

adult

COOPER'S
HAWK

adult

juvenile

adult

NORTHERN
GOSHAWK

glide
(tail folded)

full soar
(tail spread)

accipiter flight
silhouettes
(Cooper's Hawk)

103

BUTEOS AND BUTEO-LIKE HAWKS

Large, thickset hawks, with broad wings and wide, rounded tail. Many buteos habitually soar high in wide circles. Much variation; sexes similar, females slightly larger. Young birds usually streaked below. Dark morphs often occur. **FOOD:** Small mammals, sometimes small birds, reptiles, grasshoppers. **RANGE:** Widespread in New and Old Worlds.

HARRIS'S HAWK   Uncommon M130
Parabuteo unicinctus (see also p. 120)
20–21 in. (50–53 cm); wingspan 3½ ft. (107 cm). A blackish brown hawk of *Buteo* type, with flashing *white rump* and *white band* at tip of tail. Often hunts cooperatively in small groups. *Adult:* Chestnut areas on thighs and shoulders. *Immature:* Light, streaked underparts, *rusty shoulders;* conspicuous *white* at base of tail. **VOICE:** Low-pitched, harsh *raaaah!* **SIMILAR SPECIES:** Dark forms of Ferruginous and Red-tailed hawks lack bold rusty shoulders and white tail base. **HABITAT:** Mesquite, cactus deserts.

ZONE-TAILED HAWK   Uncommon M136
Buteo albonotatus (see also p. 120)
20 in. (51 cm); wingspan 4 ft. (122 cm). Dull *black,* with more *slender* wings than most other buteos. Often mistaken for Turkey Vulture because of proportions, two-toned underwing, and up-tilted wings — but hawk has larger feathered head, square-tipped tail, barred underwing, yellow cere and legs. *Adult: White tail bands* (pale gray on topside). *Immature:* Narrower tail bands, *small white spots* on breast. **VOICE:** Nasal, drawn-out *keeeeah.* **SIMILAR SPECIES:** Turkey Vulture, Common Black-Hawk, other dark-morph buteos. **HABITAT:** Riparian woodlands, mountains, canyons.

GRAY HAWK *Buteo plagiatus* (see also p. 116)   Scarce, local M133
17 in. (43 cm); wingspan 3 ft. (91 cm). A small buteo. *Adult:* Distinguished by its buteo-like proportions, gray back, *thickly barred gray* breast, white rump band, and *banded* tail (similar to Broad-winged Hawk's). *Immature:* Narrowly barred tail, striped buffy breast, bold face pattern, *white U-shaped bar* across rump. **VOICE:** Drawn-out whistles, *ka-lee-oh* or *kleeeeoo.* **SIMILAR SPECIES:** Young Broad-winged Hawk has weaker face pattern, lacks white U on rump, has shorter tail, more pointed wings. **HABITAT:** Riparian woodlands.

COMMON BLACK-HAWK   Scarce, local M129
Buteogallus anthracinus (see also p. 120)
21 in. (53 cm); wingspan 4 ft. (122 cm). A buteo-type hawk with chunky shape, exceptionally wide wings, and *long* yellow legs. *Adult:* All black with broad white *band* crossing middle of short tail. In flight, whitish spot shows at base of primaries. *Immature:* Dark-backed with heavily striped *buffy* head and underparts; tail white with five or six wavy dark bands. **VOICE:** Series of loud whistles. **SIMILAR SPECIES:** Zone-tailed Hawk. **HABITAT:** Wooded river and stream bottoms.

adult

juvenile

HARRIS'S
HAWK

GRAY HAWK

juvenile

adult

juvenile

adult

juvenile

adult

ZONE-TAILED
HAWK

adult

juvenile

COMMON
BLACK-HAWK

ROUGH-LEGGED HAWK
Uncommon M139

Buteo lagopus (see also pp. 118 and 120)

21–22 in. (53–55 cm). This hawk of open country often *hovers on beating wings,* more so than other buteos. Longer, narrower wings and tail than other buteos except Ferruginous Hawk. Many birds show *dark belly* and *black patch* at "wrist" (carpal joint) of underwing. Some adult males have dark bib but lack blackish belly band. Tail *white,* with *broad black band or bands* toward tip. White flash on upperwing. Legs feathered, feet small. Dark morph may lack extensive white on tail, but broad terminal band and extensive white on underwing are good field marks. **VOICE:** High-pitched squeal, mostly near nest site. **SIMILAR SPECIES:** Red-tailed Hawk, Northern Harrier, dark-morph Ferruginous Hawk. **HABITAT:** Nests on tundra escarpments, Arctic coasts; in winter, open fields, plains, marshes.

RED-SHOULDERED HAWK
Uncommon to fairly common M131

Buteo lineatus (see also p. 118)

16–20 in. (40–50 cm). In flight, note *translucent* "window" across primaries, longish tail. *Adult:* Black-and-white bands on wings and tail, *rufous shoulders,* wing linings, and underparts. *Immature:* Streaked below; recognized by proportions and, in flight, wing "windows." Western birds darker with quicker wingbeats; seldom soar. **VOICE:** Two-syllable scream, *kee-yer,* repeated in series. **SIMILAR SPECIES:** Broad-winged Hawk has paler wing linings, more pointed wing, lacks wing "windows." **HABITAT:** Woodlands in valleys, canyons, along rivers. Also residential areas.

BROAD-WINGED HAWK
Uncommon M132

Buteo platypterus (see also pp. 118 and 120)

15–16 in. (38–41 cm). A chunky crow-size buteo. *Adult:* Note tail banding: high overhead shows one obvious white band (Red-shouldered shows multiple bands). Underwings whitish, trimmed with black. *Immature:* Streaked along sides of breast and belly; chest often unmarked. Terminal tail band twice as wide as the rest. Rare dark morph, which breeds in Prairie Provinces, has dark wing linings but shows usual Broad-winged tail pattern. **VOICE:** High-pitched, two-part whistle, *pwe-eeeeee.* **SIMILAR SPECIES:** Young Red-shouldered similar to immature Broad-winged but has streaking heaviest on breast, barred secondaries, blunter wingtips with bold pale "window." See also accipiters. **HABITAT:** Woods, groves.

SHORT-TAILED HAWK
Very rare, local M134

Buteo brachyurus (see also p. 120)

15–16 in. (38–41 cm). A crow-size buteo. Two morphs: (1) blackish brown body and black wing linings; (2) blackish above, white below, *two-toned* underwing. **VOICE:** Descending, high-pitched scream: *kleeear!* **SIMILAR SPECIES:** Dark Swainson's Hawk is larger and longer winged with pale undertail coverts. Broad-winged Hawk. **RANGE AND HABITAT:** Casual summer visitor to se. AZ mountains.

dark morph

light morph

ROUGH-LEGGED HAWK

juvenile

adult

RED-SHOULDERED HAWK

Eastern

juvenile

adult

adult

juvenile

BROAD-WINGED HAWK

light-morph juvenile

dark-morph adult

light-morph adult

light-morph adult

dark-morph adult

SHORT-TAILED HAWK

107

RED-TAILED HAWK Common M137
Buteo jamaicensis (see also pp. 118 and 120)
19–22 in. (48–56 cm). The common conspicuous hawk of roadsides and woodland edges. When soaring, adults show *rufous* on topside of tail, pale pinkish below. Also note mottled *white patches* on scapulars. Overhead, a dependable mark on all but blackish birds is *dark patagial bar* on fore edge of wing. Immatures have brownish tail with narrow, dark banding. Underparts of typical eastern Red-taileds are "zoned" (light breast, dark *belly band*). Some birds of sw. TX ("Fuertes's" Red-tailed) lack belly band. On Great Plains, pale "Krider's" morph is found. There is much variation farther west, where Red-taileds tend to be darker. One might encounter the blackish "Harlan's" as well as rufous and dark brown birds. The latter usually have telltale rust on tail. **VOICE:** Asthmatic squeal, *keeer-r-r* (slurring downward). **SIMILAR SPECIES:** Rough-legged, Ferruginous, Swainson's, Red-shouldered, and Broad-winged hawks. **HABITAT:** Open country, woodlands, prairie groves, mountains, plains, roadsides.

SWAINSON'S HAWK Common M135
Buteo swainsoni (see also pp. 118 and 120)
19–21 in. (48–53 cm). A buteo of the plains. Slimmer than Red-tailed Hawk, with narrower, more pointed wings. When gliding, holds wings slightly above horizontal. When perched, *wingtips extend to tail tip.* In light and intermediate morphs, overhead, *pale wing linings contrast with dark flight feathers. Adult:* Typical adults have dark breast-band; tail gray-brown above, often pale toward base; dark and rufous morph birds best identified by shape and shaded flight feathers. *Immature:* Variably streaked below, white band across rump; best identified by shape and wing pattern. Many subadults are distinctly pale-headed. **VOICE:** Shrill, plaintive whistle, *kreeeeeeer.* **SIMILAR SPECIES:** Swainson's wing shape distinctive for a buteo. Lacks white scapular patches of bulkier Red-tailed. **HABITAT:** Plains, grasslands, agricultural land, open hills, sparse trees.

FERRUGINOUS HAWK Uncommon M138
Buteo regalis (see also pp. 116 and 120)
23–24 in. (58–61 cm). A large buteo of plains. Note large bill, long gape line, *long tapered wings* with *pale panel* on upper surface of primaries, *mostly white tail. Adult:* Rufous above, mostly whitish head and breast, rufous wash on tail, rufous thighs form *dark V* on birds overhead. Dark morphs are rufous brown with whitish flight feathers and whitish tail. *Immatures:* Lack rufous tones; best identified by shape as well as wing and tail patterns. **SIMILAR SPECIES:** Red-tailed Hawk and dark-morph Rough-legged Hawk. **HABITAT:** Plains, grasslands, agricultural fields.

RED-TAILED HAWK

rufous adult

Western juvenile

dark adult

Western adult

"KRIDER'S" juvenile

"HARLAN'S" adult

"HARLAN'S" adult

light morph adult

SWAINSON'S HAWK

dark morph

juvenile

adult light morph

light morph

light morph

dark morph

adult light morph

FERRUGINOUS HAWK

CARACARAS AND FALCONS Family Falconidae

Caracaras are large, long-legged birds of prey, some with naked face. **FOOD:** Our one U.S. species feeds mostly on carrion. **RANGE:** S. U.S. to Tierra del Fuego. Falcons are streamlined birds of prey with pointed wings, longish tail. **FOOD:** Birds, rodents, reptiles, insects. **RANGE:** Almost worldwide.

CRESTED CARACARA
Uncommon, local M141

Caracara cheriway (see also p. 120)

23 in. (58 cm). A large, long-legged, big-headed, long-necked bird of prey, often seen feeding with vultures. *Adult: Black crest* and *red face* distinctive. In flight, underbody presents alternating areas of light and dark: white chest, black belly, and whitish, dark-tipped tail. Note combination of *pale wing patches, pale chest, and pale tail panel,* giving impression of "white at all four corners." *Immature:* Browner, streaked on breast. **VOICE:** Weird, guttural series of croaks and rattles. **HABITAT:** Agricultural land, rangeland, deserts.

PRAIRIE FALCON
Uncommon M146

Falco mexicanus (see also p. 114)

16–19 in. (41–50 cm). Like a sandy-colored Peregrine, with *white eyebrow, narrower mustache, blackish* axillars ("wingpits"). **VOICE:** Harsh *kak-kak-kak* around nest. **SIMILAR SPECIES:** Peregrine Falcon. Female Prairie Merlin *(richardsoni)* same color above but much smaller, lacks dark underwing patch. **HABITAT:** Open country, from alpine tundra to grasslands, agricultural land, deserts, marshes.

GYRFALCON *Falco rusticolus* (see also p. 114)
Scarce M144

20–25 in. (51–64 cm). A very large Arctic falcon, larger and more robust than Peregrine; slightly broader tailed. On perched birds, wingtips do not reach near tail tip. Thinner mustache. There are brown, gray, and white color morphs. Darker immature birds are more prone to wander south. **VOICE:** Harsh *kak-kak-kak* series. **SIMILAR SPECIES:** Peregrine and Prairie falcons. **HABITAT:** Arctic barrens, seacoasts; in winter, open country.

PEREGRINE FALCON
Uncommon M145

Falco peregrinus (see also p. 114)

16–20 in. (41–51 cm). Formerly endangered; reintroduced in many regions. Size of a crow, but longer looking. Note *wide black mustache.* Known as a falcon by pointed wings, narrow tail, and quick, powerful wingbeats. Size and strong face pattern indicate this species. *Adult:* Slaty-backed, light-chested, barred and spotted below. Northwestern population, "Peale's" *(pealei),* breeding off s. AK and BC *darker* and more heavily marked on breast. Adults of Tundra race *(tundrius)* have pale forehead and upper breast. *Immature:* Brown, heavily streaked below. **VOICE:** At eyrie, a repeated *we'chew;* a rapid *kek kek kek kek.* **SIMILAR SPECIES:** Merlin, Gyrfalcon, Prairie Falcon. **HABITAT:** Nests on cliffs and ledges, in cities also on bridges and buildings; open country, from mountains to coasts.

CARACARA AND LARGE FALCONS

juvenile

CRESTED CARACARA

adults

gray morph

PRAIRIE FALCON

gray morph

own rph

white morph

YRFALCON

brown morph

enile

Pacific ("Peale's") adult

Tundra adult

PEREGRINE FALCON

adults

AMERICAN KESTREL   Fairly common M142
Falco sparverius (see also p. 114)
9½–10½ in. (24–27 cm). A falcon the size of a large jay. No other *small* hawk has *rufous back or tail*. Male has blue-gray wings. Both sexes have black-and-white face with double mustache. *Hovers* for prey on rapidly beating wings, kingfisher-like. Sits fairly erect, occasionally lifting tail. **VOICE:** Rapid, high *klee klee klee* or *killy killy killy*. **SIMILAR SPECIES:** Merlin (which only rarely perches on wires). Sharp-shinned Hawk has rounded wings, gray or brown back and tail. Neither species hovers. **HABITAT:** Open country, farmland, wood edges, residential areas, dead trees, wires, roadsides.

MERLIN *Falco columbarius* (see also p. 114)   Uncommon M143
11–12 in. (28–31 cm). Slightly larger than kestrel. Note dark coloration, weak face pattern, banded tail. Faster and steadier in flight than kestrel. *Male:* Blue-gray above, with black and gray tail bands. *Female and immature:* Dusky brown, with banded tail; boldly streaked below. Prairie subspecies *(richardsoni)* paler than widespread taiga form *(columbarius)*, lacks mustache. Coastal Northwest subspecies, "Black" *(suckleyi)*, very dark, lacks light eyebrow stripe. **VOICE:** High, rapid *kee-kee-kee-kee*. **SIMILAR SPECIES:** Other falcons. **HABITAT:** Open woods, cliffs, grasslands, tundra; in migration and winter, also open country, marshes, beaches, locally in neighborhoods.

EURASIAN KESTREL *Falco tinnunculus*   Casual
13½–14 in. (34–36 cm). Similar to American Kestrel, but slightly larger. *Adult male:* Dusky mustache on grayish head, pale chestnut upperparts and wing coverts, dusky outer wing; gray rump and tail. *Female:* Similar to female American but note single dusky mustache line, larger size. **RANGE:** Eurasian species. Casual vagrant along West Coast from w. AK to CA.

EURASIAN HOBBY *Falco subbuteo*   Casual
12½–13 in. (31–33 cm). Most aerial of the falcons; sickle-shaped wings and short tail produce a swiftlike outline. Flight dashing, with rapid, clipped wingbeats; when patrolling, action slower, more rowing, recalling Peregrine; never hovers. *Adult:* Dark mustache, cap, and upperparts contrasting with cream throat, heavily streaked underparts, chestnut thighs and vent. *Juvenile:* Lacks chestnut areas. **SIMILAR SPECIES:** Peregrine Falcon. **RANGE:** Eurasian species. Casual vagrant to w. AK; accidental in WA.

APLOMADO FALCON *Falco femoralis* (see also p. 114)   Rare, local
15–16½ in. (38–42 cm). Slightly smaller than Peregrine. *Long wings and tail.* Note *dark underwing* and *belly*, contrasting with pale breast. **RANGE:** Formerly a casual visitor and breeder from Mex., but population in U.S. growing because of reintroduction program in w. TX and s. NM. **HABITAT:** Arid brushy deserts and grasslands, yucca flats.

SMALL FALCONS

AMERICAN KESTREL

♀

♂

♀

♂

♀

♂

♂

♂

Pacific
(Black)

Taiga

Prairie

MERLIN

ARE FALCONS

EURASIAN KESTREL

EURASIAN HOBBY

juvenile

adult

♂

APLOMADO FALCON

adult

♂

Accipiters and Falcons Overhead

Accipiters (bird hawks) have short rounded wings and a long tail. They fly with several rapid beats and a short glide. They are better adapted to hunting in the woodlands than most other hawks. Females are larger than males. Immatures (not shown) have a streaked breast. Frequently soar.

COOPER'S HAWK *Accipiter cooperii*   p. 102
Underparts rusty (adult). Tail rounded and tipped with broad white terminal band. Note head and neck projecting noticeably beyond leading edge of wing.

NORTHERN GOSHAWK *Accipiter gentilis*   p. 102
Adult with bold facial pattern, underbody heavily barred with pale gray. Tail and wings broad.

SHARP-SHINNED HAWK *Accipiter striatus*   p. 102
Small. When folded, tail square or notched, with narrow pale tip. Fanned tail slightly rounded. Note small head and short neck barely projecting beyond wing.

Falcons have long, pointed wings and a relatively long tail. Wing strokes are typically rapid and continuous. Frequently soar.

PEREGRINE FALCON *Falco peregrinus*   p. 110
Falcon shape; large; bold face pattern; longer wings than Merlin or Kestrel.

AMERICAN KESTREL *Falco sparverius*   p. 112
Small; banded rufous tail. Paler underwing and less heavily marked underparts than Merlin.

MERLIN *Falco columbarius*   p. 112
Small; heavily marked underparts and dark checkered underwing; heavily banded tail.

GYRFALCON *Falco rusticolus*   p. 110
Larger than Peregrine Falcon; without that bird's contrasting facial pattern, and with broader wings and tail. Varies in color from brown to gray to white.

APLOMADO FALCON *Falco femoralis*   p. 112
Black belly band or vest, light chest, orange undertail. Tail barred with black. Very long wings and tail.

PRAIRIE FALCON *Falco mexicanus*   p. 110
Size of Peregrine Falcon. *Dark axillars* ("wingpits") and inner coverts.

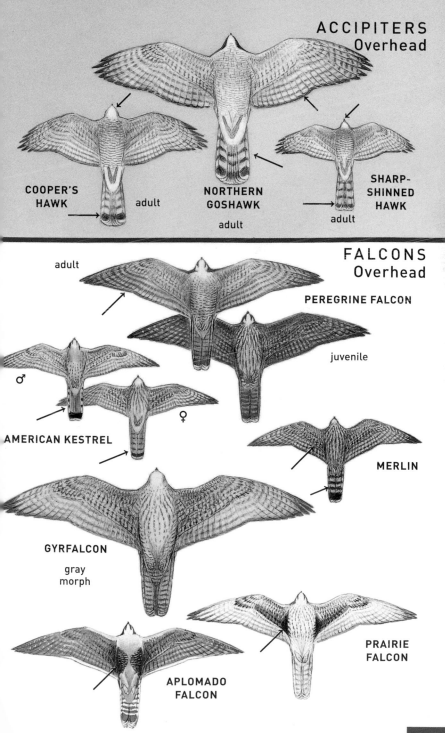

ACCIPITERS
Overhead

COOPER'S HAWK
adult

NORTHERN GOSHAWK
adult

SHARP-SHINNED HAWK
adult

FALCONS
Overhead

adult

PEREGRINE FALCON

juvenile

♂

♀

AMERICAN KESTREL

MERLIN

GYRFALCON
gray morph

APLOMADO FALCON

PRAIRIE FALCON

BUTEOS, HARRIER, AND KITES OVERHEAD

FERRUGINOUS HAWK *Buteo regalis*   p. 108
Whitish underparts, with dark V formed by reddish thighs in adult. Wings and tail long for a buteo. A bird of western plains and open range.

GRAY HAWK *Buteo plagiatus*   p. 104
Stocky. Broadly banded tail (suggestive of Broad-winged Hawk); adults have gray-barred underparts. S. AZ and sw. TX.

NORTHERN HARRIER *Circus cyaneus*   p. 100
Male: Whitish wings with black tips and dark trailing edge. Gray hood.
Female: Brown, heavily streaked; note long, slim wings and tail.
Immature (not shown): Warm brown, unstreaked body, dark head. From above, all plumages have white rump.

WHITE-TAILED KITE *Elanus leucurus*   p. 100
Adult: Falcon-shaped. White body; whitish tail; dark underside to primaries.

MISSISSIPPI KITE *Ictinia mississippiensis*   p. 100
Falcon-shaped. *Adult:* Pale gray head, black tail, dark gray and blackish wings, gray body.
Immature: Streaked breast (youngest birds only); banded square-tipped or notched tail.

Kites (except Snail Kite and Hook-billed Kite) are falcon-shaped but, unlike falcons, are buoyant gliders, not power fliers. All are southern.

BUTEOS
Overhead

adult

FERRUGINOUS HAWK

adult

GRAY HAWK

HARRIER
Overhead

adult ♂

adult ♀

NORTHERN HARRIER

KITES
Overhead

adult

adult

WHITE-TAILED KITE

juvenile

MISSISSIPPI KITE

RED-TAILED HAWK *Buteo jamaicensis* p. 108
Dark patagial bar at fore edge of wing is best mark from below. *Adult:*
Light chest, streaked belly (often forming belly band); tail plain, with
hint of red and little or no banding.
Immature: Streaked below, has light tail banding; primaries translucent.

SWAINSON'S HAWK *Buteo swainsoni* p. 108
Adult: Dark breast-band. Long, pointed, two-toned wings.
Immature: Similar, but has streaks on underbody.

RED-SHOULDERED HAWK *Buteo lineatus* p. 106
Adult: Tail strongly banded (white bands narrower than dark ones).
Strongly barred with rusty coloring on body and underwing coverts.
Immature: Chest and belly heavily streaked. Both immature and adult
show light crescent "window" just before wingtip, longish tail.

BROAD-WINGED HAWK *Buteo platypterus* p. 106
Smaller and chunkier than Red-shouldered with shorter tail, more
pointed wings. *Adult:* Widely banded tail (white bands wider); underwing
pale with dark rear margin and tip.
Immature: Body usually streaked, tail narrowly banded. Pale underwings
may show lighter "window" near wingtips when molting in first
spring.

ROUGH-LEGGED HAWK *Buteo lagopus* p. 106
Note black carpal patch contrasting with white flight feathers. Broad,
blackish band ("cummerbund") across belly is distinctive in female
and immature. Tail light, with broad, dark subterminal band. Adult
male darker chested, has multiple bands on tail, less bold belly
patch.

Buteos are chunky, with broad wings and a broad, rounded tail.
They soar and wheel high in the air.

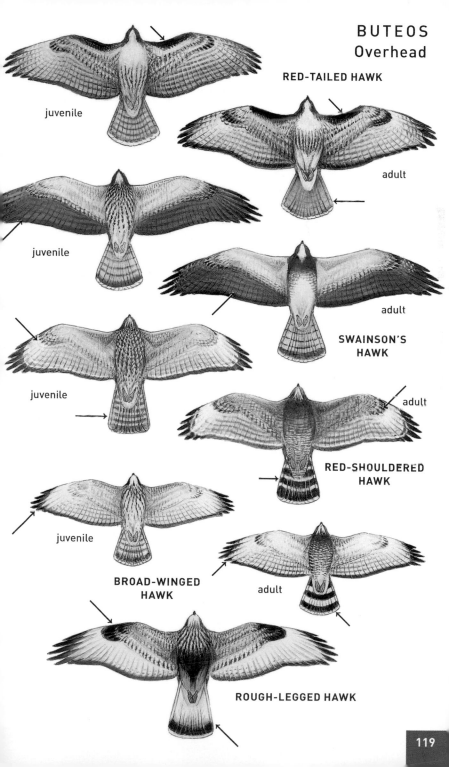

BUTEOS
Overhead

RED-TAILED HAWK

juvenile

adult

juvenile

adult

SWAINSON'S HAWK

juvenile

adult

RED-SHOULDERED HAWK

juvenile

BROAD-WINGED HAWK

adult

ROUGH-LEGGED HAWK

DARK BIRDS OF PREY OVERHEAD

CRESTED CARACARA *Caracara cheriway*   p. 110
Whitish chest, black belly, large *pale patches* in primaries, white tail with black band. Elongated neck, stiff-winged flight.

ROUGH-LEGGED HAWK *Buteo lagopus* (dark morph)   p. 106
Dark body and wing linings; *whitish flight feathers;* tail light from below, with one broad, *black terminal band* in female; additional bands in male.

FERRUGINOUS HAWK *Buteo regalis* (dark morph)   p. 108
Similar to dark-morph Rough-legged Hawk, but tail whitish, without dark banding. Note also white wrist marks, or "commas."

SWAINSON'S HAWK *Buteo swainsoni* (dark morph)   p. 108
In dark morph, fairly pointed wings are usually dark throughout, *including flight feathers;* tail narrowly banded, whitish undertail coverts. Rufous morph may be rustier, with lighter rufous wing linings.

RED-TAILED HAWK *Buteo jamaicensis* (dark morph)   p. 108
Typical chunky shape of Red-tailed; tail reddish above, pale tinged with rusty below; variable. Dark patagial bar on leading edge of wing obscured.

"HARLAN'S" RED-TAILED HAWK   p. 108
Buteo jamaicensis harlani (dark morph)
Similar to dark-morph Red-tailed Hawk. Breast mottled white; tail tends to be mottled with gray and whitish and with dusky subterminal band, lacks obvious red; primary tips barred dark and light.

BROAD-WINGED HAWK *Buteo platypterus* (dark morph)   p. 106
Typical size and shape of Broad-winged. Tail pattern and flight feathers as in light morph, but body and wing linings dark. Note whiter flight feathers than Short-tailed.

ZONE-TAILED HAWK *Buteo albonotatus* (immature)   p. 104
Slim and longish, *two-toned wings* (suggesting Turkey Vulture) with barred flight feathers. Several white bands on slim tail (only one visible on folded tail). Yellow legs.

SHORT-TAILED HAWK *Buteo brachyurus* (dark morph)   p. 106
Jet-black body and wing linings. Lightly banded tail; flight feathers more shaded than in dark Broad-wing. Casual in se. AZ.

COMMON BLACK-HAWK *Buteogallus anthracinus*   p. 104
Thickset black wings; faint light patches near wingtips. Short, broad tail with broad white band at *midtail* and very broad black subterminal band. Whereas Zone-tailed Hawk seems to mimic Turkey Vulture, a deceptive ploy when it is hunting, chunkier Common Black-Hawk may be compared to Black Vulture.

HARRIS'S HAWK *Parabuteo unicinctus*   p. 104
Chocolate brown body, chestnut wing linings. Very broad white band at base of black tail, narrow white terminal band.

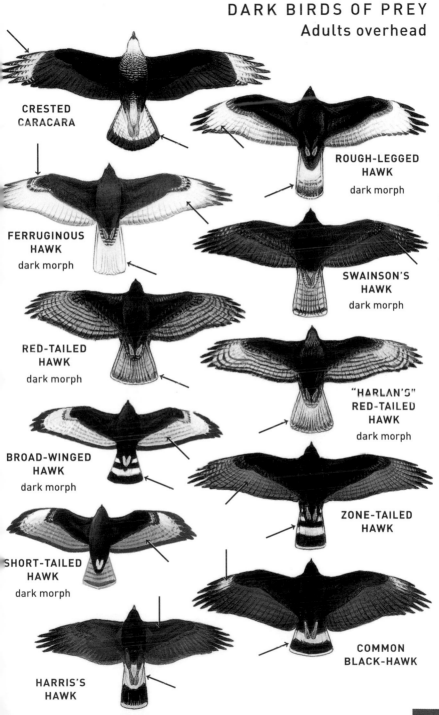

CRESTED
CARACARA

ROUGH-LEGGED
HAWK

dark morph

FERRUGINOUS
HAWK

dark morph

SWAINSON'S
HAWK

dark morph

RED-TAILED
HAWK

dark morph

"HARLAN'S"
RED-TAILED
HAWK

dark morph

BROAD-WINGED
HAWK

dark morph

ZONE-TAILED
HAWK

SHORT-TAILED
HAWK

dark morph

COMMON
BLACK-HAWK

HARRIS'S
HAWK

EAGLES, OSPREY, AND VULTURES OVERHEAD

BALD EAGLE *Haliaeetus leucocephalus*   p. 98
Adult: White head and tail.
Immature: Some white in wing linings, often on body.

GOLDEN EAGLE *Aquila chrysaetos*   p. 98
Adult: Almost uniformly dark; wing linings dark.
Immature: White patch at base of primaries and tail; no white on body.

OSPREY *Pandion haliaetus*   p. 98
White body and coverts; black wrist patch; crooked wing.

TURKEY VULTURE *Cathartes aura*   p. 94
Mostly brownish black. Two-toned wings held in distinct dihedral. Small head, red in adult, gray in immature. Longish tail. Tips and teeters in flight.

BLACK VULTURE *Coragyps atratus*   p. 94
Blackish overall. Silver wing patch. Wings held flat or in very slight dihedral. Rapid, shallow wingbeats. Stubby tail. Gray head.

Where the Bald Eagle, Turkey Vulture, and Osprey all are found, they can be separated at a great distance by their manner of soaring: the Bald Eagle with flat wings; the Turkey Vulture with a dihedral; the Osprey often with a gull-like kink or crook in its wings.

Turkey Vulture (p. 94)

Black Vulture (p. 94)

EAGLES, OSPREY, AND VULTURES
Overhead

BALD EAGLE
adult

Bald Eagle
juvenile

GOLDEN EAGLE
adult

Golden Eagle
juvenile

OSPREY
adult

Coots, Gallinules, and Rails
Family Rallidae

Rails are rather hen-shaped marsh birds, many of secretive habits and mysterious voices, more often heard than seen. Flight is brief and reluctant, with legs dangling. Gallinules and coots are much easier to see; they swim and might be confused with small ducks except for smaller head, forehead shield, and chickenlike bill. They spend most of their time swimming but may also feed on shores. Often vocal, giving loud squawks, grunts, and peeps. **FOOD:** Aquatic plants, seeds, insects, frogs, crustaceans, mollusks. **RANGE:** Nearly worldwide.

AMERICAN COOT *Fulica americana*   Common M153
15–15½ in. (38–39 cm). A slaty, ducklike bird with blackish head and neck, slate gray body, *white bill,* and divided white patch under tail. No side striping. Its big feet are lobed ("scallops" on toes). Gregarious. When swimming, pumps head back and forth; dabbles but also dives from surface. Taking off, it skitters, flight labored, big feet trailing beyond short tail, narrow white border showing along rear of wings. Aberrant birds may show some additional white or yellowish on forehead above bill. *Juvenile:* Slightly paler, with duller bill. Downy young has hairy, *orange-red* head and shoulders. **VOICE:** Grating *kuk-kuk-kuk-kuk; kakakakakaka;* etc.; also a measured *ka-ha, ha-ha;* various cackles, croaks. **SIMILAR SPECIES:** Common Gallinule slightly smaller, browner above, has thin white band on flanks, different-colored bill. Coots flock more on open water and land. **HABITAT:** Ponds, lakes, marshes; in winter, also fields, park ponds, lawns, salt bays.

COMMON GALLINULE *Gallinula galeata*   Uncommon M152
14 in. (36 cm). Note adult's rather chickenlike *red bill with yellow tip, red forehead shield,* and white band on flanks. When walking, flicks white undertail coverts; while swimming, pumps head like a coot. *Juvenile:* Duller bill. **VOICE:** Croaking *kr-r-ruk,* repeated; a froglike *kup;* also *kek, kek, kek* (higher than coot's call); loud, complaining, henlike notes. **SIMILAR SPECIES:** American Coot. **HABITAT:** Freshwater marshes, reedy ponds.

PURPLE GALLINULE *Porphyrio martinicus*   Casual
13 in. (33 cm). Very colorful; swims, wades, and climbs bushes. *Adult:* Head and underparts *deep violet-purple,* back bronzy green. Shield on forehead *pale blue;* bill red with yellow tip. Legs *yellow,* conspicuous in flight. *Juvenile:* Buffy brown below, dark above tinged greenish; bill dark; sides unstriped. **VOICE:** Henlike cackling, *kek, kek, kek;* also guttural notes, sharp reedy cries. **SIMILAR SPECIES:** Common Gallinule has *red* frontal shield, lacks greenish plumage, has duller legs and white side stripe; young moorhen also has whitish side stripe. Young American Coot much darker overall, has pale bill. **RANGE:** Casual visitor to Southwest. **HABITAT:** Freshwater marshes, ponds.

COOTS AND GALLINULES

coots skitter on takeoff

lobed foot of coot

AMERICAN COOT

juvenile

adult

adult

adult

coot chick

moorhen chick

juvenile

COMMON GALLINULE

adult

juvenile

adult

adult

PURPLE GALLINULE

CLAPPER RAIL *Rallus longirostris* Uncommon, local M149
14½ in. (37 cm). The large "marsh hen" of coastal and interior marshes. Sometimes swims. Note henlike appearance; strong legs; long, slightly decurved bill; barred flanks; and white patch under short cocked tail, which it flicks nervously. Breast rusty orange; upperparts and cheeks dull gray-brown. **VOICE:** Clattering *kek-kek-kek-kek,* etc., or *cha-cha-cha,* etc. **SIMILAR SPECIES:** Virginia Rail smaller and more richly colored. **HABITAT:** Coastal populations in salt marshes; in interior Southwest, freshwater marshes.

YELLOW RAIL Scarce, local, secretive M147
Coturnicops noveboracensis
7¼ in. (18 cm). Note *white wing patch* (in flight). A small buffy-and-black rail, suggesting a week-old chick. Bill very short, greenish or yellowish. Back dark, striped, barred, and checkered with buff, white, and black. *Mouselike; very difficult to see.* **VOICE:** Nocturnal ticking notes, often in long series: *tic-tic, tic-tic-tic, tic-tic, tic-tic-tic,* etc., in alternating groups of two and three. Compared to hitting two small stones together. **SIMILAR SPECIES:** Young Sora somewhat larger, buffier overall, lacks dark barring and checkering above, has thin pale trailing edge to wing. **HABITAT:** Grassy marshes, wet meadows; winters mostly in salt marshes and grain fields.

VIRGINIA RAIL *Rallus limicola* Fairly common M150
9½ in. (24 cm). A small rusty rail with gray cheeks, black bars on flanks, and long, slightly decurved, reddish bill with dark tip. Near size of meadowlark; only small rail with *long slender* bill. Juvenile in late summer shows much black. **VOICE:** Descending grunt, *wuk-wuk-wuk-wuk,* etc.; also *kidick, kidick,* etc.; various "kicking" and grunting sounds. **SIMILAR SPECIES:** Sora has small stubby bill, unbarred undertail coverts. Clapper Rail much larger. **HABITAT:** Fresh and brackish marshes; in winter, also salt marshes.

BLACK RAIL *Laterallus jamaicensis* Scarce, local, secretive M148
6 in. (15 cm). A tiny blackish rail with small *black* bill; about the size of a young sparrow. Nape deep chestnut. *Very difficult to glimpse. Caution:* All young rails in downy plumage are black. **VOICE:** Male (mostly at night), *kiki-doo* or *kiki-krrr* (or *kitty go*). Also a growl. **HABITAT:** Salt marshes, freshwater marshes, wet grassy meadows.

SORA *Porzana carolina* Fairly common M151
8½ in. (22 cm). Note *short yellow* bill. *Adult:* A small, plump, gray-brown rail with *black patch* on face and throat. Short, cocked tail reveals white or buff undertail coverts. *Immature:* Lacks dark throat patch and is browner. **VOICE:** Descending whinny, *whee-ee-ee-ee-ee-ee-e-e-e.* Also a plaintive whistled *keu-wee?* Clapping one's hands causes startled birds to utter a sharp *keek.* **SIMILAR SPECIES:** Immature may be confused with smaller and rarer Yellow Rail, which has large white wing patches and blacker-centered feathers above. Virginia Rail has slender bill. **HABITAT:** Freshwater marshes; in migration, also wet meadows; in winter, also salt marshes.

RAILS

CLAPPER
RAIL

chick

YELLOW RAIL

adult

juvenile

VIRGINIA RAIL

BLACK RAIL

adult

immature

SORA

chick

127

SHOREBIRDS

Many shorebirds (or "waders," as they are called in the Old World) are real puzzlers to the novice, and to many experienced birders as well! There are 10 plovers in our area, and about 35 sandpipers and their allies. Most species have two or three different plumages: breeding adult, nonbreeding adult, and juvenal. Being able to properly age many species is an important part of correctly identifying them. Noting size, shape, and feeding style is also a critical part of the identification process.

Plovers are usually more compact and thicker necked than most sandpipers, with a pigeonlike bill and larger eyes. They walk or run in short starts and stops.

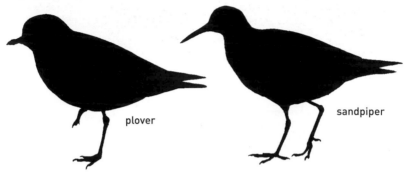

plover

sandpiper

Bill Shapes of Shorebirds

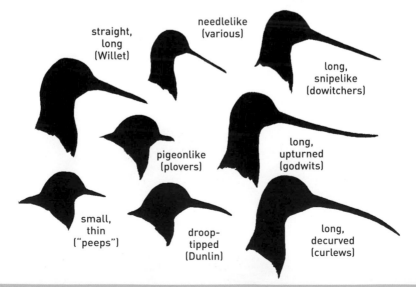

straight, long (Willet)

needlelike (various)

long, snipelike (dowitchers)

pigeonlike (plovers)

long, upturned (godwits)

small, thin ("peeps")

droop-tipped (Dunlin)

long, decurved (curlews)

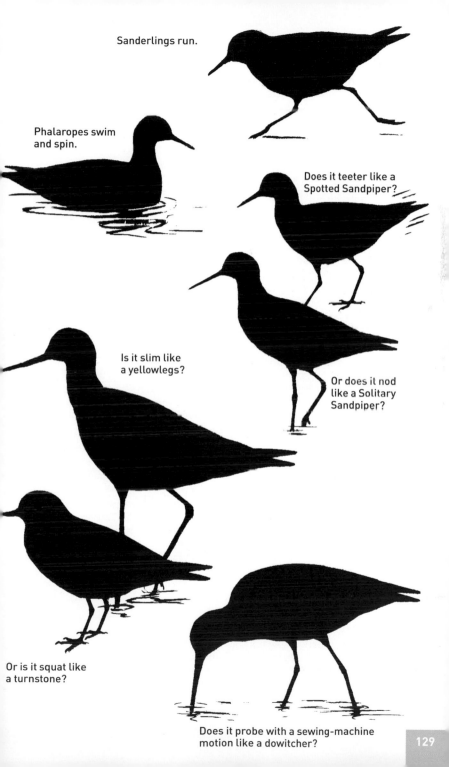

Sanderlings run.

Phalaropes swim and spin.

Does it teeter like a Spotted Sandpiper?

Is it slim like a yellowlegs?

Or does it nod like a Solitary Sandpiper?

Or is it squat like a turnstone?

Does it probe with a sewing-machine motion like a dowitcher?

129

PLOVERS Family Charadriidae

Wading birds, more compact than most sandpipers, with shorter, pigeonlike bill and larger eyes. Calls assist identification. Unlike most sandpipers, plovers run in short starts and stops. Sexes alike or differ slightly. FOOD: Small marine life, insects, some vegetable matter. RANGE: Nearly worldwide.

BLACK-BELLIED PLOVER — Common M156
Pluvialis squatarola (see also p. 154)
11½ in. (29 cm). A large stocky plover with hunched posture and short, thick bill. *Breeding adult: Black face and breast (slightly duller in female) and pale speckled back. Nonbreeding adult and immature:* Mottled tan-gray with white belly. In flight, in any plumage, note *black wingpits* and white rump and tail. VOICE: Plaintive slurred whistle, *tlee-oo-eee* (middle note lower). SIMILAR SPECIES: American and Pacific golden-plovers slightly smaller, slimmer, smaller billed, buffier or more golden cast, have more distinct supercilium, and *lack pattern of white in wings and tail.* Their wingpits are gray, not black. HABITAT: Mudflats, marshes, beaches, rocks, short-grass habitats; in summer, tundra.

AMERICAN GOLDEN-PLOVER — Uncommon to rare M157
Pluvialis dominica (see also p. 154)
10¼–10½ in. (26–27 cm). Size of Killdeer. Note long wingtip extension, well beyond tail tip. *Breeding adult:* Dark, spangled above with *whitish and yellow spots;* underparts black (mottled in female). *Broad white stripe* runs over eye to sides of breast. *Nonbreeding adult and juvenile:* Gray-brown, darker above, with distinct pale supercilium, dark crown. VOICE: Whistled *queedle* or *que-e-a* (dropping at end). SIMILAR SPECIES: Black-bellied Plover, Pacific Golden-Plover. HABITAT: Mudflats, shores, short-grass pastures, sod farms; in summer, tundra.

PACIFIC GOLDEN-PLOVER — Uncommon, local M158
Pluvialis fulva (see also p. 154)
10–10¼ in. (25–26 cm). Very similar to American Golden-Plover. Note shorter wingtips, *barely extending past tail tip;* bill slightly larger, legs slightly longer. *Breeding adult:* White neck stripe *extends down to flanks* and undertail coverts (but molting American may have this look). Golden spangles on back brighter. *Nonbreeding adult and juvenile:* Brighter gold wash than on American, especially on face and breast. VOICE: Whistled *chu-wee* or *chu-wee-dle.* HABITAT: Same as American, though typically breeds in lower, wetter tundra.

MOUNTAIN PLOVER *Charadrius montanus* — Scarce, local M163
9 in. (23 cm). Plain sandy-brown above with white forehead and eyebrow, darker crown; lacks mottling and speckling of golden-plovers. Has pale blue-gray legs, light wing stripe, and dark tail band. VOICE: Low whistle, variable. SIMILAR SPECIES: Killdeer, Black-bellied Plover, golden-plovers, Buff-breasted Sandpiper. HABITAT: Short-grass plains; in winter, also plowed fields, dry sod farms where large flocks may gather.

PLOVERS

nonbreeding

nonbreeding

breeding

juvenile

BLACK-BELLIED PLOVER

nbreeding

nonbreeding

dlng

breeding

AMERICAN GOLDEN-PLOVER

nonbreeding

breeding

non-breeding

PACIFIC GOLDEN-PLOVER

breeding

MOUNTAIN PLOVER

COMMON RINGED PLOVER *Charadrius hiaticula*   Rare, local
7½ in. (19 cm). A Eurasian species, very similar to Semipalmated Plover; best distinguished by *voice*. Slightly longer and slimmer bill, darker cheeks. Lacks obvious orbital ring. Breeding adults have bolder supercilium. **VOICE:** Softer, more minor *poo-eep*. **RANGE:** Breeds on St. Lawrence I., AK; winters in Old World. Casual migrant elsewhere in w. AK.

SEMIPALMATED PLOVER   Common M160
Charadrius semipalmatus (see also p. 154)
7¼ in. (18 cm). A small, plump, brown-backed plover, half the size of Killdeer, with *single dark breast-band. Adult:* Bill orangey with black tip or (nonbreeding) nearly all dark. Orangey orbital ring. Legs bright orange or yellow. *Juvenile:* Slightly browner above, and breast-band may be incomplete. **VOICE:** Plaintive, upward-slurred *chi-we* or *too-li.* **SIMILAR SPECIES:** Piping and Snowy plovers, Killdeer. **HABITAT:** Shores, tidal flats, wet fields; in summer, tundra.

PIPING PLOVER   Uncommon, local M161
Charadrius melodus (see also p. 154)
7¼ in. (18 cm). As pallid as dry sand. Complete or incomplete dark breastband. Legs orange. *Breeding adult:* Bill has orange base, black tip. *Nonbreeding and juvenile:* Black on collar lacking, bill all dark. Note tail pattern. Adults perform stiff-winged "bat-flight" on breeding territory. **VOICE:** Plaintive whistle: *peep-lo* (first note higher). **SIMILAR SPECIES:** Snowy and Semipalmated plovers. **HABITAT:** Nests on sandy lakeshores and river islands; winters on beaches and dry mudflats.

SNOWY PLOVER   Uncommon M159
Charadrius nivosus (see also p. 154)
6¼–6½ in. (16–17 cm). A pale plover of beaches and alkaline flats. *Male:* Has *slim black bill*, dark (sometimes pale) legs, and *dark ear patch. Female and juvenile:* May lack black in plumage. **VOICE:** Musical whistle, *pe-wee-ah* or *o-wee-ah;* also a low *prit.* **SIMILAR SPECIES:** Juvenile and nonbreeding Piping Plovers may also have dark (though thicker) bill, but they have *white on rump,* visible in flight, and orange legs. **HABITAT:** Beaches, sandy flats, alkaline lakeshores.

WILSON'S PLOVER *Charadrius wilsonia* (see also p. 154)   Casual
7¾–8 in. (19–20 cm). A "ringed" plover, larger than Semipalmated with *wider breast-band* and longer, *heavier black bill.* Legs pinkish gray. **VOICE:** Emphatic whistled *whit!* or *wheet!* **RANGE:** Casual visitor to s. CA, accidental elsewhere. **HABITAT:** Open beaches, tidal flats.

KILLDEER *Charadrius vociferus* (see also p. 154)   Common M162
10½ in. (27 cm). The common, noisy plover of farm country and playing fields. Note *two black breast-bands* (chick has only one band and might be confused with Wilson's Plover). In flight or distraction display near nest, shows *rusty orange rump*, longish tail. **VOICE:** Noisy, and often heard at night. Loud, insistent *kill-deeah*, repeated; plaintive *dee-ee* (rising). **SIMILAR SPECIES:** Other banded plovers smaller, have single breast-band. **HABITAT:** Fields, airports, mudflats, shores.

BANDED PLOVERS

breeding

COMMON RINGED PLOVER

nonbreeding

breeding

SEMIPALMATED PLOVER

nonbreeding

breeding

♂

non-breeding

SNOWY PLOVER

breeding

PIPING PLOVER

♀

♂

WILSON'S PLOVER

KILLDEER

chick

Piping

Common Ringed

Killdeer

owy

Wilson's

Semipalmated

133

Oystercatchers Family Haematopodidae

Large waders with long, laterally flattened, chisel-tipped, red bill. Sexes alike. **FOOD:** Mollusks, crabs, marine worms. **RANGE:** Widespread on coasts of world; inland in some areas of Europe and Asia.

BLACK OYSTERCATCHER   Uncommon M164
Haematopus bachmani
17–17½ in. (43–44 cm). A very noisy, heavily built, blackish shorebird of rocky coastlines. Bill straight and *orange-red,* flattened laterally. Thickish legs are pale pinkish. *Immature:* Bill dark-tipped. **VOICE:** Piercing, sharply repeated, whistled *wheep!* or *kleep!,* often in descending series. **SIMILAR SPECIES:** American Oystercatcher *(Haematopus palliatus),* a casual vagrant to s. CA, has white underparts, wing stripe, and rump. **HABITAT:** Rocky coasts, sea islets.

Stilts and Avocets Family Recurvirostridae

Slim waders with very long legs and very slender bill (bent upward in avocets). Sexes fairly similar. **FOOD:** Insects, crustaceans, other aquatic life. **RANGE:** N., Cen., and S. America, Africa, s. Eurasia, Australia, Pacific region.

BLACK-NECKED STILT   Fairly common M165
Himantopus mexicanus
14 in. (36 cm). A large, extremely slim wader; black above (female and immature tinged brown), white below. Note *extremely long pinkish red legs,* needlelike bill. In flight, black *unpatterned* wings contrast strikingly with white rump, tail, and underparts. **VOICE:** Sharp yipping: *kyip, kyip, kyip.* **SIMILAR SPECIES:** Nonbreeding American Avocet. **HABITAT:** Marshes, mudflats, pools, shallow lakes (fresh and alkaline), flooded fields.

AMERICAN AVOCET *Recurvirostra americana* Fairly common M166
18 in. (46 cm). A large, slim shorebird with very slender, *upturned bill,* more upturned in female. This and striking white-and-black pattern make this bird unique. In breeding plumage, head and neck pinkish tan or orangey buff; in nonbreeding plumage, this color replaced by pale gray. Avocets feed with scythelike sweep of head and bill. **VOICE:** Sharp *wheek* or *kleet,* excitedly repeated. **HABITAT:** Mudflats, shallow lakes, marshes, prairie ponds.

OYSTERCATCHER, STILT, AND AVOCET

American
Oystercatcher
for comparison

BLACK OYSTERCATCHER

BLACK-NECKED STILT

breeding

breeding

nonbreeding

AMERICAN AVOCET

SANDPIPERS, PHALAROPES, AND ALLIES
Family Scolopacidae

Small to large shorebirds. Bills more slender than those of plovers. Sexes mostly similar, except in phalaropes. FOOD: Insects, crustaceans, mollusks, worms, etc. RANGE: Cosmopolitan.

WILLET *Tringa semipalmata* (see also p. 156) Fairly common M171
15–16 in. (38–41 cm). Stockier than Greater Yellowlegs; has heavier bill, *blue-gray legs.* In flight, note *striking black-and-white wing pattern.* At rest, this large wader is rather nondescript. VOICE: Musical, repetitious *pill-will-willet* (in breeding season); a loud *kay-ee* (second note lower). Also a rapidly repeated *kip-kip-kip,* etc. In flight, *kree-ree-ree.* SIMILAR SPECIES: Greater Yellowlegs, dowitchers, Wandering Tattler. HABITAT: Marshes, wet meadows, mudflats, beaches.

GREATER YELLOWLEGS Common M170
Tringa melanoleuca (see also p. 158)
14 in. (36 cm). Note *bright yellow legs, long bill,* often *pale-based.* A slim gray sandpiper with speckled look above. Often teeters body. In flight, appears *dark-winged,* with *whitish rump and tail.* VOICE: Strident whistle, *dear! dear! dear!,* usually three notes. SIMILAR SPECIES: Lesser Yellowlegs, Willet. HABITAT: Marshes, mudflats, streams, ponds, flooded fields; in summer, wooded muskeg, spruce bogs.

LESSER YELLOWLEGS Uncommon to fairly common M172
Tringa flavipes (see also p. 158)
10½ in. (27 cm). Like Greater Yellowlegs, but smaller. Lesser's shorter, slimmer bill is *straight* and about *equal to length of head;* Greater's appears slightly uptilted, paler based, and longer than bird's head. Readily separated by voice. VOICE: *Yew* or *yu-yu;* less forceful than usual three-syllable call of Greater. SIMILAR SPECIES: Solitary and Stilt sandpipers, Wilson's Phalarope. HABITAT: Marshes, mudflats, ponds, flooded fields; in summer, boreal woods and taiga.

SOLITARY SANDPIPER Uncommon to scarce M168
Tringa solitaria (see also p. 158)
8½ in. (22 cm). Note *dark wings* and *white sides of tail.* Whitish below, with *light eye-ring* and greenish legs. Nods like a yellowlegs. Usually alone, seldom in groups. VOICE: *Peet!* or *peet-weet-weet!* (higher and more strident than Spotted Sandpiper's call). SIMILAR SPECIES: Lesser Yellowlegs has bright yellow legs, white rump, is paler overall. Spotted Sandpiper teeters tail (not head), has white wedge at breast-side, different wing and tail patterns. HABITAT: Streamsides, brushy ponds, rainpools; in summer, moist boreal woods, bogs.

STILT SANDPIPER *Calidris himantopus* See p. 148
Nonbreeding: Long yellow-green legs, slight droop to bill, white rump; distinct light eyebrow (supercilium).

WILSON'S PHALAROPE *Phalaropus tricolor* See p. 152
Nonbreeding: Straight needle bill, clear white underparts, pale gray back, dull yellow legs.

nonbreeding

breeding

WILLET

Lesser
Yellowlegs

**LESSER
YELLOW-
LEGS**

**GREATER
YELLOWLEGS**

**SOLITARY
SANDPIPER**

nonbreeding

onbreeding

Stilt
Sandpiper
(p. 148)
for comparison

Wilson's
Phalarope
(p. 152)
for comparison

HUDSONIAN GODWIT · Scarce M176
Limosa haemastica (see also p. 156)
15–15½ in. (38–39 cm). Rather large size and long, *slightly upturned* bill mark this wader as a godwit; *blackish wing linings* proclaim it as this species. Black tail *ringed broadly with white. Breeding:* Male ruddy-breasted, female duller. *Nonbreeding:* Both sexes gray-backed, pale-breasted. **VOICE:** *Tawit!* (or *godwit!*); higher pitched than Marbled Godwit's call. **SIMILAR SPECIES:** Bar-tailed Godwit has different wing and tail patterns; see Black-tailed Godwit, a vagrant from Eurasia. **HABITAT:** Mudflats, prairie pools; in summer, taiga and tundra.

MARBLED GODWIT · Fairly common M178
Limosa fedoa (see also p. 156)
17½–18½ in. (44–46 cm). Rich, mottled *buff brown* color identifies this species. Underwing linings *cinnamon.* **VOICE:** Accented *kerwhit!* (*godwit!*); also *raddica, raddica.* **SIMILAR SPECIES:** When head tucked in, may be difficult to tell from Long-billed Curlew except by leg color (blackish in godwit, blue-gray in curlew); in AK, see Bar-tailed Godwit. Hudsonian Godwit has white on wings and tail, blackish wing linings. **HABITAT:** Shores, mudflats, beaches; in summer, prairies, pools.

LONG-BILLED CURLEW · Uncommon M175
Numenius americanus (see also p. 156)
22–24 in. (55–60 cm). Note *long, sickle-shaped bill* (4–8½ in.; 10–21 cm). Larger than Whimbrel and more buffy overall; lacks distinct dark crown stripes. Overhead shows *cinnamon wing linings.* In young birds, bill may be scarcely longer than that of Whimbrel. **VOICE:** Loud *cur-lee* (rising inflection); rapid, whistled *kli-li-li-li.* "Song" a trilled, liquid *curleeeeeeeeuuu.* **SIMILAR SPECIES:** Marbled Godwit. **HABITAT:** High plains, rangeland; in winter, cultivated land, mudflats, salt marshes.

WHIMBREL · Fairly common M174
Numenius phaeopus (see also p. 156)
17–18 in. (43–46 cm). A large gray-brown wader with long *decurved bill.* Much grayer brown than Long-billed Curlew; bill shorter (2¾–4 in.; 7–10 cm); crown *striped.* **VOICE:** Five to seven short, rapid whistles: *hee-hee-hee-hee-hee-hee.* **SIMILAR SPECIES:** Long-billed Curlew. **HABITAT:** Mudflats, beaches, marshes, pastures, short-grass habitats; in summer, tundra.

Basic Flight Patterns of Sandpipers

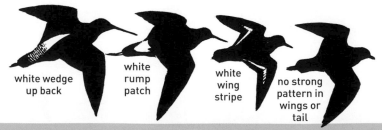

white wedge up back

white rump patch

white wing stripe

no strong pattern in wings or tail

LARGE SANDPIPERS

breeding

nonbreeding

nonbreeding

HUDSONIAN GODWIT

breeding ♂

MARBLED GODWIT

LONG-BILLED CURLEW

WHIMBREL

WANDERING TATTLER *Tringa incana*   Uncommon M169
11 in. (28 cm). A slim, solitary shorebird that bobs and teeters like
Spotted Sandpiper. Recognized from other rock-loving shorebirds by
lack of pattern in flight. Solid grayish above; light line over eye, dark
line through it. Legs yellowish. *Breeding:* Underparts *barred. Nonbreeding:* Gray-chested, with no barring. **VOICE:** Clear *whee-he-he-
he-he,* less sharp than Greater Yellowlegs, and all on same pitch; or
tweet-tweet-tweet, similar to Spotted Sandpiper's call. **SIMILAR SPE-
CIES:** Willet. In w. AK, see Gray-tailed Tattler. **HABITAT:** Rocky coasts,
pebbly beaches, more rarely mudflats and sandy beaches; nests
near mountain streams above timberline.

SURFBIRD *Aphriza virgata*   Uncommon M181
10 in. (25 cm). A stocky, dark sandpiper of wave-washed rocks. Note
conspicuous *white rump and tail tipped with broad black band;* legs
yellowish. Breeding: Heavily streaked and spotted with blackish above
and below; orangey scapulars. *Nonbreeding:* Solid gray above and
across breast. Bill short, yellow at base. **VOICE:** Sharp *pee-weet* or
key-a-weet. **SIMILAR SPECIES:** Rock Sandpiper smaller and slimmer,
with longer, slimmer bill, different tail pattern. Black Turnstone
smaller, darker, has slimmer bill, white stripe up back, and reddish
brown legs. **HABITAT:** Rocky coasts; nests on mountain tundra.

ROCK SANDPIPER *Calidris ptilocnemis*   Scarce to uncommon M190
8¾–9¼ in. (22–24 cm). *Breeding:* Suggests Dunlin, with rusty back,
black splotch on breast (but Dunlin redder, with black splotch lower,
black legs). *Nonbreeding:* Slate gray with white belly, short yellowish
legs, dull yellowish base of bill. Pribilof Islands subspecies slightly
larger and paler than other subspecies. **VOICE:** Flickerlike *du-du-du.*
When breeding, a trill. **SIMILAR SPECIES:** Black Turnstone, Surfbird.
HABITAT: Rocky shores; nests on mossy tundra.

RUDDY TURNSTONE   Fairly common M179
Arenaria interpres (see also p. 154)
9½ in. (24 cm). A squat, robust, *orange-legged* shorebird, with *harlequin pattern. Breeding:* Russet back and curious face and breast pattern. *Nonbreeding and juvenile:* Duller, but retain enough of basic
pattern to be recognized. **VOICE:** Staccato *tuk-a-tuk* or *kut-a-kut;* also
a single *kewk.* **SIMILAR SPECIES:** Black Turnstone. **HABITAT:** Beaches,
mudflats, rocky shores, jetties; in summer, tundra.

BLACK TURNSTONE   Fairly common M180
Arenaria melanocephala (see also p. 154)
9¼ in. (23 cm). A squat, blackish shorebird with blackish chest and
white belly. In breeding plumage, oval white spot before eye, and
white speckling. Flight pattern similar to Ruddy Turnstone's. Legs
darkish. **VOICE:** Rattling call, higher and longer than that of Ruddy
Turnstone. **SIMILAR SPECIES:** Nonbreeding Ruddy Turnstone has
brighter legs, browner back, more rounded and less solid breast
patches. Some juvenile Ruddy Turnstones are unusually dark. See
also Surfbird. **HABITAT:** Rocky shores, surf-pounded islets, sometimes sandy beaches and mudflats; nests on coastal tundra.

ROCK-LOVING SHOREBIRDS

nonbreeding

WANDERING TATTLER

breeding

SURFBIRD

breeding

nonbreeding

breeding

nonbreeding

ROCK SANDPIPER

nonbreeding

breeding

RUDDY TURNSTONE

nonbreeding

breeding

BLACK TURNSTONE

RED KNOT *Calidris canutus* (see also p. 160)   Uncommon M182
10½ in. (27 cm). Larger than Sanderling. Stocky, with medium-length, straight bill and short legs, plain rump. *Breeding:* Face and underparts *pale robin red;* back mottled with black, gray, and russet. *Nonbreeding:* A dumpy wader with washed-out gray look and mottled flanks; greenish legs. *Juvenile:* May show *pale feather edgings* above and pale buff wash on breast. **VOICE:** Low *knut;* also a low, mellow *tooit-wit* or *wah-quoit.* **SIMILAR SPECIES:** Dowitchers. **HABITAT:** Tidal flats, sandy beaches, shores; in summer, tundra.

SANDERLING *Calidris alba* (see also p. 160)   Common M183
8 in. (20 cm). A plump, active sandpiper of outer beaches, where it chases retreating waves like a wind-up toy. Note bold *white wing stripe* in flight. *Breeding:* Bright rusty about head, back, and breast. *Nonbreeding:* The palest sandpiper; snowy white underparts, plain pale gray back, *black shoulders. Juvenile:* Differs from nonbreeding adults in having salt-and-pepper pattern on back and breast sides. **VOICE:** Short *kip* or *quit.* **SIMILAR SPECIES:** Western Sandpiper, Red-necked Stint. **HABITAT:** Beaches, mudflats, also lakeshores in migration; in summer, stony tundra.

DUNLIN *Calidris alpina* (see also p. 160)   Common M191
8½–8¾ in. (22–23 cm). Slightly larger than a peep or Sanderling, with *longish, droop-tipped bill.* Black legs. *Breeding: Rusty red above,* with *black patch on belly. Nonbreeding:* Unpatterned gray or gray-brown above, with *grayish wash across breast* (not clean white as in Sanderling or Western Sandpiper). *Juvenile* (this plumage rarely seen away from nesting areas): Rusty above, with buffy breast and suggestion of belly patch. **VOICE:** Nasal, rasping *cheezp* or *treezp.* **SIMILAR SPECIES:** Nonbreeding Sanderling and Western Sandpiper have clean white breast; Sanderling also paler above and has straighter bill; Western Sandpiper slightly smaller. See also Rock Sandpiper. **HABITAT:** Tidal flats, beaches, muddy pools; in summer, moist tundra.

SANDPIPERS

nonbreeding

juvenile

RED KNOT

nonbreeding

breeding

juvenile

SANDERLING

breeding

nonbreeding

juvenile

nonbreeding

breeding

DUNLIN

143

"Peep"

Collectively, the three common small sandpipers resident in N. America are nicknamed "peep." Sometimes somewhat larger *Calidris* are also called peep. In Old World, small peep are called "stints."

LEAST SANDPIPER
Common M186

Calidris minutilla (see also p. 160)

6 in. (15 cm). Distinguished from the other two peep by its slightly smaller size, *browner* look, and *yellowish or greenish* — not blackish — legs (but which might appear dark if caked in mud). *Bill finer and slightly drooped at tip. Adult:* Mostly brownish (breeding) or brownish gray (nonbreeding). *Juvenile:* Much brighter, with extensive rufous on upperparts and buff wash across breast. **VOICE:** Thin *krreet* or *kree-eet.* **SIMILAR SPECIES:** Western and Semipalmated sandpipers have blackish legs, thicker bill, paler upperparts, and different voice; whitish breast in nonbreeding plumage. **HABITAT:** Mudflats, marshes, rain pools, shores; in summer, taiga wetlands.

SEMIPALMATED SANDPIPER
Uncommon to rare M184

Calidris pusilla (see also p. 160)

6¼ in. (16 cm). Very similar to Western Sandpiper, the "Semi" is a small black-legged peep with a *straight,* somewhat *tubular bill* of variable length. *Breeding:* Gray-brown above, many birds with a tinge of russet to cheeks and back; dark streaks on breast. *Nonbreeding:* Rarely seen in our area. Uniformly plain gray across upperparts. *Juvenile:* Scaly look to upperpart; dark cap, breast and upperparts tinged buff when fresh. **VOICE:** Call *chit* or *chirt* (lacks *ee* sound of Least and Western sandpipers). **SIMILAR SPECIES:** Typical Western Sandpiper (especially female) has *longer bill, slightly drooped* at tip. Breeding Western more rufous above, more heavily speckled below. Juvenile has rusty scapulars and slightly paler face. Least Sandpiper smaller, browner, and thinner billed; has *yellowish or greenish* legs; in nonbreeding plumage, has darker breast. **RANGE:** Most migrate east of Rocky Mts. **HABITAT:** Mudflats, marshes, shores, beaches; in summer, tundra.

WESTERN SANDPIPER *Calidris mauri*
Common M185

6½ in. (17 cm). Legs black. In typical female, bill thicker at base and *longer* than Semipalmated's and *droops near tip* (male's bill shorter, less drooped). *Breeding: Heavily spotted* on breast and flanks; *rusty scapulars, crown, and ear patch. Nonbreeding:* Gray above, perhaps the palest peep, unmarked whitish below. *Juvenile:* Like juvenile Semipalmated but with distinct rusty scapulars, paler cap. **VOICE:** Distinct high-pitched *jeet* or *cheet,* unlike lower, soft *chirt* of Semipalmated. **SIMILAR SPECIES:** Semipalmated and Least sandpipers, Dunlin. Because of their shorter bill, many male Westerns may be particularly difficult to separate from Semipalmated; see also voice. Semipalmated is rare in most of the West; Western is a common migrant and winterer. **HABITAT:** Shores, beaches, mudflats, marshes; in summer, tundra.

SMALL "PEEP" SANDPIPERS

nbreeding

juvenile

LEAST SANDPIPER

breeding

nbreeding

juvenile

breeding

SEMIPALMATED SANDPIPER

nbreeding ♀

WESTERN SANDPIPER

juvenile

breeding ♀

Least   Semipalmated   Western

WHITE-RUMPED SANDPIPER   Rare to casual M187
Calidris fuscicollis (see also p. 160)
7½ in. (19 cm). Larger than Semipalmated Sandpiper, smaller than Pectoral Sandpiper. The only peep with completely *white rump.* At rest, this long-winged bird has *tapered* look, with *wingtips extending well beyond tail.* Distinct pale supercilium. *Breeding:* Some rusty on back. *Dark streaks and chevrons on sides extend to flanks.* Bill reddish at base of lower mandible. *Nonbreeding:* Gray upperparts and *breast, gray smudging down flanks,* bold *white eyebrow. Juvenile:* Rusty edges on crown and back. **VOICE:** High, thin, mouselike *jeet,* like two flint pebbles scraping. **SIMILAR SPECIES:** Long wings and very attenuated look shared only by Baird's Sandpiper among other peeps, but Baird's browner, has dark center to rump, lacks bold supercilium and dark streaks on flanks, and has much lower pitched call. **RANGE:** Breeds in n. AK and nw. Canada; migrates east of Rocky Mts.; casual along West Coast. **HABITAT:** Prairie pools, shores, mudflats, marshes; in summer, tundra.

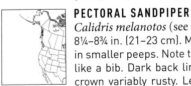

BAIRD'S SANDPIPER   Uncommon M188
Calidris bairdii (see also p. 160)
7½ in. (19 cm). Larger than Semipalmated or Western sandpiper, with more *long-winged, tapered look* (wings extend ½ in., 1 cm, beyond tail tip). *Breeding and juvenile:* Brown or *buff* across breast (warmer buff in juvenile). Suggests large, long-winged Least Sandpiper with black legs. Back of juvenile has *scaled* look. **VOICE:** Call a low *kreep* or *kree;* a rolling trill. **SIMILAR SPECIES:** White-rumped and Pectoral sandpipers. Buff-breasted Sandpiper buffier below, without streaks, and has *yellowish* (not *blackish*) legs. **HABITAT:** Pond margins, grassy mudflats, shores, upper beaches; in summer, tundra.

PECTORAL SANDPIPER   Uncommon M189
Calidris melanotos (see also p. 158)
8¼–8¾ in. (21–23 cm). Medium sized (but variable); neck longer than in smaller peeps. Note that heavy breast streaks end rather *abruptly,* like a bib. Dark back lined with white. Wing stripe faint or lacking; crown variably rusty. Legs usually dull yellowish. Bill may be pale yellow-brown at base. *Juvenile:* Brighter upperparts and crown, buffy wash on breast under streaking. **VOICE:** Low, reedy *churrt* or *trrip, trrip.* **SIMILAR SPECIES:** Sharp-tailed, Baird's, and Least sandpipers. **HABITAT:** Prairie pools, sod farms, muddy shores, fresh and tidal marshes; in summer, tundra.

nonbreeding

WHITE-RUMPED SANDPIPER

breeding

juvenile

breeding

BAIRD'S SANDPIPER

breeding ♂

venile

PECTORAL SANDPIPER

breeding

SPOTTED SANDPIPER Common M167

Actitis macularius (see also p. 160)

7½ in. (19 cm). The most widespread sandpiper along shores of small lakes and streams. Teeters rear body up and down nervously. Note relatively *long tail*. Breeding: Note *round breast spots*. *Nonbreeding and juvenile:* No spots; brown above, with white line over eye. Dusky smudge enclosing white wedge near shoulder is a good aid. Flight distinctive: wings beat in a *shallow arc*, giving a stiff, bowed appearance. Underwing striped. **VOICE:** Clear *peet* or *peet-weet!* or *peet-weet-weet-weet-weet*. **SIMILAR SPECIES:** Solitary Sandpiper. **HABITAT:** Pebbly shores, ponds, streamsides, marshes; in winter, also seashores, rock jetties.

STILT SANDPIPER Scarce M192

Calidris himantopus (see also pp. 136 and 158)

8½ in. (22 cm). Slight *droop* to tip of bill. Legs long and greenish yellow. Feeds like a dowitcher (sewing-machine motion) but *tilts tail up* more than a dowitcher while feeding. Breeding: Heavily marked below with *transverse bars*. Note *rusty cheek patch*. Nonbreeding: Yellowlegs-like; gray above, white below; dark-winged and *white-rumped*; note more *greenish legs* and *white eyebrow*. Juvenile: Slight buffy wash to breast and pale edgings above. **VOICE:** Single *whu* (like Lesser Yellowlegs but lower, hoarser), although often silent. **SIMILAR SPECIES:** Yellowlegs. Dowitchers pudgier, have longer, yellowish-based, less drooped bills, and in flight show white wedge up back. See also Curlew Sandpiper. **HABITAT:** Shallow pools, mudflats, marshes; in summer, tundra.

BUFF-BREASTED SANDPIPER Rare M193

Tryngites subruficollis (see also p. 158)

8¼ in. (21 cm). No other small shorebird is as *buffy* below (paling to whitish on undertail coverts). A tame, buffy bird, with erect stance, small head, short bill, and yellowish legs. Dark eye stands out on plain face. In flight or in "display," buff body contrasts with underwing (*white* with marbled tip). Juvenile: Scaly above, paler on belly (most fall birds along coasts are in this plumage). **VOICE:** Low, trilled *pr-r-r-reet*. Sharp *tik*. **SIMILAR SPECIES:** Juvenile Ruff. **HABITAT:** Dry dirt, sand, and short-grass habitats, including drying lakeshores, pastures, sod farms; in summer, drier tundra ridges.

UPLAND SANDPIPER Scarce, local M173

Bartramia longicauda (see also p. 158)

12 in. (30–31 cm). A "pigeon-headed" brown sandpiper; larger than Killdeer. Short bill, *small head,* shoe-button eye, thin neck, and *long tail* are helpful points. Often perches with erect posture on fenceposts and poles; on alighting, holds wings elevated. **VOICE:** Mellow, whistled *kip-ip-ip-ip,* often heard at night. Song a weird windy whistle: *whoooleeeeee, wheeloooooooooo.* **SIMILAR SPECIES:** Buff-breasted Sandpiper, yellowlegs. **HABITAT:** Grassy prairies, open meadows, fields, airports, sod farms.

SANDPIPERS

nonbreeding

nonbreeding

breeding

SPOTTED SANDPIPER

juvenile

nonbreeding

STILT SANDPIPER

breeding

UPLAND SANDPIPER

BUFF-BREASTED SANDPIPER

WILSON'S SNIPE
Uncommon to fairly common M196

Gallinago delicata (see also p. 158)

10¼–10½ in. (26–27 cm). A tight-sitting bog and wet-field prober; on nesting grounds may be seen standing on posts. Note *extremely long bill*. Brown, with *buff stripes on back* and a *striped head*. When flushed, flies off in *zigzag*, showing *short rusty orange tail* and uttering rasping note. **VOICE:** When flushed, a rasping *scaip.* Song a measured *chip-a, chip-a, chip-a,* etc. In high aerial display, a winnowing *huhuhuhuhuhuhu.* **SIMILAR SPECIES:** Dowitchers. **HABITAT:** Marshes, bogs, ditches, wet fields and meadows.

SHORT-BILLED DOWITCHER
Common M194

Limnodromus griseus (see also p. 160)

11–11¼ in. (27–28 cm). A snipelike bird of open mudflats. Note very long bill, sewing-machine feeding motion, and, in flight, *long white wedge up back. Breeding:* Breast rich rusty with some barring on flanks. Underbelly in Pacific subspecies *(caurinus)* shows extensive white, which helps separate from lookalike Long-billed Dowitcher. Bill length not a dependable mark for separation. Great Plains subspecies *(hendersoni)* more extensively rusty below but color paler orange than Long-billed and fades toward belly. *Nonbreeding:* Gray with white belly and barred flanks. *Juvenile:* Brighter upperparts, buff wash to neck and breast; *patterned tertial feathers* an important distinction from juvenile Long-billed. **VOICE:** Staccato *tu-tu-tu;* pitch of Lesser Yellowlegs. **SIMILAR SPECIES:** Long-billed Dowitcher, Stilt Sandpiper. In nonbreeding plumage, see Red Knot. **HABITAT:** Mudflats, tidal marshes, pond edges. More frequent on large tidal mudflats than Long-billed Dowitcher. In summer, taiga and tundra.

LONG-BILLED DOWITCHER
Common M195

Limnodromus scolopaceus (see also p. 160)

11½ in. (29 cm). When feeding, shows more round-bodied profile than Short-billed; dark tail bars average wider; bill averages longer — but bill lengths of the two dowitchers overlap, so only extreme birds are distinctive. *Breeding:* Underparts *evenly bright rusty to lower belly* (white or very pale lower belly in Short-billed Dowitcher), with dark spotting on neck and barring on sides. Dark bars on tail broader, giving tail a darker look. *Nonbreeding:* Averages darker than Short-billed with smoother gray breast and darker centers to scapulars. *Juvenile: Solid gray tertials with pale fringe;* Short-billed has *internal rusty markings* similar to "tiger barring." **VOICE:** Single sharp, high *keek,* occasionally given in twos or threes. **SIMILAR SPECIES:** The two dowitcher species are most easily separated by voice. **HABITAT:** Mudflats, shallow pools, marshes. In summer, tundra. More partial to fresh water than Short-billed, but extensive overlap.

winnowing display flight

snipe

SHORT-BILLED DOWITCHER

juvenile

nonbreeding

coastal breeding

central breeding

WILSON'S SNIPE

juvenile

non-breeding

breeding

probing

LONG-BILLED DOWITCHER

PHALAROPES

Sandpipers with lobed toes; equally at home wading or swimming. Placed by some taxonomists in a family of their own, Phalaropodidae. When feeding, phalaropes often spin like tops, rapidly dabbling at disturbed water for plankton, brine shrimp, and other marine invertebrates; mosquito larvae; and insects. Females slightly larger and more colorful than males. **RANGE:** Two of the three species are circumpolar, wintering at sea; the other species breeds in N. American interior, winters mostly in S. America.

WILSON'S PHALAROPE   Fairly common M197
Phalaropus tricolor (see also pp. 136 and 158)
9¼ in. (23½ cm). This trim phalarope is plain-winged, with white rump. In addition to spinning in water, may also feed by dashing about on shorelines. *Breeding:* Female unique, with *broad black face and neck stripe blending into cinnamon.* Male duller, with just a wash of cinnamon on sides of neck and white spot on hindneck. *Nonbreeding:* Suggests Lesser Yellowlegs, but whiter below, with no speckling; bill *needlelike;* legs greenish or straw colored. *Juvenile:* Shows buffy and brown pattern above, buffy wash on breast. **VOICE:** Low nasal *wurk;* also *check, check, check.* **SIMILAR SPECIES:** Other two phalaropes show white wing stripe, dark central tail, and bolder dark patch through eye. See also yellowlegs, which may swim for brief periods of time. **HABITAT:** Shallow lakes, freshwater marshes, pools, shores, mudflats; in migration, also salt marshes.

RED-NECKED PHALAROPE   Uncommon to fairly common M198
Phalaropus lobatus (see also p. 160)
7¾ in. (20 cm). A shorebird far out to sea is most likely a phalarope. Note dark patch through eye and needlelike black bill. *Breeding:* Female gray above, with *rufous chestnut on neck,* white throat and eyebrow. Male duller, but similar in pattern. *Nonbreeding:* Both sexes gray above with whitish streaks, white below. *Juvenile:* Has distinct buff stripes on back. **VOICE:** Sharp *kit* or *whit,* similar to call of Sanderling. **SIMILAR SPECIES:** Red Phalarope. **HABITAT:** Common offshore, uncommon inland. Ocean, bays, lakes, ponds; in summer, tundra.

RED PHALAROPE   Uncommon to rare M199
Phalaropus fulicarius (see also p. 160)
8¼–8½ in. (21–22 cm). Seagoing habits and buoyant swimming (like a tiny gull) distinguish this as a phalarope. *Breeding:* Female mostly deep *reddish with white face.* Male duller. *Nonbreeding:* Plain gray above, white below; in flight suggest Sanderling, but with *dark patch* through eye. *Juvenile:* Has peach-buff wash on neck; acquires adult's pale gray back-feathering quickly. **VOICE:** *Whit* or *kit,* higher than Red-necked Phalarope's call. **SIMILAR SPECIES:** Red-necked Phalarope slightly smaller, has more needlelike bill; nonbreeding birds darker gray above with thin pale back stripes. Slightly thicker bill of Red may have yellowish base. **HABITAT:** Uncommon offshore, very rare onshore. Ocean, bays, lakes; more strictly pelagic than Red-necked. In summer, tundra.

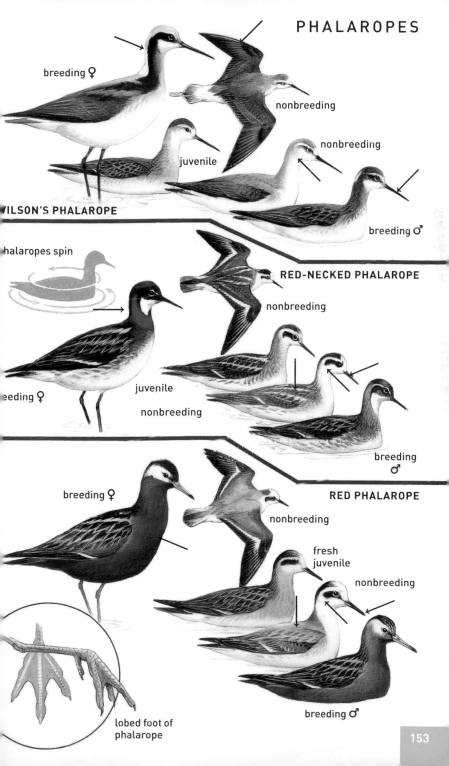

PHALAROPES

breeding ♀

nonbreeding

juvenile

nonbreeding

nonbreeding

WILSON'S PHALAROPE

breeding ♂

halaropes spin

RED-NECKED PHALAROPE

nonbreeding

breeding ♀

juvenile

nonbreeding

nonbreeding

breeding ♂

RED PHALAROPE

breeding ♀

nonbreeding

fresh juvenile

nonbreeding

lobed foot of phalarope

breeding ♂

Plovers and Turnstone in Flight

Learn their distinctive flight calls.

PIPING PLOVER *Charadrius melodus*   p. 132
Pale sand color above, wide black tail spot, whitish rump.
Call a plaintive whistle, *peep-lo* (first note higher).

SNOWY PLOVER *Charadrius nivosus*   p. 132
Pale sand color above; tail with dark center, white sides; rump not white.
Call a musical whistle, *pe-wee-ah* or *o-wee-ah*.

SEMIPALMATED PLOVER *Charadrius semipalmatus*   p. 132
Mud brown above; dark tail with white borders.
Call a plaintive upward-slurred *chi-we* or *too-li.*

WILSON'S PLOVER *Charadrius wilsonia*   p. 132
Similar in pattern to Semipalmated; larger with big bill.
Call an emphatic whistled *whit!* or *wheet!*

KILLDEER *Charadrius vociferus*   p. 132
Tawny orange rump, longish tail.
Noisy; a loud *kill-deeah* or *killdeer;* also *dee-dee-dee,* etc.

BLACK-BELLIED PLOVER *Pluvialis squatarola*   p. 130
Breeding: Black below, white undertail coverts.
Year-round: Black wingpits, white in wing and tail.
Call a plaintive slurred whistle, *tlee-oo-eee* or *whee-er-ee.*

AMERICAN GOLDEN-PLOVER *Pluvialis dominica*   p. 130
Breeding: Black below, black undertail coverts.
Nonbreeding: Speckled brown above, grayish below.
Year-round: Underwing grayer than Black-bellied Plover's; no black in wingpits.
Call a querulous whistled *queedle* or *que-e-a.*

PACIFIC GOLDEN-PLOVER *Pluvialis fulva* (not shown) p. 130
Like American, but with slightly longer legs. Breeding birds show some white along flanks and undertail; nonbreeding birds more gold-washed on face.
Call a loud, whistled *chu-whee* or *chu-wee-dle.*

RUDDY TURNSTONE *Arenaria interpres*   p. 140
Harlequin pattern distinctive.
Call a low chuckling *tuk-a-tuk* or *kut-a-kut.*

BLACK TURNSTONE *Arenaria melanocephala* (not shown) p. 140
Boldly patterned in black and white. Fairly similar to nonbreeding Ruddy Turnstone, but brown replaced by black, head mostly dark.
Call a short series of rattling notes.

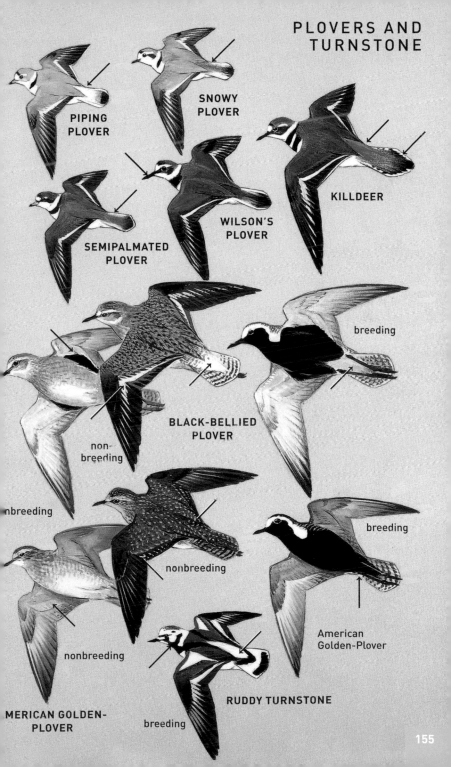

PLOVERS AND TURNSTONE

PIPING PLOVER

SNOWY PLOVER

SEMIPALMATED PLOVER

WILSON'S PLOVER

KILLDEER

BLACK-BELLIED PLOVER

nonbreeding

breeding

nonbreeding

nonbreeding

breeding

American Golden-Plover

MERICAN GOLDEN-PLOVER

nonbreeding

RUDDY TURNSTONE

breeding

Large Waders in Flight

Learn to know their flight calls, which are distinctive.

HUDSONIAN GODWIT *Limosa haemastica*   p. 138
Upturned bill, white wing stripe, ringed tail. Blackish wing linings.
Flight call *tawit!,* higher pitched than Marbled Godwit's.

WILLET *Tringa semipalmata*   p. 136
Contrasty black, gray, and white wing pattern. Overhead, wing pattern is even more striking.
Flight call a whistled one- to three-note *kree-ree-ree.*

MARBLED GODWIT *Limosa fedoa*   p. 138
Long upturned bill, tawny brown color. Cinnamon wing linings.
Flight call an accented *kerwhit!* (or *godwit!*).

WHIMBREL *Numenius phaeopus*   p. 138
Decurved bill, gray-brown overall color, striped crown. Grayer than next species, lacks cinnamon wing linings.
Flight call five to seven short, rapid whistles: *hee-hee-hee-hee-hee-hee.*

LONG-BILLED CURLEW *Numenius americanus*   p. 138
Very long, sicklelike bill; no head striping. Bright cinnamon wing linings. Juvenile's bill shorter but note head patterns.
Flight call a loud *cur-lee* (rising inflection).

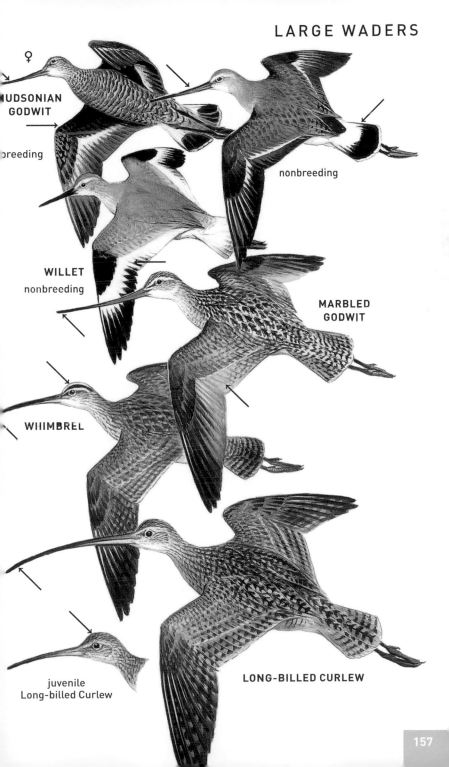

LARGE WADERS

♀

HUDSONIAN
GODWIT

breeding

nonbreeding

WILLET
nonbreeding

MARBLED
GODWIT

WIIIMBREL

LONG-BILLED CURLEW

juvenile
Long-billed Curlew

SNIPELIKE WADERS AND SANDPIPERS IN FLIGHT

These species and those on the next plate show their basic flight patterns. Most of these have unpatterned wings, lacking a pale stripe. Learn their distinctive flight calls.

WILSON'S SNIPE *Gallinago delicata*   p. 150
Long bill, pointed wings, rusty orange tail, zigzag flight.
Flight call, when flushed, a rasping *scaip.*

SOLITARY SANDPIPER *Tringa solitaria*   p. 136
Very dark unpatterned wings (underwing dark also — pale in yellow-legs), conspicuous bars on white sides of tail.
Flight call *peet!* or *peet-weet-weet!* (higher than Spotted Sandpiper's).

LESSER YELLOWLEGS *Tringa flavipes*   p. 136
Similar to Greater Yellowlegs, but smaller, with smaller bill.
Flight call *yew* or *yu-yu* (rarely three), softer than Greater's call.

GREATER YELLOWLEGS *Tringa melanoleuca*   p. 136
Plain unpatterned wings, whitish rump and tail, long bill.
Flight call a forceful typically three-note whistle, *dear! dear! dear!*

WILSON'S PHALAROPE *Phalaropus tricolor*   p. 152
Nonbreeding: Suggests Lesser Yellowlegs; smaller, whiter, bill needlelike.
Flight call a low nasal *wurk.*

BUFF-BREASTED SANDPIPER *Tryngites subruficollis*   p. 148
Buff below, contrasting with white wing linings; plain upperparts.
Flight call a low, trilled *pr-r-r-reet;* usually silent.

STILT SANDPIPER *Calidris himantopus*   p. 148
Suggests Lesser Yellowlegs, but legs greenish yellow, bill longer and drooped.
Flight call a single *whu,* lower than Lesser Yellowlegs'; usually silent.

UPLAND SANDPIPER *Bartramia longicauda*   p. 148
Brown; small head, long tail.
Often flies "on tips of wings," like Spotted Sandpiper.
Flight call a mellow whistled *kip-ip-ip-ip.*

PECTORAL SANDPIPER *Calidris melanotos*   p. 146
Like an oversized Least Sandpiper. Wing stripe faint or lacking.
Flight call a low, reedy *churrt* or *trrip, trrip.*

SNIPELIKE WADERS AND SANDPIPERS IN FLIGHT

WILSON'S SNIPE

SOLITARY SANDPIPER

GREATER YELLOWLEGS

LESSER YELLOWLEGS

WILSON'S PHALAROPE
nonbreeding

BUFF-BREASTED SANDPIPER

STILT SANDPIPER
nonbreeding

UPLAND SANDPIPER

PECTORAL SANDPIPER

Sandpipers and Phalaropes in Flight

SHORT-BILLED DOWITCHER *Limnodromus griseus*   p. 150
Long bill, long wedge of white up back. (Long-billed very similar.)
Flight call a staccato mellow *tu-tu-tu.*

DUNLIN *Calidris alpina*   p. 142
Nonbreeding: Slightly larger than peeps, darker than Sanderling.
Flight call a nasal rasping *cheezp* or *treezp.*

RED KNOT *Calidris canutus*   p. 142
Nonbreeding: Washed-out gray look, pale rump.
Flight call a low *knut.*

WHITE-RUMPED SANDPIPER *Calidris fuscicollis*   p. 146
White rump; other peep have white rumps with dark divide.
Flight call a mouselike squeak, *jeet.*

CURLEW SANDPIPER *Calidris ferruginea*   p. 168
Nonbreeding: Suggests Dunlin, but rump white.

RUFF *Philomachus pugnax*   p. 160
If seen well, oval white patch on each side of dark tail distinctive.
Usually silent.

SPOTTED SANDPIPER *Actitis macularius*   p. 148
Shallow wing stroke gives stiff, bowed effect; longish tail.
Flight call a clear *peet* or *peet-weet.*

SANDERLING *Calidris alba*   p. 142
The most contrasting wing stripe of any small shorebird.
Flight call a sharp *kip* or *quit.*

RED PHALAROPE *Phalaropus fulicarius*   p. 152
Nonbreeding: Paler above than Red-necked Phalarope; bill slightly
thicker.

RED-NECKED PHALAROPE *Phalaropus lobatus*   p. 152
Nonbreeding: Sanderling-like, but with dark eye patch.
Flight call (both pelagic phalaropes) a sharp *kit* or *whit.*

LEAST SANDPIPER *Calidris minutilla*   p. 144
Very small, brown with short wings and tail; faint wing stripe.
Flight call a thin single or doubled *krreet, krreet.*

SEMIPALMATED SANDPIPER *Calidris pusilla*   p. 144
Grayer than Least Sandpiper.
Flight call a soft *chit* or *chirt* (lacks *ee* sound of Least).

BAIRD'S SANDPIPER *Calidris bairdii*   p. 146
Larger and longer winged than above two. Buffy color.
Flight call a low, raspy *kreep* or *kree.*

SANDPIPERS AND PHALAROPES

SHORT-BILLED DOWITCHER
long-billed has similar pattern

nonbreeding

DUNLIN
nonbreeding

nonbreeding

RED KNOT

nonbreeding

WHITE-RUMPED SANDPIPER

CURLEW SANDPIPER

nonbreeding

RUFF

nonbreeding

SPOTTED SANDPIPER

SANDERLING

nonbreeding

RED PHALAROPE

RED-NECKED PHALAROPE
nonbreeding

LEAST SANDPIPER

SEMIPALMATED SANDPIPER

BAIRD'S SANDPIPER

EURASIAN DOTTEREL
Charadrius morinellus   Vagrant or very rare breeder

8¼–8½ in. (21–22 cm). Narrow white stripe crossing midbreast identifies this dark plover. Broad *white eyebrow stripes* join in broad V on nape. **VOICE:** Repeated piping, *titi-ri-titi-ri,* running into a trill. **RANGE:** Very rare Asian visitor to w. AK, casual farther south along Pacific Coast. A few pairs may breed locally on high tundra of nw. AK.

LESSER SAND-PLOVER (MONGOLIAN PLOVER)   Vagrant
Charadrius mongolus

7½ in. (19 cm). Asian. Slightly larger and larger-billed than Semipalmated Plover. *Breeding:* Very distinctive, with *broad rufous breastband.* Female duller. *Nonbreeding:* Breast-band gray-brown. *Juvenile:* Pale peachy buff breast. **VOICE:** Calls include a ploverlike whistle and a rolling trill. **RANGE:** Rare but regular migrant on Aleutians and Bering Sea islands. Casual vagrant from mainland AK to CA.

SPOTTED REDSHANK *Tringa erythropus*   Vagrant

12½ in. (32 cm). A slender, long-legged, long-billed shorebird. *Breeding: Sooty black,* with small white speckles on back and wings, making bird appear a trifle paler above. Long legs *dark red;* long black bill *reddish basally,* has *slight droop at tip. Nonbreeding and juvenile:* Gray and somewhat yellowlegs-like, but legs *orange-red,* bill *orange-red* basally. In flight, shows *long white wedge* on back, white underwing. **VOICE:** Sharp, whistled *tcheet,* with rising inflection. **RANGE:** Casual Eurasian visitor; records widely scattered.

COMMON GREENSHANK *Tringa nebularia*   Vagrant

13½ in. (34 cm). Size and shape of Greater Yellowlegs, but legs *dull greenish* (not bright yellow). Wedgelike white rump patch runs up back, as in a dowitcher. **VOICE:** Ringing, whistled *tew tew tew,* similar to Greater Yellowlegs. **RANGE:** Eurasian species; annual visitor on w. AK islands, accidental elsewhere.

WOOD SANDPIPER *Tringa glareola*   Very rare, local

8 in. (20 cm). Shape of Solitary Sandpiper, but has pale (not dark) underwings. Pale supercilium. Upperparts slightly paler and browner, *heavily spotted* with pale buff. Rump patch *white* (Solitary has dark rump). Legs dull yellow. Overall, looks very short in rear. **VOICE:** Sharp, high *chew-chew-chew* or *chiff-chiff-chiff.* **RANGE:** Regular migrant on w. AK islands, accidental elsewhere.

EURASIAN
DOTTEREL

breeding

♀

juvenile

nonbreeding

LESSER
SAND-
PLOVER

nonbreeding

breeding

COMMON
GREENSHANK

nbreeding

breeding

SPOTTED
EDSHANK

nonbreeding

breeding

WOOD
SANDPIPER

RARE SHOREBIRDS
(MOST FROM EURASIA)

BAR-TAILED GODWIT *Limosa lapponica* Scarce, local **M177**
16–17 in. (41–44 cm). Note *mottled rump* and *whitish tail* crossed by narrow dark bars. *Breeding:* Male rich *reddish orange* head and underparts. Female duller. *Nonbreeding:* Both sexes grayish above, white below. *Juvenile:* Underparts washed buffy, back with neat buff-and-black pattern. **VOICE:** Flight call a harsh *kirrick;* alarm a shrill *krick.* **SIMILAR SPECIES:** Marbled and Hudsonian godwits. Bar-tailed has slightly shorter bill and legs, underwing dusky. **RANGE:** Nests in w. AK; vagrant along West Coast. **HABITAT:** Mudflats, shores, tundra.

BLACK-TAILED GODWIT *Limosa limosa* Vagrant
16½ in. (42 cm). This elegant Eurasian godwit resembles Hudsonian Godwit (white rump, white wing stripe, black tail), but bill straighter and has *white underwings* (black in Hudsonian). In breeding plumage, has chestnut head and neck, black-and-white barred belly. **VOICE:** Flight call a clear *reeka-reeka-reeka.* **RANGE:** Casual visitor to w. AK. **HABITAT:** Lakes with muddy shores.

"EURASIAN" WHIMBREL *Numenius phaeopus variegatus* Vagrant
Asian subspecies of Whimbrel, *variegatus,* is a rare but regular migrant in w. AK; casual farther south along Pacific Coast. Differs from N. American Whimbrel by showing mottled *white rump* and whiter underwing. **VOICE:** Calls similar to N. American Whimbrel.

BRISTLE-THIGHED CURLEW *Numenius tahitiensis* Rare, local
17½–18 in. (44–46 cm). Very similar to Whimbrel, but *tawnier,* especially about *tail and unbarred rump.* Breast less streaked. Call very different. **VOICE:** Slurred *chi-u-it* (Inuit name) or *whee-oo-wheep;* suggests call of Black-bellied Plover. Also a wolf whistle–like *whee-wheeo.* **RANGE:** Nests locally in w. AK; accidental farther south. **HABITAT:** In summer, tundra; in winter, reefs and beaches.

ESKIMO CURLEW *Numenius borealis* Probably extinct
14 in. (36 cm). Last documented record in early 1960s. Much smaller and buffier than Whimbrel, with weak head pattern, shorter, thinner bill. *Wing linings cinnamon-buff. Primaries extend well past tail tip* at rest. **VOICE:** Call has been described as *tee-dee-dee* or repeated *tee-dee* or a note suggestive of Common Tern. **SIMILAR SPECIES:** Upland Sandpiper, Little Curlew. **RANGE:** Formerly bred in nw. Canada, migrating through Great Plains in spring. **HABITAT:** Open grasslands, coastal areas; in summer, tundra.

LITTLE CURLEW *Numenius minutus* Vagrant
12 in. (30 cm). The tiniest curlew. Bill *short and gently decurved.* Breast washed with buff, finely streaked. At rest, *wingtips even with tail tip* (extend beyond tail in Eskimo Curlew); note difference in *underwing* (pale buff, not cinnamon) and *flanks* (lightly barred, not heavy chevrons). **RANGE:** Casual along West Coast.

RARE SHOREBIRDS

nonbreeding

BAR-TAILED GODWIT

nonbreeding

nonbreeding

juvenile

nonbreeding

breeding

BLACK-TAILED GODWIT

breeding

BRISTLE-THIGHED CURLEW

Eurasian"

WHIMBREL

underwing

LITTLE CURLEW

underwing

ESKIMO CURLEW

COMMON SANDPIPER *Actitis hypoleucos*   **Vagrant**
8 in. (20 cm). At all seasons resembles nonbreeding Spotted Sandpiper (no spots). Best feature is *longer tail.* At rest, wingtips of Common reach only halfway to tail tip, those of Spotted closer to tip.
Common has grayer legs, longer white wing stripe. **VOICE:** In flight,
twee-see-see, thinner than Spotted's call. **RANGE:** Very rare but regular, mostly in spring, on Aleutians and Bering Sea islands.

TEREK SANDPIPER *Xenus cinereus*   **Vagrant**
9 in. (23 cm). Note *upturned bill* and short *orange-yellow legs, jagged
black stripe* along scapulars. Often bobs like Spotted Sandpiper. In
flight, wing has dark leading edge and broad *white band* at rear.
VOICE: Fluty *dudududu* or sharp piping, *twita-wit-wit-wit.* **RANGE:** Casual in w. AK islands, accidental farther south.

LITTLE STINT *Calidris minuta*   **Vagrant**
6 in. (15 cm). Size of Semipalmated Sandpiper, but bill slightly finer.
Breeding: Rusty orange above and on breast. Similar to some Red-
necked Stints, but *dark breast markings washed with orange.* **RANGE:**
Widespread casual visitor, mostly to coasts.

RED-NECKED STINT   **Rare visitor and breeder, local**
Calidris ruficollis
6¼ in. (17 cm). Size of Semipalmated Sandpiper but bill finer. Recognized in breeding plumage by *bright rusty head and neck, bordered
below by dark streaks.* **RANGE:** Rare but regular migrant in w. AK,
where very rare breeder; casual migrant elsewhere in N. America.

GRAY-TAILED TATTLER *Tringa brevipes*   **Rare visitor, local**
10 in. (25 cm). Very similar to Wandering Tattler; best told by voice.
Breeding: Compared with Wandering, barring on underparts finer
and less extensive; supercilium somewhat bolder. *Juvenile:* Gray-
tailed has more extensive whitish spots and notches to scapulars,
coverts, and tertials than Wandering, is slightly paler gray above
(sometimes tinged brownish), and flanks paler. **VOICE:** Up-slurred
whistle, *too-weet?* or *tu-whip?,* with accent on second syllable. **RANGE:**
Regular visitor to w. AK islands, accidental elsewhere.

TEMMINCK'S STINT *Calidris temminckii*   **Vagrant**
6¼ in. (16 cm). A brownish gray stint with *irregular black spots* on
scapulars. Has *elongated,* crouching look; *short dull yellow legs.* In
flight, shows *white outer tail feathers.* **VOICE:** In flight, a dry *trree,* often repeated in cricketlike trill. **SIMILAR SPECIES:** Least and Baird's
sandpipers. **RANGE:** Very rare visitor to w. AK islands, accidental farther south.

LONG-TOED STINT *Calidris subminuta*   **Vagrant**
6 in. (15 cm). Much like Least Sandpiper, but *brighter* above, with
more erect stance, *longer legs* and *toes,* dark forehead. May suggest
miniature Sharp-tailed Sandpiper. **VOICE:** Purring *prrp.* **RANGE:** Rare
but regular migrant on w. AK islands, accidental farther south.

COMMON
SANDPIPER

TEREK SANDPIPER

breeding

juvenile

nonbreeding
Spotted Sandpiper
(p. 148)
for comparison

Wandering Tattler
(p. 140)
for comparison

breeding   LITTLE
STINT

nonbreeding

breeding

O-NECKED
STINT

breeding

early spring
(breeding)

GRAY-TAILED
TATTLER

juvenile

juvenile

breeding

breeding

breeding   TEMMINCK'S
STINT

LONG-TOED
STINT

SHARP-TAILED SANDPIPER
Rare to casual visitor

Calidris acuminata

8½ in. (22 cm). Similar to Pectoral Sandpiper, but shows bolder whitish supercilium and brighter rusty crown. Most birds in N. America are juveniles, which have rich *orangey buff breast,* finely streaked on sides only. Breeding adults have heavy *dark chevrons* extending to flanks. Undertail coverts streaked. In no plumage is there as sharp a demarcation between white belly and streaked breast as in Pectoral. **VOICE:** Trilled *prreeet* or *trrit-trrit,* sometimes twittered. **SIMILAR SPECIES:** Juvenile Ruff. **RANGE:** Regular fall migrant in w. AK, very rare farther south; casual in spring; accidental elsewhere. **HABITAT:** Marshy and grassy borders of wetlands, muddy shores, wet pastures; in summer, tundra.

CURLEW SANDPIPER
Very rare visitor

Calidris ferruginea (see also p. 160)

8½–8¾ in. (21–22 cm). A Eurasian species with slim downcurved bill, blackish legs, and white rump in flight. *Breeding:* Male variably rich rufous red; female duller with thin pale barring. *Nonbreeding:* Resembles Dunlin, but slightly longer legged, bolder pale supercilium; bill curved slightly throughout; whitish rump. *Juvenile:* Buff edges on feathers of back give it a very scaly look; breast washed with buff. Similar to juvenile Stilt Sandpiper, but Curlew's legs black rather than greenish, and bill curves downward throughout its length. **VOICE:** Liquid *chirrip.* **SIMILAR SPECIES:** In breeding plumage, see also Red Knot. **RANGE:** Casual migrant inland and along West Coast. **HABITAT:** Marshy pools, mudflats; in summer, tundra.

RUFF *Philomachus pugnax* (see also p. 160)
Very rare visitor

Male (Ruff) 12–13 in. (30–32 cm); female (known informally as Reeve) 9 in. (23 cm). *Breeding male:* Unique, with erectile *ruffs* and *ear tufts* that may be black, brown, rufous, buff, white, or barred, in various combinations. Legs may be greenish, yellow, or orange. Bill color also variable. *Breeding female:* Smaller than male; lacks ruffs, breast *heavily blotched* with dark. *Nonbreeding:* Rather plain, with short bill, small head, thick neck, mottling of gray across breast. Note *erect stance* and (in flight) *oval white patch* on each side of dark tail. *Juvenile:* Buffy below, very scaly on back. **VOICE:** Often silent; flight call a low *too-i* or *tu-whit.* **SIMILAR SPECIES:** Juvenile Sharp-tailed Sandpiper, adult Buff-breasted Sandpiper. **RANGE:** Very rare but regular migrant along Pacific Coast; casual inland. **HABITAT:** Marshes, tundra in summer. Mudflats, marshes, coastal pools, wet agricultural fields in migration.

COMMON SNIPE *Gallinago gallinago*
Rare, local visitor

10½ in. (27 cm). Compared with Wilson's Snipe, has paler underwing, bolder white trailing edge to secondaries, weaker flank barring, slightly buffier overall color, and lower-pitched winnowing in flight display. **RANGE:** Regular visitor to w. AK islands. **HABITAT:** Similar to Wilson's Snipe.

juvenile

**SHARP-TAILED
SANDPIPER**

nonbreeding

breeding

breeding
dress of ♂
variable

♂

nonbreeding

♂

nonbreeding
♀

juvenile ♂

CURLEW
SANDPIPER

breeding

RUFF

breeding ♀

COMMON
SNIPE

GULLS Family Laridae

Long-winged swimming birds with superb flight. Most are more robust, wider winged, and longer legged than terns, and most have slightly hooked bills. Tails square or rounded (terns usually have forked tail). Gulls seldom dive (most terns hover, then plunge headfirst). FOOD: Omnivorous; marine life, plant and animal food, refuse, carrion. RANGE: Nearly worldwide.

AGING GULLS

It is often important to determine the age of a gull before identifying it. Knowing what a gull looks like in both its adult and first-year plumages is helpful in identifying the bird to species in its intermediate stages. Note that the molt of a gull from one plumage to the next is a gradual process. Therefore, a single "molt cycle" (which takes about a year in gulls) from, for example, fresh juvenal plumage in August to "first winter" plumage in January to "first summer" plumage in June will result in a range of appearances (particularly in larger species). Only one point in that range is pictured here.

SEQUENCE OF PLUMAGES IN A TWO-YEAR GULL

On the top of the opposite page, the Bonaparte's Gull illustrates the transition of plumages from first year to adult. Species in this category are mostly smaller gulls, including Bonaparte's, Black-headed, Little, Ross's, Sabine's, and Ivory gulls, and Red-legged Kittiwake.

SEQUENCE OF PLUMAGES IN A THREE-YEAR GULL

In the middle of the opposite page, the Ring-billed Gull, widespread and abundant both coastally and inland, illustrates the transition of plumages from first year to adult. Species in this category are mostly medium-sized gulls, including Ring-billed, Laughing, Franklin's, and Mew gulls and Black-legged Kittiwake.

SEQUENCE OF PLUMAGES IN A FOUR-YEAR GULL

On the bottom of the opposite page, the Herring Gull, a widespread species, illustrates the transition of plumages from first year to adult. Species in this category are most of the larger gulls, including California, Herring, Lesser Black-backed, Great Black-backed, Slaty-backed, Western, Glaucous-winged, Glaucous, Iceland, and Thayer's gulls. These species attain full maturity in 3½ to 4½ years. Surprisingly, the medium-sized Heermann's Gull is also a four-year species.

In this field guide, intended for identification on the species level, no other four-year gull receives similarly full treatment. That is the province of a larger text specifically on gulls. For in-depth analysis of other species, consult the *Peterson Reference Guide to Gulls of the Americas.*

Caution: There is extensive variation within species (particularly the immatures), resulting from several factors including dimorphism (males are larger than females), molt, variation in wear and bleaching, albinism, and other factors. In addition, hybridization is a regular phenomenon among most four-year species. Even expert birders leave some gulls unidentified.

BONAPARTE'S GULL

Plumage Transition of a Two-Year Gull

first year

adult

RING-BILLED GULL

first year

second year

adult

...mage ...nsition of ...hree-Year Gull

Plumage Transition of a Four-Year Gull

HERRING GULL

first year

second year

third year

adult

LAUGHING GULL *Leucophaeus atricilla* Uncommon, very local M206
16–16½ in. (41–42 cm). *Dark mantle blends into black wingtips.* Head *black* in breeding plumage; pale in nonbreeding plumage, with dark gray smudge. Bill longish, often with slight droop; reddish when breeding, mostly dark when not breeding. *Immature:* See p. 180. **VOICE:** Nasal *ha-a* and strident laugh, *ha-ha-ha-ha-ha-haah-haah-haah,* etc. **SIMILAR SPECIES:** Franklin's Gull slightly smaller, shorter billed, has broader white eye-arcs, paler underwing, and *different wingtip pattern.* **HABITAT:** Shorelines, farm fields.

FRANKLIN'S GULL *Leucophaeus pipixcan* Fairly common M207
14½–15 in. (37–38 cm). Note *white band* near wingtip, separating black from gray. In breeding plumage, head black; breast has rosy bloom; bill red. In nonbreeding plumage, head paler but with extensive *blackish "half hood"*; bill mostly dark. *Immature:* See p. 180. **VOICE:** Shrill *kuk-kuk-kuk;* also mewing, laughing cries. **SIMILAR SPECIES:** Laughing and Bonaparte's gulls. **HABITAT:** Prairies, inland marshes, lakes; in migration, also coasts, ocean.

SABINE'S GULL *Xema sabini* Scarce M203
13½–14 in. (34–36 cm). A small, *ternlike* gull with slightly *forked tail.* Note *bold upperwing pattern* of black outer primaries and *triangular white wing patch.* Bill black with *yellow tip. Immature:* See p. 180. **VOICE:** Various grating or buzzy ternlike calls. **HABITAT:** Ocean; mostly pelagic in migration; casual inland; nests on tundra pools.

BLACK-HEADED GULL *Chroicocephalus ridibundus* Very rare
15¾–16 in. (40–41 cm). This rare Eurasian visitor is similar to Bonaparte's Gull and often associates with it or with Ring-billed Gull. Slightly larger than Bonaparte's; mantle slightly paler; much *blackish on underside of primaries;* bill *dark red.* In nonbreeding plumage, loses dark brown hood and has black ear spot. *Immature:* See p. 180. **RANGE:** Rare visitor to AK; casual farther south. **HABITAT:** Same as Bonaparte's Gull.

BONAPARTE'S GULL Uncommon to fairly common M204
Chroicocephalus philadelphia
13–13½ in. (33–34 cm). A petite, ternlike gull. Note *wedge of white* on *fore edge* of wing. Legs pinkish; bill small, black. In breeding plumage, head blackish. In nonbreeding plumage, head whitish with *black ear spot. Immature:* See p. 180. Also see Sequence of Plumages in a Two-Year Gull, p. 170. **VOICE:** Nasal, grating *cheeer* or *cherr.* **SIMILAR SPECIES:** Black-headed and Little gulls. **HABITAT:** Ocean, bays, lakes, sewage-treatment ponds; in summer, muskeg.

LITTLE GULL *Hydrocoloeus minutus* Casual
11 in. (28 cm). This casual visitor is the smallest gull. Note *blackish undersurface* of *rather rounded wing* and absence of black above. In breeding plumage, head black. In nonbreeding plumage, head *dark-capped, black ear spot. Immature:* See p. 180. **VOICE:** Series of one- or two-syllable *key* notes. **SIMILAR SPECIES:** Bonaparte's Gull. **RANGE:** Casual visitor to West. **HABITAT:** Lakes, bays, coastal waters, sewage-treatment ponds; usually with Bonaparte's Gulls.

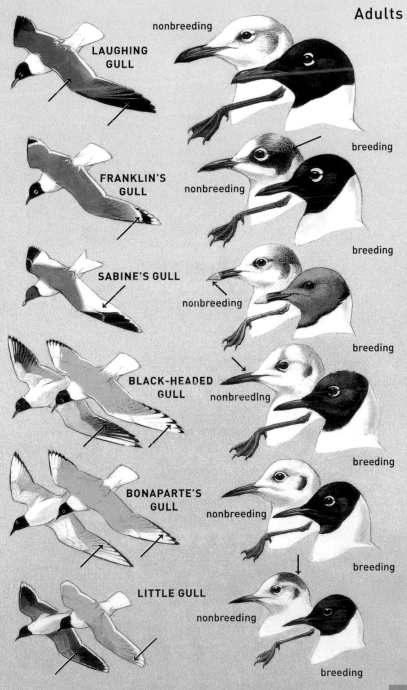

SMALL HOODED GULLS

Adults

LAUGHING GULL
nonbreeding
breeding

FRANKLIN'S GULL
nonbreeding
breeding

SABINE'S GULL
nonbreeding
breeding

BLACK-HEADED GULL
nonbreeding
breeding

BONAPARTE'S GULL
nonbreeding
breeding

LITTLE GULL
nonbreeding
breeding

HEERMANN'S GULL *Larus heermanni*   Common M208
19 in. (48 cm). The easiest gull in West to identify. *In all plumages, has black legs and feet.* Adult has *dark gray body, black tail* with thin white tip, whitish head, *red bill with black tip.* In fall and early winter, white head becomes gray. A few birds have white patches on upperwing. *Immature:* See p. 180. **VOICE:** Whining *whee-ee;* also a repeated *cow-auk.* **SIMILAR SPECIES:** May be confused with jaegers because of Heermann's habit of chasing other birds for food, overall dark coloration, and occasional adult with white wing patch. **HABITAT:** Ocean and immediate coastlines, including parks.

CALIFORNIA GULL *Larus californicus*   Common M213
21–21½ in. (53–55 cm). Resembles larger Herring Gull, but note darker mantle, *darker eye, yellowish legs.* Shows more white and black in wingtips than Herring. In nonbreeding plumage, head streaked or mottled brownish, dark spot on bill may extend to upper mandible, legs slightly duller. *Immature:* See p. 182. **VOICE:** Like Herring Gull's but higher, more hoarse. **HABITAT:** Ocean and coasts, lakes, farms, dumps, parks, urban centers.

RING-BILLED GULL *Larus delawarensis*   Common M210
17–17½ in. (43–45 cm). A small gull, with *pale eye* and *light gray mantle* (similar to Herring's); *legs yellow or greenish yellow* (may be duller in nonbreeding plumage). Note complete *black ring* encircling bill. In nonbreeding plumage, shows some *fine dark streaking* on head. *Immature:* See p. 180. Also see Sequence of Plumages in a Three-Year Gull, p. 170. **VOICE:** Higher pitched than Herring Gull's. **SIMILAR SPECIES:** Mew Gull. **HABITAT:** Lakes, bays, coasts, piers, dumps, plowed fields, sewage outlets, parks, shopping malls, fast-food restaurants.

MEW GULL *Larus canus*   Common M209
16–17 in. (41–44 cm). Similar to Ring-billed Gull but slightly smaller, with more greenish yellow legs and smaller, *unmarked greenish yellow bill.* (Birds in full breeding condition have yellow bill and legs.) *Darkish eye. Mantle noticeably darker than Ring-billed's.* More extensive dark mottling on head and neck in winter. Mew shows larger white "mirrors" in its black wingtips than either California or Ring-billed gull. *Immature:* See p. 180. **VOICE:** Low, mewing *queeu* or *meeu.* Also *hiyah-hiyah-hiyah,* etc., higher than voice of other gulls. **HABITAT:** In winter, ocean, coastlines, parks, dumps, wet fields, tidal rivers; in summer, lakes, taiga, tundra.

BLACK-LEGGED KITTIWAKE *Rissa tridactyla*   Uncommon M200
16–17 in. (41–43 cm). A small, buoyant oceanic gull. Wingtips are *solid black,* as if dipped in ink. Bill small, pale yellow, and unmarked. Legs and feet *black. Eyes dark.* In nonbreeding plumage, rear head and nape dusky. *Immature:* See p. 180. **VOICE:** At nesting colony, a raucous *kaka-week* or *kitti-waak.* **SIMILAR SPECIES:** Mew, Ring-billed, and Sabine's gulls; in w. AK, Red-legged Kittiwake. **HABITAT:** Chiefly oceanic; rarely on beaches and in harbors, casual inland. Nests on sea cliffs.

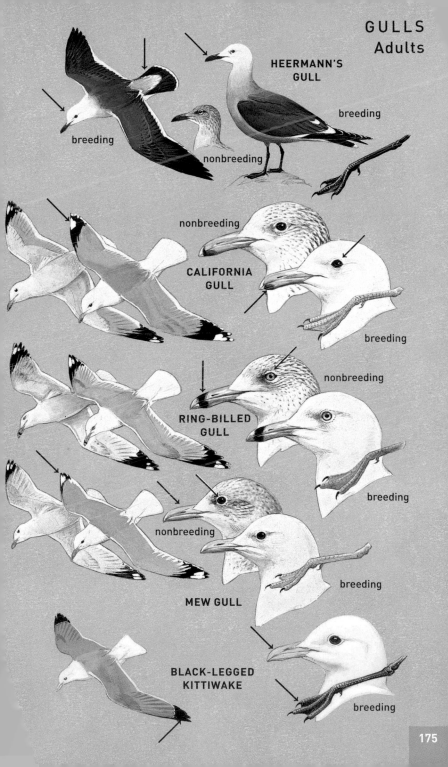

GULLS
Adults

HEERMANN'S
GULL

breeding

nonbreeding

breeding

nonbreeding

CALIFORNIA
GULL

breeding

nonbreeding

RING-BILLED
GULL

breeding

nonbreeding

MEW GULL

breeding

BLACK-LEGGED
KITTIWAKE

breeding

HERRING GULL *Larus argentatus*   Uncommon M214
24–25 in. (61–64 cm). A widespread large gull. Regularly hybridizes with Glaucous-winged Gull in AK. *Pale gray* mantle, *pinkish* legs, *pale eye*. Outer primaries *black* with white spots or "mirrors." Bill yellow with red spot. In nonbreeding plumage, head and neck mottled with brownish. *Immature:* See p. 182. Also see Sequence of Plumages in a Four-Year Gull, p. 170. VOICE: A loud *hiyak . . . hiyak . . . hiyah-hyak* or *yuk-yuk-yuk-yuk-yuckle-yuckle.* Mewing squeals. Anxiety call *gah-gah-gah.* SIMILAR SPECIES: Thayer's and California gulls. HABITAT: Ocean, coasts, bays, lakes, dams, piers, farmland, dumps.

THAYER'S GULL *Larus thayeri*   Scarce M215
23–24 in. (58–61 cm). Formerly thought to be a race of Herring Gull. Now designated as a full species, but regarded by some as a subspecies of Iceland Gull. Very similar to Herring Gull. Typical adult has *pale to dark brown* eyes, *only a thin trailing edge of black* on *grayish* underside of primaries, slightly darker mantle, slightly deeper pink legs, and somewhat slighter bill, often with greenish-tinged base. *Immature:* See p. 184. VOICE: Similar to Herring Gull. SIMILAR SPECIES: Iceland Gull; Glaucous-winged × Western gull hybrid larger, has larger, thicker bill. HABITAT: Similar to Herring Gull.

GLAUCOUS-WINGED GULL *Larus glaucescens*   Common M218
25–26 in. (63–66 cm). A *very large pinkish-legged* gull, with large bill, pale gray mantle, and *medium gray* primaries. *Immature:* See p. 184. Hybridizes with Western Gull in Pacific Northwest, and with Herring Gull in AK. VOICE: Low *kak-kak-kak;* a low *wow;* a high *keer, keer.* SIMILAR SPECIES: Adult Glaucous Gull has whitish primaries, thinner bill, paler eye. See also Western, Thayer's, and Herring gulls. HABITAT: Ocean, coastlines, bays, parks, dumps, lakeshores.

GLAUCOUS GULL *Larus hyperboreus*   Rare to uncommon M219
27–28 in. (68–72 cm). A large, chalky white gull with pinkish legs. Note "frosty" wingtips. Has pale gray mantle and *unmarked white outer primaries. Light eye. Immature:* See p. 184. VOICE: Much like Herring Gull's. SIMILAR SPECIES: Iceland and Glaucous-winged gulls. HABITAT: Mainly coastal; a few inland at large lakes and dumps.

ICELAND GULL *Larus glaucoides*   Casual
22–23 in. (56–60 cm). A pale ghostly gull, slightly smaller than Herring Gull. Mantle pale gray; primaries whitish and extending *well beyond tail. Immature:* See p. 184. "Kumlien's" Gull *(Larus glaucoides kumlieni),* the subspecies that breeds in e. Arctic Canada, is the one seen in U.S.; has gray or dark markings, variable in extent, toward tips of whitish primaries (not black with white "mirrors" as in Herring Gull). VOICE: Similar to Herring Gull but higher pitched; rarely heard away from breeding grounds. SIMILAR SPECIES: Glaucous Gull larger, has larger bill, shorter primary extension. At very close range, adult Glaucous shows narrow *yellow* eye-ring (*red* in Iceland). Adult Thayer's Gull has slightly darker mantle, blacker primaries, dark eye. RANGE: Casual visitor to West. HABITAT: Ocean, shorelines, lakes, dumps.

GULLS
Adults

HERRING GULL

nonbreeding

breeding

nonbreeding

THAYER'S GULL

breeding

breeding

GLAUCOUS-WINGED GULL

nonbreeding

breeding

GLAUCOUS GULL

nonbreeding

breeding

ICELAND GULL

"Kumlien's" (typical)

pale extreme

WESTERN GULL *Larus occidentalis*   Common M211

25–26 in. (64–66 cm). A large, large-billed gull. Note *very dark* back and wings (called *"mantle"*) contrasting with snowy underparts. Legs and feet dull pinkish. Northern race (cen. CA to WA) has paler mantle, but it is still noticeably darker than that of California Gull. Southern race is blacker backed and paler eyed, appears cleaner headed in winter. *Immature:* See p. 182. *Note:* There is much hybridization with Glaucous-winged Gull where their breeding ranges overlap. Hybrids have intermediate mantle and wingtip coloration. They are found in winter south to cen. CA, with a few inland as well. **VOICE:** Guttural *kuk kuk kuk;* also *whee whee whee* and *ki-aa.* **SIMILAR SPECIES:** Glaucous-winged and Herring gulls. **HABITAT:** Offshore and coastal waters, beaches, piers, city waterfronts, parks, dumps, lower reaches of tidal rivers.

YELLOW-FOOTED GULL *Larus livens*   Uncommon, very local M212

27 in. (69 cm). In U.S., this species found regularly only at Salton Sea. This large gull closely resembles Western Gull, but adult has *yellow* (not pinkish) legs and feet and slightly darker mantle and thicker bill. It matures in its third year, not fourth as Western Gull does. *Immature:* Brown juvenile has whitish belly, and by first winter already has some black on back. Yellow legs and feet are attained by second winter. **VOICE:** Deeper than Western's. **HABITAT:** Same as Western Gull.

LESSER BLACK-BACKED GULL *Larus fuscus*   Casual to rare M216

21–22½ in. (53–57 cm). Slightly smaller than Herring Gull and slimmer, with longer wings and smaller bill. Distinguished by yellowish (not pink) legs and slate gray mantle. *Extensive head and neck streaking* in nonbreeding plumage. Pale eye. Oblong red spot on bill. *Immature:* See p. 182. **VOICE:** Harsh *kyah.* **SIMILAR SPECIES:** California and Western gulls. **RANGE:** Rare but regular visitor in the Great Plains; casual to West Coast. **HABITAT:** Same as Herring Gull.

GREAT BLACK-BACKED GULL *Larus marinus*   Casual

29–30 in. (73–76 cm). Largest gull in the world, with broad wings and heavy body and bill. Black back and wings, snow-white underparts, no head streaking in winter. Legs and feet *pale* pinkish. *Immature:* See p. 182. **VOICE:** Harsh deep seal-like *kyow* or *owk.* **SIMILAR SPECIES:** Western, Lesser Black-backed, and Slaty-backed gulls. **RANGE:** Casual visitor from East to plains; accidental farther west. **HABITAT:** Shorelines, large lakes, dumps.

Dark-backed Adults

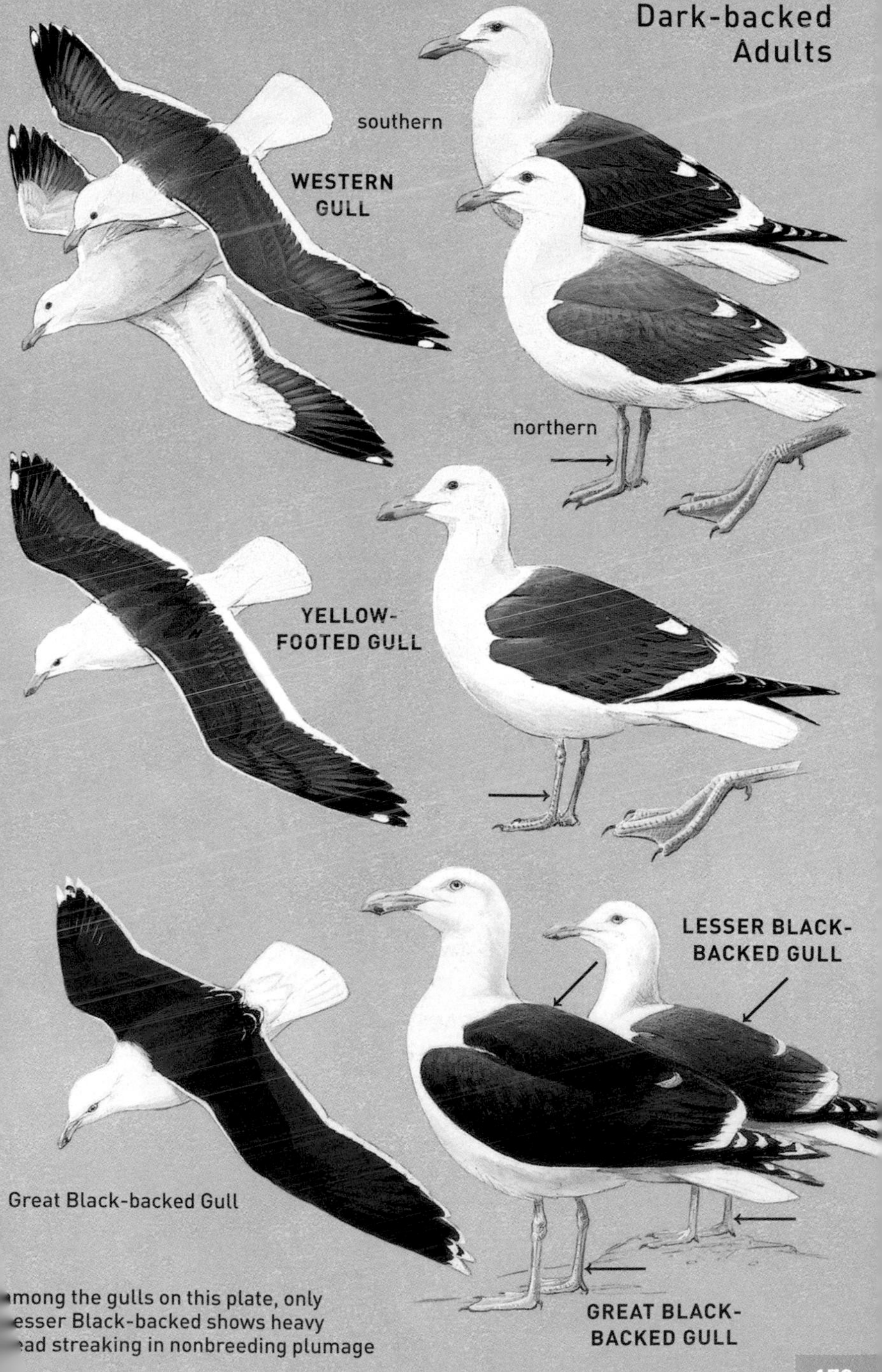
southern
WESTERN GULL
northern
YELLOW-FOOTED GULL
LESSER BLACK-BACKED GULL
Great Black-backed Gull
GREAT BLACK-BACKED GULL

mong the gulls on this plate, only esser Black-backed shows heavy ead streaking in nonbreeding plumage

IMMATURE SMALL GULLS

Immatures of many gull species are more difficult to identify than adults. They are usually darkest the first year, lighter the second, when some species show adult eye and back color. (See pp. 170–71.) Identify mainly by pattern, size, and structure. The most typical plumages are shown here; intermediate and successive stages can be expected.

LAUGHING GULL *Leucophaeus atricilla*   Adult, p. 172
A three-year gull. *Juvenile:* Dark brown with black tail, white rump. *First winter:* Neck and back become extensively smudged with gray. *Second year:* Similar to adult, but with trace of black in tail. **SIMILAR SPECIES:** Franklin's Gull.

FRANKLIN'S GULL *Leucophaeus pipixcan*   Adult, p. 172
A three-year gull. *First year:* Similar to first-year Laughing, but more petite with *smaller bill, blackish half-hood, white neck, white* outer tail feathers. *Second year:* Close to second winter Laughing but with blackish half hood, pale underside to primaries.

BLACK-HEADED GULL *Chroicocephalus ridibundus*   Adult, p. 172
A two-year gull. *First year:* Similar to first-year Bonaparte's but slightly larger; bill *orange* at base; *sooty underwing;* dusky trailing edge to upperwing.

BONAPARTE'S GULL *Chroicocephalus philadelphia*   Adult, p. 172
A two-year gull. Petite, ternlike. *First year:* Note dark ear spot, narrow black tail band, neat dark trailing edge to wings. Pale underwing. See Sequence of Plumages in a Two-Year Gull, p. 170.

LITTLE GULL *Hydrocoloeus minutus*   Adult, p. 172
A two-year gull. *First year:* Slightly smaller than Bonaparte's, with *blacker M pattern, white trailing edge* to wings, *dusky cap.*

SABINE'S GULL *Xema sabini*   Adult, p. 172
A two-year gull. *Juvenile:* Dark grayish brown on back, but with adult's bold *triangular wing pattern.* Note also *forked* tail.

HEERMANN'S GULL *Larus heermanni*   Adult, p. 174
A four-year gull. Readily told by *black legs and feet* and overall *dark brown or sooty gray color.* Note two-toned bill.

BLACK-LEGGED KITTIWAKE *Rissa tridactyla*   Adult, p. 174
A three-year gull. *First year:* Note *dark bar on nape, black M across back and wings;* slightly notched tail; white trailing edge to wings.

MEW GULL *Larus canus*   Adult, p. 174
A three-year gull. *First year:* Smaller than Ring-billed with slimmer bill, rounder head, browner primaries, broader tail band; heavily mottled tail coverts, darker gray back, usually dark underparts.

RING-BILLED GULL *Larus delawarensis*   Adult, p. 174
A three-year gull. *First year:* Usually *bicolored bill,* mostly whitish underneath and on rump and upper tail, *pale gray back.* Subterminal tail band usually narrow; contrasty wing pattern.

SMALL GULLS
Immatures

juvenile

first year

juvenile

Laughing Gull

first year

LAUGHING GULL

first year

FRANKLIN'S GULL

Franklin's Gull first year

first year

BONAPARTE'S GULL

first year

BLACK-HEADED GULL

first year

LITTLE GULL

first year

SABINE'S GULL

juvenile

first year

first year

second year

BLACK-LEGGED KITTIWAKE

first year

HEERMANN'S GULL

first year

first year

RING-BILLED GULL

first year

MEW GULL

181

DARK IMMATURE LARGE GULLS

Immatures of many gull species are more difficult to identify than adults. They are usually darkest in the first year and progressively lighter and more adultlike as they get older. Most large gulls do not develop their full adult plumage until the fourth year (see pp. 170–71). Identify mainly by pattern, size, and structure. Typical plumages of the younger stages are shown here. Intermediate and successive stages can be expected, but because of variables such as molt, wear, age, individual variation, hybridization, and occasional albinism, some birds may remain a mystery even to the expert.

WESTERN GULL *Larus occidentalis*   Adult, p. 178

A four-year gull. Compared with first-year Herring Gull, first-year Western is larger, larger-billed, sootier brown, lacks pale inner primaries.

HERRING GULL *Larus argentatus*   Adult, p. 176

A four-year gull. *First year:* Brownish overall, with brownish black wingtips and dark brown tail. Often shows much mottling or checkering on upperwing coverts and rump. *Pale area on inner primaries visible in flight.* Bill all dark at first, becoming paler at base later. *Second and third years:* Head and underparts whiter; eye pale; back pale gray; rump white; bill pale, dark-tipped. See Sequence of Plumages in a Four-Year Gull, p. 170.

CALIFORNIA GULL *Larus californicus*   Adult, p. 174

A four-year gull. *First year:* Like Herring Gull, but slightly smaller, with smaller bicolored bill. In flight, shows double dark bar on wing and lacks pale area on inner primaries. *Second year:* Legs and bill base often dull gray-green-blue. Much like first-winter Ring-billed Gull, but somewhat larger, retains dark eye, darker gray on back, and tail mostly dark rather than with only a dark subterminal band.

LESSER BLACK-BACKED GULL *Larus fuscus*   Adult, p. 178

A four-year gull. Smaller, slimmer than Herring Gull. *First year:* Like miniature first-year Herring but with broader tail band, darker wings, more heavily streaked (and spotted) breast; colder brown than Herring with white tail base, paler head and underparts, darker wings.

GREAT BLACK-BACKED GULL *Larus marinus*   Adult, p. 174

A four-year gull. *First year:* Larger and more salt-and-pepper patterned than first-year Herring Gull. They show more contrast, being paler on head, rump, and underparts. Pale belly contrasts with dark underwing. More checkered looking than Herring. *Second year:* The "saddle-back" pattern is suggested; they may resemble later immature stages of Herring Gull, but back darker, head and bill larger.

LARGE GULLS
Dark Immatures

second year

first year

WESTERN GULL

second year

first year

second year

California Gull

first year

LESSER BLACK-
BACKED GULL

first year

GREAT BLACK-
BACKED GULL

first year

first year

HERRING
GULL

second year

CALIFORNIA
GULL

first year

first year

HERRING
GULL

second year

Pale Immature Large Gulls

THAYER'S GULL *Larus thayeri*   Adult, p. 176

A four-year gull. *First year:* Tan-brown and checkered; similar to first year Herring Gull but lighter; primaries paler, usually *light tan-brown* (not brownish black) *with pale edges to tips; bill entirely or almost entirely blackish, more petite; underside of primaries pale.* Often shows dark smudge through eye. *Second year:* Paler and grayer; primaries gray-brown with darker outer webs. See Iceland Gull.

ICELAND GULL *Larus glaucoides*   Adult, p. 176

Sequence of plumages similar to Glaucous Gull's, but Iceland is smaller (smaller than Herring Gull) with smaller bill and proportionately longer wings (projecting beyond tail at rest). Bill of most first-year Iceland Gulls mostly dark, only very rarely as sharply demarcated as in Glaucous. Most birds show a hint of a tail band as well as some dark in outer primaries, both lacking in Glaucous; darkest birds approach Thayer's in appearance (some may be indistinguishable).

GLAUCOUS GULL *Larus hyperboreus*   Adult, p. 176

A four-year gull. *First year:* Recognized by its large size, pale tan or off-whitish (particularly by late winter) coloration, and unmarked *frosty primaries,* a shade lighter than rest of wing. Brownish barring on undertail coverts and mottling in wing coverts and tail. Bill *pale pinkish* with dark tip — *sharply demarcated. Second year:* Pale gray back and pale eye acquired.

GLAUCOUS-WINGED GULL *Larus glaucescens*   Adult, p. 176

A four-year gull. Variable. Slightly larger than Herring Gull, and with similar sequence of plumages (see p. 182), but primaries are close to same tone as rest of wing, not markedly darker as in Western and Herring gulls, or paler or translucent as in Glaucous Gull. Hybrids with Western or Herring gulls have intermediate-colored primaries. Worn Glaucous-wingeds in spring and summer may appear very white, but lack clean-cut two-toned bill and tan mottling to wing coverts and undertail coverts of Glaucous.

LARGE GULLS
Pale Immatures

THAYER'S
GULL

second
year

first year

second
year

first
year

first year

ICELAND
GULL

GLAUCOUS
GULL

d year

second
year

Glaucous Gull
first year

Iceland Gull
first year

first year

second
year

second
year

first year

GLAUCOUS-WINGED GULL

185

Rare Gulls

BLACK-TAILED GULL *Larus carassirostris* Vagrant
18–18½ in. (46–47 cm). Slightly larger than Ring-billed Gull, and with slightly longer wings and bill. Adult has red tip to black-banded bill, slate gray mantle, and wide black subterminal band on tail. **RANGE:** Casual visitor from e. Asia, with widely scattered records across much of N. America.

SLATY-BACKED GULL *Larus schistisagus* Scarce, local M217
25–26 in. (64–67 cm). Any large, very dark backed gull in Bering Sea is likely to be this Asian species. Adult similar to Western Gull, but with slightly slimmer bill, paler eye, deeper pinkish feet, *extensive head streaking in nonbreeding plumage.* Note how broad white trailing edge of wing invades outer wing, forming *thin white bar* crossing dark primaries (best seen across underwing). Primaries *gray* beneath. **SIMILAR SPECIES:** Siberian subspecies of Herring Gull *(vegae)*, found in same areas of w. AK, is darker mantled than typical N. American Herring Gull. **RANGE:** Regular visitor to w. AK, very rare to Pacific Northwest, casual elsewhere. **HABITAT:** Seacoasts, dumps.

RED-LEGGED KITTIWAKE Uncommon, very local M201
Rissa brevirostris
15 in. (38 cm). *Adult:* Similar to Black-legged Kittiwake but smaller, with *darker gray mantle* (very noticeable when both species seen together); *shorter bill and rounder head* give it a more dove-headed look; legs *bright red.* Has similar wing pattern above (although white trailing edge broader); *darkish gray underwing. Immature:* Wing pattern more similar to Sabine's Gull; tail lacks black terminal band. Legs duller than in adult. **VOICE:** High-pitched *tuu-WEE* near nesting colony. **HABITAT:** Open ocean, where it often forages at night. Nests in colonies on steep, rocky ocean cliffs.

ROSS'S GULL *Rhodostethia rosea* Very rare M205
13–13½ in. (33–35 cm). A rare Arctic gull of drift ice. Note *wedge-shaped tail, medium gray wing linings,* and *small black bill.* A two-year gull. *Breeding: Rosy* blush on underparts, *fine black collar. Nonbreeding:* Rosy blush duller or lacking, lacks black collar, neck washed with gray. *First winter:* Similar in pattern to immature Black-legged Kittiwake or Little Gull, but intermediate in size and note *wedge-shaped tail* and *gray* linings of underwing; lacks dark nape of young kittiwake. **HABITAT:** Arctic waters, tundra in summer.

IVORY GULL *Pagophila eburnea* Very rare, threatened M202
17 in. (43 cm). A declining species of Arctic pack ice. Most individuals that wander south of normal range are immatures. A two-year gull. *Adult:* The only all-white gull with black legs. Pigeon sized with dove-like head; wings long, flight ternlike. Bill greenish with yellow tip. *Immature:* White, with dark *smudge on face,* a *sprinkling of black spots* above, black spots on primary tips, and narrow black tip to tail. Legs and feet black, a distinction from all other white gulls. **HABITAT:** Open Arctic waters usually near pack ice.

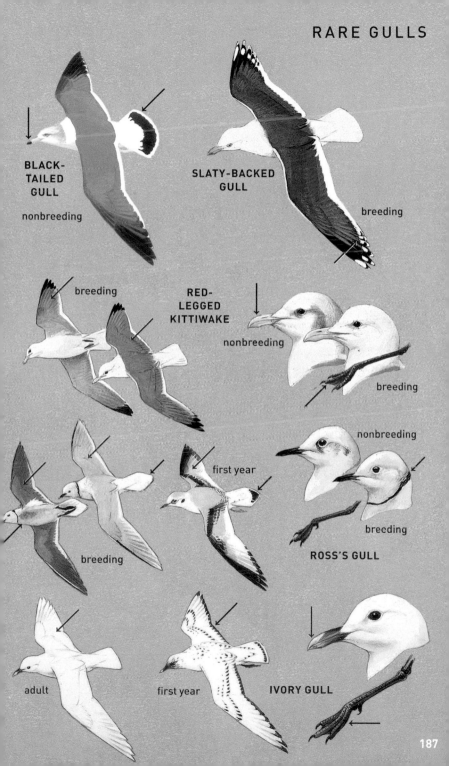

RARE GULLS

BLACK-TAILED GULL

nonbreeding

SLATY-BACKED GULL

breeding

RED-LEGGED KITTIWAKE

breeding

nonbreeding

breeding

breeding

first year

nonbreeding

breeding

ROSS'S GULL

adult

first year

IVORY GULL

187

TERNS Subfamily Sterninae

Graceful waterbirds, more streamlined than gulls; wings more pointed, tail usually forked. Bill sharp-pointed, often tilted toward water when bird is flying. Most terns are whitish with black cap; in nonbreeding plumage, black of forehead replaced by white. Sexes alike. Terns often hover and plunge headfirst for fish. Normally do not swim (gulls do). FOOD: Small fish, marine life, large insects. RANGE: Almost worldwide.

FORSTER'S TERN *Sterna forsteri*   Common M227

14½ in. (37 cm). Very similar to Common Tern, but adult Forster's paler; all adults have frosty wingtips (lighter than rest of wing; darkening in Common). Whitish below in all plumages, lacking gray wash of breeding Common. Tail grayer; bill slightly thicker and more orange than red. Nonbreeding adult and immature have isolated *black mask* and lack dark carpal ("shoulder") bar of Common in similar plumages. See also Arctic Tern. **VOICE:** Harsh, nasal *za-a-ap* and nasal *kyarr*. **HABITAT:** Fresh and salt marshes, lakes, bays, beaches, nearshore ocean; nests in marshes.

COMMON TERN *Sterna hirundo*   Uncommon M225

14 in. (36 cm). A graceful, small, black-capped, slim bird with deeply forked tail. *Breeding adult:* Pearl gray mantle and black cap; bill red with black tip; feet orange-red. Similar to Forster's Tern, but several outer primaries form *dark wedge on upperwing, grayer below, bill slightly smaller and redder, legs shorter. Nonbreeding adult and immature:* Cap, nape, and bill blackish. *Show dark shoulder (carpal) bar.* Asian subspecies *(longipennis),* a very rare visitor in w. AK, darker, with *black bill* in breeding plumage and *blackish legs and feet.* **VOICE:** Drawling *kee-arr* (downward inflection); also *kik-kik-kik;* a quick *kirri-kirri.* **HABITAT:** Lakes, ocean, bays, marshes, beaches; nests colonially on small islands.

ARCTIC TERN *Sterna paradisaea*   Uncommon M226

15 in. (38 cm). A pelagic (seagoing) tern. Similar to Forster's and particularly Common terns. Bill and neck shorter, head rounder. *Legs shorter.* Overhead, note *translucent* effect of primaries and *narrow* black trailing edge; from above, secondaries pale. *Breeding adult:* Bill usually *blood red* to tip, uniform pale gray upperwing, extensive wash of *gray below,* setting off white cheeks. (*Caution:* Breeding Common Terns are fairly similar below.) *Nonbreeding and juvenile:* Like Common, but black on head slightly more extensive, shoulder bar somewhat *weaker, secondaries whitish,* and same structural differences as in breeding. **VOICE:** *Kee-yak,* similar to Common Tern's cry, but less slurred, higher. A high *keer-keer* is characteristic. **HABITAT:** Open ocean, coasts, islands; in summer, also taiga lakes, tundra.

adult

nonbreeding

breeding

nature

FORSTER'S TERN

adult

nonbreeding

dult

immature

breeding

COMMON TERN

Asian race

breeding

adult

dult

nonbreeding

breeding

immature

ARCTIC TERN

GULL-BILLED TERN

Uncommon, very local M222

Gelochelidon nilotica

14 in. (36 cm). Note *stout black* bill. Stockier and paler than Common Tern; tail much less forked; feet *black*. In nonbreeding plumage, head white with smudgy dark ear patch, pale dusky on nape; suggests a small gull with notched tail. *Immature:* Similar to nonbreeding adult. This tern plucks food from water's surface and often hawks for insects over marshes and fields, swooping (rarely diving) after prey. **VOICE:** *Kay-weck, kay-weck;* also a throaty, rasping *za-za-za.* **SIMILAR SPECIES:** Midsized gulls. **HABITAT:** Marshes, fields, coastal bays.

ELEGANT TERN *Thalasseus elegans*

Fairly common, local M229

17 in. (43 cm). This Mexican species has recently expanded its breeding range to include San Diego and Orange counties in CA. North of there it should be looked for primarily between midsummer and late fall. In size, slightly smaller than Royal Tern. Bill orange or orange-yellow, proportionately *longer, more slender,* and slightly droopier than deeper orange bill of Royal. Elegant's black crown extends farther down nape. In nonbreeding plumage, dark of head *includes eye.* **VOICE:** Nasal *karrik* or *kerr-rik.* **SIMILAR SPECIES:** Royal and Caspian terns. **HABITAT:** Ocean, coasts, beaches, salt bays.

ROYAL TERN *Thalasseus maximus*

Fairly common, local M228

20 in. (51 cm). A large tern, slimmer than Caspian, with large *orange* bill (Caspian's bill heavier, redder, and has dark mark near tip). Tail forked. Although some Royal Terns in spring show solid black crown, for most of year they have *much white on forehead,* black crown feathers forming a crest. In nonbreeding plumage, black feathers behind eye usually *do not encompass eye* as they do in nonbreeding Elegant Tern. Dusky upperside and *pale underside to primaries,* opposite of Caspian. **VOICE:** Sonorous *karr-rik,* mellower (slower and lower-pitched) than Elegant or Sandwich; also *kaak* or *kak.* **SIMILAR SPECIES:** Caspian and Elegant terns. **HABITAT:** Ocean, coasts, beaches, salt bays. More closely tied to coastal waters than Caspian, which is common inland.

CASPIAN TERN

Uncommon to fairly common M223

Hydroprogne caspia

21 in. (53 cm). Large size and *stout reddish bill with small dark mark near tip* set Caspian apart from all other terns. Tail of Caspian *shorter;* head and bill larger, crest shorter. Royal's forehead is usually *clear white* (in adult nonbreeding plumage, Caspian has *streaked* forehead). Caspian shows obvious *grayish black on undersurface of primaries, but pale upper surface.* Caspian ranges inland, Royal does not. **VOICE:** Raspy, low *kraa-uh* or *karr,* also repeated *kak;* juveniles give whistled *wheee-oo.* **SIMILAR SPECIES:** Royal and Elegant terns. **HABITAT:** Large lakes, rivers, coastal waters, beaches, bays.

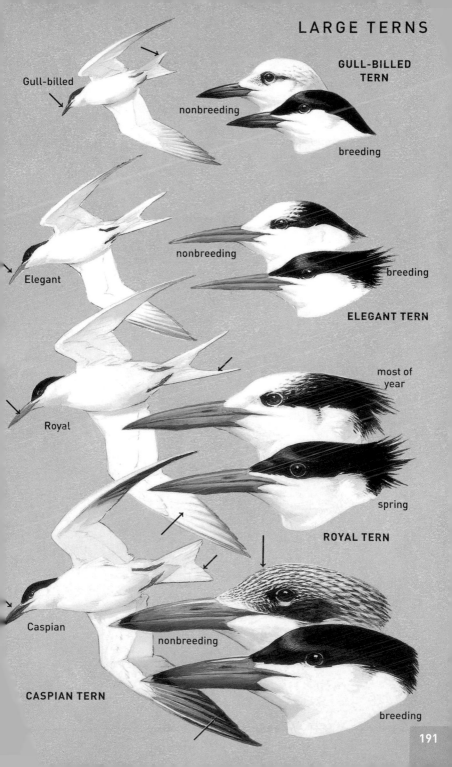

LARGE TERNS

GULL-BILLED TERN

Gull-billed

nonbreeding

breeding

nonbreeding

Elegant

breeding

ELEGANT TERN

most of year

Royal

spring

ROYAL TERN

Caspian

nonbreeding

CASPIAN TERN

breeding

LEAST TERN *Sternula antillarum*　　　　　　Uncommon M221
9 in. (23 cm). A *very small,* pale tern, with rapid wingbeats (quicker than other terns). *Breeding adult:* Dark-tipped *yellow bill, yellow legs and feet* (in fall, all birds may have dark bill, but feet show yellow), and *white forehead. Long black wedge on outer wing. Immature:* Dark bill, dark cheek and nape, dusky crown, dark shoulder (carpal) bar, duller legs. **VOICE:** Sharp, repeated *kit;* a harsh, squealing *zree-eek* or *k-zeek;* also a rapid *kitti-kitti-kitti.* **SIMILAR SPECIES:** Forster's Tern. **HABITAT:** Nearshore ocean waters, beaches, bays, ponds, large rivers, sandbars.

ALEUTIAN TERN *Onychoprion aleuticus*　　　　Scarce, local M220
13½–14 in. (34–36 cm). A lead-colored tern of Alaskan coastal waters. Told from Arctic Tern by its *blackish bill and legs, clean-cut white forehead, dark bar along underside of secondaries.* Lead gray body and mantle contrast with white tail. *Juvenile:* Boldly edged with rusty orange above; legs orangey red. **VOICE:** Three-syllable whistle, suggesting a shorebird or House Sparrow. **HABITAT:** Open ocean; nests along AK coast on islands, sandbars.

BLACK TERN *Chlidonias niger*　　　　　　　　Uncommon M224
9½–9¾ in. (24–25 cm). A black-bodied tern. Short tail only slightly forked. *Breeding adult:* Head and underparts (except undertail coverts) *black; back, wings, and tail dark gray;* wing linings whitish. *Nonbreeding adult:* By midsummer, molting birds are mottled, with black largely replaced by white. Note pied head, with dark smudge from crown to ear coverts and on sides of breast. *Immature:* Similar to nonbreeding adult. **VOICE:** Sharp *kik, keek,* or *klea.* **HABITAT:** Freshwater marshes, lakes; in migration, also coastal waters, including open ocean.

WHITE-WINGED TERN *Chlidonias leucopterus*　　　　Accidental
9¼–9½ in. (23–24 cm). *Breeding:* Similar to Black Tern but *underwing lining black, upperwing mostly white,* tail paler. *Nonbreeding:* Paler than Black Tern; lacks dark shoulder spot. **RANGE:** Eurasian species. Accidental in AK and CA.

SOOTY TERN *Onychoprion fuscatus*　　　　　　　　Casual
16 in. (41 cm). A dark tropical tern of the open ocean. *Adult:* A cleanly patterned tern, black above and white below. Cheeks and patch on forehead white; bill and feet black. *Immature:* Dark brown; back spotted with white; note forked tail. **VOICE:** Nasal *wide-a-wake* or *wacky-wack.* **SIMILAR SPECIES:** Black Tern. **RANGE:** Casual visitor to s. CA coast, accidental elsewhere. **HABITAT:** Warm ocean waters.

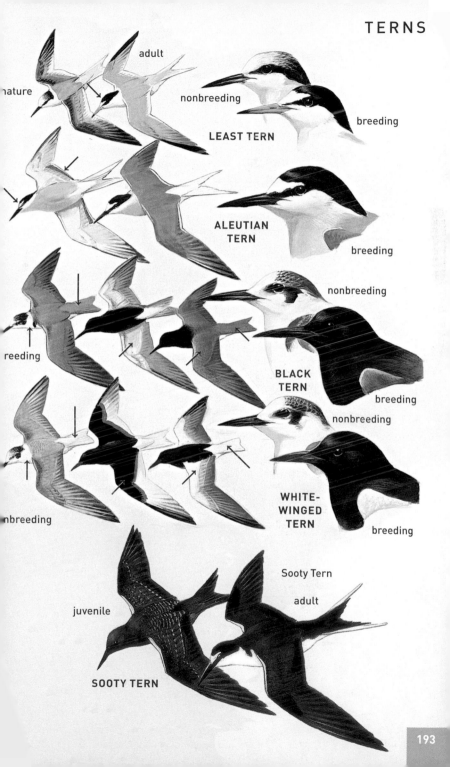

TERNS

adult

nature

nonbreeding

breeding

LEAST TERN

**ALEUTIAN
TERN**

breeding

breeding

nonbreeding

reeding

**BLACK
TERN**

breeding

nonbreeding

nbreeding

**WHITE-
WINGED
TERN**

breeding

Sooty Tern

adult

juvenile

SOOTY TERN

193

SKIMMERS Subfamily Rynchopinae

Slim, short-legged relatives of gulls and terns. Scissorlike red bill; *lower mandible longer than upper.* **FOOD:** Small fish, crustaceans. **RANGE:** Coasts, ponds, marshes, beaches, rivers of warmer parts of world.

BLACK SKIMMER *Rhynchops niger*   Uncommon, local M230
18–18½ in. (46–47 cm). More slender than a gull, with very long wings. Skims low, dipping lower mandible in water, snapping shut when it comes in contact with a food item. Forages mostly at night. *Adult:* Black above; white face and underparts. Bright red bill (tipped with black) is long and flat vertically; *lower mandible juts a third beyond upper.* Reddish legs. *Immature:* Brownish and speckled above, bill smaller, bill and legs duller. **VOICE:** Soft, short, barking notes. Also *kaup, kaup.* **HABITAT:** Bays, marshes, beaches, protected ocean waters.

SKUAS AND JAEGERS Family Stercorariidae

Falconlike seabirds that harass gulls and terns, forcing them to disgorge or drop their food. Light, intermediate, and dark morphs exist in at least two species; all have flash of white in primaries. Adult jaegers have two projecting central tail feathers, which are sometimes broken or missing. Young birds lack these feathers. Separating jaegers in most plumages can be very difficult. Skuas are larger, lack tail points, and are broader winged. Sexes alike. **FOOD:** In Arctic, lemmings, eggs, young birds. At sea, food taken from other birds or from water. **RANGE:** Seas of world, breeding in subpolar regions.

SOUTH POLAR SKUA *Stercorarius maccormicki*   Scarce M231
21 in. (53 cm). Near size of Herring Gull, but stockier, with deep-chested, hunch-backed look. Dark, with short, slightly wedge-shaped tail and *conspicuous white wing patch at base of primaries* visible on both upper- and underwing. "Blond" morph has *pale head and underparts* contrasting with darker wings; dark morph uniform gray-brown with *paler nape.* **SIMILAR SPECIES:** Dark jaegers (particularly Pomarine Jaeger) may lack tail points, but skuas larger, their wings wider, and they have more striking white wing patches. **HABITAT:** Open ocean. Breeds in Antarctic region.

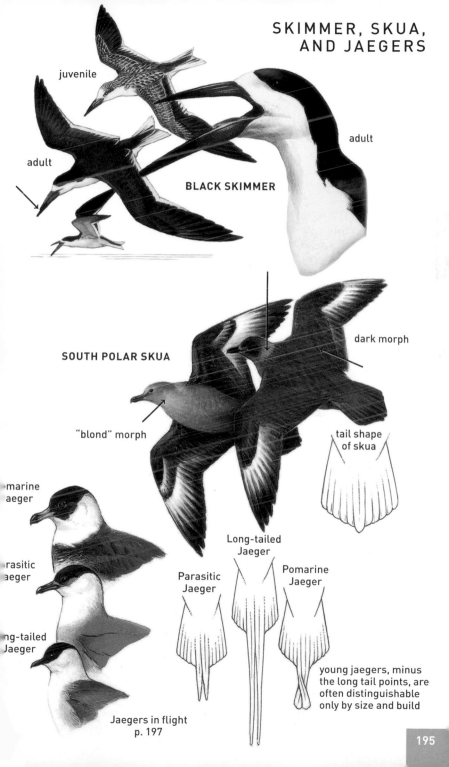

SKIMMER, SKUA, AND JAEGERS

juvenile

adult

adult

BLACK SKIMMER

SOUTH POLAR SKUA

dark morph

"blond" morph

tail shape of skua

marine aeger

rasitic aeger

ng-tailed Jaeger

Parasitic Jaeger

Long-tailed Jaeger

Pomarine Jaeger

young jaegers, minus the long tail points, are often distinguishable only by size and build

Jaegers in flight
p. 197

195

PARASITIC JAEGER *Stercorarius parasiticus*   **Uncommon M233**
17–19 in. (44–49 cm). This is the jaeger most frequently seen from shore. Flies with strong, falconlike wing strokes. Like other jaegers, it shows white wing-flash. *Adult:* Dark crown, pale underparts. Sharp tail points project up to 3½ in. (9 cm). Shows small *pale spot* above base of bill. Varies from light to dark morphs. *Juvenile:* Juvenile jaegers show heavy barring, especially on underwing. Juvenile Parasitic is usually *warmer brown* than other juvenile jaegers, often with *more distinct white patch on upperwing*. Up close, look for *streaked head* and *pale-edged primary tips*. **SIMILAR SPECIES:** Pomarine and Long-tailed jaegers, Heermann's Gull (which also often harasses terns, small gulls). **HABITAT:** Primarily ocean, regularly seen from shore in small numbers; in summer, tundra.

POMARINE JAEGER *Stercorarius pomarinus*   **Uncommon M232**
19–21 in. (48–53 cm). Like Parasitic Jaeger, but slightly heavier with more gull-like flight style. *Adult:* Broad and twisted central tail feathers project 2–7 in. (5–18 cm). Dark cap extends *farther down* through face to "jowls." Bill heavy and *pink-based;* breast-band *darker* and more barred than in Parasitic. *Juvenile:* Plumage variable, but compared with juvenile Parasitic it lacks warm tones, and very short central tail feathers are blunt-tipped. Look for white-based primary coverts creating *double white flash* on underwing. **HABITAT:** Open ocean, seen from shore in small numbers; in summer, tundra.

LONG-TAILED JAEGER *Stercorarius longicaudus*   **Scarce M234**
17–22 in. (44–56 cm). The smallest, slimmest jaeger with buoyant, ternlike flight style. *Adults:* Paler and grayer above than other jaegers with distinctly *two-toned upperwing* in flight; *long tail streamers* project 3–6 in. (8–15 cm); black cap neat and *sharply defined; no breast-band; very limited white in wings. Juvenile:* Varies from light to dark morph. All show very *limited white on upperwing* (two or three primary shafts), *stubby bill,* and longer, blunter-tipped central tail feathers than other juvenile jaegers. Light morph has distinctively *pale grayish head and breast* and extensively *white belly.* Dark morph cold gray-brown and often with pale nape and *pale lower breast patch.* **HABITAT:** Open ocean; tundra in summer. Most pelagic of the jaegers.

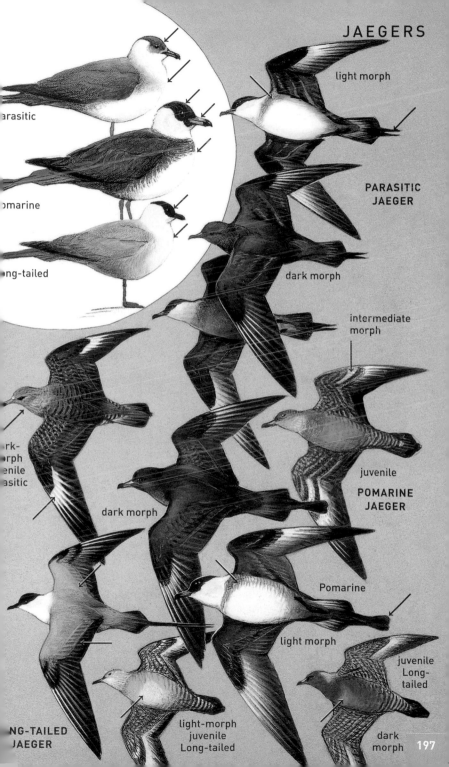

JAEGERS

light morph

PARASITIC
JAEGER

dark morph

intermediate
morph

parasitic

pomarine

long-tailed

dark-
morph
juvenile
Parasitic

dark morph

juvenile

POMARINE
JAEGER

Pomarine

light morph

juvenile
Long-
tailed

LONG-TAILED
JAEGER

light-morph
juvenile
Long-tailed

dark
morph

197

Auks, Murres, and Puffins Family Alcidae

The northern counterparts of penguins, but alcids can fly, beating their small narrow wings in a whir, often veering. They are chunky-bodied and short-necked with various bill shapes. Alcids swim and dive expertly. Most species nest on sea cliffs or in burrows, often in crowded colonies; most winter on ocean. Mostly silent away from breeding grounds. Sexes alike. FOOD: Fish, squid, zooplankton. RANGE: N. Atlantic, N. Pacific, and Arctic oceans.

THICK-BILLED MURRE *Uria lomvia*   Uncommon, local M237
18 in. (46 cm). Similar to Common Murre, but *blacker above.* Bill slightly shorter, thicker, with *whitish line along gape.* Overall a bit stockier than Common with bigger head and thicker neck. *Breeding:* White of foreneck forms inverted V. *Nonbreeding:* Dark on head extends *well below eye.* White bill mark less evident. VOICE: Guttural calls and moans, hence the name "murre." SIMILAR SPECIES: Common Murre. HABITAT: Nests on coastal cliff ledges. Spends non-breeding season on offshore ocean waters.

COMMON MURRE *Uria aalge*   Uncommon to common M236
17–17½ in. (43–45 cm). Size of a small duck, with slender pointed bill. *Breeding:* Head and upperparts *tinged brownish;* underparts white with *dusky markings on flanks. Nonbreeding:* Throat and cheeks white. *Black mark behind eye.* Murres often raft on water, fly in lines, stand erect on sea cliffs. Chicks may be mistaken for Xantus's Murrelet. SIMILAR SPECIES: Thick-billed Murre, Long-tailed Duck. HABITAT: Same as Thick-billed Murre, but regularly seen from shore throughout year.

PIGEON GUILLEMOT *Cepphus columba*   Fairly common M239
13½ in. (34 cm). *Breeding:* A small, black, pigeonlike waterbird, with large *white wing patches* (subdivided by variable black bar or wedge, sometimes rather indistinct), *red feet,* pointed black bill, orange-red mouth lining, and mostly dark or dirty underwing. *Nonbreeding:* Pale with white underparts and blackish wings with large white patches as in summer. *Juvenile:* Similar to nonbreeding adult, but white wing patches mottled; underwing may have center third or more pale. VOICE: Feeble wheezy or hissing whistle, *peeeeee.* SIMILAR SPECIES: Marbled Murrelet, Black Guillemot. HABITAT: Inshore ocean waters, harbors; less pelagic than most other alcids.

BLACK GUILLEMOT *Cepphus grylle*   Scarce, local M238
13 in. (33 cm). Very similar to Pigeon Guillemot. Black Guillemot's white wing patch lacks dark bar; underwing linings *white* with thin dark border (at least half dusky in Pigeon). Nonbreeding and juvenile Black Guillemots paler than most, but not all, Pigeon Guillemots. HABITAT: Inshore ocean waters; breeds in small groups or singly in holes in ground or under rocks on rocky shores, islands. Less pelagic than most other alcids.

ALCIDS (AUKS)

Common

breeding

nonbreeding

THICK-BILLED MURRE

nonbreeding

COMMON MURRE

Common
breeding

Thick-billed
breeding

PIGEON
GUILLEMOT

nonbreeding

breeding

BLACK
GUILLEMOT

nonbreeding

breeding

breeding

199

TUFTED PUFFIN *Fratercula cirrhata*　　　　　Uncommon M252
15–16 in. (38–40 cm). A stocky, dark seabird with massive bill. *Breeding:* Blackish, with *large, triangular, orange-red* bill; white face; and *long, curved, ivory yellow ear tufts.* Feet orange. *Nonbreeding:* White face and ear tufts much reduced (a trace of dull buffy-yellowish); duller orange-red bill not as triangular as in summer. *Immature:* Body grayer, bill smaller, with no red. **VOICE:** Throaty growling in nesting colony; silent at sea. **SIMILAR SPECIES:** Compare immature with Rhinoceros Auklet. **HABITAT:** Same as Horned Puffin.

HORNED PUFFIN *Fratercula corniculata* Fairly common, local M251
15 in. (38 cm). A puffin with *clear white underparts* and broad black collar. Feet bright orange. *Breeding:* Cheeks *white,* with small, dark erectile horn above each eye. Bill massive, *triangular,* laterally flat; *yellow with red tip. Nonbreeding:* Cheeks dusky; bill blackish with red tip. *Immature:* Resembles nonbreeding adult with dusky cheeks, but bill smaller and all dark. **VOICE:** Low, growling *arr.* **HABITAT:** Nests on rocky ocean cliffs. Forages in offshore waters.

CASSIN'S AUKLET *Ptychoramphus aleuticus*　　Fairly common M245
9 in. (23 cm). A small stubby seabird; entirely dark gray except for white crescent above eye and white belly; note pale spot at base of lower mandible. **VOICE:** Usually silent. In nesting colony, a series of harsh *kueek-kueek* notes. **SIMILAR SPECIES:** In winter, all other small alcids in its range show more white. See Rhinoceros Auklet. **HABITAT:** Nests on sea cliffs. Forages in open ocean.

RHINOCEROS AUKLET　　　　　　　　　Fairly common M250
Cerorhinca monocerata
15 in. (38 cm). A dark stubby seabird. *Breeding* (plumage acquired in late winter): *White mustache,* narrow *white plume* behind eye, *short erect horn* at base of yellowish bill. *Nonbreeding:* Note size and *uniform dark color with paler lower vent.* White plumes shorter, horn absent. *Immature:* Similar to nonbreeding adult, with smaller, darker bill. **VOICE:** Wide array of barks, growls, groans. **SIMILAR SPECIES:** Cassin's Auklet, immature Tufted Puffin. **HABITAT:** Nests colonially in burrows on islands. Found in both inshore and offshore ocean waters.

ALCIDS

ature

non-
eeding

TUFTED
PUFFIN

breeding

immature

nonbreeding

CASSIN'S
AUKLET

adult

HORNED
PUFFIN

breeding

immature

nonbreeding

breeding

RHINOCEROS AUKLET

Tufted
Puffin

Horned
Puffin

breeding
Tufted Puffin

Tufted Puffin
breeding

Horned Puffin
breeding

Horned Puffin

breeding

Rhinoceros
Auklet

breeding

201

LONG-BILLED MURRELET *Brachyramphus perdix*   Vagrant
10–11 in. (25–28 cm). *Breeding:* Paler brown than Marbled Murrelet; white throat. *Nonbreeding:* Like Marbled, but *lacks white collar* and shows two small pale *oval patches* on nape. **RANGE AND HABITAT:** Casual visitor (mostly between late summer and early winter) from Asia to West Coast and at lakes, reservoirs, and rivers far inland.

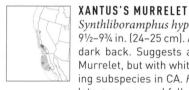

MARBLED MURRELET   Uncommon, threatened M240
Brachyramphus marmoratus
9¾–10 in. (24–25 cm). *Breeding: Dark brown; heavily mottled* on underparts. The only alcid south of AK so colored (in AK, see Kittlitz's Murrelet). *Nonbreeding:* A small neckless-looking seabird, dark above and white below, with *strip of white on scapulars,* white collar. **VOICE:** Sharp *keer, keer* or lower *kee.* **SIMILAR SPECIES:** Nonbreeding Pigeon Guillemot slightly larger, and white patch is on wing, not scapulars. See Long-billed Murrelet. **HABITAT:** Coastal ocean waters, bays. Breeds short distance inland, mainly high on limbs of mossy old-growth conifers if available.

KITTLITZ'S MURRELET   Scarce, local M241
Brachyramphus brevirostris
9¼–9½ in. (23–24 cm). *Breeding:* Buffy or tan overall except for whitish vent, *mottled and freckled with white* above, giving a pale look. *Nonbreeding:* Similar to Marbled Murrelet, but *white on face surrounds eyes.* White outer tail feathers in all plumages. **SIMILAR SPECIES:** Marbled Murrelet, nonbreeding Pigeon Guillemot. **HABITAT:** Glacial and other nearshore waters; nests presumably on barren slopes above timberline in coastal mountains.

XANTUS'S MURRELET   Uncommon, local M242
Synthliboramphus hypoleucus
9½–9¾ in. (24–25 cm). A small brown-black and white alcid with solid dark back. Suggests a miniature murre. Very similar to Craveri's Murrelet, but with white wing linings. *Scrippsi* race is regular breeding subspecies in CA. *Hypoleucus* subspecies of Baja CA, a very rare late-summer and fall visitor north to BC, has white arc around eye. **HABITAT:** Offshore waters; breeds on offshore islands.

CRAVERI'S MURRELET *Synthliboramphus craveri* Rare, local M243
9¼–9½ in. (23–24 cm). Very similar to Xantus's Murrelet, but with *black partial collar* on breast, slight black chin (below bill), and *dusky* (not white) underwing linings. Bill very slightly longer. **HABITAT:** Same as Xantus's Murrelet.

ANCIENT MURRELET *Synthliboramphus antiquus*   Scarce M244
10 in. (25 cm). In all plumages, *gray back contrasts with black cap.* *Breeding:* Note sharply cut *black throat patch* and *white stripe over eye.* Bill yellow. *Nonbreeding:* Weaker head stripe. **SIMILAR SPECIES:** Other similarly sized alcids lack back/crown contrast. **HABITAT:** Offshore waters; breeds on rocky and debris-strewn slopes.

LONG-BILLED MURRELET

nonbreeding

MARBLED MURRELET

eeding adult

reeding adult

KITTLITZ'S MURRELET

XANTUS'S MURRELET

northern *(scrippsi)*

inset above left, thern *(hypoleucus)*

CRAVERI'S MURRELET

nonbreeding

eding ult

breeding

ANCIENT MURRELET

CRESTED AUKLET *Aethia cristatella*   Fairly common, local M249

9½–10½ in. (24–27 cm). A droll auklet of Bering Sea. *Adult:* Completely slate gray, darker on back; thin white plume behind eye. In breeding plumage, stubby bill is *bright orange* and a curious crest *curls forward* over bill. In nonbreeding plumage, orange gape on bill is lost and crest is shorter. *Immature:* Paler gray overall, with dark bill. **VOICE:** Doglike bark in nesting colony. **SIMILAR SPECIES:** Whiskered and Cassin's auklets. **HABITAT:** Nests on islands and coastal areas of Bering Sea. Forages in open ocean.

WHISKERED AUKLET *Aethia pygmaea*   Scarce, local M248

7¾–8 in. (20 cm). Similar to slightly larger Crested Auklet, but in addition to curled black plume on forehead, this bird has *three thin white plumes* (whiskers) on each side of face. In nonbreeding plumage, plumes shorter. At all times has *pale lower belly and undertail coverts.* **HABITAT:** Nearshore ocean waters, especially tidal rips; rocky coasts.

PARAKEET AUKLET *Aethia psittacula*   Uncommon, local M246

10 in. (25 cm). A small alcid with *stubby, red bill* (like colorful bill of a parakeet) and whitish underparts. *Breeding:* Entire head black, with thin white plume behind eye. *Nonbreeding and immature:* Mostly whitish underneath, and bill shows less red. **VOICE:** At nesting colony, a high whinny. **SIMILAR SPECIES:** Crested Auklet entirely dark. Least Auklet much smaller. **HABITAT:** Offshore occurs singly or in small groups (not in large flocks like other small alcids); nests in scattered pairs or in colonies on sea cliffs and rubble slopes.

LEAST AUKLET *Aethia pusilla*   Fairly common, local M247

6–6¼ in. (15–16 cm). The tiniest alcid; chubby, neckless. Black above, white below. In flight, a whirring ping-pong ball. In breeding plumage, dark band across upper breast. Nonbreeding strongly contrasting blackish above and white below. Tiny size and small stubby bill separate it from other alcids except Dovekie. **VOICE:** High-pitched chattering in colony. **SIMILAR SPECIES:** Dovekie. **HABITAT:** Nests on rocky islands in colonies with other auklets. Forages in open ocean.

DOVEKIE *Alle alle*   Scarce, very local M235

8–8¼ in. (20–21 cm). A very small alcid, about the size of European Starling. Chubby and seemingly neckless, with very stubby bill. Contrasting alcid pattern — black above, white below. Black-hooded in breeding plumage, white-chested in nonbreeding plumage. **VOICE:** Shrill chatter. Noisy on nesting grounds. **SIMILAR SPECIES:** Parakeet Auklet slightly larger and with larger bill, less clean-cut, and lacks white line on rear edge of wing. See nonbreeding Least Auklet. **HABITAT:** Nests in high Arctic on coastal cliffs. Winters at sea.

CRESTED AUKLET

WHISKERED AUKLET

PARAKEET AUKLET

LEAST
AUKLET

nonbreeding
adult

breeding adult

nonbreeding

nbreeding

breeding

DOVEKIE

breeding

PIGEONS AND DOVES Family Columbidae

Plump, fast-flying birds with small head and low, cooing voice; nod their head as they walk. Two types: (1) birds with fanlike tails (e.g., Rock Pigeon) and (2) smaller birds with rounded or pointed tail (e.g., Mourning Dove). Sexes mostly similar. **FOOD:** Seeds, waste grain, fruit, insects. **RANGE:** Nearly worldwide in tropical and temperate regions.

BAND-TAILED PIGEON *Patagioenas fasciata*   Fairly common M254
14½–15 in. (37–38 cm). Heavily built; might be mistaken for Rock Pigeon except for its woodland habitat and tendency to alight in trees. Note *broad pale band* across end of tail; *white band* on nape. Feet *yellow.* Bill *yellow* with *dark tip.* **VOICE:** Hollow owl-like *oo-whoo* or *whoo-oo-whoo,* repeated. **SIMILAR SPECIES:** Rock Pigeon. **HABITAT:** Oak canyons, foothills, chaparral, mountain forests; also some residential areas, parks.

AFRICAN COLLARED-DOVE *Streptopelia roseogrisea*   Exotic
12 in. (30 cm). Escaped cage bird. A very pale dove with dark bill and eye and black partial collar. In flight, white tail tip obvious. **VOICE:** Soft series of two-syllable cooing notes. **SIMILAR SPECIES:** Eurasian Collared-Dove darker overall, with medium gray undertail coverts, darker primaries, and *three*-syllable notes. Hybrids with Eurasians occur mixed in with pure birds in the wild. **HABITAT:** Urban areas, suburban yards, power lines, feeders.

EURASIAN COLLARED-DOVE   Common, exotic M255
Streptopelia decaocto
12½–13 in. (32–33 cm). Recent colonizer of N. America from Caribbean but native to Eurasia; rapidly increasing and spreading. Slightly chunkier than Mourning Dove, *paler beige,* and with *square-cut tail.* Note *narrow black ring on hindneck. Grayish undertail coverts.* Three-toned wing pattern in flight. **VOICE:** *Three*-noted *coo-COOO-cup.* **SIMILAR SPECIES:** African Collared-Dove. **HABITAT:** Towns, field edges, cultivated land.

SPOTTED DOVE *Streptopelia chinensis*   Scarce, local, exotic M256
12 in. (30–31 cm). Note *broad collar of black and white spots* on hindneck. A bit larger than Mourning Dove; tail rounded with much white in corners. *Juvenile:* Lacks collar, but can be told by shape of spread tail. **VOICE:** *Coo-who-coo;* resembles cooing of White-winged Dove. **SIMILAR SPECIES:** Mourning Dove. **RANGE:** Introduced from Asia, formerly widespread in s. CA, now much reduced. **HABITAT:** Residential areas, parks.

ROCK PIGEON (ROCK DOVE, DOMESTIC PIGEON)
Columba livia   Common, exotic M253
12½ in. (32 cm). Typical birds are gray with *whitish rump, two black wing bars,* and broad, dark tail band. Domestic stock or feral birds may have many color variants. **VOICE:** Soft, gurgling *coo-roo-coo.* **SIMILAR SPECIES:** Band-tailed Pigeon. **HABITAT:** Cities, farms, cliffs, bridges.

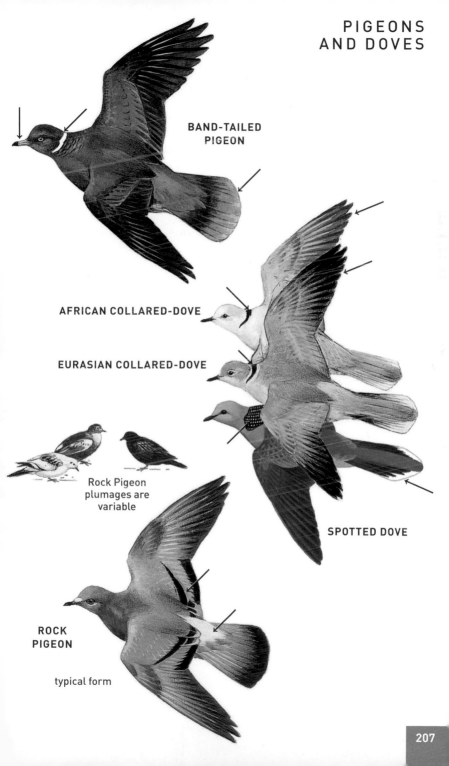

PIGEONS
AND DOVES

**BAND-TAILED
PIGEON**

AFRICAN COLLARED-DOVE

EURASIAN COLLARED-DOVE

Rock Pigeon
plumages are
variable

SPOTTED DOVE

**ROCK
PIGEON**

typical form

207

WHITE-WINGED DOVE *Zenaida asiatica*   Common M257
11½–12 in. (29–30 cm). A dove of desert, readily known by *white wing patches, large when bird is in flight, narrow when at rest.* Otherwise similar to Mourning Dove, but tail *rounded* and tipped with broad white corners, bill slightly longer, eye orangey red. **VOICE:** Harsh cooing, *who cooks for you?;* also, *ooo-uh-CUCK oo.* Sounds vaguely like crowing of a young rooster. **SIMILAR SPECIES:** Mourning Dove. **HABITAT:** River woods, mesquite, saguaros, desert oases, groves, towns, feeders.

MOURNING DOVE *Zenaida macroura*   Common M258
12 in. (30–31 cm). In most regions, the common widespread wild dove. Brown; smaller and slimmer than Rock Pigeon. Note *pointed tail* with large white spots. Juvenile slightly smaller and shows scaly pattern. **VOICE:** Hollow, mournful *coah, cooo, coo, cooo.* At a distance, only the three *coo*s are audible. **SIMILAR SPECIES:** White-winged Dove. Juvenile Mourning Dove might be confused with Inca Dove or Common Ground-Dove. **HABITAT:** Farms, towns, open woods, fields, scrub, roadsides, grasslands, feeders.

RUDDY GROUND-DOVE *Columbina talpacoti*   Very rare M261
6½–6¾ in. (16–17 cm). This rare but regular visitor (and very rare breeder) to border states from Mex. is similar to Common Ground-Dove but is slightly larger, longer tailed, and longer billed; has *dark, grayish base* to bill; *lacks all scaliness.* Has *blackish* spots and streaks on wing coverts and *scapulars. Male:* Washed rufous. *Female and immature:* Plain brown and gray. *Caution:* A bright male Common Ground-Dove may be misidentified as a Ruddy. **VOICE:** Cooing similar to Common Ground-Dove's, but faster and more repetitive: *pity-you pity-you pity you.* **SIMILAR SPECIES:** Inca Dove, Common Ground-Dove. **HABITAT:** Farms, livestock pens, fields, brushy areas. Often found with Inca Dove and Common Ground-Dove.

INCA DOVE *Columbina inca*   Fairly common M259
8¼–8½ in. (21–22 cm). A very small, slim dove with *scaly look. Rufous* in primaries (as in ground-doves), but has *longer tail* with *white sides.* **VOICE:** Monotonous *coo-hoo* or *no-hope.* **SIMILAR SPECIES:** Common Ground-Dove has short tail without obvious white, lacks scaling on back. Juvenile Mourning Dove. **HABITAT:** Towns, parks, farms.

COMMON GROUND-DOVE *Columbina passerina*   Uncommon M260
6¼–6½ in. (15–16 cm). A very small dove. Note *stubby black tail,* scaly breast, pinkish or orangey base of bill, and rounded wings that flash *rufous* in flight, *bronzy* spots and streaks on wing coverts. Feet yellow or pink. Adult male's body washed pinkish. **VOICE:** Soft, monotonously repeated *woo-oo, woo-oo,* etc. May sound monosyllabic — *wooo,* with rising inflection. **SIMILAR SPECIES:** Inca Dove, Ruddy Ground-Dove, juvenile Mourning Dove. **HABITAT:** Farms, orchards, brushy areas, roadsides.

DOVES

WHITE-WINGED DOVE

MOURNING DOVE

RUDDY GROUND-DOVE
adult ♂

INCA DOVE

COMMON GROUND-DOVE

PARAKEETS AND PARROTS Family Psittacidae

Noisy and gaudily colored. Compact, short-necked birds with stout, hooked bill. Parakeets smaller, with long, pointed tail. Feet zygodactyl (two toes fore, two aft). RANGE: Worldwide in Tropics and subtropics. Several exotic species have been released or have escaped, especially around Los Angeles.

YELLOW-CHEVRONED PARAKEET *Brotogeris chiriri*
(S. America) 9 in. (23 cm). Found at a few locations in CA.

RED-CROWNED PARROT *Amazona viridigenalis* Locally established
12 in. (30 cm). Large, with red crown (reduced in first year), blue nape, red wing panels. Established in several southern cities, including Los Angeles, from introductions.

ROSE-RINGED PARAKEET *Psittacula krameri*
(Africa, India) 16 in. (41 cm). A few in s. CA.

MITRED PARAKEET *Aratinga mitrata*
(S. America) 15 in. (38 cm). Found in Los Angeles area.

LILAC-CROWNED PARROT *Amazona finschi*
(Mex.) 12½–13½ in. (30–34 cm). Like first-year Red-crowned but darker. Red forehead, *lilac* crown, longer tail. A few live in Los Angeles area.

YELLOW-HEADED PARROT *Amazona oratrix*
(Mex. and Belize) 14–15 in. (36–38 cm). Escapees found in several areas; established locally in Los Angeles region.

RED-LORED PARROT *Amazona autumnalis*
(Cen. and S. America) 12–13 in. (30–33 cm). Small numbers seen in CA.

WHITE-FRONTED PARROT *Amazona albifrons*
(Cen. America) 9–10 in. (23–25 cm). Found in small numbers in CA.

PARAKEETS AND PARROTS

RED-CROWNED
PARROT

YELLOW-
CHEVRONED
PARAKEET

MITRED
PARAKEET

LILAC-CROWNED
PARROT

ROSE-RINGED
PARAKEET

WHITE-FRONTED
PARROT

YELLOW-HEADED
PARROT

RED-LORED
PARROT

CUCKOOS, ROADRUNNERS, AND ANIS
Family Cuculidae

Slender, long-tailed birds; feet zygodactyl (two toes forward, two backward). Sexes alike. **FOOD:** Cuckoos eat caterpillars, other insects; roadrunners eat reptiles, rodents, large insects, small birds; anis eat seeds, fruit. **RANGE:** Warm and temperate regions of world. N. American cuckoos are not parasitic.

BLACK-BILLED CUCKOO *Coccyzus erythropthalmus*   Scarce M263
11½–12 in. (29–30 cm). *Adult:* Similar to Yellow-billed Cuckoo, but *bill dark gray to blackish;* narrow *red orbital ring. No rufous in wing;* undertail spots small. *Immature:* Has yellow orbital ring and may have small amount of rufous in wing; thus more like Yellow-billed Cuckoo, but has *all-dark bill.* **VOICE:** Fast, rhythmic *cucucu, cucucu, cucucu,* etc. The grouped rhythm (three or four) is typical, but often employs irregular cadences. May sing at night. **HABITAT:** Wood edges, groves, thickets.

YELLOW-BILLED CUCKOO *Coccyzus americanus*   Uncommon M262
12 in. (30–31 cm). Known as a cuckoo by slim sinuous look, brown back, and white underparts; as this species by *rufous* in wings, *large white* spots at tips of dark undertail feathers, and *yellow* lower mandible on slightly curved bill. **VOICE:** Song a rapid throaty *ka-ka-ka-ka-ka-ka-ka-ka-ka-ka-ka-ka-kow-kow-kowlp-kowlp — kowlp — kowlp* (slowing toward end). **SIMILAR SPECIES:** Black-billed Cuckoo. **HABITAT:** Riparian woodlands (particularly cottonwoods).

GREATER ROADRUNNER   Fairly common M264
Geococcyx californianus
22–23 in. (56–58 cm). The familiar cuckoo that runs on ground (tracks show two toes forward, two backward). A large, slender, streaked bird, with long, white-edged tail; shaggy crest; long legs. White crescent on wing (visible when spread). **VOICE:** Six to eight low, dovelike *coos,* descending in pitch. **SIMILAR SPECIES:** Thrashers in same habitat also run on the ground and are streaky and brown but are much smaller. **HABITAT:** Deserts, open country with scattered cover, chaparral, brush.

GROOVE-BILLED ANI *Crotophaga sulcirostris*   Casual M265
13–13½ in. (33–34 cm). A coal black, grackle-sized bird with long, loose-jointed tail, short wings, and *huge puffin-like bill.* At close range, bill shows fine grooves (lacking in juvenile). **VOICE:** Repeated *whee-o* or *tee-ho,* first note slurring up. **RANGE:** Casual visitor to Southwest from Mex. **HABITAT:** Thickets.

CUCKOOS, ETC.

immature

BLACK-
BILLED
CUCKOO

adult

YELLOW-BILLED
CUCKOO

adults

GROOVE-
BILLED
ANI

GREATER
ROADRUNNER

Owls Families Tytonidae (Barn Owls) and Strigidae (Typical Owls)

Chiefly nocturnal birds of prey, with large heads and flattened faces forming facial disk; large, forward-facing eyes; hooked bill and claws; usually feathered feet (outer toe reversible). Flight noiseless, mothlike. Some species have "horns," or ear tufts. Sexes similar; female larger. **FOOD:** Rodents, birds, reptiles, fish, large insects. **RANGE:** Nearly worldwide.

SHORT-EARED OWL *Asio flammeus*　　　　Uncommon M282
15 in. (38 cm). An owl of open country; often abroad by day, particularly at dawn and dusk or when cloudy. Often tussles with Northern Harrier. Streaked, tawny brown color and irregular flopping flight identify it. Large buffy wing patch and black carpal ("wrist") patch show in flight. *Dark facial disk* emphasizes yellow eyes. **VOICE:** Emphatic, sneezy bark: *kee-yow!, wow!,* or *waow!* **SIMILAR SPECIES:** Long-eared Owl similar in flight, but with jerkier wing action. **HABITAT:** Grasslands, marshes, dunes, tundra. Roosts on ground, rarely in trees. Winter range and numbers vary from year to year.

BARN OWL *Tyto alba*　　　　Uncommon M266
16 in. (41 cm). A long-legged, knock-kneed, pale, monkey-faced owl. *White heart-shaped face and dark eyes;* no ear tufts. In flight, note large head, unstreaked white or buff underparts (ghostly at night), warm brown upperparts; shallower wingbeats and steadier flight path than Short-eared. **VOICE:** Shrill, rasping hiss or snore: *kschh* or *shiiish.* **SIMILAR SPECIES:** Short-eared Owl. **HABITAT:** Open country, groves, farms, barns, towns, cliffs.

LONG-EARED OWL *Asio otus*　　　　Scarce to uncommon M281
15 in. (38 cm). A slender, crow-sized owl with long ear tufts. Usually seen "frozen" close to trunk of a tree. Much smaller than Great Horned Owl; underparts streaked *lengthwise,* not barred crosswise. Ears *closer together, erectile;* much black around eyes. **VOICE:** One or two long *hooo*s; usually silent. Also a catlike whine and doglike bark. **SIMILAR SPECIES:** In flight, similar to Short-eared Owl, which has more mothlike, meandering flight. See Great Horned Owl. **HABITAT:** Coniferous and deciduous woodlands, desert groves. Often roosts in groups in nonbreeding season. Hunts over open country.

GREAT HORNED OWL *Bubo virginianus*　　　　Common M271
21–22 in. (54–56 cm). A *very large* owl with ear tufts, or "horns." Heavily *barred* beneath; conspicuous *white throat bib.* Varies regionally from very dark to rather pale. Often active just before dark. **VOICE:** Male usually utters five or six resonant hoots: *hu-hu-hu-hu, hoo! hoo!* Female's hoots slightly higher pitched than male's, in shorter sequence. Young birds make catlike screams, especially when begging or when separated from adults in spring and summer. **SIMILAR SPECIES:** Long-eared Owl smaller (crow-sized in flight), with lengthwise streaking rather than crosswise barring beneath; ears closer together; lacks white bib. **HABITAT:** Forests, woodlots, deserts, residential areas, open country.

SHORT-EARED OWL

BARN OWL
female
(male is whiter below)

LONG-EARED OWL

subarctic

GREAT HORNED OWL

typical

SPOTTED OWL *Strix occidentalis*   Scarce M278

17½–18 in. (45–46 cm). A large, dark brown forest owl with puffy round head. Large *dark eyes* (all other large western owls except Barn and Barred owls have yellow eyes) and *heavily spotted chest and barred belly* identify this endangered bird, which in many areas may eventually be displaced by Barred Owl. **VOICE:** High-pitched hoots, like barking of a small dog; usually in groups of three *(hoo, hoo-hoo)* or four *(hoo, who-who-whooo)*. Also a longer series of rapid hoots in crescendo, and a rising whistle. **SIMILAR SPECIES:** See Barred Owl. **HABITAT:** In north, mature old-growth forests; in south, more varied habitats, including conifers, mixed woods, wooded canyons.

BARRED OWL *Strix varia*   Uncommon M279

20–21 in. (51–53 cm). A large, brown, puffy-headed woodland owl with large *brown* eyes. Barred *across* chest and streaked *lengthwise* on belly; this combination separates it from Spotted Owl. **VOICE:** Usually eight accented hoots, in two groups of four: *hoohoo-hoohoo, hoo-hoohooHOOaaw.* The *aaw* at end is characteristic. Sometimes rendered as *who cooks for you, who cooks for you-all.* Also simply a *hoo-aww.* **SIMILAR SPECIES:** Other large owls, except Barn and Spotted, have yellow eyes. **HABITAT:** Coniferous, deciduous, and mixed woodlands.

GREAT GRAY OWL *Strix nebulosa*   Scarce M280

26–28 in. (67–73 cm). Our largest owl; very tame. Dusky gray, heavily striped *lengthwise* on underparts. Round-headed, without ear tufts; large, *strongly lined facial disk* dwarfs *yellow* eyes. Note *black chin spot* bordered by two broad white patches like *white mustaches.* Tail long for an owl. **VOICE:** Deep *whoo-hoo-hoo.* Also deep single *whoo*s. **SIMILAR SPECIES:** Barred and Spotted owls much smaller. **HABITAT:** Coniferous forests, adjacent meadows, bogs. Often hunts by day, particularly in winter. Rarely appears outside normal range.

SNOWY OWL *Bubo scandiacus*   Scarce, irregular M272

22–24 in. (56–61 cm). An irruptive, large, mostly *white,* Arctic, day-flying owl; variably flecked or barred with dusky. Round head, *yellow eyes.* Adult males much whiter than females and young birds. **VOICE:** Usually silent. Flight call when breeding a loud, repeated *krow-ow;* also a repeated *rick.* **SIMILAR SPECIES:** Barn Owl whitish on underparts only; much smaller and has dark eyes. Many young owls are whitish when in down. See Gyrfalcon (white morph). **HABITAT:** Prairies, fields, marshes, beaches; in summer, Arctic tundra. Perches on dunes, posts, haystacks, ground in open country, sometimes buildings. Has cyclic winter irruptions southward into lower 48 states.

SPOTTED OWL

Barred

Spotted

BARRED OWL

GREAT GRAY OWL

SNOWY OWL

WESTERN SCREECH-OWL *Megascops kennicottii* Uncommon M268
8½ in. (22 cm). A widespread small owl with conspicuous ear tufts.
Yellow eyes. Usually *gray* overall, but n. Great Basin population has
two color morphs, *gray* and *brown*. Birds in northwestern humid regions are *usually* darker brown; those in arid regions paler, grayer.
Bill dark with pale tip. **VOICE:** Series of hollow whistles on one pitch,
running into a tremolo (rhythm of a small ball bouncing to a stand-
still). **SIMILAR SPECIES:** Eastern Screech-Owl has paler bill; best told
by voice and range. See Whiskered Screech-Owl. Flammulated Owl
smaller, plumage tinged rusty, has dark eyes. **HABITAT:** Wooded canyons, farm groves, shade trees, well-vegetated residential areas,
pinyon-juniper and cactus woodlands.

WHISKERED SCREECH-OWL Uncommon, local M270
Megascops trichopsis
7¼–7½ in. (18–19 cm). Very similar to Western Screech-Owl. Has
large white spots on scapulars, coarser black spots on underparts,
longer facial bristles, *yellow-green bill, smaller legs and feet.* Readily
identified by voice. **VOICE:** *Boo-boo, booboo-boo-boo, booboo-boo-boo,*
etc.; arrangement of this "code" may vary. At times a repeated, four-
syllable *chooyoo-coo-cooo,* vaguely suggestive of White-winged Dove.
SIMILAR SPECIES: Western Screech-Owl. **HABITAT:** Canyons, pine-oak
woods, sycamores; typically at higher elevation than Western
Screech-Owl.

FLAMMULATED OWL *Otus flammeolus* Uncommon M267
6–7 in. (15–18 cm). Smaller than a screech-owl. *Our only small owl
with dark eyes.* Largely gray, with *tawny scapulars* and inconspicuous
ear tufts. Southern birds rustier. **VOICE:** Mellow *hoot* (also *hoo-hoot* or
hu-hu, hoot), low in pitch for so small an owl; repeated steadily at intervals of two or three seconds. Ventriloquial. **SIMILAR SPECIES:**
Screech-owls. **HABITAT:** Open pine and fir forests in mountains and
canyons.

EASTERN SCREECH-OWL *Megascops asio* Uncommon M269
8½ in. (22 cm). Two color morphs: red and gray. No other owl is bright
foxy red. Young birds may lack conspicuous ear tufts. **VOICE:** Mournful whinny or wail; tremulous, *descending* in pitch. Sometimes a series of notes on one pitch. **SIMILAR SPECIES:** Like Western Screech-
Owl, but separated by voice and, usually, range. Bill paler (greenish,
versus gray-black in Western). Also differs in having bright *red-brown*
morph. **HABITAT:** Deciduous woodlands, shade trees.

ELF OWL *Micrathene whitneyi* Uncommon M276
5¾ in. (15 cm). A tiny, small-headed, short-tailed, earless owl. Underparts softly striped with rusty; eyebrows white. Hides by day in
woodpecker holes in saguaros, telephone poles, or trees. Found at
night by call. **VOICE:** Rapid, high-pitched *whi-whi-whi-whi-whi-whi* or
chewk-chewk-chewk-chewk, etc., often becoming higher and more
yipping or puppylike, and chattering in middle of series. **SIMILAR SPE-
CIES:** Western Screech-Owl. **HABITAT:** Saguaro and mesquite woodlands and deserts, wooded canyons.

Northwest

WESTERN
SCREECH-
OWL

WHISKERED
CREECH-OWL

red morph

EASTERN
SCREECH-OWL

gray morph

gray morph

FLAMMULATED
OWL

red morph

ELF
OWL

NORTHERN HAWK OWL *Surnia ulula*   Scarce M273
16 in. (41 cm). A medium-sized day-flying owl, with *long, rounded tail* and *barred underparts.* Often *perches at tip of tree.* Shrikelike, it flies low, rising abruptly to perch. VOICE: A rapid series of whistled notes, faster and longer than Boreal. Also a falcon-like chattering *kikikiki* and a harsh scream. HABITAT: Open coniferous forests, birch scrub, tamarack bogs, field edges. Rarely appears south of normal range.

BURROWING OWL *Athene cunicularia*   Uncommon M277
9½ in. (24 cm). A small long-legged owl of open country, often seen by day standing erect on ground or low perches. Frequently seen with prairie dogs. VOICE: Rapid, chattering *quick-quick-quick.* At night, a mellow *co-hoo,* higher than Mourning Dove's *coo.* Young in burrow rattle like rattlesnake to deter predators. HABITAT: Open grasslands, unplowed prairies, farmland, airfields. Nests in burrows in ground or in pipes.

NORTHERN SAW-WHET OWL *Aegolius acadicus*   Uncommon M284
8 in. (20 cm). A very tame little owl; smaller than a screech-owl, without ear tufts. Underparts have blotchy, reddish brown streaks. Bill black. Forehead streaked white. *Juvenile:* Chocolate brown in summer, with white eyebrows; belly *tawny.* VOICE: Song a mellow, whistled note repeated in endless succession, often 100 to 130 times per minute. Longer, faster than Northern Pygmy-Owl, which is also more apt to vary tempo. Also raspy, squirrel-like yelps. SIMILAR SPECIES: Boreal Owl. HABITAT: Coniferous and mixed woods, swamps.

BOREAL OWL *Aegolius funereus*   Scarce M283
10 in. (25 cm). Tame but seldom seen. Similar to Northern Saw-whet Owl, but a bit larger; facial disk pale, *framed with black;* bill *pale;* forehead *spotted* with white. *Juvenile:* Sooty brown with dirty white eyebrows. VOICE: "Song" an accelerating series of hoots, similar to a winnowing snipe; call includes a raspy *skew.* HABITAT: Forests primarily of spruce, fir, and lodgepole pine; muskeg.

NORTHERN PYGMY-OWL *Glaucidium gnoma*   Uncommon M274
6¾–7 in. (17–18 cm). A very small earless owl, active during daytime (especially early and late). Note "eyes on back of the head," *sharply streaked underparts, spotted crown,* and *rather long tail barred with white.* Often mobbed by birds. VOICE: Single mellow whistle, repeated every two or three seconds. Also a rolling series, ending with two or three deliberate notes: *too-too too-too-too-too-too-too-took-took-took.* Birds in se. AZ mountain canyons double the notes. SIMILAR SPECIES: Northern Saw-whet Owl, Ferruginous Pygmy-Owl. HABITAT: Open coniferous and mixed woods, wooded canyons.

FERRUGINOUS PYGMY-OWL   Rare, local M275
Glaucidium brasilianum
6½–6¾ in. (16–17 cm). Similar to Northern Pygmy-Owl. Note rusty tail barred with black, browner breast streaks, and streaked (not spotted) crown. VOICE: Whistled notes repeated monotonously two or three times per second. Calls both in day and at night. SIMILAR SPECIES: Northern Pygmy-Owl (note habitat). HABITAT: Saguaro desert.

BURROWING
OWL

NORTHERN
HAWK OWL

juvenile

NORTHERN
SAW-WHET
OWL

adult

FERRUGINOUS
PYGMY-OWL

BOREAL
OWL

gray
morph

NORTHERN
PYGMY-OWL

note "eye
pattern" on nape

221

GOATSUCKERS (NIGHTJARS)
Family Caprimulgidae

Nocturnal birds with ample tail, large eyes, tiny bill, large bristled gape, and very short legs. By day, they rest on limbs or on ground, camouflaged by their "dead-leaf" pattern. Best identified at night by voice. FOOD: Nocturnal insects. RANGE: Nearly worldwide in temperate and tropical land regions.

COMMON NIGHTHAWK
Uncommon to fairly common M286
Chordeiles minor
9½ in. (24 cm). A slim-winged bird, often seen high in air; flies with easy strokes, changing gear to quicker erratic strokes. Prefers dusk, but may be abroad at midday. Note *broad white bar* across pointed wing. At rest, *tertial feathers extend well past white wing patch;* wingtips extend to or beyond tail tip. VOICE: Nasal *peer.* In aerial display, male dives, then zooms up sharply with sudden deep whir of wings. SIMILAR SPECIES: Lesser Nighthawk. HABITAT: Open country from mountains to lowlands; open pine woods; sagebrush; towns. Also over ponds. Sits on ground, posts, limbs.

LESSER NIGHTHAWK *Chordeiles acutipennis*   Fairly common M285
8½–9 in. (21–23 cm). Slightly smaller than Common Nighthawk; white bar (*buffy* in female) *closer to tip of wing* (at rest, this bar even with tips of tertial feathers). More extensive brown spotting on inner primaries. VOICE: Low *chuck chuck* and soft purring sound, much like trilling of a toad. HABITAT: Arid scrub, dry grasslands, farm fields, deserts. Also over ponds. Sits on branches and ground.

COMMON POORWILL *Phalaenoptilus nuttallii*   Uncommon M287
7½–7¾ in. (19–20 cm). Best known by its night cry in arid hills. Smaller and more compact than an Eastern Whip-poor-will; has shorter, more rounded wings, and shorter tail with *white corners.* VOICE: At night, a loud, repeated *poor-will* or *poor-jill.* HABITAT: Dry or rocky hills, including open pine forests, and chaparral. Sits on ground, roadsides.

BUFF-COLLARED NIGHTJAR
Rare, local M288
Antrostomus ridgwayi
8¾–9 in. (22–23 cm). Similar to Eastern Whip-poor-will, but with *buff collar* across hindneck. Best told by voice. VOICE: Staccato notes, terminating with strongly accented phrase, *cuk-cuk-cuk-cuk-cuk-cuk-cuk-cukacheea.* RANGE: Annual spring and summer visitor to se. AZ. HABITAT: Rocky slopes and washes near mesquite or junipers.

EASTERN WHIP-POOR-WILL
Uncommon, local M289
Antrostomus vociferous
9½–9¾ in. (24–25 cm). A voice in the night woods. When flushed by day, flops away on rounded wings. Male shows large *white tail patches;* in female these are buffy. At rest, tail extends beyond wings, unlike nighthawk's. VOICE: At night, a rolling, tiresomely repeated *WHIP poor-WEEL.* Birds in Southwest give much burrier song. SIMILAR SPECIES: Common Poorwill. HABITAT: Montane and canyon woodlands, especially oak and pine.

GOATSUCKERS

COMMON
NIGHTHAWK

♂

♀

♂

LESSER
NIGHTHAWK

♂

COMMON
POORWILL

♀

♂

EASTERN
WHIP-POOR-
WILL

♂

♂

♀

BUFF-COLLARED
NIGHTJAR

♂

223

HUMMINGBIRDS Family Trochilidae

The smallest birds. Iridescent, with needlelike bill for sipping nectar. Jewel-like gorget (throat feathers) adorns most adult males; in poor light, however, iridescence may not show and throat will appear dark. Hummingbirds hover when feeding; their wing motion is so rapid that wings appear as a blur. They can fly backward. Pugnacious. **FOOD:** Nectar (red flowers favored), small insects, spiders. **RANGE:** W. Hemisphere; majority in Tropics.

ANNA'S HUMMINGBIRD *Calypte anna*   Common M302
4 in. (10 cm). *Male:* The only U.S. hummer with rose *red crown* and throat. *Female:* Slightly larger than other West Coast hummers. Overall a bit "messier" than female Costa's or Black-chinned with more heavily mottled flanks; throat more heavily spotted, often with red central patch. The only hummingbird commonly found along Pacific Coast in midwinter. **VOICE:** Feeding call *chick.* Chase call a raspy chatter. Song (from a perch) squeaking, grating notes. When diving in its aerial "pendulum display," male makes *sharp popping sound* at bottom of arc. Vocal differences important. **HABITAT:** Gardens, parks, feeders, chaparral, open woods.

COSTA'S HUMMINGBIRD *Calypte costae*   Uncommon M303
3½ in. (9 cm). *Male:* Note *purple* throat and crown. Feathers of gorget *project* at sides. **VOICE:** Series of ticking notes. Male in display, a rising *zing.* **SIMILAR SPECIES:** Female very similar to female Black-chinned, but duller above, shorter bill and tail, *voices differ.* Female Anna's slightly larger, more mottled below. **HABITAT:** Deserts, coastal sage scrub, chaparral, arid hillsides, feeders.

BLACK-CHINNED HUMMINGBIRD   Fairly common M301
Archilochus alexandri
3¾ in. (10 cm). *Male:* Note *black throat* and conspicuous white collar. Violet of lower throat shows only in certain lights. *Caution:* Throat of other hummers may look black until it catches the light. *Female:* See Ruby-throated and Costa's hummingbirds. **VOICE:** Like Ruby-throated. **SIMILAR SPECIES:** Ruby-throated, Costa's, and Anna's hummingbirds. **HABITAT:** Riparian woodlands, wooded canyons, semiarid country, chaparral, suburbs, feeders.

RUBY-THROATED HUMMINGBIRD   Uncommon, local M300
Archilochus colubris
3¾ in. (10 cm). A primarily eastern species. *Male: Fiery red throat,* green back, forked tail. *Female:* White throat; tail blunt, with white spots. **VOICE:** Male's wings hum in courtship display. Chase calls high, squeaky. Other call a soft *chew.* **SIMILAR SPECIES:** Male Broad-tailed Hummingbird lacks forked tail, typically makes wing-trill sound. Female and immature similar to Black-chinned but have *crown brighter green,* bill slightly shorter, throat whiter, pump tail less. *Outermost primary narrower and straighter at tip (more club-shaped in Black-chinned).* Adult male Black-chinned has shallower tail fork than male Ruby-throated (both look black-throated in poor light). **HABITAT:** Flowers, gardens, feeders, wood edges, over streams.

HUMMINGBIRDS

ANNA'S
HUMMINGBIRD

♂

♀

COSTA'S
HUMMINGBIRD

♂

♀

BLACK-CHINNED
HUMMINGBIRD

♂

♀

♂

♀

sphinx moths resemble
hummingbirds

RUBY-THROATED
HUMMINGBIRD

BROAD-TAILED HUMMINGBIRD
Fairly common M305

Selasphorus platycercus

4 in. (10 cm). *Male:* Crown and back green; throat bright *rose red.* *Female:* Slightly larger and larger-tailed than female Black-chinned Hummingbird; sides tinged with buffy; touch of rufous at basal corners of tail. VOICE: Produces a variety of vocal and nonvocal sounds. *Chi-chewee chi-chewee* often given in flight. Male's wings produce distinctive high trill (except when in molt). Call a sharp *chit!* SIMILAR SPECIES: Female Calliope smaller, with smaller bill; at rest *wingtips extend beyond short tail.* Female Rufous Hummingbird has slightly smaller tail, usually more sharply defined rufous on sides, more well-defined pale semi-collar, and usually more rufous in tail. Male Ruby-throated Hummingbird smaller with forked tail. HABITAT: Mountains and canyons; numerous at feeders.

RUFOUS HUMMINGBIRD *Selasphorus rufus*
Fairly common M306

3¾ in. (9–10 cm). *Male:* No other N. American hummingbird has *rufous back.* Throat flaming orange-red. Aerial display is a closed ellipse, slowing on return climb. *Female and immature:* Green-backed; dull *rufous on sides and at base of outer tail feathers* (visible when tail is spread). Adult females often have a few orange-red feathers on throat. VOICE: Produces a variety of vocal and nonvocal sounds. Aggressive flight call a buzzy *zeee chippity chippity.* Displaying male utters low hum. Male's wings make high trill in flight (higher than Broad-tailed). SIMILAR SPECIES: Allen's, Calliope, and Broad-tailed hummingbirds. HABITAT: Wooded or brushy areas, parks, gardens, feeders; in southbound migration, also mountain meadows.

CALLIOPE HUMMINGBIRD *Selasphorus calliope*
Uncommon M304

3¼ in. (8 cm). The smallest hummer normally found in U.S. and Canada. *Adult male: Throat with purple-red rays on white background* (may be folded like a dark inverted V on white throat); the only U.S. hummingbird with this effect. *Female and immature:* Similar to female Broad-tailed and Rufous hummingbirds (which have buffy sides, some rufous at base of tail), but Calliope *shorter tailed (wingtips extend beyond square-tipped tail at rest),* slightly smaller, and shorter billed; rust on sides paler, face pattern shows weak *pale line over base of bill.* VOICE: High-pitched chips and buzzes in series. HABITAT: Mountains and canyons, feeders; in migration, also lowlands.

ALLEN'S HUMMINGBIRD *Selasphorus sasin*
Uncommon M307

3¾ in. (9–10 cm). *Male:* Like Rufous Hummingbird, but back *green.* (*Note:* Some male Rufous have a mix of green and rufous.) Aerial "pendulum display" starts in a shallow arc and after several swoops goes into a steep climb, than swoops back, with an air-splitting *vrrrip. Female and immature:* Not safely distinguishable in field from female Rufous (when measured in the hand, Allen's has narrower outermost tail feathers). VOICE: Similar to Rufous. SIMILAR SPECIES: Adult male and some molting young male Rufous have largely or entirely rufous back. See also female Broad-tailed and Calliope hummingbirds. HABITAT: Wooded or brushy canyons, riparian woodlands, parks, feeders; in migration south, also mountain meadows.

**BROAD-TAILED
HUMMINGBIRD**

♂

♀

♂

♀

**RUFOUS
HUMMINGBIRD**

♂

♀

**CALLIOPE
HUMMINGBIRD**

♂

**ALLEN'S
HUMMINGBIRD**

BROAD-BILLED HUMMINGBIRD

Uncommon, local M294

Cynanthus latirostris

4 in. (10 cm). *Male:* Dark green above and below, with *blue throat* (bird may look all black at a distance or in poor light). Bill *reddish* with black tip. Tail notched and *bluish black,* often flicked when hovering. *Female:* Identified by combination of *dull orange-red base to bill* (often restricted to lower mandible), *dark tail,* and *unmarked, pearly gray* throat; thin white line behind eye. Voice important. **VOICE:** Distinctive rough chattering. **SIMILAR SPECIES:** White-eared Hummingbird. **HABITAT:** Desert canyons, mountain slopes, riparian woodlands, agaves, mesquite, feeders.

VIOLET-CROWNED HUMMINGBIRD

Scarce, local M296

Amazilia violiceps

4½ in. (11 cm). A medium-sized hummer with *immaculate white underparts, including throat;* bill *red* with dark tip. Sexes similar, but *crown violet-blue* in male, *dull greenish blue* in female and immature. No iridescent gorget on male. **VOICE:** Aggressive call a series of squeaky notes. Call note *chak.* **SIMILAR SPECIES:** Anna's Hummingbird. **HABITAT:** Riparian woodlands, lower canyons, sycamores, agaves, feeders.

BLUE-THROATED HUMMINGBIRD

Uncommon, local M297

Lampornis clemenciae

5 in. (13 cm). Note large tail with *large white patches. Male:* A very large hummingbird, with black and white stripes about eye and light *blue throat;* big black tail with large white patches at corners. *Female:* Large, with *evenly gray* underparts, white marks on face, and big, blue-black tail with *large white corners,* as in male. **VOICE:** Call a distinctive squeaking *seek.* **SIMILAR SPECIES:** Magnificent Hummingbird. **HABITAT:** Near wooded streams in mountain canyons; feeders.

MAGNIFICENT HUMMINGBIRD *Eugenes fulgens*   Uncommon M298

5¼ in. (13 cm). *Male:* A very large hummingbird with *blackish belly, bright green throat,* and *purple crown.* Looks all black at a distance. Wingbeats discernible; sometimes the bird briefly glides on set wings. *Female:* Large; greenish above, washed with greenish or dusky below. **VOICE:** Call a thin, sharp *chip;* distinctive. **SIMILAR SPECIES:** Told from female Blue-throated Hummingbird by voice, more mottled underparts, short eye stripe, and dark greenish tail with obscure pale corners. **HABITAT:** Mountain glades, pine-oak woods, canyons, feeders.

VIOLET-CROWNED
HUMMINGBIRD

BROAD-
BILLED
HUMMINGBIRD

MAGNIFICENT
HUMMINGBIRD

BLUE-THROATED
HUMMINGBIRD

229

WHITE-EARED HUMMINGBIRD   Rare, local   M295
Hylocharis leucotis
3¾ in. (10 cm). A rare but regular summer visitor to s. AZ mountains, very rare in w. TX. *Male: Bill short, orangey red,* with black tip; *broad white stripe behind eye.* Underparts dark greenish, throat blue and green, crown purple. *Female:* Orangey red bill, bold white stripe behind eye. Note small *green spots* on throat. **VOICE:** Makes a variety of thin chips, sometimes in rapid series. **SIMILAR SPECIES:** Female Broad-billed Hummingbird often mistaken for rarer White-eared (reddish-based bill and pronounced white eye stripe), but note *vocal differences* and Broad-billed's slightly longer bill, slightly shorter white eyebrow, more forked tail, and evenly gray throat and underparts. **HABITAT:** Montane pine-oak woods near streams; feeders.

BERYLLINE HUMMINGBIRD *Amazilia beryllina*   Rare, local
4¼ in. (11 cm). *Male: Glittering green* on underparts; *deep rich rufous* in *wings,* rump, and tail. Bill partly red. *Female:* Duller; belly gray. **VOICE:** All vocal sounds very scratchy and buzzy. **SIMILAR SPECIES:** Buff-bellied Hummingbird. **RANGE AND HABITAT:** Mexican species; rare visitor and casual breeder in oak-clad mountain canyons of se. AZ, often at feeders.

LUCIFER HUMMINGBIRD *Calothorax lucifer*   Scarce, local   M299
3½ in. (9 cm). A small hummingbird. Note pronounced *decurved bill. Male: Purple throat, rusty or buffy sides. No* purple on crown (as in Costa's Hummingbird); tail *deeply forked,* often folded. *Female: Decurved bill, underparts extensively buff,* rufous at base of outer tail feathers. **VOICE:** Series of dry twitters. Male in courtship display makes "playing-card shuffle" sound. **SIMILAR SPECIES:** Black-chinned and Costa's hummingbirds may show slight curve to bill. **HABITAT:** Arid slopes, agaves, feeders.

PLAIN-CAPPED STARTHROAT *Heliomaster constantii*   Casual
5 in. (13 cm). A large, *long-billed* hummer, with red throat, *white facial stripes, white rump.* **VOICE:** Variety of strong *chips* given singly or in series. **SIMILAR SPECIES:** Magnificent and Anna's hummingbirds. **RANGE AND HABITAT:** Mexican species, casual visitor at lower elevations in s. AZ, usually at feeders.

♂

♀

BERYLLINE HUMMINGBIRD

♂

♀

WHITE-EARED HUMMINGBIRD

adult

♂

♀

tail may fold in a spikelike point

PLAIN-CAPPED STARTHROAT

LUCIFER HUMMINGBIRD

SWIFTS Family Apodidae

Aerial, swallowlike birds. Fly with rapid "twinkling" wingbeats mixed with glides on slender, stiffly bowed wings. **FOOD:** Flying insects. **RANGE:** Nearly worldwide.

VAUX'S SWIFT *Chaetura vauxi* Uncommon M292
4¾ in. (12 cm). A small, dark, swallowlike bird with very short tail, narrow, pointed wings, and "twinkling" flight. **VOICE:** High-pitched chippering notes, often run into an insectlike trill. **SIMILAR SPECIES:** Chimney Swift (very rare west of Rocky Mts.) is slightly larger, longer winged, and darker; calls differ. **HABITAT:** Open sky over woodlands, lakes, and rivers; nests in tree cavities, more rarely chimneys.

CHIMNEY SWIFT *Chaetura pelagica* Uncommon M291
5¼ in. (13 cm). Like a cigar with wings. Very similar to Vaux's Swift but no range overlap. **VOICE:** Rapid twittering notes lower and louder than Vaux's. **HABITAT:** Open sky, especially over cities, towns; nests and roosts in chimneys (originally in large hollow trees and cliff crevices).

BLACK SWIFT *Cypseloides niger* Uncommon, local M290
7¼ in. (18 cm). A large *blackish* swift with notched tail (sometimes fanned). Slower wingbeats than other swifts. **VOICE:** Sharp *plik-plik-plik-plik-plik*, etc., rarely heard away from nest site. **SIMILAR SPECIES:** Vaux's Swift much smaller. **HABITAT:** Open sky; favors mountain country, coastal cliffs; nests on sea cliffs and behind waterfalls.

WHITE-THROATED SWIFT *Aeronautes saxatalis* Uncommon M293
6½ in. (17 cm). Known from other N. American swifts by its contrasting *black-and-white pattern*. In poor light look for long slim tail. **VOICE:** Shrill, excited *jejejejeje*, in descending scale. **SIMILAR SPECIES:** Other swifts and swallows. **HABITAT:** Open sky. Breeds mainly in dry mountains, canyons, cliffs; locally on sea cliffs.

TROGONS Family Trogonidae

Solitary, brightly colored woodland birds with stubby bill, long tail, and very small feet. Erect when perched. May remain motionless for long periods. Flutter when plucking berries. **FOOD:** Small fruit, insects. **RANGE:** Mainly tropical areas.

EARED QUETZAL (EARED TROGON) Very rare, local
Euptilotis neoxenus
13½–14 in. (35–36 cm). Note *black* bill, *lack of white breast-band,* and mostly *white* underside of blue tail. "Ears" of male inconspicuous. **VOICE:** High-pitched, rising squeal; series of whistled notes. **RANGE AND HABITAT:** Very rare visitor from Mex., mostly in late summer and fall, to mountains and canyons in se. AZ, casual to cen. AZ.

ELEGANT TROGON *Trogon elegans* Uncommon, local M308
12–12½ in. (31–32 cm). Note *red belly, white breast-band,* yellow bill, and *finely barred underside of tail* (coppery above). Female has *white mark* on cheek. **VOICE:** Series of low, coarse notes, suggesting a hen turkey: *koa, koa, koa,* etc. **HABITAT:** Mountain forests, pine-oak and sycamore canyons.

roosting
swifts

SWIFTS

WHITE-
THROATED
SWIFT

CHIMNEY
SWIFT

VAUX'S
SWIFT

BLACK
SWIFT

TROGONS

♀

♀

♂

EARED
QUETZAL

♂

ELEGANT
TROGON

233

KINGFISHERS Family Alcedinidae

Solitary birds with large head, long pointed bill, and small syndactyl feet (two toes partially joined). Most eat fish, perching above water or hovering and plunging headfirst. FOOD: Fish; some eat insects, lizards. RANGE: Almost worldwide.

BELTED KINGFISHER *Ceryle alcyon*   Fairly common M309
13 in. (33 cm). Hovering on rapidly beating wings, or flying with uneven wingbeats (as if changing gear), rattling as it goes, Belted Kingfisher is easily recognized. *Male:* Shows single broad gray breast-band. *Female:* Has an additional rusty breast-band. VOICE: Loud dry rattle. SIMILAR SPECIES: Green Kingfisher. HABITAT: Streams, lakes, bays, coasts; nests in banks, perches on wires.

GREEN KINGFISHER *Chloroceryle americana*   Scarce, local M310
8½–8¾ in. (22 cm). This small kingfisher flies low over water; perches on low branches. Deep green above, white below. *Male:* Has *rusty* breast-band. *Female:* Has one or two greenish bands. VOICE: Sharp clicking; also a sharp squeak. SIMILAR SPECIES: Belted Kingfisher. HABITAT: Small rivers, streams, and ponds with clear water.

WOODPECKERS AND ALLIES Family Picidae

Chisel-billed, wood-boring birds with strong zygodactyl feet (usually two toes front, two rear), remarkably long tongue, and stiff tail that acts as prop for climbing. Flight usually undulating. FOOD: Tree-boring insects; also ants, flying insects, berries, acorns, sap. RANGE: Most wooded parts of world.

PILEATED WOODPECKER *Dryocopus pileatus*   Uncommon M331
16½–17 in. (42–44 cm). A spectacular black, *crow-sized* woodpecker, with flaming red *crest.* Flies with sweeping wingbeats, flashing white underwing. Large *oblong* holes in dead or dying trees indicate its presence. VOICE: Call resembles a flicker, but louder, irregular: *kik-kik-kikkik-kik-kik,* etc. HABITAT: Coniferous, mixed, and hardwood forests.

ARIZONA WOODPECKER *Picoides arizonae* Uncommon, local M325
7½ in. (19 cm). A dark, *brown-backed* woodpecker with *white-striped face;* spotted and barred below. Male has red nape patch. Our only woodpecker with *solid brown* back. VOICE: Sharp *spik;* a hoarse whinny. Fairly similar to Hairy Woodpecker's calls. SIMILAR SPECIES: Northern Flicker has *barred brown back,* white rump, is larger. Also see Ladder-backed, Downy, and Hairy woodpeckers. HABITAT: Canyon woodlands of oak, juniper, and pine-oak.

WHITE-HEADED WOODPECKER   Uncommon M326
Picoides albolarvatus
9¼ in. (23 cm). Our only woodpecker with *white head.* Male has red patch on nape; otherwise black overall, with large white patch in primaries. No white on rump (as in Acorn Woodpecker). VOICE: Sharp, *doubled ki-dik,* sometimes rapidly repeated, *chick-ik-ik-ik;* also a rattle similar to Downy Woodpecker's. SIMILAR SPECIES: Downy and Hairy woodpecker calls are *single, not double,* notes. HABITAT: Mountain pine forests, particularly ponderosa, Jeffrey, and sugar pines.

KINGFISHERS

hovering

plunging

♀

♂

BELTED KINGFISHER

→ ♂

GREEN KINGFISHER

♀

WOODPECKERS

Pileated below

♀

♂

♂

♀

ARIZONA WOODPECKER

♂

♀

PILEATED WOODPECKER

WHITE-HEADED WOODPECKER

RED-HEADED WOODPECKER
Uncommon, local M312

Melanerpes erythrocephalus

9¼ in. (24 cm). *Adult:* A black-backed woodpecker with *entirely red* head. Back *solid black,* rump white. Large, square *white patches* conspicuous on wing (making lower back look white when bird is on a tree). Sexes similar. *Immature:* Dusky-headed; wing patches mottled with dark. **VOICE:** Loud *queer* or *queeah.* **SIMILAR SPECIES:** Red-bellied Woodpecker has partially red head. **HABITAT:** Groves, farm country, shade trees in towns, large scattered trees.

LEWIS'S WOODPECKER *Melanerpes lewis*
Uncommon M311

10¾–11 in. (27–28 cm). A large, dark woodpecker with extensive *pinkish red belly.* Has *wide gray collar* and dark red face patch. Sexes similar. Has straight *crowlike flight.* **VOICE:** Usually silent. Occasionally a harsh *churr* or *chee-ur.* **SIMILAR SPECIES:** Red-headed and Acorn woodpeckers. **HABITAT:** Open, burned, or logged forests, usually of ponderosa pine or oak, river groves, oak savanna.

ACORN WOODPECKER *Melanerpes formicivorus*
Common M313

9 in. (23 cm). Social, usually found in clans. Note *clownish black, white, and red head pattern.* A black-backed woodpecker showing conspicuous white rump and *white wing patches* in flight. Both sexes have whitish eyes, red on crown. Stores acorns in holes drilled in bark and wooden building sides. **VOICE:** *Whack-up, whack-up, whack-up,* or *ja-cob, ja-cob.* **HABITAT:** Oak woods, mixed oak-pine forests, foothills, well-vegetated residential areas.

RED-BELLIED WOODPECKER
Uncommon M316

Melanerpes carolinus

9¼ in. (24 cm). *Adult:* A *zebra-backed* woodpecker with *red cap, white rump.* Red covers both crown and nape in male, *only nape in female.* *Juvenile:* Also zebra-backed, but has brown head, devoid of red. **VOICE:** Call *kwirr, churr,* or *chaw;* also *chiv, chiv.* Also a muffled flickerlike series. **SIMILAR SPECIES:** Golden-fronted and Red-headed woodpeckers. **HABITAT:** Woodlands, groves, orchards, towns.

GILA WOODPECKER *Melanerpes uropygialis*
Fairly common M314

9¼ in. (24 cm). *Male:* Note *round red cap.* A zebra-backed woodpecker; in flight, shows *white wing patch.* Head and underparts graybrown. *Female:* Lacks red cap. **VOICE:** Rolling *churr* and a sharp *pit* or *yip.* **SIMILAR SPECIES:** Ladder-backed Woodpecker has striped face, lacks white wing patch. See female Williamson's Sapsucker. **HABITAT:** Desert washes, saguaros, riparian woodlands, towns.

GOLDEN-FRONTED WOODPECKER
Fairly common M315

Melanerpes aurifrons

9½ in. (25 cm). *Male:* Note *multicolored head* (yellow near bill, red on crown, orange nape). A zebra-backed woodpecker with light underparts and white rump. Shows white wing patch in flight. *Female:* Lacks red crown. *Immature:* Lacks color patches on head. **VOICE:** Tremulous *churrrr;* flickerlike *kek-kek-kek-kek.* **SIMILAR SPECIES:** Red-bellied Woodpecker. **HABITAT:** Mesquite, woodlands, groves.

WOODPECKERS

juvenile

RED-HEADED WOODPECKER

LEWIS'S WOODPECKER

juvenile

ACORN WOODPECKER

♂

♀

RED-BELLIED WOODPECKER

♂

♀

GILA WOODPECKER

♂

♀

GOLDEN-FRONTED WOODPECKER

♂

♀

NORTHERN FLICKER *Colaptes auratus*   Common M329

12–12½ in. (30–32 cm). In undulating flight, note conspicuous *white rump* and *salmon red* or *golden yellow* underwing flash. Close up, it shows barred brown back and *black patch* across chest. Often hops awkwardly on ground, feeding on ants. Two subspecies groups are recognized: "Yellow-shafted" Flicker, the northern and eastern form, and "Red-shafted" Flicker, the widespread western form. Note differences in underwing and tail colors and head patterns. Where ranges overlap (western edge of plains), intergrades occur. **VOICE:** Loud *wick wick wick wick wick,* etc. Also a loud *klee-yer* and a squeaky *flick-a, flick-a,* etc. (see also Pileated Woodpecker). **SIMILAR SPECIES:** Gilded Flicker. **HABITAT:** Open forests, woodlots, towns.

GILDED FLICKER *Colaptes chrysoides*   Uncommon, local M330

11–11½ in. (28–29 cm). Some overlap with Northern Flicker. Wing and tail linings usually *yellow,* crown mustard brown, male has *red* mustache. Black breast patch slightly thicker, dark barring on back slightly narrower. **VOICE:** Same as Northern's, but slightly higher pitched. **HABITAT:** Cactus deserts, riparian woodland corridors.

WILLIAMSON'S SAPSUCKER   Uncommon M317
Sphyrapicus thyroideus

9 in. (23 cm). *Male:* Mostly *black with long white shoulder patch,* white rump, white facial stripes, *red throat, yellow belly. Female:* A brownish *zebra-backed* woodpecker with white rump, *brown head,* yellow belly. **VOICE:** Nasal *cheeer.* Drum is several rapid thumps followed by three or four slow, accented thumps. **SIMILAR SPECIES:** Gila Woodpecker. **HABITAT:** Coniferous forests, rarely other types of trees.

RED-BREASTED SAPSUCKER *Sphyrapicus ruber*   Uncommon M320

8½ in. (22 cm). Note *entirely red head and breast, sapsucker wing stripe.* Northern birds have blacker back, less white and black in face than birds from CA. Hybridizes regularly with Red-naped Sapsucker. Hybrids show more face pattern, some black on breast. **VOICE:** Similar to Red-naped Sapsucker. **HABITAT:** Coniferous and mixed woods, groves.

RED-NAPED SAPSUCKER   Fairly common M319
Sphyrapicus nuchalis

8½ in. (22 cm). Sapsuckers drill orderly rows of small holes in trees for sap and the insects it attracts. Note *longish wing patch* and *striped head.* Hybridizes with Red-breasted Sapsucker. **VOICE:** Nasal mewing note, *cheerrrr;* drum is several rapid taps followed by several slow, rhythmic taps. **SIMILAR SPECIES:** Yellow-bellied Sapsucker. **HABITAT:** Coniferous, mixed, and deciduous woodlands; in summer, particularly aspen groves.

YELLOW-BELLIED SAPSUCKER   Uncommon M318
Sphyrapicus varius

8½ in. (22 cm). Very similar to Red-naped Sapsucker but note lack of red nape, broader white head stripes, more solid black frame around throat patch. Female has all-white throat. **VOICE:** Like Red-naped. **HABITAT:** Coniferous, mixed, and deciduous woods, shade trees.

WOODPECKERS

♀

"Red-
shafted"

"Red-
hafted"

"Red-
shafted"

"Yellow-
shafted"

♂

"Yellow-
shafted"

Gilded
Flicker

**NORTHERN
FLICKER**

**GILDED
FLICKER** ♂

♂

"Red-
shafted"

mmature

♂

♂

**LIAMSON'S
PSUCKER**

♀

juvenile

southern

**RED-BREASTED
SAPSUCKER**

northern

♀

♂

juvenile

**RED-NAPED
SAPSUCKER**

♂

♀

**YELLOW-
BELLIED
SAPSUCKER**

239

NUTTALL'S WOODPECKER *Picoides nuttallii*   Fairly common M322

7½ in. (19 cm). The only small "zebra-backed" woodpecker west of deserts. Similar to Ladder-backed but has thinner white stripes on face and back; ranges barely overlap (hybrids are known). **VOICE:** High-pitched whinny or rattle. Call a low *pa-teck,* lower and raspier than Ladder-backed. **SIMILAR SPECIES:** Ladder-backed and Downy woodpeckers. **HABITAT:** Riparian, canyon, and mixed montane woodlands, particularly those with oaks.

LADDER-BACKED WOODPECKER   Fairly common M321
Picoides scalaris

7¼ in. (18 cm). The only "zebra-backed" woodpecker with *black-and-white-striped face* in arid country *east of Sierra Nevada.* **VOICE:** Rattling series, *chikikikikikikikikikik,* diminishing. Call a sharp *pick* or *chik.* **SIMILAR SPECIES:** Nuttall's Woodpecker. **HABITAT:** Deserts, canyons, pinyon-juniper, riparian woodlands, arid brush.

HAIRY WOODPECKER *Picoides villosus*   Fairly common M324

9–9¼ in. (23–24 cm). A mid-sized black-and-white woodpecker with *white back* and *large bill.* Downy and Hairy woodpeckers are almost identical in pattern, but Hairy is *larger* with *longer bill* and *white outer tail feathers. Juvenile:* May show orangey crown patch. **VOICE:** Kingfisher-like rattle, run together more than that of Downy. Call a sharp *peek!* **SIMILAR SPECIES:** Downy Woodpecker. American Three-toed Woodpecker has some barring on back and barred sides. **HABITAT:** Forests, woodlands, shade trees, suet feeders.

DOWNY WOODPECKER *Picoides pubescens*   Common M323

6½–6¾ in. (17 cm). Note *white back* and *small bill.* This industrious bird is like a small edition of Hairy Woodpecker. Outer tail feathers *spotted.* Amount of white spotting in wings varies regionally, as it does in Hairy. **VOICE:** Rapid whinny of notes, descending in pitch. Call a flat *pick,* not as sharp as Hairy's *peek!* **SIMILAR SPECIES:** Hairy and Ladder-backed woodpeckers. **HABITAT:** Forests, woods, residential areas, suet feeders, even corn and cattail stems.

AMERICAN THREE-TOED WOODPECKER   Scarce M327
Picoides dorsalis

8½–8¾ in. (22 cm). Males of this and next species have *yellow caps* and *barred sides.* This species is distinguished by irregular white patch on back (Rockies) or *bars* (farther north). Female lacks yellow cap and suggests Downy or Hairy woodpecker, but note *barred sides.* **VOICE:** A level-pitched whinny and a flat *pyik.* **SIMILAR SPECIES:** Black-backed Woodpecker, Hairy Woodpecker. **HABITAT:** Coniferous forests, particularly where deadwood is present.

BLACK-BACKED WOODPECKER *Picoides arcticus*   Scarce M328

9½ in. (24 cm). Note *black back* and *barred sides.* Male has *yellow cap.* This and preceding species (both have three toes) inhabit boreal and montane forests; their presence revealed by patches of bark scaled from dead conifers. **VOICE:** Low flat *puk* and a short buzzy call. **SIMILAR SPECIES:** American Three-toed and Hairy woodpeckers. **HABITAT:** Coniferous forests, particularly where deadwood is present.

WOODPECKERS

NUTTALL'S
WOODPECKER

♂

♀

LADDER-BACKED
WOODPECKER

♂

♀

Northwest

Rockies

♂

♀

DOWNY
WOODPECKER

♂

♂

st

Northwest

Rockies

♂

♀

HAIRY
WOODPECKER

Rockies

♀

♂

North

♂

AMERICAN
THREE-TOED
WOODPECKER

♂

♀

BLACK-BACKED
WOODPECKER

TYRANT FLYCATCHERS Family Tyrannidae

New World Flycatchers, or Tyrant Flycatchers, make up the largest family of birds in the world, with approximately 425 known species. Found chiefly in the Neotropics. Many are very similar and require attention to fine points to identify. Most species perch quietly, sitting upright, and sally forth to snap up insects. Bill flattened, with bristles at base. FOOD: Mainly flying insects. Some species also eat fruit in fall and winter. RANGE: New World; majority in Tropics.

OLIVE-SIDED FLYCATCHER *Contopus cooperi*   Uncommon M333
7½ in. (19 cm). A stout, large-headed flycatcher; often perches on dead snags at tops of trees. Note large bill and *dark chest patches* separated by narrow strip of white (like unbuttoned vest). A *cottony tuft* may poke from behind wing (often not visible). VOICE: Call a two- or three-note *pip-pip-pip*. Song a spirited whistle, *I SAY there* or *Quick three beers!*, middle note highest, last one sliding. SIMILAR SPECIES: Wood-pewees, Greater Pewee. HABITAT: Coniferous forests, bogs, burns. In migration, usually seen on dead branches at tips of trees.

GREATER PEWEE *Contopus pertinax*   Uncommon, local M334
7¾ in. (20 cm). Resembles Olive-sided Flycatcher, but more obvious crest, breast more uniformly gray with *no white stripe* down center. *Lower mandible brighter and more extensively orangey.* VOICE: Thin, plaintive whistle, *ho-say, re-ah* or *ho-say, ma-re-ah* (nickname, "José Maria"). Call *pip-pip*. SIMILAR SPECIES: Western Wood-Pewee. HABITAT: Pine and pine-oak forests of mountains, canyons.

WESTERN WOOD-PEWEE   Fairly common M335
Contopus sordidulus
6¼ in. (16 cm). A dusky, sparrow-sized flycatcher that perches motionless on open treetops or dead branches. Shows long wings, two narrow wing bars, and *no eye-ring*. Often appears "vested" below (with "top button buttoned"). Some fresh fall birds tinged yellow on belly. Bill shows small amount of pale on lower mandible. VOICE: Nasal *peeyee* or *peeeer*. SIMILAR SPECIES: Eastern Wood-Pewee. Olive-sided Flycatcher larger, more strongly "vested," different voice. *Empidonax* flycatchers are slightly smaller, have shorter wingtips, flick tails regularly, most have eye-rings. HABITAT: Pine-oak forests, open conifers, canyon and riparian woodlands.

EASTERN WOOD-PEWEE *Contopus virens*   Uncommon, local M336
6¼ in. (16 cm). The eastern counterpart of Western Wood-Pewee, this species barely enters our area. Very similar to Western Wood-Pewee, but slightly greener above and paler below (vest "not buttoned"); best distinguished by voice, range. VOICE: Sweet plaintive whistle, *pee-a-wee*, slurring down, then up. Also *pee-ur*, slurring down, and a *chip*. SIMILAR SPECIES: Western Wood-Pewee. Eastern Phoebe lacks wing bars; bobs tail downward. HABITAT: Woodlands, groves.

OLIVE-SIDED
FLYCATCHER

GREATER
PEWEE

WESTERN
WOOD-PEWEE

EASTERN
WOOD-PEWEE

EMPIDONAX FLYCATCHERS

Several small, drab flycatchers share the characters of light eye-ring and two pale wing bars. When breeding, some of these birds may be separated by habitat and manner of nesting. Voice is *always* the best means of identification. Silent individuals are very tough to identify, so many may have to be let go simply as "empids." Distinguishing characters to emphasize are subtle and include size and shape of bill and color of lower mandible; shape and boldness of eye-ring; pattern of underparts; primary (wingtip) projection; tail length; direction of tail wag; and calls.

LEAST FLYCATCHER *Empidonax minimus* Uncommon M340

5¼ in. (13 cm). A small empid, *grayish* above and *pale* below with *bold white eye-ring,* short wingtip projection, and short, wide-based bill. Whitish wing bars on mostly blackish wing. Actively flicks tail. **VOICE:** Emphatic, sharply snapped *che-bek!* Call a sharp, dry *whit.* **SIMILAR SPECIES:** Alder Flycatcher is browner above with bigger bill, longer wingtips, and weaker eye-ring. Hammond's and Dusky flycatchers have darker throat and underparts, duller wings. Hammond's also has *thinner, darker bill,* more teardrop-shaped eye-ring, and longer wingtips. **HABITAT:** Deciduous and mixed woodlands, poplars, aspens.

YELLOW-BELLIED FLYCATCHER Uncommon M337
Empidonax flaviventris

5½ in. (14 cm). Yellowish underparts (including *throat*) separate this from all other empids except Cordilleran and Pacific-slope flycatchers. (*Caution:* All other empids may show yellow belly but *not throat.*) **VOICE:** Song a simple, spiritless *chi-lek;* also a rising *chu-wee,* whistled *chew.* **SIMILAR SPECIES:** Greener than other western empids. Cordilleran and Pacific-slope flycatchers slightly browner, with peaked head; *teardrop-shaped eye-ring,* often broken above eye; duller wings. **HABITAT:** In summer, boreal forests, muskeg, bogs. Migrates east of Rockies.

WILLOW FLYCATCHER *Empidonax traillii* Fairly common M339

5¾ in. (15 cm). Alder and Willow flycatchers (formerly lumped as one species) are almost identical in appearance, a bit larger, longer billed, and browner than Least Flycatcher. They may be separated from each other mainly by voice and breeding habitat. Willow averages paler and browner (less olive) than Alder and shows little or no eye-ring (weak to moderately bold in Alder). **VOICE:** Song a sneezy *fitz-bew,* unlike *fee-BE-o* of Alder. Call a soft *whit.* **HABITAT:** Bushes, willow thickets, etc.

ALDER FLYCATCHER *Empidonax alnorum* Fairly common M338

5¾ in. (15 cm). The northern counterpart of Willow Flycatcher, with which it was formerly lumped as Traill's Flycatcher. Safely separated only by voice. (See Willow Flycatcher.) **VOICE:** Song an accented *fee-BE-o* or *rree-BE-o.* Call *kep* or *pit.* **HABITAT:** Willows, alders, brushy swamps, swales.

EMPIDONAX FLYCATCHERS

che-BEK or *chebek*

Pewees tend to sit motionless on open perches. Empids tend to stay more within vegetation and flick tail.

chi-lek

coniferous woods, bogs; Canada, n. edge of U.S.

arms, orchards, groves, pen woods; n. U.S. and anada

LEAST FLYCATCHER

grayest of the group

YELLOW-BELLIED FLYCATCHER

throat and breast washed with yellow

pewee

Empidonax

fitz-bew

fee-bee'-o

wet and dry thickets, brushy pastures, old orchards, willows; U.S., s. Canada

alder swamps, wet thickets, usually near water; n. U.S., Canada

WILLOW FLYCATCHER

ALDER FLYCATCHER

BUFF-BREASTED FLYCATCHER

Scarce, local M346

Empidonax fulvifrons

5 in. (13 cm). Distinguished from the other empids by its small size and *rich buffy breast.* **VOICE:** Accented *chee-lik.* Call a dry *pit* or *whit.* **SIMILAR SPECIES:** Northern Beardless-Tyrannulet. **HABITAT:** High-elevation canyons, open pine forests.

PACIFIC-SLOPE FLYCATCHER

Fairly common M344

Empidonax difficilis

5½ in. (14 cm). This and Cordilleran Flycatcher were formerly considered conspecific, as Western Flycatcher. Silent birds are impossible to tell apart. Voice and range are best identification clues. Both species have *yellowish* underparts, *including throat,* and *teardrop-shaped* eye-ring, broken above. Other empids in their ranges may have wash of yellow, but their throats are gray or whitish. **VOICE:** Song of both is a thin, squeaky *pit-PEET SWEEE;* variable. Call an upslurred *tsueet.* **SIMILAR SPECIES:** Cordilleran and Yellow-bellied flycatchers. **HABITAT:** In summer, riparian, mixed, or coniferous woodlands.

CORDILLERAN FLYCATCHER

Uncommon M345

Empidonax occidentalis

5½ in. (14 cm). Nearly identical to Pacific-slope Flycatcher. Identify by voice and range. **VOICE:** Song like Pacific-slope. Call a two-noted *soo-seet.* **HABITAT:** In summer, riparian, mixed, or coniferous woodlands and shaded canyons, often with rock walls.

HAMMOND'S FLYCATCHER

Uncommon M341

Empidonax hammondii

5½ in. (14 cm). Both Hammond's and Dusky flycatchers breed in coniferous and mixed woods; Hammond's prefers more closed canopy. Hammond's has more *teardrop-shaped eye-ring;* slightly *shorter, thinner* mostly *dark bill* (kingletlike); is more prone to flick wings; has slightly *shorter tail* and *longer wings.* **VOICE:** Song typically three-part and similar to Dusky but slightly lower pitched. Abrupt *tse-beek.* Call a sharp, thin *peep* or *peek.* **SIMILAR SPECIES:** Dusky and Least flycatchers. **HABITAT:** Breeds in woodlands with coniferous component; in migration through lowlands, other trees, thickets.

DUSKY FLYCATCHER *Empidonax oberholseri*   Uncommon M343

5¾ in. (15 cm). Very similar to Hammond's Flycatcher; see that account. **VOICE:** Three-part song ends in a high *preet.* Call a dry *whit.* **HABITAT:** Breeds in open pine forests, montane scrub with scattering of trees, brushy meadow and stream edges.

GRAY FLYCATCHER *Empidonax wrightii*   Uncommon M342

6 in. (15 cm). Similar to Dusky and Hammond's flycatchers, but paler and grayer overall, with *longer tail,* and *longer, narrow bill* with *pinkish* lower mandible. Has habit of *wagging its tail downward* like a phoebe, then bringing it back up (all other empids *flick tail upward*). *Direction of tail wag best noted immediately after bird lands.* **VOICE:** Two-syllable *chewip* or *cheh-we.* Call a dry *whit.* **SIMILAR SPECIES:** Other empids. **HABITAT:** Dry pine forests with sagebrush; in winter, willows, mesquite. Often drops to ground to grab prey.

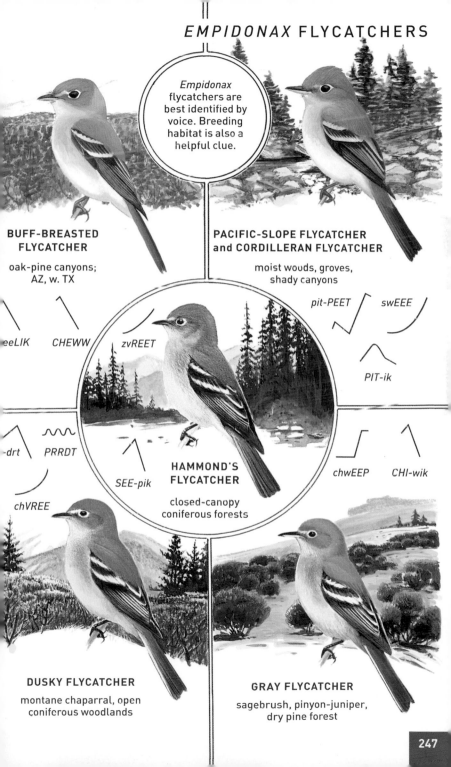

EMPIDONAX FLYCATCHERS

Empidonax flycatchers are best identified by voice. Breeding habitat is also a helpful clue.

BUFF-BREASTED FLYCATCHER

oak-pine canyons; AZ, w. TX

eeLIK   *CHEWW*

PACIFIC-SLOPE FLYCATCHER and CORDILLERAN FLYCATCHER

moist woods, groves, shady canyons

pit-PEET   *swEEE*

PIT-ik

zvREET

-drt   *PRRDT*

chVREE

SEE-pik

HAMMOND'S FLYCATCHER

closed-canopy coniferous forests

chwEEP   *CHI-wik*

DUSKY FLYCATCHER

montane chaparral, open coniferous woodlands

GRAY FLYCATCHER

sagebrush, pinyon-juniper, dry pine forest

MISCELLANEOUS FLYCATCHERS

BLACK PHOEBE *Sayornis nigricans*   Fairly common M347
6¾–7 in. (17–18 cm). Our only *black-breasted* flycatcher; belly white.
Has typical phoebe tail-bobbing habit. *Immature:* Wing bars cinnamon-buff. **VOICE:** Thin, strident *fi-bee, fi-bee,* rising then dropping;
also a sharp slurred *chip.* **SIMILAR SPECIES:** Eastern Phoebe, juncos
(which are ground-loving birds). **HABITAT:** Streams, dams, walled
canyons, farmyards, towns, parks; usually near water.

EASTERN PHOEBE *Sayornis phoebe*   Scarce M348
7 in. (18 cm). Note *downward tail-bobbing.* A grayish, sparrow-sized
flycatcher *without eye-ring or strong wing bars* (thin buff wing bars on
immature); small, *all-dark bill* and dark head; yellowish belly in fall.
VOICE: Song a well-enunciated *phoe-be* or *fi-bree* (second note alternately higher or lower). Call a sharp *chip.* **SIMILAR SPECIES:** Eastern
Wood-Pewee and smaller *Empidonax* flycatchers have conspicuous
wing bars; bills partly yellowish or horn colored on lower mandible.
All *Empidonax* except Gray Flycatcher flick tail *upward.* **HABITAT:**
Streamsides, pond and field edges, bridges, farms.

SAY'S PHOEBE *Sayornis saya*   Fairly common M349
7½ in. (19 cm). A midsized, brownish flycatcher with contrasty black
tail and pale *orange-buff belly.* **VOICE:** Plaintive, down-slurred *pweer*
or *pee-ee.* **SIMILAR SPECIES:** Ash-throated and Dusky-capped flycatchers, Eastern Phoebe. **HABITAT:** Open country, scrub, canyons,
ranches, parks.

NORTHERN BEARDLESS-TYRANNULET   Uncommon, local M332
Camptostoma imberbe
4¼ in. (11 cm). A very small, nondescript flycatcher that may suggest
a kinglet, Bell's Vireo, or immature Verdin. Grayish olive, with *slight
crested* look. *Dull wing bars* and indistinct pale supercilium. Distinguished from *Empidonax* flycatchers by its smaller size, smaller
head, stubby bill, and voice. **VOICE:** Thin *peeee-yuk.* A gentle, descending *ee, ee, ee, ee, ee.* **SIMILAR SPECIES:** Buff-breasted Flycatcher, *Empidonax* flycatchers. **HABITAT:** Lowland woods, mesquite,
stream thickets, lower canyons. Builds a globular nest with entrance
on side.

BLACK
PHOEBE

EASTERN
PHOEBE

SAY'S
PHOEBE

NORTHERN
BEARDLESS-
TYRANNULET

Myiarchus Flycatchers

BROWN-CRESTED FLYCATCHER
Uncommon M354
Myiarchus tyrannulus
8¾ in. (22 cm). Similar to Ash-throated Flycatcher, but larger, with noticeably larger bill. Underparts brighter yellow. Tail rusty, a bit less so than in Ash-throated. Voice important. **VOICE:** Sharp *whit* and rolling, throaty *purreeer.* Voice much more vigorous and raucous than Ash-throated's. **SIMILAR SPECIES:** Great Crested Flycatcher. **HABITAT:** Sycamore-dominated canyons, cottonwood groves, saguaros.

GREAT CRESTED FLYCATCHER
Uncommon, local M353
Myiarchus crinitus
8½–8¾ in. (21–22 cm). A kingbird-sized flycatcher with cinnamon wings and tail, dark olive back, *mouse gray breast,* and bright yellow belly. Often erects bushy crest. Note *strongly contrasting tertial pattern* and pink-based bill. **VOICE:** Loud whistled *wheeep!* Also a rolling *prrrrreet!* **SIMILAR SPECIES:** Brown-crested Flycatcher equal in size but has all-dark bill, paler gray breast, paler yellow belly, less contrasting tertials. Ash-throated Flycatcher has grayer back, much paler below. Vocal differences important. **HABITAT:** Deciduous woodlands, groves.

DUSKY-CAPPED FLYCATCHER
Uncommon, local M351
Myiarchus tuberculifer
7 in. (18 cm). Similar to Ash-throated Flycatcher, but slightly smaller overall with proportionately larger bill; cap and throat darker, belly brighter yellow, and *almost no rusty* in tail. Voice distinctive. **VOICE:** Mournful, down-slurred whistle, *pweeeur.* **HABITAT:** Pine-oak and deciduous canyons.

ASH-THROATED FLYCATCHER
Fairly common M352
Myiarchus cinerascens
8–8¼ in. (20–21 cm). A medium-sized flycatcher, smaller than a kingbird, with two wing bars, *whitish* throat, *pale* gray breast, *pale yellowish belly,* and *rufous tail.* Head slightly bushy. Except for prairie and southwest border areas, this is normally the only flycatcher in West with rusty tail. **VOICE:** *Prrt;* also a rolling *chi-queer* or *prit-wheer.* **SIMILAR SPECIES:** Great Crested, Brown-crested, and Dusky-capped flycatchers; Say's Phoebe. **HABITAT:** Semiarid country, deserts, brush, mesquite, pinyon-juniper, chaparral, open woods.

Miscellaneous Flycatchers

SULPHUR-BELLIED FLYCATCHER
Uncommon, local M355
Myiodynastes luteiventris
8½ in. (22 cm). A large flycatcher with *bright rufous tail* and dark patch through eye; underparts *pale yellowish, with black streaks.* No other U.S. flycatcher is streaked *above and below.* **VOICE:** High, penetrating *kee-ZEE ick! kee-ZEE ick!* (like squeezing a bathroom rubber duckie). **HABITAT:** Midelevation canyons, often with sycamores.

FLYCATCHERS

BROWN-CRESTED FLYCATCHER

Most have extensively rusty tails

GREAT CRESTED FLYCATCHER

DUSKY-CAPPED FLYCATCHER

SULPHUR-BELLIED FLYCATCHER

ASH-THROATED FLYCATCHER

KINGBIRDS

WESTERN KINGBIRD *Tyrannus verticalis*   Common M359
8¾ in. (22 cm). The most widespread kingbird in West. Note *pale gray head and breast,* white throat, *yellowish belly.* Western's *black tail* has *narrow white edges.* **VOICE:** Shrill, bickering calls; a sharp *kip* or *whit-ker-whit;* dawn song *pit-PEE-tu-whee.* **SIMILAR SPECIES:** Eastern, Cassin's, and Tropical kingbirds. **HABITAT:** Farms, shelterbelts, semi-open country, roadsides, fences, wires.

EASTERN KINGBIRD *Tyrannus tyrannus*   Common M360
8½ in. (22 cm). The *white band* across tail tip marks Eastern Kingbird. Red crown mark is concealed and rarely seen. Often seems to fly quiveringly on tips of wings. Harasses crows, hawks. **VOICE:** Rapid sputter of high, bickering electric-shock notes: *dzee-dzee-dzee,* etc., and *kit-kit-kitter-kitter,* etc. Also a nasal *dzeep.* **SIMILAR SPECIES:** The yellow on some worn Western Kingbirds is very pale. Eastern Phoebe. **HABITAT:** Wood edges, river groves, farms, shelterbelts, roadsides, fences, wires.

CASSIN'S KINGBIRD   Uncommon to fairly common M357
Tyrannus vociferans
9 in. (23 cm). Like Western Kingbird, but *darker head and chest contrast with whitish chin and upper throat,* darker olive-gray back; *no distinct white sides* on dark brown (not truly black) tail, which may be *lightly tipped with gray-buff.* Wing coverts often edged in pale gray. **VOICE:** Low, nasal *queer, chi-queer,* or *chi-beer;* also an excited *ki-ki-ki-dear, ki-dear, ki-dear.* **SIMILAR SPECIES:** Some worn Western Kingbirds may lack white sides on tail, but head, breast, and back *paler, lack contrasty pale chin* and pale edges to wing coverts, and have *different call.* In much of interior, Cassin's prefers higher elevations. **HABITAT:** Semiopen country, pine-oak mountains, pinyon-juniper, ranch groves, parks, eucalyptus.

THICK-BILLED KINGBIRD   Scarce, local M358
Tyrannus crassirostris
9½ in. (24 cm). A large kingbird with *oversized bill;* differs from similar kingbirds in having extensive *dark cap.* Entirely dark tail. *Adult:* Upperparts *brownish,* underparts *whitish* with pale yellow wash on belly. *Fall adult and immature:* May be quite yellow below. **VOICE:** Quick, shrill *brrr-zee* or *kut'r-eet.* **SIMILAR SPECIES:** Bright, fresh fall birds told from Tropical Kingbird by bill size, dark head. **HABITAT:** Riparian woodlands, particularly sycamores.

TROPICAL KINGBIRD   Uncommon, local M356
Tyrannus melancholicus
9¼ in. (23 cm). Similar to Western and Cassin's kingbirds, but *bill larger and longer,* tail *notched* and *brownish;* bright yellow on underparts *includes breast.* **VOICE:** Insectlike twittering. **HABITAT:** Breeds in groves along streams and ponds.

KINGBIRDS

WESTERN
KINGBIRD

EASTERN
KINGBIRD

CASSIN'S
KINGBIRD

THICK-
BILLED
KINGBIRD

fall

TROPICAL
KINGBIRD

More Tyrant Flycatchers and Becard

ROSE-THROATED BECARD
Rare, local M362
Pachyramphus aglaiae
7¼ in. (18 cm). Big-headed and thick-billed. *Male:* Dark gray above, pale to dusky below, with *blackish cap and cheeks* and lovely *rose-colored throat* (lacking in some males). *Female:* Brown above, with *dark cap* and *light buffy collar* around nape. Underparts strong buff. **VOICE:** Thin, slurred whistle, *seeoo.* **SIMILAR SPECIES:** Kingbirds, Say's Phoebe. **HABITAT:** Riparian woodlands, particularly sycamores.

SCISSOR-TAILED FLYCATCHER
Uncommon M361
Tyrannus forficatus
13–15 in. (33–38 cm). A beautiful bird, pale pearly gray, with *extremely long, scissorlike tail* that is usually folded. Flanks orange-buff, wing linings salmon pink. *Immature:* Shorter tail and duller sides may suggest Western Kingbird. Hybrids are known. **VOICE:** Harsh *keck* or *kew;* a repeated *ka-leep;* also shrill, kingbirdlike bickerings and stutterings. **SIMILAR SPECIES:** Western Kingbird. **HABITAT:** Semiopen country, ranches, farms, roadsides, fences, wires.

VERMILION FLYCATCHER *Pyrocephalus rubinus*   Uncommon M350
6 in. (15 cm). *Adult male:* Crown (often raised in slight bushy crest) and underparts *flaming vermilion;* upperparts brown and tail blackish. *Immature male:* Breast whitish, with some streaks; crown, belly, and undertail coverts washed with vermilion. *Female:* Breast whitish, narrowly streaked; belly washed with pinkish or yellowish. **VOICE:** *P-p-pit-zee* or *pit-a-zee.* **SIMILAR SPECIES:** Female told from Say's Phoebe by shorter tail, pale supercilium, and dusky streaks on breast. See also male Scarlet Tanager (which has scarlet back and black wings), a vagrant in West. **HABITAT:** Moist areas in arid country, such as streams, ponds, pastures, golf courses, ranches.

FLYCATCHERS

♀

♂

SCISSOR-TAILED FLYCATCHER

♂

immature

ROSE-THROATED BECARD

Immature
♂

immature
♀

adult
♂

adult
♀

VERMILION FLYCATCHER

SHRIKES Family Laniidae

Songbirds with hook-tipped bill. Perch watchfully on bush tops, treetops, wires; impale prey on thorns, barbed wire. FOOD: Insects, lizards, small rodents, small birds. RANGE: Widespread in Old World; two species in N. America.

NORTHERN SHRIKE *Lanius excubitor*   Scarce M364
10–10¼ in. (25–26 cm). An irregular winter visitor south of Canada. Similar to Loggerhead, but slightly larger, paler; *narrower mask with more white around eye, faintly barred* breast, longer, more hooked bill with *pale base.* VOICE: Song a disjointed, thrasherlike succession of harsh musical notes. Call *shek-shek;* a grating *jaaeg.* SIMILAR SPECIES: Loggerhead Shrike, Northern Mockingbird. HABITAT: Semiopen country with lookout posts; in summer, taiga, muskeg, tundra.

LOGGERHEAD SHRIKE *Lanius ludovicianus*   Uncommon M363
9 in. (23 cm). Similar to a mockingbird but note *hooked bill, black mask, black wings,* more *flickering wingbeats. Juvenile:* Faint barring below *briefly in late summer.* VOICE: Song consists of harsh, deliberate notes and phrases, repeated 3 to 20 times, suggesting mockingbird's song; *queedle, queedle* or *tsurp-see, tsurp-see.* Call *shack shack* or *jeeer jeeer.* SIMILAR SPECIES: Northern Shrike, Northern Mockingbird. HABITAT: Semiopen country with lookout posts: wires, fences, trees, shrubs.

VIREOS Family Vireonidae

Small olive- or gray-backed birds, much like wood-warblers, usually less active. Bill slightly thicker, with hook to tip. FOOD: Mostly insects, also fruit in winter. RANGE: Canada to Argentina.

BELL'S VIREO *Vireo bellii*   Uncommon M366
4¾ in. (12 cm). Small, nondescript. Usually stays concealed in dense cover. Southwestern birds grayer, flick tail like gnatcatchers; eastern birds more yellow-green, pump tail like Palm Warbler. VOICE: Sings as if through clenched teeth; husky phrases at short intervals: *cheedle cheedle chee? cheedle cheedle chew!* SIMILAR SPECIES: Immature White-eyed Vireo has bolder wing bars, yellow lores. Gray Vireo slightly larger with complete eye-ring; note voice and habitat. HABITAT: Willows, streamsides, hedgerows, mesquite.

BLACK-CAPPED VIREO *Vireo atricapilla*   Scarce, local M367
4½ in. (11 cm). Cap *glossy black* in male, slate gray in female. Note wing bars, white spectacles, *red* eyes. VOICE: Song hurried, harsh, restless. Call a harsh *chit-ah.* SIMILAR SPECIES: Blue-headed Vireo larger with dark eyes. HABITAT: Oak scrub, brushy hills, rocky canyons. Often hard to see. Endangered.

WHITE-EYED VIREO *Vireo griseus*   Uncommon, local M365
5 in. (13 cm). Note *yellow spectacles, whitish throat,* wing bars, white eye (dark in immature). Skulking. VOICE: Song a sharply enunciated *CHICK-a-per-weeoo-CHICK.* Variable. SIMILAR SPECIES: Bell's Vireo. HABITAT: Wood edges, brush, brambles, dense undergrowth.

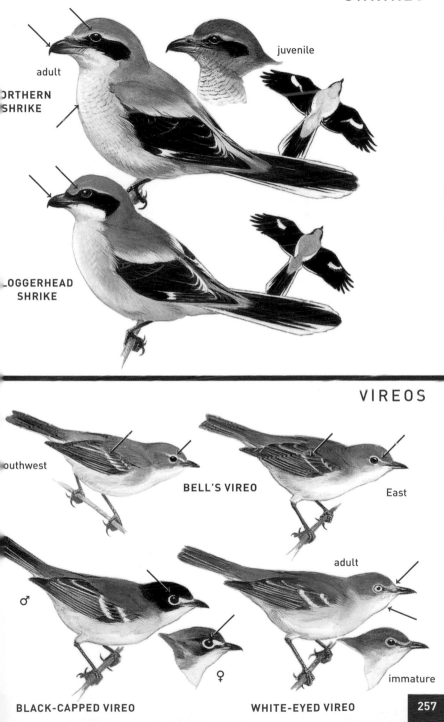

SHRIKES

adult

**NORTHERN
SHRIKE**

juvenile

**LOGGERHEAD
SHRIKE**

VIREOS

Southwest

BELL'S VIREO

East

♂

adult

immature

BLACK-CAPPED VIREO

♀

WHITE-EYED VIREO

257

BLUE-HEADED VIREO *Vireo solitarius*   Uncommon M372

5¼ in. (14 cm).The northern/eastern representative of the "Solitary Vireo" complex. Note *sharply demarcated* blue-gray cap, *bright white* spectacles, strong yellow and green tones. **VOICE:** Song of sweet high-pitched phrases with deliberate pauses: *wee-ay, chweeo, chuweep*. Also gives a whiny chatter. **SIMILAR SPECIES:** Cassin's Vireo. **HABITAT:** Coniferous, mixed, and deciduous woods.

CASSIN'S VIREO *Vireo cassinii*   Uncommon M371

5¼ in. (14 cm). The Pacific/northwest representative of the "Solitary Vireo" complex. Brighter yellow-green tones than Plumbeous. Duller with less contrasting face pattern than Blue-headed. **VOICE:** Similar to Plumbeous. **SIMILAR SPECIES:** Dull Blue-headeds difficult to separate from bright Cassin's; dull Cassin's difficult to separate from Plumbeous. See Gray Vireo. **HABITAT:** Coniferous, mixed, and deciduous woods.

PLUMBEOUS VIREO *Vireo plumbeus*   Uncommon M370

5½ in. (15 cm). The Rocky Mountain/Great Basin representative of the "Solitary Vireo" complex. Although nesting ranges barely overlap, all three species may occur together on migration. Grayest of the group with yellow-green tones *faint or lacking*. **VOICE:** Song of slurred phrases with deliberate pauses. Blue-headed phrases sweeter. Cassin's and Plumbeous have burrier phrases, e.g., *wee-ay, chweeo, chuweep*. (Plumbeous is slowest, burriest.) All three species give a whiny chatter. **SIMILAR SPECIES:** Cassin's and Gray vireos. **HABITAT:** Coniferous, mixed, and deciduous woods, pinyon-juniper.

YELLOW-THROATED VIREO   Uncommon, local M369
Vireo flavifrons

5½ in. (14 cm). Bright yellow throat, yellow spectacles, and white wing bars. **VOICE:** Song similar to Blue-headed Vireo's, but lower pitched with *burry quality*; swings back and forth with phrases that sound like *ee-yay, three-eight*. **HABITAT:** Deciduous woodlands, shade trees, particularly oaks.

GRAY VIREO *Vireo vicinior*   Scarce M368

5½ in. (14 cm). This plain, gray-backed vireo of arid mountains has *complete, narrow, white eye-ring* and only *one faint wing bar*. Though drab, it has character, flipping tail like a gnatcatcher. **VOICE:** Song similar to Plumbeous Vireo's, but sweeter, more rapid, in regular series. **SIMILAR SPECIES:** Plumbeous Vireo stockier, has shorter tail that is not flipped, bold spectacles rather than just eye-ring, and two, thicker wing bars. See Bell's Vireo. **HABITAT:** Pinyon-juniper woodlands, brushy slopes, chamise-dominated chaparral, scrub oak.

HUTTON'S VIREO *Vireo huttoni*   Fairly common M373

5 in. (13 cm). Note *incomplete eye-ring*, broken *above*, and large light loral spot. **VOICE:** Buzzy, rising *zu-weep* or falling *zee-ur*, oft-repeated; a hoarse, deliberate *day dee dee*. **SIMILAR SPECIES:** Ruby-crowned Kinglet smaller with skinny black legs, quicker movements, black "highlight bar" behind wing bars. See also Cassin's Vireo. **HABITAT:** Woodlands, parks, particularly with oaks.

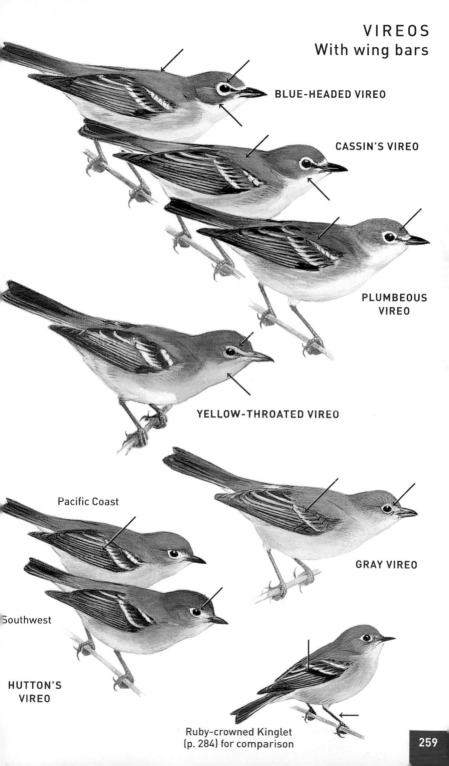

VIREOS
With wing bars

BLUE-HEADED VIREO

CASSIN'S VIREO

PLUMBEOUS VIREO

YELLOW-THROATED VIREO

Pacific Coast

Southwest

HUTTON'S VIREO

GRAY VIREO

Ruby-crowned Kinglet
(p. 284) for comparison

RED-EYED VIREO *Vireo olivaceus*   Uncommon M376

6 in. (15 cm). Note *gray cap* contrasting with olive back, and strong, *black-bordered white eyebrow stripe (supercilium)*. Red iris may not be obvious at a distance. Iris is brown in immature birds in fall. **VOICE:** Song is abrupt, robinlike phrases, monotonous. Faster than Blue-headed's song, with more notes per phrase. Call a nasal, whining *chway.* **SIMILAR SPECIES:** Warbling Vireo slightly smaller, duller and less contrasty above, with pale lores and arching supercilium. See Yellow-green Vireo, a vagrant. **HABITAT:** Deciduous woodlands, shade trees, groves.

YELLOW-GREEN VIREO *Vireo flavoviridis*   Casual

6–6¼ in. (15–16 cm). This tropical species is very similar to Red-eyed Vireo, but has *strong yellow tones* on sides, flanks, and undertail coverts; back *yellower* green; head stripes *less distinct;* bill slightly *longer* and paler. (Immature Red-eyed Vireos may have yellow on flanks and undertail coverts.) **VOICE:** Song slower than Red-eyed's, suggestive of House Sparrow. **RANGE:** Casual in summer in s. AZ and as a fall vagrant in CA. **HABITAT:** Deciduous woods, ornamental plantings.

WARBLING VIREO *Vireo gilvus*   Fairly common M374

5½ in. (14 cm). One of the widespread vireos that lack wing bars. In this *very plain* species, note *whitish breast, pale lores,* and *lack of black borders* on eyebrow stripe that arches slightly above dark eye. Back tinged dull greenish. Immature and western birds have more yellow on sides than eastern birds. **VOICE:** Song distinctive: a languid warble, unlike broken phrases of other vireos; suggests Purple Finch's song, but less spirited, with burry undertone. Call a wheezy querulous *twee* and short *vit.* **SIMILAR SPECIES:** Philadelphia Vireo yellowish on throat and breast, as bright in middle as on sides, has slate gray line through lores. Red-eyed Vireo larger, greener above, and has bolder eyebrow stripe. See also Tennessee Warbler. **HABITAT:** Deciduous and mixed woods, aspen groves, cottonwoods, riparian woodlands, shade trees.

PHILADELPHIA VIREO *Vireo philadelphicus*   Scarce M375

5¼ in. (13 cm). This smallish vireo has a face pattern reminiscent of Warbling Vireo, but with more distinct dark eye line (including lores), slightly greener back, and single faint wing bar. Underparts pale and vary from a small wash of pale yellow on lower throat and upper breast in duller adults to more extensive yellow in bright immatures. **VOICE:** Song very similar to Red-eyed Vireo's; higher, slower. Call, a quick, husky *niff-niff-niff-niff.* **SIMILAR SPECIES:** Bright Warbling Vireos in fall tinged green above and have yellow on sides, but that yellow is *dull or lacking in center of breast and throat;* also *lack Philadelphia's dark line through lores.* Different song. Tennessee Warbler slightly smaller, has finer bill, clear white (not yellow) undertail coverts, blackish rather than blue-gray legs. **HABITAT:** Second-growth woodlands, poplars, willows, alders.

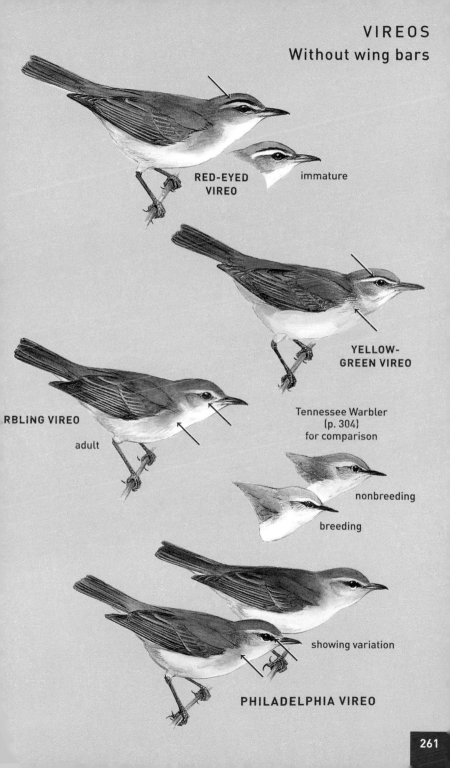

**RED-EYED
VIREO**

immature

**YELLOW-
GREEN VIREO**

RBLING VIREO

adult

Tennessee Warbler
(p. 304)
for comparison

nonbreeding

breeding

showing variation

PHILADELPHIA VIREO

Jays, Crows, and Allies Family Corvidae

Large perching birds with strong, longish bill, nostrils covered by forward-pointing bristles. Crows and ravens are very large and black. Jays are often colorful (usually blue). Magpies are black and white, with long tail. Sexes alike. Most immatures resemble adults. FOOD: Almost anything edible. RANGE: Worldwide except s. S. America, some islands, Antarctica.

WESTERN SCRUB-JAY *Aphelocoma californica*　　Common M381
11–11¼ in. (29 cm). *Crestless* with blue head, wings, and tail, *brownish* back, white throat with *necklace*. Interior populations ("Woodhouse's" Scrub-Jay) slightly duller than coastal birds. VOICE: Rough, rasping *kwesh . . . kwesh*. Also a harsh *shreck-shreck-shreck-shreck* and a rasping *zhreek, zhreek*. SIMILAR SPECIES: Mexican Jay. HABITAT: Oaks, pine-oak, oak-chaparral of foothills and lower mountains, riparian woodlands, pinyon-juniper, residential areas, parks.

MEXICAN JAY　　　　　　　Fairly common, local M382
Aphelocoma wollweben
11½ in. (29 cm). A blue crestless jay of Southwest. Resembles Western Scrub-Jay, but *more uniform;* back and breast grayer. *No strong contrast* between throat and breast. Also *lacks narrow whitish line over eye.* In AZ, juveniles may have partly yellow bill. VOICE: Rough, querulous *wink? wink?* or *zhenk?* SIMILAR SPECIES: Western Scrub-Jay. HABITAT: Pine-oak and oak-juniper woodlands.

BLUE JAY *Cyanocitta cristata*　　　　Fairly common M379
11 in. (28 cm). A showy, noisy, *crested jay.* Bold *white spots on wings and tail;* whitish or dull gray underparts; *black necklace.* VOICE: Harsh slurring *jeeah* or *jay;* a musical *queedle, queedle;* also many other notes. Mimics calls of Red-shouldered and Red-tailed hawks. SIMILAR SPECIES: Steller's Jay. HABITAT: Oak and pine woods, suburban gardens, groves, towns, feeders.

STELLER'S JAY *Cyanocitta stelleri*　　　　Common M378
11½ in. (29 cm). In coniferous woodlands between Rockies and Pacific, this is the resident jay with a crest. Foreparts *blackish;* rear parts (wings, tail, belly) *deep blue.* Some interior birds have white eyebrow. VOICE: Loud *shook-shook-shook* or *shack-shack-shack* or *wheck-wek-wek-wek-wek* or *kwesh kwesh kwesh;* harsh *jjaairr* and many other notes. Frequently mimics hawks. SIMILAR SPECIES: Other "blue jays" show some white below. HABITAT: Coniferous and pine-oak forests; also some residential areas, feeders.

ISLAND SCRUB-JAY　　　　Uncommon, very local M380
Aphelocoma insularis (not shown)
12½–13 in. (31–33 cm). Recently elevated to full species status. Found only on Santa Cruz I. off coast of s. CA, most restricted range of any species in N. America. VOICE: Same as Western Scrub-Jay. SIMILAR SPECIES: Almost identical to Pacific Coast Western Scrub-Jay (no range overlap), but slightly larger and larger billed, deeper blue, darker cheek. HABITAT: Woodlands and scrubby habitat.

JAYS

nterior

Pacific
Coast

**WESTERN
SCRUB-JAY**

AZ juvenile

**MEXICAN
JAY**

BLUE JAY

**STELLER'S
JAY**

263

PINYON JAY *Gymnorhinus cyanocephalus* **Uncommon M383**
10½ in. (27 cm). Looks *like a small dull blue crow,* but nearer size of a robin, though chunkier, with long, sharp bill. Readily told from other jays by its short tail, uniform pale blue coloration, and crowlike flight. Pinyon Jays are gregarious, often gathering in large noisy flocks and walking about like small crows. **VOICE:** Nuthatchlike *nasal* cawing, *kaa-ah* or *karn-ah* (descending inflection); has mewing effect. Also jaylike notes; chattering. **SIMILAR SPECIES:** Other western jays. **HABITAT:** Primarily pinyon-juniper; also dry, open ponderosa and Jeffrey pine woodlands; ranges into sagebrush.

CLARK'S NUTCRACKER **Fairly common M384**
Nucifraga columbiana
12 in. (30–31 cm). Built like a small crow, with *light gray* or tan-gray body and large *white patches* in black wings and tail. If these patches are seen, it should be confused with no other bird of high mountains. Long bill. Tame birds often can be fed by hand. **VOICE:** Flat, drawn-out, grating *caw, khaaa* or *khraa.* **SIMILAR SPECIES:** Gray Jay has shorter bill, lacks white patches. **HABITAT:** Coniferous forests in mountains as high as near tree line, mountain resorts, pinyon pine.

GRAY JAY *Perisoreus canadensis* **Uncommon M377**
11¼–11½ in. (28–29 cm). A large, fluffy, gray bird of cool northern and montane forests. Called "Whiskey Jack" by woodsmen. *Adult: Black* patch or partial cap across back of head and *white forehead* (or crown); suggests a huge overgrown chickadee. *Juvenile: Dark sooty,* almost blackish; only distinguishing mark is *whitish whisker.* Pacific Coast and far northern birds have dark on heads. Rocky Mt. birds have mostly white heads. **VOICE:** Soft *whee-ah;* also many other notes, some harsh. **SIMILAR SPECIES:** Clark's Nutcracker. **HABITAT:** Spruce and fir forests. Becomes tame around campgrounds, picnic areas.

YELLOW-BILLED MAGPIE *Pica nuttalli* **Fairly common, local M386**
16½–17 in. (42–43 cm). Similar to Black-billed Magpie, but *bill yellow.* At close range shows crescent of bare yellow skin below eye. **VOICE:** Similar to Black-billed Magpie's *maag?,* etc. **HABITAT:** Oak savanna, riparian groves, ranches, farms. Usually in small to medium-sized flocks.

BLACK-BILLED MAGPIE *Pica hudsonia* **Fairly common M385**
18½–19½ in. (47–49 cm); tail 9½–12 in. (24–30 cm). A large, slender, *black-and-white bird,* with *long, graduated tail.* In flight, iridescent greenish black tail streams behind and large *white patches flash in wings.* **VOICE:** Harsh, rapid *queg queg queg queg* or *wah-wah-wah.* Also a querulous, nasal *maag?* or *aag-aag?* **SIMILAR SPECIES:** Yellow-billed Magpie; ranges do not overlap, although escapees may occur. **HABITAT:** Rangeland, brushy country, conifers, streamsides, forest edges, farms. Often in flocks.

JAYS AND MAGPIES

PINYON JAY

CLARK'S NUTCRACKER

adult

North and Pacific

GRAY JAY

Rockies

Gray Jay juvenile

YELLOW-BILLED MAGPIE

BLACK-BILLED MAGPIE

NORTHWESTERN CROW *Corvus caurinus*   Uncommon, local M388
16 in. (41 cm). This small beachcombing crow of Northwest is very similar to American Crow but is slightly smaller and has slightly quicker wingbeats. It replaces the latter on the narrow northwestern coastal strip. There is apparently integration with American Crow in Puget Sound area; hence some believe they may be conspecific. **VOICE:** *Khaaa* or *khaaw*. Usually more resonant than American Crow's *caw*. Also, *cowp-cowp-cowp*. **SIMILAR SPECIES:** American Crow. **HABITAT:** Near tidewater, shores, coastal towns.

AMERICAN CROW *Corvus brachyrhynchos*   Common M387
17–17½ in. (43–45 cm). A large, chunky, ebony bird. Completely black; glossed with purplish in strong sunlight. Bill and feet strong and black. Often gregarious. **VOICE:** Loud *caw, caw, caw* or *cah* or *kahr*. **SIMILAR SPECIES:** Common Raven larger, has wedge-shaped tail, more sweptback wings, different call. See also Chihuahuan Raven, Northwestern Crow. **HABITAT:** Woodlands, farms, fields, river groves, shores, towns, dumps.

CHIHUAHUAN RAVEN *Corvus cryptoleucus*   Fairly common M389
19–19½ in. (48–50 cm). Slightly larger than American Crow; a small raven of plains and deserts. Flies with typical flat-winged glide of a raven; has somewhat wedge-shaped tail. White feather bases on neck and breast sometimes show when feathers are ruffled by the wind, hence former name White-necked Raven. **VOICE:** Hoarse *kraak,* flatter and higher than Common Raven's. **SIMILAR SPECIES:** Difficult to tell from Common Raven, particularly when separate, but slightly smaller and tail slightly less wedge-shaped, calls higher pitched, and bristles extend farther down upper mandible. **HABITAT:** Arid and semiarid scrub and grasslands, deserts, yucca, mesquite, towns, dumps.

COMMON RAVEN *Corvus corax*   Common M390
23½–24 in. (59–61 cm). Note *wedge-shaped tail.* Much larger than American Crow; has heavier voice and is not inclined to be as gregarious, often solitary or in family groups. More hawklike in flight, it alternates flapping and sailing, gliding on flat, somewhat sweptback wings (crow glides much less and with slight upward dihedral). When bird is perched and not too distant, note "goiter" look created by shaggy throat feathers and heavier "Roman-nose" bill. **VOICE:** Croaking *cr-r-ruck* or *prruk;* also a metallic *tok*. **SIMILAR SPECIES:** Chihuahuan Raven. **HABITAT:** Boreal and mountain forests, desert lowlands (particularly in winter), cliffs, tundra, towns, dumps.

CROWS AND RAVENS

American
Crow

**NORTHWESTERN
CROW**

**AMERICAN
CROW**

show white
nape when
hers are
led

ravens have
wedge-
shaped tails

**CHIHUAHUAN
RAVEN**

**COMMON
RAVEN**

Swallows Family Hirundinidae

Slim, streamlined form and graceful flight characterize these sparrow-sized birds. Pointed wings; short bill with very wide gape; tiny feet. **FOOD:** Mostly flying insects. **RANGE:** Worldwide except for polar regions, some islands.

TREE SWALLOW *Tachycineta bicolor*   Common M393
5¾ in. (15 cm). *Adult:* Male *steely blue,* tinged green, above; *white below.* Female slightly duller than male. *Juvenile:* Dusky gray-brown back and dusky smudge across breast. Tree Swallows have distinctly notched tail; glide in circles, ending glide with quick flaps and a short climb. **VOICE:** Rich *cheet* or *chi-veet;* a liquid twitter, *weet, trit, weet,* etc. **SIMILAR SPECIES:** May be confused with Northern Rough-winged Swallow (dingy throat, different flight style) or Bank Swallow (bolder dark breast-band than juvenile Tree, smaller overall, browner above). See Violet-green Swallow. All species also have different calls. **HABITAT:** Open country near water, marshes, meadows, streams, lakes, wires. Nests in holes in trees, birdhouses.

BANK SWALLOW *Riparia riparia*   Fairly common M396
5 in. (12 cm). Our smallest swallow. Brown-backed with slightly darker wings and paler rump. Note *distinct dark breast-band.* Wing-beats rapid and shallow. **VOICE:** Dry, trilled chitter, *brrt* or *trr-tri-tri.* **SIMILAR SPECIES:** Northern Rough-winged Swallow and juvenile Tree Swallow. When perched in mixed-species flocks, Bank's smaller size stands out. **HABITAT:** Near water; fields, marshes, lakes. Nests colonially in dirt and sand banks.

NORTHERN ROUGH-WINGED SWALLOW   Fairly common M395
Stelgidopteryx serripennis
5¼ in. (12 cm). *Adult: Brown-backed;* does not show contrast above that Bank Swallow does; *throat and upper breast dusky;* no breast-band. Flight more languid; wings pulled back at end of stroke. *Juvenile:* Has cinnamon-rusty wing bars. **VOICE:** Call a low, liquid *trrit,* lower and less grating than Bank Swallow's. **SIMILAR SPECIES:** Bank Swallow and juvenile Tree Swallow. **HABITAT:** Near streams, lakes, rivers. Nests in banks, pipes, and crevices, but not colonially as Bank Swallow does.

VIOLET-GREEN SWALLOW   Fairly common M394
Tachycineta thalassina
5¼ in. (13 cm). Note *white patches that almost meet* over base of tail. *Male:* Dark and shiny above; adults glossed with beautiful *green on back and purple on rump and uppertail;* clear white below. *White of face partially encircles eye. Female and immature:* Somewhat duller above, and white above eye tinged grayish or brownish. **VOICE:** A twitter; a thin *ch-lip* or *chew-chit;* rapid *chit-chit-chit wheet, wheet.* **SIMILAR SPECIES:** Separated from Tree Swallow by pale feathering above eye, greener back, white patches on sides of rump, slightly smaller size, and longer wings. See also White-throated Swift. **HABITAT:** Widespread when foraging. Nests in holes in cliffs and in trees in open forests, foothill woods, mountains, canyons, towns.

SWALLOWS

TREE SWALLOW

adult

nests in e holes nest oxes

juvenile

BANK SWALLOW

Bank Swallow colony

NORTHERN ROUGH-WINGED SWALLOW

VIOLET-GREEN SWALLOW

adult ♂

Purple Martin (p. 270)

Barn (p. 270)

Cliff (p. 270)

Violet-green

Northern Rough-winged

Tree

Bank

Swallows on a wire

269

PURPLE MARTIN *Progne subis*   Uncommon and local M392
8 in. (20 cm). The largest N. American swallow. *Male:* Uniformly blue-black *above and below;* no other swallow is dark-bellied. *Female and juvenile:* Light-bellied; throat and breast grayish, often with faint gray collar. Glides in circles, alternating quick flaps and glides; often spreads tail. **VOICE:** Throaty and rich *tchew-wew,* etc., or *pew, pew.* Song gurgling, ending in a succession of rich, low guttural notes. **SIMILAR SPECIES:** Tree and Violet-green swallows, much smaller than female Purple Martin, are cleaner white below. In flight, male martin might be confused with European Starling. **HABITAT:** Towns, farms, open or semiopen country, often near water. Nests in cavities in trees (e.g., sycamores, ponderosa pines), posts, and, in s. AZ, saguaros; rarely martin houses.

CAVE SWALLOW *Petrochelidon fulva*   Uncommon, local M398
5½ in. (14 cm). Similar to Cliff Swallow (rusty rump, square-cut tail), but face colors reversed: *throat and cheeks buffy* (not dark), forehead *dark chestnut* (not pale, although Cliff Swallows in Southwest have chestnut forehead). *Buff color sets off dark mask and cap.* **VOICE:** Clear, sweet *weet* or *cheweet;* a loud, accented *chu, chu.* **SIMILAR SPECIES:** Cliff Swallow; Cave has buffier throat and face, more deeply colored rump, different call. **HABITAT:** Open country. Cuplike nest placed in caves, culverts, and under bridges; nests colonially.

CLIFF SWALLOW *Petrochelidon pyrrhonota*   Common M397
5½ in. (14 cm). Note *rusty* or *buffy rump.* Overhead, appears square-tailed, with dark throat patch. Glides in a long ellipse, ending each glide with a roller coaster–like climb. **VOICE:** *Zayrp;* a low *chur.* Alarm call *keer!* Song consists of creaking notes and guttural gratings; harsher than Barn and Cave swallows' songs. **SIMILAR SPECIES:** Barn and Cave swallows. **HABITAT:** Open to semiopen land, farms, cliffs, lakes. Nests colonially on cliffs, barn sides, under eaves and bridges; rarely on trees. Builds mud jug, or gourdlike, nest. Barn and Cave swallows build cuplike open nest; and Barn Swallows often but not always nest *inside* the barn.

BARN SWALLOW *Hirundo rustica*   Common M399
6¾ in. (17 cm). Our only swallow that is truly *swallow-tailed;* also the only one with *white tail spots. Adult:* Blue-black above; cinnamon-buff below, with darker throat. *Immature:* More whitish below. Flight direct, often close to ground; wingtips pulled back at end of stroke; not much gliding. **VOICE:** Soft *vit* or *kvik-kvik, vit-vit.* Also *szee-szah* or *szee.* Anxiety call a harsh, irritated *ee-tee* or *keet.* Song a long, musical twitter interspersed with guttural notes. **SIMILAR SPECIES:** Most other N. American swallows have notched (not deeply forked) tail. Cliff Swallow is colonial, building mud jugs under eaves or cliffs. See Cave Swallow. **HABITAT:** Open or semiopen land; farms, fields, marshes, lakes; often perches on wires; usually near habitation. Builds *cuplike nest inside* barns or under eaves, not in tight colonies like Cliff Swallow.

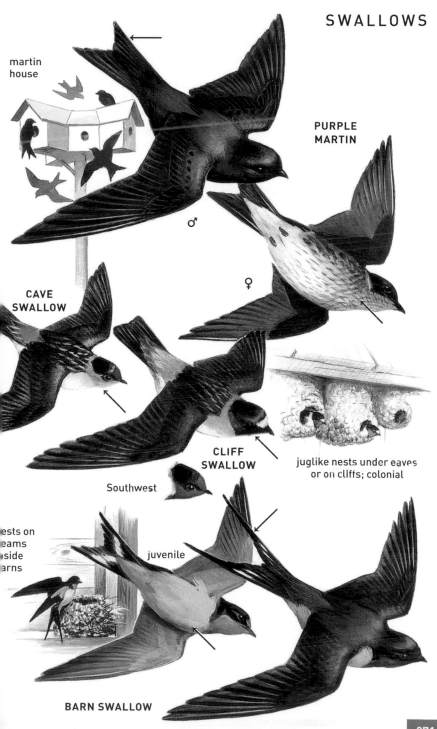

SWALLOWS

martin
house

PURPLE
MARTIN

♂

♀

CAVE
SWALLOW

CLIFF
SWALLOW

juglike nests under eaves
or on cliffs; colonial

Southwest

ests on
eams
side
arns

juvenile

BARN SWALLOW

271

LARKS Family Alaudidae

Brown terrestrial birds with long hind claws. Gregarious in nonbreeding season, when they may be joined by longspurs and Snow Buntings. Larks often sing in high display flights. **FOOD**: Seeds, insects. **RANGE**: Mainly Old World.

SKY LARK (EURASIAN SKYLARK) *Alauda arvensis*   Scarce, local
7¼ in. (19 cm). Like a drab, streaky Horned Lark. *Trailing edge of broad-based wing and sides of tail white.* Short *crest*, heavier bill than pipits. **VOICE**: Call a clear, liquid *chir-r-up*. Song, in hovering flight, high-pitched, with long-sustained runs and trills. **RANGE**: Introduced birds from Europe are resident on s. Vancouver I., BC. Vagrants from Asia reach w. AK islands. **HABITAT**: Open country, fields, airports.

HORNED LARK *Eremophila alpestris*   Uncommon to common M391
7–7¼ in. (18–19 cm). A pale bird of open ground. *Walks,* does not hop. Overhead, pale with *black* tail. *Adult:* Distinctive face pattern with tiny "horns"; black breast patch; varies from pales to darker races. *Juvenile:* Very different, *streaked below;* note heavier bill than pipits. **VOICE**: Song tinkling, irregular, high-pitched, from ground or air. Call a clear *tsee-titi.* **HABITAT**: Prairies, short-grass and dirt fields, golf courses, airports, shores, tundra.

BUSHTITS AND VERDIN
Families Aegithalidae and Remizidae

Bushtits are nearly always found in flocks except during breeding season, often mixing with small birds of other species. Verdin are found singly or in pairs. **FOOD**: Insects, fruit, berries. **RANGE**: Bushtits from sw. BC to s. Guatemala; Verdin in desert regions of sw. N. America.

BUSHTIT *Psaltriparus minimus*   Uncommon to common M411
4½ in. (11 cm). A very small, plain bird with longish tail and stubby bill. Except briefly during nesting season, travels in *straggling talkitive flocks,* often joined by warblers and other species. Some males in s. NM and w. TX have black cheeks. **VOICE**: Insistent light *tsit*s, *pit*s, and *clenk*s. **SIMILAR SPECIES**: Verdin, Wrentit. **HABITAT**: Oak scrub, chaparral, mixed woods, riparian woodland, pinyon-juniper, parks, residential areas.

VERDIN *Auriparus flaviceps*   Uncommon to fairly common M410
4½ in. (11 cm). Tiny. *Adult:* Gray, with *yellowish head, rufous bend of wing* (often hidden). *Juvenile:* Plain gray. **VOICE**: Insistent *see-lip.* Rapid chipping. Song a three-note whistle, *tsee see-see.* **SIMILAR SPECIES**: Bushtit longer tailed; not usually found in desert lowlands. See also Lucy's Warbler, Northern Beardless-Tyrannulet. **HABITAT**: Brushy desert and semiarid lowlands, mesquite.

LARKS

overhead

towering
flight

**HORNED
LARK**

**SKY
LARK**

adult

juvenile

prairie

northern

BUSHTIT AND
VERDIN

Pacific
Coast

VERDIN

adult

interior

juvenile

males have
yellow eyes

juvenile

BUSHTIT

juvenile ♂
"Black-eared"

CHICKADEES AND TITMICE Family Paridae

Small, plump, small-billed birds. Acrobatic when feeding. Often found in mixed-species flocks during nonbreeding season with other parids, kinglets, warblers, etc. **FOOD:** Insects, seeds, acorn mast, berries; at feeders, suet, sunflower seeds. **RANGE:** Widespread in N. America, Eurasia, Africa.

BLACK-CAPPED CHICKADEE   Fairly common M400
Poecile atricapillus
5–5¼ in. (12–13 cm). This small, tame acrobat can be separated from other widespread western chickadees by its *solid black cap* in conjunction with *gray back* and buffy sides. **VOICE:** Clearly enunciated *chick-a-dee-dee-dee*. Song a clear whistle, *fee-bee-ee* or *fee-bee*, first note higher. **HABITAT:** Mixed and deciduous woods; willow thickets, shade trees, residential areas, feeders.

MOUNTAIN CHICKADEE *Poecile gambeli*   Fairly common M401
5¼ in. (13 cm). Similar to Black-capped Chickadee, but note *white line over eye*. **VOICE:** Song a clear whistled *fee-bee-bee* or *fee-ee-bee-bee*, first note(s) usually higher; also *tsick-a-zee-zee-zee*, huskier than Black-capped's, and a rolling *deedleedleoo*. **HABITAT:** Mountain forests, conifers; irregularly moves to lower elevations in winter.

CHESTNUT-BACKED CHICKADEE   Fairly common M403
Poecile rufescens
4¾ in. (12 cm). The cap, bib, and white cheeks indicate a chickadee; the *chestnut back and rump*, this species. Sides *chestnut* (or *gray* along coast of cen. CA). **VOICE:** Hoarser and more rapid than Black-capped Chickadee, e.g., *sick-a-see-see*. No whistled song. **HABITAT:** Moist coniferous and mixed forests, oaks, willows, parks.

MEXICAN CHICKADEE *Poecile sclateri*   Uncommon, local M402
5 in. (13 cm). Similar to Black-capped Chickadee, but *black of throat more extensive*, spreading across upper breast. Note *dark gray sides*. Lacks whitish supercilium of Mountain Chickadee. The only chickadee in its local U.S. range. **VOICE:** Nasal and husky for a chickadee: a low *dzay-dzeee*. **HABITAT:** Montane coniferous forests; sometimes moves to lower canyons in winter.

GRAY-HEADED CHICKADEE (SIBERIAN TIT)   Rare, local M405
Poecile cinctus
5½ in. (14 cm). This subarctic chickadee can be separated from Boreal Chickadee by its *grayer cap* and *more extensive white cheek*. **VOICE:** Peevish *dee-deer* or *chee-ee*. **HABITAT:** Spruce forests, particularly at border with riparian willow and alder thickets and cottonwoods; isolated stands of trees at tundra edge.

BOREAL CHICKADEE *Poecile hudsonicus*   Uncommon M404
5½ in. (14 cm). Note *dull brown cap*, rich brown to pinkish brown flanks, extensively *grayish cheeks*. **VOICE:** Wheezy *chick-che-day-day*; notes slower, more raspy and drawling than lively *chick-a-dee-dee-dee* of Black-capped Chickadee. **SIMILAR SPECIES:** Gray-headed Chickadee. **HABITAT:** Coniferous forests.

CHICKADEES

BLACK-CAPPED CHICKADEE

MOUNTAIN CHICKADEE

Rockies

CHESTNUT-BACKED CHICKADEE

cen. CA coast

MEXICAN CHICKADEE

GRAY-HEADED CHICKADEE

BOREAL CHICKADEE

BLACK-CRESTED TITMOUSE
Fairly common M409

Baeolophus atricristatus

6¼ in. (16 cm). A small gray bird with *black crown and crest*. Forehead and underparts pale, sides rusty. Juveniles have mostly gray crest briefly in summer. **VOICE:** Chickadee-like calls. Song a whistled *peter peter peter peter* or *hear hear hear hear*. Varied. **SIMILAR SPECIES:** Bridled Titmouse has harlequin face pattern. **HABITAT:** Woodlands, canyons, towns, feeders.

OAK TITMOUSE *Baeolophus inornatus*
Fairly common M407

5¾ in. (15 cm). This is the sole titmouse west of Sierra Nevada. Very like Juniper Titmouse, but slightly browner. Plain Titmouse was split into Oak and Juniper titmice. **VOICE:** Call a scratchy *sissi-chee*. Song a whistled *weety weety* or *tee-wit tee-wit tee-wit;* highly variable. **SIMILAR SPECIES:** Other titmice, but separated by range. **HABITAT:** Oak and oak-pine woods; locally in riparian woodlands, shade trees, residential areas.

JUNIPER TITMOUSE *Baeolophus ridgwayi*
Uncommon M408

5¾ in. (15 cm). Birds bearing the name "titmouse" are our only *small, gray-backed* birds with pointed crest. Juniper and Oak titmice were once combined as a single species, Plain Titmouse. The two are very similar, although Juniper is slightly grayer. **VOICE:** Call more rapid than Oak's, *si-dee-dee-dee-dee*. **SIMILAR SPECIES:** Juniper Titmice reported from Big Bend and Edwards Plateau areas of TX are probably young Black-crested Titmice, which have short gray crest. **HABITAT:** Pinyon-juniper and oak-juniper woodlands.

BRIDLED TITMOUSE *Baeolophus wollweberi*
Fairly common M406

5¼ in. (13 cm). Crest and black-and-white *"bridled" face* identify this small gray titmouse of Southwest. **VOICE:** Similar to other titmice and chickadees, but higher and faster. Song a repeated two-syllable phrase. **SIMILAR SPECIES:** Black-crested Titmouse. **HABITAT:** Oak, pine-oak, and sycamore canyons, riparian woodlands, feeders.

TITMICE

BLACK-
CRESTED
TITMOUSE

JUNIPER
TITMOUSE

OAK
ITMOUSE

BRIDLED
TITMOUSE

Mountain Chickadee
(p. 274)
for comparison

277

NUTHATCHES Family Sittidae

Small, stubby tree climbers with strong, woodpecker-like bill and strong feet. Short, square-cut tail is not braced like a woodpecker's tail during climbing. Nuthatches habitually go down trees headfirst. Sexes similar, or mostly so. **FOOD:** Bark insects, seeds, nuts; attracted to feeders by suet, sunflower seeds. **RANGE:** Most of N. Hemisphere.

WHITE-BREASTED NUTHATCH　　　　Fairly common M413
Sitta carolinensis
5¾ in. (15 cm). This, the most widespread nuthatch, is known by its *black cap* (gray in female) and beady black eye on white face. Undertail coverts chestnut. **VOICE:** Song a rapid series of low, nasal, whistled notes on one pitch: *whi, whi, whi, whi, whi, whi* or *who, who, who,* etc. Notes of birds in interior West higher pitched and given in rapid series. Call a distinctive nasal *yank, yank, yank;* also a nasal *tootoo.* **SIMILAR SPECIES:** Red-breasted Nuthatch. **HABITAT:** Forests, woodlots, groves, river woods, shade trees, feeders.

RED-BREASTED NUTHATCH *Sitta canadensis*　　Common M412
4½ in. (11 cm). A small nuthatch with *broad black line* through eye and white line above it. Underparts washed with rusty (deeper in male). **VOICE:** Call higher, more nasal than White-breasted Nuthatch, *ank* or *enk,* sounding like a baby nuthatch or tiny tin horn. **SIMILAR SPECIES:** Pygmy Nuthatch has gray-brown crown, lacks white supercilium, has very different call. **HABITAT:** Coniferous forests; in winter, also other trees, feeders.

PYGMY NUTHATCH *Sitta pygmaea*　　Fairly common M414
4¼ in. (11 cm). A very small, pine-loving nuthatch, with *gray-brown cap coming down to eye* and a whitish spot on nape. Usually roams about in little flocks. **VOICE:** High, piping *peep-peep* or *pit-pi-dit-pi-dit.* Also a high *ki-dee;* incessant, sometimes becoming an excited chatter. Often heard before it is seen. **SIMILAR SPECIES:** Red-breasted Nuthatch. **HABITAT:** Favors ponderosa, Jeffrey, and Monterey pines, Douglas-fir.

CREEPERS Family Certhiidae

Small, slim, stiff-tailed birds, with slender, slightly curved bill used to probe bark of trees. **FOOD:** Bark insects. **RANGE:** Cooler parts of N. Hemisphere.

BROWN CREEPER *Certhia americana*　　Uncommon M415
5¼ in. (13 cm). A very small, slim, camouflaged tree climber. Brown above, whitish below, with *slender decurved bill* and *stiff tail,* which is used as a brace during climbing. Ascends trees spirally from base, hugging bark closely. **VOICE:** Call a single high, thin *seee,* similar to quick three-note call *(see-see-see)* of Golden-crowned Kinglet. Song a high, thin, sibilant *see-ti-wee-tu-wee* or *trees, trees, trees, see the trees.* **SIMILAR SPECIES:** Pygmy Nuthatch. **HABITAT:** Nests in variety of coniferous and mixed woodlands; in nonbreeding season, also in deciduous woods, groves, shade trees.

WHITE-BREASTED
NUTHATCH

♀

♂

BROWN
CREEPER

♀

♂

RED-
BREASTED
NUTHATCH

PYGMY
NUTHATCH

WRENS Family Troglodytidae

Mostly small, energetic brown birds; stumpy, with slim, slightly curved bill; tail often cocked. FOOD: Insects, spiders. RANGE: N., Cen., and S. America; also in Eurasia.

HOUSE WREN *Troglodytes aedon*   Fairly common M421
4½–4¾ in. (11–12 cm). A small, energetic, gray-brown wren with light eye-ring and no strong eyebrow stripe. VOICE: Stuttering, gurgling song rises in a musical burst, then falls at end; calls a rolled *prrrrr* and harsh *cheh, cheh.* SIMILAR SPECIES: Winter Wren. HABITAT: Open woods, thickets, towns, gardens; often nests in bird boxes.

PACIFIC WREN *Troglodytes pacificus*   Uncommon M422
4 in. (10 cm). A *very small, dark* wren, told from House Wren by its smaller size, *much stubbier tail,* and *heavily barred belly.* Often bobs body. Mouselike and secretive; stays near ground. VOICE: Song a rapid succession of high tinkling warbles, trills. Call a hard, two-syllable *timp-timp* (suggests Wilson's Warbler) west of Rockies, or *kip-kip* (suggests Song Sparrow) east of Rockies. HABITAT: Dense, shaded woodland underbrush, ferns, fallen trees; in summer, also coniferous forests.

BEWICK'S WREN *Thryomanes bewickii*   Fairly common M420
5¼ in. (13 cm). Note longish tail with *white corners* and bold *white eyebrow stripe.* Mouse brown above. VOICE: Song suggests Song Sparrow's, but thinner, starting on two or three high notes, dropping lower, ending on a thin trill; calls sharp *vit, vit* and buzzy *dzzzzt.* SIMILAR SPECIES: Some Carolina Wrens have limited buff below but have *rufous tails without white corners.* HABITAT: Thickets, underbrush, gardens; often nests in bird boxes.

CAROLINA WREN *Thryothorus ludovicianus*   Scarce, local M419
5½ in. (14 cm). A large wren, near size of a sparrow. *Warm rusty brown* above, variably buff below; conspicuous *white eyebrow stripe.* VOICE: Two- or three-syllable chant. Variable; *tea-kettle, tea-kettle, tea kettle,* or *chirpity, chirpity, chirpity, chirp.* Variety of *chip*s and *churr*s. SIMILAR SPECIES: Bewick's and Marsh wrens. HABITAT: Tangles, undergrowth, gardens; often nests in bird boxes.

SEDGE WREN *Cistothorus platensis*   Uncommon, secretive M423
4½ in. (11 cm). Stubbier than Marsh Wren; buffier, with *buffy* undertail coverts, *barred wings,* and *finely streaked* crown. VOICE: Song a dry staccato chattering: *chap chap chapper-rrrrr.* Call a single or double *chap,* like first note of song. SIMILAR SPECIES: House Wren. HABITAT: Grassy and sedgy marshes and meadows.

MARSH WREN *Cistothorus palustris*   Fairly common M424
5 in. (13 cm). *White stripes on back* and white eyebrow stripe identify this marsh dweller. VOICE: Song reedy, gurgling, often ending in a guttural rattle: *cut-cut-turrrrrrrrr-ur;* often heard at night. Call a low *tsuck-tsuck.* SIMILAR SPECIES: Sedge Wren. HABITAT: Fresh and brackish marshes; in winter, also salt marshes.

HOUSE
WREN

PACIFIC
WREN

BEWICK'S
WREN

CAROLINA
WREN

SEDGE
WREN

MARSH
WREN

CANYON WREN *Catherpes mexicanus*   Uncommon M418

5¾–6 in. (15 cm). Rusty, with dark rufous belly contrasting with *white breast and throat.* Long, slightly decurved bill. **VOICE:** Gushing cadence of clear, curved notes tripping down scale: *tee tee tee tee tew tew tew tew.* Call a shrill *beet.* **SIMILAR SPECIES:** Rock and Bewick's wrens. **HABITAT:** Cliffs, canyons, rockslides, stone buildings.

ROCK WREN *Salpinctes obsoletus*   Fairly common M417

6 in. (15 cm). A gray western wren with *finely streaked breast,* rusty rump, and *buffy terminal tail band.* Frequently bobs. **VOICE:** Song a harsh chant. A loud dry trill; also *ti-keer.* **SIMILAR SPECIES:** Canyon Wren. **HABITAT:** Rocky slopes, canyons, rubble.

CACTUS WREN   Fairly common M416
Campylorhynchus brunneicapillus

8½ in. (22 cm). A very large wren of arid country. Distinguished from other wrens by *much larger size and heavy spotting.* **VOICE:** Monotonous *chug-chug-chug-chug,* on one pitch, gaining speed. **SIMILAR SPECIES:** Sage Thrasher. **HABITAT:** Arid areas of cactus, mesquite, yucca; coastal birds in coastal scrub with prickly-pear cactus.

BABBLERS Family Timaliidae

Long-tailed denizens of brushy cover. This Old World family is represented in N. America by just one species. **FOOD:** Insects, fruit. **RANGE:** Widespread in temperate and tropical Old World.

WRENTIT *Chamaea fasciata*   Fairly common M444

6½ in. (17 cm). Hard to see as it slips through brush; heard far more often. Note *long,* rounded, slightly cocked tail, obscurely streaked breast, and *pale eye.* **VOICE:** Song (heard year-round) consists of staccato level-pitched ringing notes that accelerate in a "bouncing ball" pattern. Female gives slower, double-note version. Call a soft *prr.* **SIMILAR SPECIES:** Bushtit much smaller, usually in flocks. **HABITAT:** Chaparral, coastal sage scrub, brush, parks, dense garden shrubs.

DIPPERS Family Cinclidae

Plump, stub-tailed; like very large wrens. Solitary or in family groups. Dippers dive and swim underwater, where they walk on bottom. **FOOD:** Insects, larvae, aquatic invertebrates, small fish. **RANGE:** Eurasia, w. N. America, Andes of S. America.

AMERICAN DIPPER *Cinclus mexicanus*   Uncommon M425

7½ in. (19 cm). A chunky, thrush-sized, *slate-colored* bird of rushing mountain streams, *tail stubby.* Flies low over water; perches on rocks; dives, submerges. **VOICE:** Call a sharp, buzzy *zeet.* Song clear and ringing, mockingbird-like (much repetition of notes), but higher, more wrenlike. **SIMILAR SPECIES:** Wrens. **HABITAT:** Fast-flowing streams in mountains and canyons; more rarely pond edges. Nests under bridges, behind waterfalls. Some birds move to lower elevations in winter.

WRENS, WRENTIT, AND DIPPER

CANYON WREN

ROCK WREN

CACTUS WREN

juvenile

adult

WRENTIT

northern

southern

AMERICAN DIPPER

adult

juvenile

KINGLETS Family Regulidae

Tiny active birds with small slender bill, short tail, bright crown. In nonbreeding season, often found in mixed-species flocks with chickadees and warblers. **FOOD:** Insects, larvae. **RANGE:** N. America and Eurasia.

RUBY-CROWNED KINGLET *Regulus calendula*   Common M427
4¼ in. (11 cm). Smaller than warblers; *flicks wings constantly.* Male has *scarlet crown patch* (erect when excited). **VOICE:** Husky *ji-dit.* Song is several high notes, lower notes, and a chant, *tee tee tee-tew tew tew — ti-didee, ti-didee, ti-didee.* **SIMILAR SPECIES:** See Hutton's Vireo. **HABITAT:** Coniferous forests; in migration and winter, woodlands.

GOLDEN-CROWNED KINGLET   Fairly common M426
Regulus satrapa
4 in. (10 cm). Similar to Ruby-crowned but note *boldly striped face.* **VOICE:** High, wiry *see-see-see.* Song several high thin notes, dropping into a little chatter. **SIMILAR SPECIES:** Ruby-crowned Kinglet. **HABITAT:** Conifers; in migration and winter, also other trees.

OLD WORLD WARBLERS AND GNATCATCHERS Family Sylviidae

Active birds with slender bill. Gnatcatchers have long, mobile tail. **FOOD:** Insects, larvae. **RANGE:** Worldwide.

BLUE-GRAY GNATCATCHER   Fairly common M429
Polioptila caerulea
4½ in. (11 cm). A tiny, slim mite, blue-gray above, whitish below, with narrow *white eye-ring. Long tail* is *mostly white underneath* and often flipped about and cocked. **VOICE:** Call a thin, peevish *zpee;* often doubled, *zpee-zee.* Song a thin, squeaky, wheezy series of notes. **HABITAT:** Open woods; also brushy habitats in winter.

BLACK-TAILED GNATCATCHER   Uncommon M431
Polioptila melanura
4½ in. (11 cm). Similar to Blue-gray, but underparts grayer, undertail *largely black.* Breeding male has *black cap.* **VOICE:** Call a thin harsh *chee,* repeated two or three times; soft *chip-chip-chip* series. **HABITAT:** Desert brush, ravines, dry washes, mesquite.

BLACK-CAPPED GNATCATCHER *Polioptila nigriceps*   Rare, local
4¼ in. (11 cm). Visitor to se. AZ; recently a very local breeder there. Note *largely white undertail; bill longer* and eye-ring weaker than Blue-gray. Breeding male has *black cap.* **VOICE:** Rough *meeeer.* **HABITAT:** Brushy washes and riparian habitat in desert.

CALIFORNIA GNATCATCHER   Scarce, local M430
Polioptila californica
4½ in. (11 cm). Similar to Black-tailed Gnatcatcher but no range overlap. *Grayer below,* less white on undertail. **VOICE:** Kittenlike *meew,* rising then falling; harsher *jih-jih-jih.* **SIMILAR SPECIES:** Blue-gray Gnatcatcher. **HABITAT:** Restricted to coastal sage scrub.

KINGLETS AND GNATCATCHERS

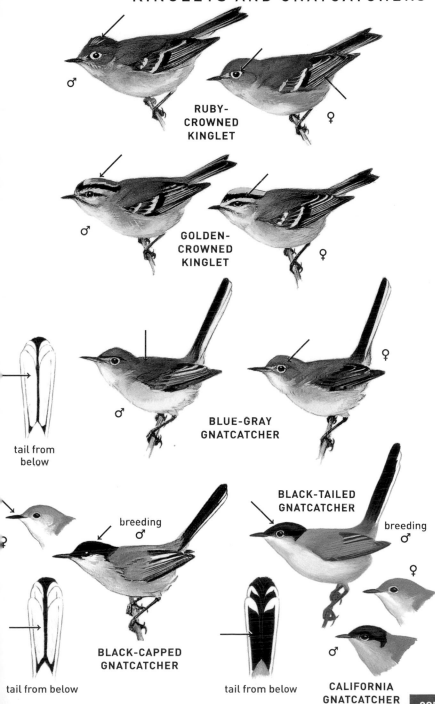

RUBY-CROWNED KINGLET

♂   ♀

GOLDEN-CROWNED KINGLET

♂   ♀

tail from below

BLUE-GRAY GNATCATCHER

♂   ♀

breeding ♂

BLACK-CAPPED GNATCATCHER

tail from below

BLACK-TAILED GNATCATCHER

breeding ♂

♀

♂

tail from below

CALIFORNIA GNATCATCHER

285

DUSKY WARBLER *Phylloscopus fuscatus*   Casual
5¼ in. (13 cm). A small, *brownish* Old World warbler; note *buffy eyebrow, plain wings*. **VOICE:** Call a hard *tik*. **SIMILAR SPECIES:** Arctic Warbler. **RANGE:** Asian species; casual vagrant to AK and CA, mostly in fall. **HABITAT:** Thick, scrubby cover.

ARCTIC WARBLER *Phylloscopus borealis*   Uncommon, local M428
5 in. (13 cm). A small, *greenish* Old World warbler; note light eyebrow, *single narrow wing bar*. Fresh birds in fall are brighter yellowgreen. **VOICE:** Song a monotonous series of buzzy notes; call a buzzy *tsik*. **SIMILAR SPECIES:** Orange-crowned and Tennessee warblers. **HABITAT:** Breeds in willow and alder scrub.

ACCENTORS Family Prunellidae

Eurasian family of thrushlike birds, more closely related to pipits. One species occurs as a vagrant in N. America. **FOOD:** Insects, seeds, fruit. **RANGE:** Palearctic regions.

SIBERIAN ACCENTOR *Prunella montanella*   Casual
5½ in. (14 cm). *Dark cheeks; bright ocher-buff eyebrow and underparts;* bill *warblerlike*. **VOICE:** Call a thin, high-pitched *sree* given in series. **RANGE:** Very rare fall visitor to St. Lawrence I., casual to other Bering Sea islands. Accidental to mainland Northwest. **HABITAT:** Thickets.

THRUSHES Family Turdidae

Large-eyed, slender-billed songbirds. Most species that bear the name "thrush" are brown-backed with spotted breasts. Robins and bluebirds, etc., suggest their relationship through their speckle-breasted young. Often fine singers. **FOOD:** Insects, worms, snails, berries, fruit. **RANGE:** Nearly worldwide.

SIBERIAN RUBYTHROAT *Luscinia calliope*   Casual
6 in. (15 cm). Brown above; white eyebrow and whiskers. *Male: Ruby red throat. Female:* White throat. **VOICE:** Series of chattering notes. Call a sharp *chak*. **SIMILAR SPECIES:** Bluethroat. **RANGE:** Asian species; very rare vagrant to w. AK. **HABITAT:** Thickets.

BLUETHROAT *Luscinia svecica*   Scarce, local M432
5½ in. (14 cm). A small, sprightly skulking bird. Note chestnut base to tail and bold supercilium. *Male: Blue throat* with *reddish patches. Female:* Whitish throat with *dark necklace*. **VOICE:** Calls a sharp *tac*, a soft *wheet*, and a cricketlike note. Song composed of repetitious notes, musical and varied. **SIMILAR SPECIES:** Siberian Rubythroat. **HABITAT:** Dwarf willows and alders, thick brush.

NORTHERN WHEATEAR   Uncommon, local M433
Oenanthe oenanthe
5¾ in. (15 cm). A small, dapper bird of Arctic barrens. Note *white rump and sides of tail. Breeding male:* Pale gray back, black wings, and *black ear patch. Female and nonbreeding:* Buffier, with brown back, reduced black. **VOICE:** Call a hard *chak-chak* and soft *heet*. **HABITAT:** Open, stony areas; in summer, rocky tundra.

ALASKA AND ARCTIC NESTERS
AND VAGRANTS

ARCTIC
WARBLER

DUSKY
WARBLER

breeding ♂

♀

BLUETHROAT

SIBERIAN
ACCENTOR

SIBERIAN
RUBYTHROAT

♀

♂

breeding ♂

nonbreeding

NORTHERN WHEATEAR

287

EASTERN BLUEBIRD *Sialia sialis*　　　　Uncommon, local M434
7 in. (18 cm). A blue bird with *rusty red breast;* appears round-shouldered when perched. Female duller than male; has rusty throat and
breast, *white* belly. *Juvenile:* Speckle-breasted. **VOICE:** Call a musical
chur-wi. Song three or four gurgling notes. **SIMILAR SPECIES:** Western Bluebird, but *throat rusty,* not blue. Belly and undertail *whiter,*
not as gray. Western Bluebird usually has some rust color on back.
Fresh female and immature Mountain Bluebirds may have warm buff
wash on throat and breast, but flanks not as bright, and they are
longer winged and slightly longer billed. **HABITAT:** Open country with
scattered trees; farms, roadsides. Often nests in bluebird boxes.

WESTERN BLUEBIRD *Sialia mexicana*　　　　Fairly common M435
7 in. (18 cm). Appears round-shouldered when perched. *Male:* Head,
wings, and tail *blue;* breast and back *rusty red.* (In some birds, back is
partially or wholly blue.) *Throat blue. Female:* Paler, duller, with rusty
breast, *grayish* throat and belly. *Juvenile:* Speckle-breasted, grayish,
devoid of red, but with some telltale blue in wings and tail. **VOICE:**
Short *pew* or *mew.* Also a hard, chattering note. **SIMILAR SPECIES:**
Eastern Bluebird. Fresh female and immature Mountain Bluebirds
have buff wash on breast, but flanks duller, blue typically slightly
paler, and bill and wings slightly longer. **HABITAT:** Scattered trees,
open pine forests, oak savanna, farms; in winter, semiopen terrain,
pinyon-juniper, mistletoe, mesquite, parks, golf courses, desert
edges. Nests in cavities, including nest boxes.

MOUNTAIN BLUEBIRD *Sialia currucoides*　　　Fairly common M436
7¼–7½ in. (18–19 cm). *Male: Turquoise blue,* paler below; belly whitish. No rusty. *Female and immature:* Dull brownish gray, with touch of
pale blue on rump, tail, and wings. **VOICE:** Low *chur* or *vhew.* Song a
short, subdued warble. **SIMILAR SPECIES:** Has straighter posture than
female Western and Eastern bluebirds, with slightly longer bill and
tail. Warm-colored birds in fresh plumage lack rusty-colored flanks.
Like other bluebirds, often forms flocks in winter, but Mountain
Bluebird flocks often very large, and this species more apt to be seen
hovering over fields in search of prey. **HABITAT:** Open country with
some trees; in winter, also treeless terrain. Often nests in bluebird
boxes.

TOWNSEND'S SOLITAIRE *Myadestes townsendi*　　Uncommon M437
8½ in. (22 cm). A slim gray bird with *white eye-ring, white sides on tail,*
and *buffy wing patches.* Pattern in wing and tail gives it a not-too-
remote resemblance to Northern Mockingbird, but note eye-ring,
darker breast, and especially buff wing patches. *Juvenile:* Dark overall with light spots and scaly belly. **VOICE:** Song a rich warbling. Call a
high-pitched *eek,* like a squeaky bicycle wheel. **SIMILAR SPECIES:**
Northern Mockingbird, shrikes. **HABITAT:** Variety of coniferous forests almost to tree line, rocky cliffs; in winter, particularly fond of junipers, also chaparral, open woods. Nests on ground.

BLUEBIRDS AND SOLITAIRE

juvenile

♀

♂

WESTERN
BLUEBIRD

♂

♂

♀

EASTERN
BLUEBIRD

MOUNTAIN
BLUEBIRD

juvenile

TOWNSEND'S
SOLITAIRE

VEERY *Catharus fuscescens*   Uncommon M438
7 in. (18 cm). Note *uniform rusty brown* cast above and grayish flanks. No strong eye-ring (may have dull whitish ring) on grayish face. Of all our brown thrushes, this is the least spotted (spots often indistinct). **VOICE:** Song liquid, breezy, ethereal, wheeling downward: *vee-ur, vee-ur, veer, veer.* Call a down-slurred *phew* or *view.* **SIMILAR SPECIES:** Easily confused with russet-backed race of Swainson's Thrush (Pacific Coast states), but latter has distinct buffy eye-ring or spectacles, more spotting on breast, browner sides and flanks, and different vocalizations. Also Gray-cheeked Thrush. **HABITAT:** Moist deciduous woods, willow and alder thickets along streams and meadows in pine forests. Migrates east of Rockies.

SWAINSON'S THRUSH *Catharus ustulatus*   Fairly common M440
7 in. (18 cm). This spotted thrush is marked by its conspicuous *buffy eye-ring* or *spectacles,* buff on cheeks and upper breast. Interior and eastern forms are dull *olivey brown* above; subspecies in Pacific Coast region much more *russet.* **VOICE:** Song is breezy, flutelike phrases, each phrase sliding *upward.* Call a liquid *whit* or *foot.* Migrants at night (in sky) give a short whistled *quee.* **SIMILAR SPECIES:** Gray-cheeked Thrush has thin, often *incomplete* grayish eye-ring on *grayish face.* Young Hermit Thrush may have buff-tinged eye-ring, but all Hermits show *contrasty rufous tail, no buffy* on breast, regularly *flick wings and raise tail,* and *vocalizations differ.* See Veery. **HABITAT:** Moist spruce and fir forests, riparian woodlands; in migration, other woods.

GRAY-CHEEKED THRUSH *Catharus minimus*   Uncommon M439
7–7¼ in. (17–18 cm). A dull, "cold-colored," *gray-brown,* furtive thrush, distinguished from Swainson's by its *grayish* cheeks, *grayish,* less conspicuous, often broken eye-ring. *Little or no buffy on breast.* **VOICE:** Song thin and nasal, downward, suggesting Veery's: *whee-wheeoo-titi-wheew.* Call a downward *pheu* much higher than Veery's call. **SIMILAR SPECIES:** Other thrushes. **HABITAT:** Boreal forests, tundra willow and alder scrub; in migration, other woodlands. Migrates east of Rockies.

HERMIT THRUSH *Catharus guttatus*   Fairly common M441
6¾ in. (17 cm). A spot-breasted brown thrush with *rufous* tail. When perched, it has habit of *flicking wings* and of *cocking tail and dropping it slowly.* Different subspecies groups vary in exact color of back and flanks, some being warmer, others grayer. **VOICE:** Call a low *chuck;* also a scolding *tuk-tuk-tuk* and a rising, whiny *pay.* Song clear, ethereal, flutelike; three or four phrases at *different pitches,* each with a *long introductory note.* **SIMILAR SPECIES:** Swainson's and Gray-cheeked thrushes. Some Fox Sparrows have rusty tail and are found in same habitat, but they are heavily streaked rather than spotted and have conical bill. **HABITAT:** Coniferous and mixed woods; in winter, woods, thickets, chaparral, parks, gardens.

SPOTTED THRUSHES

VEERY

SWAINSON'S
THRUSH

Pacific Coast

East and
interior West

GRAY-CHEEKED
THRUSH

ail-lifting

interior
West

HERMIT
THRUSH

Pacific Coast
and East

AMERICAN ROBIN *Turdus migratorius*   Common M442

10 in. (25 cm). A very familiar bird; often seen on lawns, with an erect stance, giving short runs then pauses. Recognized by dark gray back and brick red breast. Dark stripes on white throat. On male, head and tail blackish, underparts solid, deep reddish; those colors duller on female. *Juvenile:* Has speckled breast, but rusty wash identifies it. **VOICE:** Song a clear caroling; short phrases, rising and falling, often prolonged. Calls *tyeep* and *tut-tut-tut.* **SIMILAR SPECIES:** Varied Thrush, Rufous-backed Robin (rare). **HABITAT:** Wide variety of habitats, including towns, parks, lawns, farmland, shade trees, many types of forests and woodlands; in winter, also berry-producing trees.

VARIED THRUSH *Ixoreus naevius*   Uncommon M443

9½ in. (24 cm). Similar to American Robin, but with *orangish eye stripe, orange wing bars,* and *orange bar on underwing* visible in flight. *Male: Blue-gray above,* with wide *black breast-band. Female:* Duller gray above, with *gray breast-band. Juvenile:* Breast-band imperfect or speckled. **VOICE:** Song a long, eerie, quavering, whistled note, followed, after a pause, by one on a lower or higher pitch. Call a liquid *chup.* **SIMILAR SPECIES:** Orangey wing bars and eye stripe, and a breast-band, distinguish it from a robin, with which it only rarely mingles. **HABITAT:** Thick, wet coniferous and mixed forests; in winter, also other moist, dense woods, ravines, thickets.

RUFOUS-BACKED ROBIN *Turdus rufopalliatus*   Very rare visitor

9¼ in. (24 cm). This very rare Mexican winter visitor is like a pale American Robin (extensive cinnamon underparts; grayish head, wings, and tail), but with orangier tinge below, *rufous back,* and *no white around eye.* More heavily streaked throat. *Orangier bill.* A timid skulker. **VOICE:** Call a soft whistled *teeww.* Song a mellow series of warbles, each repeated two or more times. **SIMILAR SPECIES:** American Robin. **RANGE:** Most records from se. AZ, but also recorded west to CA, north to UT, and east to TX. **HABITAT:** Woods and thickets, often near water.

AZTEC THRUSH *Ridgwayia pinicola*   Casual

9¼ in. (24 cm). A robinlike thrush with *dark hood,* white belly, white rump. Wings strikingly *patched with white. Male:* Blackish on head, breast, and back. *Female and immature:* Brownish. Often sits still for long periods. **VOICE:** Nasal, wheezy *wheeeah.* Often silent. **SIMILAR SPECIES:** Northern Mockingbird, juvenile Spotted Towhee. **RANGE:** Casual late-summer visitor from Mex. to se. AZ and w. TX. **HABITAT:** Mixed montane woodlands, especially pine-oak forests.

♂

♀

juvenile

AMERICAN
ROBIN

♂

♀

juvenile

VARIED
THRUSH

♂

♂

♀

RUFOUS-BACKED
ROBIN

AZTEC
THRUSH

MOCKINGBIRDS AND THRASHERS
Family Mimidae

Often called "mimic thrushes." Excellent songsters; some mimic other birds. Strong-legged; usually longer tailed than true thrushes, bill usually longer and more decurved. **FOOD:** Insects, fruit. **RANGE:** New World.

LONG-BILLED THRASHER *Toxostoma longirostre*   Rare, local M449
11½ in. (29 cm). *Duller brown* above than Brown Thrasher, breast stripes *blacker, cheeks grayer;* bill longer, slightly more curved, and all dark. **VOICE:** Song similar to Brown Thrasher's, but more jumbled. Call a harsh *tchuk.* **SIMILAR SPECIES:** Curve-billed Thrasher. **RANGE:** Casual visitor to NM, CO. **HABITAT:** Brush, mesquite.

BROWN THRASHER *Toxostoma rufum*   Uncommon to scarce M448
11½ in. (29 cm). Slimmer but longer than a robin; *bright rufous* above, *heavily streaked* below. Note *wing bars,* slightly curved bill, long tail, and yellow eyes. **VOICE:** Song a succession of deliberate notes and phrases resembling Gray Catbird's song, but each phrase usually *in pairs.* Call a harsh *chack!* **SIMILAR SPECIES:** The various brown thrushes have shorter tails, lack distinct wing bars, are spotted (not striped), and have brown (not yellow) eyes. In s. TX see Long-billed Thrasher. **HABITAT:** Thickets, brush.

SAGE THRASHER *Oreoscoptes montanus*   Uncommon M447
8½ in. (22 cm). A bit smaller than a robin. Gray-backed, with *streaked breast, wing bars, white tail corners.* Eyes pale yellow, duller in immature. Small size, shorter tail, *shorter bill* distinguish it from other thrashers. **VOICE:** Song is clear, ecstatic warbled phrases, sometimes repeated but more often continuous, suggestive of Black-headed Grosbeak. Call a blackbirdlike *chuck.* **SIMILAR SPECIES:** Cactus Wren, Bendire's Thrasher, juvenile Northern Mockingbird. **HABITAT:** Sagebrush, mesas; in winter, also deserts.

GRAY CATBIRD *Dumetella carolinensis*   Uncommon M445
8¾ in. (23 cm). Slate gray; slim. Note *black cap. Chestnut undertail coverts.* Flips tail jauntily. **VOICE:** *Catlike mewing;* distinctive. Also a grating *tcheck-tcheck.* Song is disjointed notes and phrases; not repetitious, compared with other mimids. **SIMILAR SPECIES:** Northern Mockingbird. **HABITAT:** Riparian undergrowth, brush.

NORTHERN MOCKINGBIRD *Mimus polyglottos*   Common M446
10 in. (25 cm). A familiar and conspicuous species. Slimmer, longer tailed than a robin. Note *large white patches* on wings and tail. **VOICE:** Song a varied, prolonged succession of notes and phrases, may be repeated a half-dozen times or more before changing. Often heard at night. Mockingbirds are excellent mimics. Call a loud *tchack;* also *chair.* **SIMILAR SPECIES:** Shrikes have dark facial masks. Sage Thrasher looks similar to juvenile mockingbird but has distinct streaks, not spots, and lacks large white flashes in tail and wings. **HABITAT:** Towns, parks, gardens, farms, roadsides, thickets.

THRASHERS AND MOCKINGBIRDS

LONG-BILLED
THRASHER

BROWN
THRASHER

SAGE
THRASHER

GRAY
CATBIRD

NORTHERN
MOCKINGBIRD

wing-flashing

juvenile

shrike (p. 256)
for comparison

CALIFORNIA THRASHER
Fairly common M452

Toxostoma redivivum

12 in. (31 cm). A large, brownish thrasher, with *pale cinnamon belly and undertail coverts;* tail long; bill long and *sickle-shaped.* Eyes dark brown. **VOICE:** Call a dry *chak,* also a sharp *g-leek.* Song a long, sustained series of notes and phrases, some musical, some harsh. Phrases may be *repeated* once or twice, but not several times as in Northern Mockingbird; song more leisurely than Mocker's. **SIMILAR SPECIES:** Crissal Thrasher has chestnut undertail coverts; ranges do not overlap. **HABITAT:** Chaparral, coastal sage scrub, thickets, parks.

CRISSAL THRASHER *Toxostoma crissale*
Uncommon M453

11½ in. (29 cm). A *dark* plain thrasher of desert, with long, *deeply curved bill.* Note *chestnut undertail coverts* (or "crissum"). **VOICE:** Song sweeter and less spasmodic than in other thrashers. Call *pichoory,* repeated two or three times. **SIMILAR SPECIES:** California Thrasher. **HABITAT:** Dense brush along desert streams, mesquite, willows, locally at higher elevations in manzanita, scrub oak.

LE CONTE'S THRASHER
Uncommon to scarce M454

Toxostoma lecontei

11 in. (28 cm). A *very pale* thrasher of driest deserts. Shows contrastingly *darker tail.* Salmon-rust undertail coverts. Eyes dark and stand out on plain face. Rather shy. Runs long distances on ground. **VOICE:** Song (Jan.–Apr.) similar to other thrashers. Call *ti-reep,* rising on second syllable. **SIMILAR SPECIES:** Crissal and California thrashers much darker. **HABITAT:** Desert flats with sparse bushes, mostly saltbush *(Atriplex)* or creosote bush.

CURVE-BILLED THRASHER
Fairly common M451

Toxostoma curvirostre

11 in. (28 cm). This, the most common desert thrasher, can be told from others that have *well-curved* bill by *mottled breast.* Some individuals have narrow white wing bars. Eyes pale orange. *Juvenile:* Yellow eyes, somewhat straighter bill. **VOICE:** Call a sharp, liquid *whit-wheet!* (like a whistle to attract attention). Song a musical series of notes and phrases, almost grosbeaklike in quality but faster. Not much repetition. **SIMILAR SPECIES:** Bendire's Thrasher. **HABITAT:** Deserts, arid brush, lower canyons, ranch yards, residential areas.

BENDIRE'S THRASHER
Uncommon, local M450

Toxostoma bendirei

9¾ in. (25 cm). Similar to Curve-billed Thrasher but with *shorter, straighter bill* with *pale base;* breast spots smaller and more triangular (except when worn). Eyes usually *yellow.* **VOICE:** Song a *continuous,* clear, double-note warble, not broken into phrases. Call a soft *tirup.* **SIMILAR SPECIES:** Young Curve-billed may have a bill as short as Bendire's, and yellow eyes. Sage Thrasher has much shorter, straighter bill. **HABITAT:** Deserts, yuccas, dry brushy farmland.

CALIFORNIA
THRASHER

CRISSAL
THRASHER

LE CONTE'S
THRASHER

CURVE-BILLED
THRASHER

TX and NM

AZ

BENDIRE'S THRASHER

PIPITS AND WAGTAILS Family Motacillidae

Pipits are streaked brown ground birds with white outer tail feathers, long hind claws, thin bill. They walk briskly, and most wag their tail. Wagtails are widespread in the Old World; two species breed in AK. Long tails are wagged constantly; flight undulating. FOOD: Insects, seeds. RANGE: Nearly worldwide.

AMERICAN PIPIT *Anthus rubescens*   Fairly common M459
6½ in. (17 cm). A *slim-billed, sparrowlike* bird of open country. *Bobs tail as it walks.* Underparts buffy (breeding) or streaked (nonbreeding); *outer tail feathers white;* legs dusky. Asian subspecies *(japonicus)*, rare in w. AK, casual farther south, more boldly streaked, brighter pinkish legs. VOICE: Call a thin *jeet* or *jee-eet.* In aerial song flight, a repeated *chwee chwee chwee chwee,* etc. SIMILAR SPECIES: Red-throated and Sprague's pipits. Sparrows have thicker bills, do not wag tails. HABITAT: In summer, Arctic and alpine tundra; in migration and winter, fields, short-grass habitats, shores.

SPRAGUE'S PIPIT *Anthus spragueii*   Uncommon, secretive M460
6½ in. (17 cm). More solitary and furtive than American Pipit. When flushed, often towers high, then drops like a rock back to ground. Note *striped back, plain buffy face with beady dark eye, pinkish legs.* Does *not* wag tail. VOICE: Sings high in air; a sweet, thin jingling series, descending in pitch: *shiing-a-ring-a-ring-a-ring-a.* Flight call a distinctive *squeet* or *squeet-squeet.* SIMILAR SPECIES: Juvenile Horned Lark. HABITAT: Short- to medium-grass prairies and fields.

RED-THROATED PIPIT *Anthus cervinus*   Rare, local M458
6 in. (15 cm). Rare Pacific Coast visitor in autumn. A few nest in w. AK. *Adult:* Breeding male has *pinkish red face and breast;* less extensive in female and nonbreeding male. *Immature:* Similar to American Pipit but more *heavily streaked below; bold striping on back,* pinkish legs. VOICE: Call a high, thin *speee* and a hoarse *tzeez.* HABITAT: In summer, hillside tundra; migrants often found in flocks of American Pipits.

WHITE WAGTAIL *Motacilla alba*   Rare, local M457
7¼ in. (18 cm). Note bold head pattern, gray back, and white wing patches. "Black-backed" Wagtail *(M. a. lugens)* has *black back* in breeding plumage, *more white in wings.* VOICE: Call a lively *tchizzik,* also an abrupt *tchik.* SIMILAR SPECIES: Immature Eastern Yellow Wagtails have less white in face and wings; slightly shorter tail; different call. HABITAT: Tundra, open country, shorelines.

EASTERN YELLOW WAGTAIL   Uncommon, local M456
Motacilla tschutschensis
6½ in. (17 cm). *Adult:* Variably *yellow below. Immature:* Dull whitish below, some tinged yellow; throat outlined in dark. VOICE: Call a buzzy *tsoueep.* Song *tsip-tsip-tsipsi.* HABITAT: Willow scrub on tundra, marshy country, shorelines.

PIPITS AND WAGTAILS

American and Red-throated pipits wag their tails

breeding

AMERICAN PIPIT

nonbreeding

SPRAGUE'S PIPIT

Sprague's overhead

towering flight

breeding ♀

RED-THROATED PIPIT

immature

breeding ♂

nonbreeding

breeding ♂

WHITE WAGTAIL

breeding ♂

"Black-backed"

breeding ♂

...STERN ...LLOW ...GTAIL

immature

breeding ♂

WAXWINGS Family Bombycillidae

Pointed crest may be raised or lowered. Waxy red tips on secondaries in adults. Gregarious. **FOOD**: Berries, insects. **RANGE**: N. Hemisphere.

BOHEMIAN WAXWING Uncommon, irregular M461
Bombycilla garrulus
8¼ in. (21 cm). Similar to Cedar Waxwing, but larger and grayer, with *no yellow on belly;* wings with strong *white and yellow* markings; *rusty* undertail coverts. **VOICE**: Rougher than thin Cedar. **HABITAT**: In summer, boreal forests, muskeg; in winter, widespread in search of berries, especially fruiting trees in towns.

CEDAR WAXWING *Bombycilla cedrorum* Common M462
7¼ in. (18 cm). Note *yellow band* at tip of tail, black mark. A sleek, crested, brown bird, larger than House Sparrow. *Juvenile:* Grayer, with blurry streaks below. Waxwings are gregarious in nonbreeding season, flying and feeding in compact flocks. **VOICE**: High, thin lisp or *zeee;* slightly trilled. **SIMILAR SPECIES**: Bohemian Waxwing. **HABITAT**: Open woodlands, riparian willows and alders, orchards; in winter, widespread, including towns, fruiting trees and bushes; nomadic.

SILKY-FLYCATCHERS Family Ptilogonatidae

Slim, crested, waxwinglike birds. **FOOD**: Berries, insects. **RANGE**: Sw. U.S. to Panama.

PHAINOPEPLA *Phainopepla nitens* Uncommon M463
7¾ in. (20 cm). Both sexes are sleek, crested, with red eye. *Male:* Glossy black with conspicuous *white wing patches* in flight. *Female:* Dark gray; wing patches light, not as conspicuous as male's. Eats berries but also catches insects. **VOICE**: Call a soft, rising *wurp* and harsher *churrrr.* Song a weak, casual warble, wheezy and disconnected. **SIMILAR SPECIES**: Cedar Waxwing, Northern Mockingbird. **HABITAT**: Desert scrub, mesquite, mistletoe (especially), oak foothills, pepper trees.

STARLINGS Family Sturnidae

A varied family; some blackbirdlike. Sharp-billed, usually short-tailed. **FOOD**: Insects, seeds, berries. **RANGE**: Widespread in Old World. Introduced in New World.

EUROPEAN STARLING *Sturnus vulgaris* Common M455
8½ in. (22 cm). Introduced from Europe in 1890. A gregarious, garrulous "blackbird"; shape of a meadowlark with *short tail* and *sharply pointed bill.* In flight, has *triangular wings. Breeding:* Plumage iridescent, bill *yellow. Nonbreeding: Heavily speckled with white,* bill dark. *Juvenile:* Dusky gray-brown, a bit like a female cowbird, but tail shorter, bill longer. **VOICE**: Harsh *tseeeer;* a whistled *whooee.* Also clear whistles, clicks, chuckles; often mimics other birds. **SIMILAR SPECIES**: Cedar Waxwing, in flight. **HABITAT**: Cities, suburbs, parks, feeders, farms, livestock pens, open groves, fields. Has had substantial negative impact on several native cavity-nesting species.

WAXWINGS, PHAINOPEPLA, AND STARLING

CEDAR WAXWING

juvenile

BOHEMIAN WAXWING

♂ ♀

PHAINOPEPLA

breeding

juvenile

nonbreeding

EUROPEAN STARLING

OLIVE WARBLER Family Peucedramidae

Formerly considered a wood-warbler but now placed in its own family. Young males may take two full years to reach adult plumage. Longer winged than wood-warblers, and tail deeply notched. **FOOD**: Insects. **RANGE**: Pine and oak forests at higher elevations from se. AZ and sw. NM to Nicaragua.

OLIVE WARBLER *Peucedramus taeniatus*   Uncommon, local M464
5¼ in. (13 cm). *Male:* Note *orange-brown head* and *black ear patch.* *Female:* Crown tinged olive; head duller, paler. *Immature:* Like female, but may lack most yellow. All plumages show *deeply notched tail* and bold wing bars with *white patch at base of primaries.* **VOICE**: Song a ringing *peter peter peter peter,* variable. Call a rich *kew.* **SIMILAR SPECIES**: Female Grace's Warbler, Western Tanager. **HABITAT**: Pine and fir forests of high mountains, occasionally to lower pine-oak canyon woodland in winter.

WOOD-WARBLERS Family Parulidae

Small, active, brightly colored birds, with thin, needle-pointed bill. The majority have some yellow in plumage. **FOOD**: Mainly insects though many species also eat fruit in fall and winter. **RANGE**: AK and Canada to n. Argentina.

"LAWRENCE'S" WARBLER   Vagrant
Recessive hybrid of Blue-winged × Golden-winged warbler combination. Yellow below like Blue-winged; head pattern of Golden-winged. **VOICE**: Like either parent. **RANGE**: Accidental in West. **HABITAT**: Same as Blue-winged and Golden-winged warblers.

GOLDEN-WINGED WARBLER *Vermivora chrysoptera*   Casual
4¾ in. (12 cm). *Male: Yellow wing patch* and *black throat. Female:* Ear and throat patches grayer. **VOICE**: Song a buzzy note followed by three on a lower pitch: *bee-bz-bz-bz.* Call like Blue-winged's. **SIMILAR SPECIES**: "Brewster's," "Lawrence's," and Blue-winged warblers. **RANGE**: Casual vagrant from East. **HABITAT**: Open woodlands, swampy edges, brushy clearings, undergrowth. Declining.

"BREWSTER'S" WARBLER   Vagrant
Golden-winged and Blue-winged warblers regularly hybridize, producing two basic types, "Lawrence's" and "Brewster's" warblers ("Brewster's" is the more frequent hybrid and more variable). Typical "Brewster's" is like Blue-winged with whitish underparts. Some have white wing bars, others yellow; some are tinged with yellow below. **RANGE**: Casual vagrant from East. **VOICE**: Like either parent. **HABITAT**: Same as Blue-winged and Golden-winged warblers.

BLUE-WINGED WARBLER *Vermivora cyanoptera*   Casual
4¾ in. (12 cm). Note *narrow black line through eye.* Underparts yellow, with white undertail coverts; *white wing bars.* Female duller than male. **VOICE**: Song a buzzy *beeee-bzzz,* as if inhaled and exhaled. Call a sharp *tsik.* **SIMILAR SPECIES**: Prothonotary and Yellow warblers. **RANGE**: Casual vagrant from East. **HABITAT**: Field edges, woodland openings.

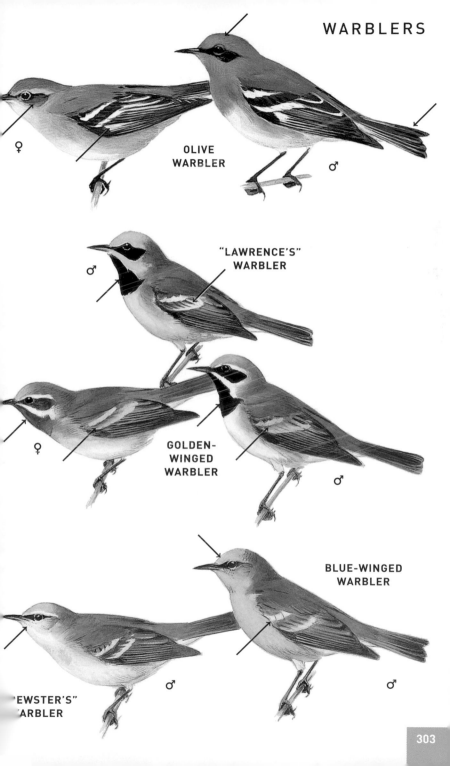

WARBLERS

♀

OLIVE
WARBLER

♂

♂

"LAWRENCE'S"
WARBLER

♀

GOLDEN-
WINGED
WARBLER

♂

BLUE-WINGED
WARBLER

♂

"BREWSTER'S"
WARBLER

♂

TENNESSEE WARBLER *Oreothlypis peregrina*   Uncommon M465
4¾ in. (12 cm). Note short tail, *bold eyebrow, white undertail coverts.*
Breeding male: Pale gray head contrasting with greenish back. *Female
and immature:* Washed with yellow-green; often showing a trace of a
single wing bar. **VOICE:** Song staccato, three-part: *ticka ticka ticka
ticka, swit swit, chew-chew-chew-chew-chew.* Call a sweet *chip.* **SIMI-
LAR SPECIES:** Orange-crowned Warbler. Warbling and Philadelphia
vireos. **HABITAT:** Deciduous and mixed forests.

ORANGE-CROWNED WARBLER *Oreothlypis celata*   Common M466
5 in. (13 cm). Usually drab *olive green* with *yellow undertail coverts*
and *blurry breast streaking.* Subspecies vary in brightness: orange of
crown seldom visible. **VOICE:** Song a colorless trill, becoming weaker
toward end. Often changes pitch, rising or dropping slightly. Call a
sharp *stik.* **SIMILAR SPECIES:** Tennessee, Yellow, and Wilson's warblers. **HABITAT:** Open woodlands, brushy clearings, willows, alders,
chaparral, parks, gardens.

COLIMA WARBLER *Oreothlypis crissalis*   Scarce, local M469
5¾ in. (15 cm). Found in Chisos Mts. in w. TX. Drab, with yellow rump
and undertail coverts. Larger than Virginia's; sides brownish; lacks
yellow on breast. **VOICE:** Song a trill, like Orange-crowned Warbler,
but more musical and ending in two lower notes. **SIMILAR SPECIES:**
Lucy's and Virginia's warblers. **HABITAT:** Oak-pine canyons.

NASHVILLE WARBLER *Oreothlypis ruficapilla*   Uncommon M467
4¾ in. (12 cm). Note *white eye-ring* in combination with *yellow* throat.
Head gray, contrasting with olive green back. No wing bars. Underparts bright yellow with white vent. Regularly bobs tail. **VOICE:** Song
two-part: *seebit, seebit, seebit, seebit, titititi* (ends like Chipping
Sparrow's song). Call a sharp *pink.* **SIMILAR SPECIES:** Connecticut
Warbler is larger, behaves very differently (*walks on limbs and
ground, does* not *flutter about actively*), and has grayish or brownish
throat. Virginia's has *gray back, white throat.* **HABITAT:** Open mixed
woods, edges, bogs; in migration, also brushy areas.

VIRGINIA'S WARBLER *Oreothlypis virginiae*   Uncommon M468
4¾ in. (12 cm). *Male:* A slim *gray* warbler with *yellowish rump* and *undertail coverts, white eye-ring,* rufous spot on crown (usually concealed), and touch of yellow on breast. Flicks or jerks tail. *Female:*
Duller. *Immature:* Lacks yellow on breast. **VOICE:** Song loose, colorless notes on nearly the same pitch: *chlip-chlip-chlip-chlip-chlip-
wick-wick.* Call like Nashville. **SIMILAR SPECIES:** Nashville and Lucy's
warblers. **HABITAT:** Oak canyons, brushy slopes, pinyon-juniper.

LUCY'S WARBLER *Oreothlypis luciae*   Uncommon M470
4¼ in. (11 cm). A small desert warbler; known by its *chestnut rump
patch.* Dull white eye-ring, small patch of chestnut on crown (difficult
to see). *Immature:* May show touch of peach-buff on breast. **VOICE:**
High *weeta weeta weeta che che che che,* on two pitches. Call a sharp
pink, like Virginia's Warbler. **SIMILAR SPECIES:** Virginia's and Colima
(very local) warblers. **HABITAT:** Mesquite along desert streams and
washes; willows, cottonwoods.

WARBLERS

♀

TENNESSEE
WARBLER

immature

breeding
♂

COLIMA
WARBLER

typical

ORANGE-CROWNED
WARBLER

northern

♀

NASHVILLE
WARBLER

♂

♀

VIRGINIA'S
WARBLER

♂

♀

LUCY'S
WARBLER

♂

NORTHERN PARULA *Parula americana*　　　　　　　　**Rare**
4½ in. (11 cm). A small, short-tailed warbler, *pale bluish above,* with
yellow throat and breast, white wing bars, *greenish patch* on back,
broken eye-ring. Adult male has *dark breast-band;* immature lacks
breast-band, has greenish wash on head. **VOICE:** Song a buzzy trill
that climbs scale and trips over the top: *zeeeeeeeee-up.* Also *zh-zh-
zh-zheeeeee.* **HABITAT:** Deciduous and mixed woodlands.

TROPICAL PARULA *Parula pitiayumi*　　　　　　**Rare, local**
4½ in. (11 cm). Similar to Northern Parula. Dark head and *black face,
lacks white eye-ring.* Note *more extensive yellow on breast.* **VOICE:** Like
Northern Parula's. **RANGE:** Rare breeder in w. TX; accidental elsewhere in Southwest. **HABITAT:** Nests in oak and mixed woodlands (in
sw. TX).

YELLOW WARBLER *Dendroica petechia*　　　　**Common M471**
5 in. (13 cm). No other warbler is so extensively yellow. Even *tail spots
are yellow* (other warblers have white tail spots or none). Male has
rusty breast streaks (in female, these are faint or lacking). Note dark
beady eye. *Immature:* Lacks breast streaks; some individuals may be
quite dull, with bright yellow restricted to lower vent and undertail
coverts. May show some very faint dusky breast streaks. All show
yellow edgings to wing and tail. **VOICE:** Song a bright cheerful *tsee-
tsee-tsee-tsee-titi-wee* or *weet weet weet weet tsee-tsee wew.* Variable. Call a soft, slurred, rich *chip.* **SIMILAR SPECIES:** Shorter tailed
than Wilson's Warbler and brighter yellow individuals of Orange-
crowned Warbler, with yellow tail spots. Note vocal differences. **HAB-
ITAT:** Riparian woodlands and understory, swamp edges, particularly
alders and willows, including bordering tundra; also parks, gardens.

CHESTNUT-SIDED WARBLER *Dendroica pensylvanica*　　**Rare M472**
5 in. (13 cm). Usually holds tail cocked up at an angle. *Breeding:* Identified by combination of *yellow crown, chestnut sides. Nonbreeding:*
Lime greenish above, whitish below; narrow white eye-ring, *two pale
yellow* wing bars. Adults retain some chestnut; immatures do not.
VOICE: Song similar to Yellow Warbler's: *see see see see Miss
BEECHer* or *please please pleased to MEETcha,* last note dropping.
Call a rich, slurred *chip,* like Yellow Warbler's. **HABITAT:** Undergrowth,
overgrown field edges, small trees.

MAGNOLIA WARBLER *Dendroica magnolia*　　　**Uncommon M473**
5 in. (13 cm). The "black-and-yellow warbler." *Breeding male:* Upperparts blackish, with large white patches on wings and tail; underparts yellow, with heavy black stripes. Note black tail crossed midway by *broad white band* (from beneath, tail is white with broad black
tip). *Female and nonbreeding male:* Duller. *Immature:* Has weak
stripes on sides, but tail pattern distinctive; often shows thin, weak
grayish band across upper breast. **VOICE:** Song suggests Yellow Warbler's but is shorter: *weeta weeta weetsee* (last note rising); or a
Hooded Warbler–like *weeta weeta wit-chew.* Call an odd nasal note.
SIMILAR SPECIES: Yellow-rumped and Black-throated Green warblers. **HABITAT:** Low conifers. Most migrate east of Rockies.

↓ WARBLERS

NORTHERN
PARULA

♀

♂

TROPICAL
PARULA

♂

YELLOW WARBLER

♀

♂

immature

CHESTNUT-SIDED
WARBLER

breeding
♀

breeding
♂

immature

MAGNOLIA
WARBLER

eeding
♀

breeding
♂

CAPE MAY WARBLER *Dendroica tigrina*   Scarce M474

5 in. (13 cm). *Breeding male:* Note *chestnut* cheeks. Yellow below, striped with black; rump yellow, crown black. *Female and nonbreeding:* Lack chestnut cheeks; duller, breast often whitish, streaked. Note dull *patch of yellow behind ear, yellowish rump,* and *one wing bar bolder than the other.* Immature female distinctly *gray.* **VOICE:** Song a very high, thin *seet seet seet seet.* May be confused with song of Bay-breasted or Black-and-white warbler. **SIMILAR SPECIES:** Dull birds in nonbreeding plumage may be confused with Yellow-rumped Warbler but have small pale patch behind ear; duller, greenish yellow rump; and shorter tail. **HABITAT:** Spruce forests; often searches out isolated spruce and fir trees in migration, also broadleaf trees. Migrates east of Rockies.

BLACK-THROATED BLUE WARBLER   Very rare
Dendroica caerulescens

5¼ in. (13 cm). *Male:* Upperparts *deep blue;* throat and sides *black,* belly white; wing with white spot. *Female:* Olive-brown, with dark cheek, eyebrow, and small *white wing spot.* Immature female may lack white "pocket handkerchief." **VOICE:** Song a husky, lazy *zur, zur, zur, zreee* or *beer, beer, bree* (ending higher). Call a hard *thip,* similar to call of Dark-eyed Junco. **SIMILAR SPECIES:** Orange-crowned Warbler shows pale crescent along leading edge of wing, not white wing spot. **RANGE:** Very rare vagrant from East. **HABITAT:** Understory of deciduous and mixed woodlands.

YELLOW-RUMPED WARBLER *Dendroica coronata*   Common M475

5½ in. (14 cm). Includes "Audubon's" and "Myrtle" warblers, two subspecies groups formerly considered separate species. Note bright *yellow rump. Breeding male:* Blue-gray above; heavy black breast patch (like an inverted U); crown and side patches yellow. "Audubon's" (breeds w. U.S., sw. Canada) differs from "Myrtle" (breeds AK, much of Canada, e. U.S.) in having *yellow throat* (which does not extend behind cheek, as white does in "Myrtle"), large white wing patches, no white supercilium. *Breeding female:* Duller. *Nonbreeding:* More brownish above; whitish below, streaked; throat yellowish (sometimes dim) in "Audubon's." **VOICE:** Variable song, junco-like but two-part, rising or dropping in pitch, *seet-seet-seet-seet-seet, trrrrrrrr.* Call a loud *check* ("Myrtle") or higher *tchip* ("Audubon's"). **HABITAT:** Nests in coniferous forests. In migration and winter, varied: open woods, brush, thickets, gardens.

BLACK-THROATED GRAY WARBLER   Fairly common M476
Dendroica nigrescens

5 in. (13 cm). *Male:* Gray above, with black throat, cheek, and crown separated by *white.* Small yellow spot in lores. *Female:* Slaty crown and cheek; dusky or light throat; loral spot duller yellow. *Immature:* May be tinged brownish above; loral spot pale. **VOICE:** Song a buzzy chant, "full of Zs," *zeedle zeedle zeedle ZEETche* (next-to-last or last note higher). Call a dull *tup.* **SIMILAR SPECIES:** Black-and-white Warbler has white stripes on back and crown, crawls around on branches and limbs. **HABITAT:** Nests in oaks, pinyon-juniper, mixed woods.

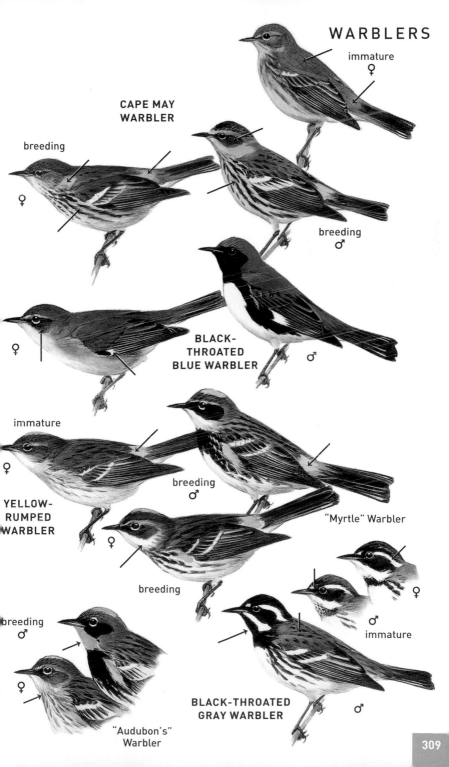

WARBLERS

immature ♀

CAPE MAY WARBLER

breeding

♀

breeding ♂

♀

BLACK-THROATED BLUE WARBLER

♂

immature ♀

YELLOW-RUMPED WARBLER

breeding ♂

"Myrtle" Warbler

♀

breeding

breeding ♂

♀

immature

♀

♂

"Audubon's" Warbler

BLACK-THROATED GRAY WARBLER

♂

309

GOLDEN-CHEEKED WARBLER *Dendroica chrysoparia*   Scarce, local
5¼ in. (14 cm). Breeds in Ashe Juniper hills of Edwards Plateau, TX.
Similar to Black-throated Green Warbler, but with *darker back* (black
in adult male), *bolder eye-line, lacks yellow tinge on flanks*. **VOICE:**
Song a hurried *tweeah, tweeah, tweesy* or *bzzzz, laysee, daysee*. Call
like Black-throated Green's. **HABITAT:** Junipers, oaks; also stream-
side trees.

HERMIT WARBLER *Dendroica occidentalis*   Uncommon M479
5 in. (13 cm). Note *yellow face with beady dark eye, gray back, unstreaked flanks*. **VOICE:** Song three high lisping notes followed by two
abrupt lower ones: *sweety, sweety, sweety, CHUP CHUP* or *seedle,
seedle, seedle, CHUP CHUP*. Call like Townsend's. **SIMILAR SPECIES:**
Townsend's Warbler. Hybrid Townsend's × Hermit warblers occur
regularly. East of Rockies, see Black-throated Green Warbler. **HABI-
TAT:** Nests in coniferous forests; in migration, coniferous and deciduous woods.

TOWNSEND'S WARBLER   Fairly common M478
Dendroica townsendi
5 in. (13 cm). *Male:* Easily distinguished by *black-and-yellow pattern
of head*, with *blackish cheek patch; underparts yellow*, with heavily
striped sides. *Female and immature:* Throat largely yellow, not black;
note *well-defined dark cheek patch*. **VOICE:** Song like Black-throated
Gray Warbler's but higher: *dzeer dzeer dzeer tseetsee* or *weazy,
weazy, seesee*. Call a soft, flat *tip*. **SIMILAR SPECIES:** Hermit and
Black-throated Green warblers. **HABITAT:** Nests in tall conifers, cool
fir forests; in migration and winter, also oaks, riparian woodlands,
parks, gardens.

BLACK-THROATED GREEN WARBLER   Uncommon M477
Dendroica virens
5 in. (13 cm). *Male:* Bright *yellow face* is framed by black throat and
olive green crown. *Female and immature:* Black on throat reduced or
lacking. Recognized by yellow face; olive green back. All birds show
small yellow spot on rear flank. **VOICE:** Lisping, weezy or buzzy *zoo
zee zoo-zoo zee* or *zee zee zee zee zoo zee; zee* notes on same pitch,
zoo notes lower. Call a flat *tip* or *tup*. **SIMILAR SPECIES:** Townsend's,
Hermit, and Golden-cheeked warblers. **HABITAT:** Mainly coniferous
or mixed woods; in migration, variety of woodlands. Migrates mostly
east of Rockies.

BLACKBURNIAN WARBLER *Dendroica fusca*   Scarce M480
5 in. (13 cm). The "fire throat." *Breeding male:* Black and white, with
flame orange on head and throat. *Female and nonbreeding:* Paler orange (adult female and immature male) or yellowish (immature female) on throat; dark cheek patch. Note head stripes, *pale back
stripes*. **VOICE:** Song *zip zip zip titi tseeeeee*, ending on a very high, up-
slurred note (inaudible to some ears). Also a two-part *teetsa teetsa
teetsa teetsa zizizizizi*, more like Nashville Warbler. Call a rich *chip*.
SIMILAR SPECIES: Yellow-rumped ("Audubon's") and Yellow-throated
warblers. **HABITAT:** Woodlands; in summer, conifers.

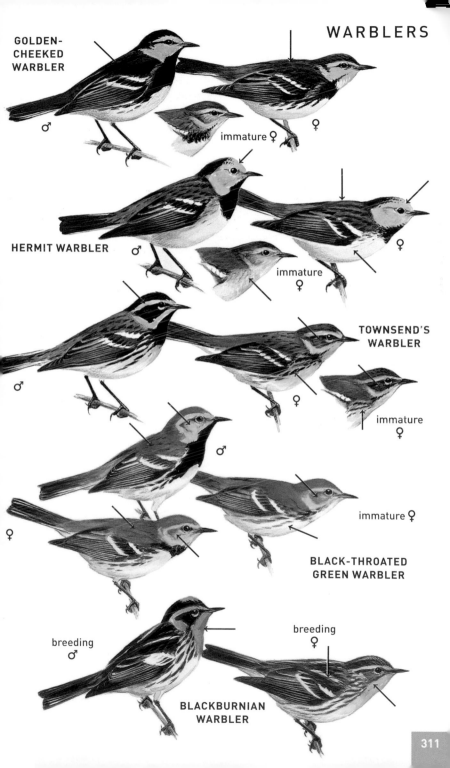

WARBLERS

GOLDEN-CHEEKED WARBLER

♂

immature ♀

♀

HERMIT WARBLER

♂

immature ♀

♀

TOWNSEND'S WARBLER

♂

immature ♀

♂

♀

immature ♀

♀

BLACK-THROATED GREEN WARBLER

breeding ♂

breeding ♀

BLACKBURNIAN WARBLER

PINE WARBLER *Dendroica pinus*   Casual
5½ in. (14 cm). All plumages show dark cheeks, blurry streaking at breast-sides, unstreaked back, and white tail spots. *Male:* Yellow-breasted, with olive green back, *white wing bars. Female:* Duller; brownish olive above; immature females often obscure. **VOICE:** Song a trill on one pitch like Chipping Sparrow's song, but more musical, slower. Call a sweet *chip.* **SIMILAR SPECIES:** Nonbreeding Blackpoll and Bay-breasted warblers. **RANGE:** Casual vagrant from East. **HABITAT:** Pines.

PRAIRIE WARBLER *Dendroica discolor*   Casual
4¾ in. (12 cm). This warbler *bobs its tail* (as does Palm Warbler); underparts yellow, paling on undertail coverts; black stripes *confined to sides and face.* **VOICE:** Song a thin *zee zee zee zee zee zee zee zee,* ascending the chromatic scale. Call a sharp *tschip.* **SIMILAR SPECIES:** Pine, Palm, and Yellow warblers. **RANGE:** Casual vagrant from East. **HABITAT:** Brushy fields, low pines, mangroves.

PALM WARBLER *Dendroica palmarum*   Uncommon M482
5¼ in. (14 cm). Note constant *bobbing* of tail. Both sexes brownish or olive above; yellowish or dirty white below, narrowly streaked; *bright yellow* undertail coverts, white spots in tail corners. In breeding plumage has *chestnut cap.* Two subspecies: Eastern breeders (casual vagrants in West) show more yellow below and on eyebrow; western breeders duller, may have yellow restricted to undertail coverts in fall. **VOICE:** Song weak, repetitious notes: *zhe-zhe-zhe-zhe-zhe-zhe.* Call a distinctive sharp *tsup.* **SIMILAR SPECIES:** Yellow-rumped Warbler. **HABITAT:** In summer, wooded borders of muskeg, bogs. In migration and winter, low trees, bushes, weedy fields. A ground-loving warbler.

YELLOW-THROATED WARBLER *Dendroica dominica*   Casual
5½ in. (14 cm). A gray-backed warbler with *yellow throat. Black eye mask,* white wing bars, black stripes on sides. Sexes similar. Creeps about branches of trees. **VOICE:** Song a series of clear slurred notes dropping slightly in pitch: *tee-ew, tew, tew, tew, tew, tew wi* (last note rising). Call a rich *chip.* **SIMILAR SPECIES:** Grace's and female Blackburnian warblers. **RANGE:** Casual vagrant from East. **HABITAT:** Open woodlands.

GRACE'S WARBLER *Dendroica graciae*   Uncommon M481
5 in. (13 cm). *Gray-backed, with yellow throat and upper breast,* two wing bars, *yellowish eyebrow stripe,* dark streaks on sides. **VOICE:** *Cheedle cheedle che che che che* (ends in a trill). Call a soft, sweet *chip.* **SIMILAR SPECIES:** Yellow-rumped ("Audubon's") Warbler. Yellow-throated Warbler, a vagrant in West, has white patch behind ear, blacker facial pattern. **HABITAT:** Pine-oak forests of canyons and mountains.

WARBLERS

immature ♀

PINE
WARBLER

♂

immature
♀

PRAIRIE
WARBLER

♀

♂

PALM
WARBLER

non-
breeding

western

breeding

western

breeding

eastern

YELLOW-
THROATED
WARBLER

GRACE'S
WARBLER

BAY-BREASTED WARBLER *Dendroica castanea* Scarce M483
5½ in. (14 cm). *Breeding male:* Dark looking, with *chestnut throat, upper breast,* and sides. Note *buff patch* on neck. *Breeding female:* Paler, with whitish throat. *Nonbreeding:* Olive green above; two white wing bars; pale *yellow breast, buff flanks and undertail coverts, dark feet; no streaks on back or breast.* **VOICE:** High, sibilant *tees teesi teesi;* resembles song of Black-and-white Warbler, but thinner, shorter, more on one pitch. Call a sharp *chip,* like Blackpoll Warbler's. **SIMILAR SPECIES:** See nonbreeding Blackpoll and Pine warblers. **HABITAT:** Woodlands; in summer, conifers. Migrates east of Rockies.

BLACK-AND-WHITE WARBLER *Mniotilta varia* Uncommon M485
5¼ in. (13 cm). *Creeping along trunks* and branches of trees, this warbler is *striped lengthwise with black and white* and has striped crown, white stripes on back. *Male:* Black throat partly or mostly lost in winter. *Female and immature:* Paler cheek, fainter streaks below, and buffy wash on flanks. **VOICE:** Song a thin *weesee weesee weesee weesee;* suggests one of American Redstart's songs, but higher pitched and longer. A second, more rambling song drops in pitch midway. Call a sharp *chip.* **SIMILAR SPECIES:** Blackpoll and Black-throated Gray warblers. **HABITAT:** Deciduous and mixed woods.

BLACKPOLL WARBLER *Dendroica striata* Uncommon M484
5½ in. (14 cm). *Breeding male:* A striped gray warbler with *black cap, white cheeks, distinct pale legs. Breeding female: Greenish gray above,* whitish below, *streaked. Nonbreeding:* Olive above, greenish yellow below, *faintly streaked* on back and on breast; two wing bars; *whitish undertail coverts;* usually *pale legs* (or at least *feet*). **VOICE:** Song a thin, deliberate, mechanical *zi-zi-zi-zi-zi-zi-zi-zi-zi* on one pitch, becoming stronger, then diminishing. Call a sharp *chip.* **SIMILAR SPECIES:** Breeding Black-and-white Warbler has white stripe through crown and on back, different behavior. Nonbreeding Bay-breasted Warbler lacks streaking on breast and flanks, has buff wash on flanks and undertail coverts, and dark feet. **HABITAT:** Nests in conifers; in migration, also broadleaf trees. Most migrate east of Rockies.

AMERICAN REDSTART *Setophaga ruticilla* Uncommon M486
5¼ in. (13 cm). Butterfly-like; actively flitting, with drooping wings and spread tail. *Adult male:* Black; *bright orange patches* on wings and tail. *Female:* Gray-olive above; *yellow flash patches* on wings and tail. *Immature male:* Like female, but tinged with orange on chest patches, sometimes with black splotches on face. **VOICE:** Songs (often alternated) *zee zee zee zee zwee* (last note higher), *tsee tsee tsee tsee tsee-o* (last syllable dropping), and *teetsa teetsa teetsa teetsa teet* (notes paired). Call a slurred, rich *chip.* **HABITAT:** Second-growth woods, riparian woodlands.

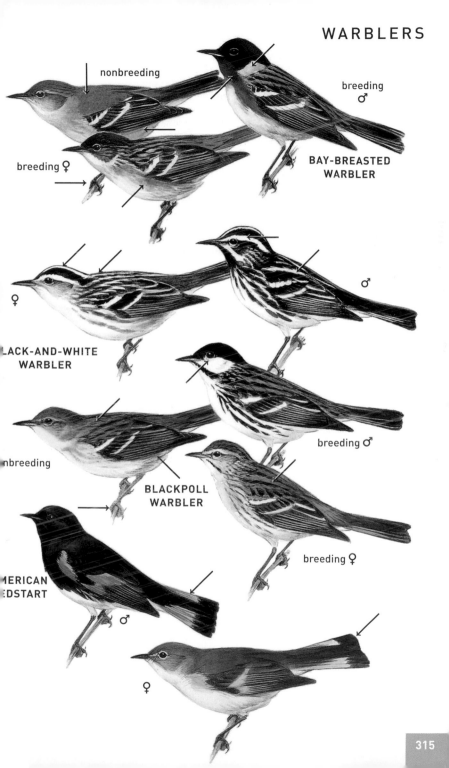

WARBLERS

nonbreeding

breeding ♂

breeding ♀

BAY-BREASTED WARBLER

♀

♂

BLACK-AND-WHITE WARBLER

breeding ♂

nbreeding

BLACKPOLL WARBLER

breeding ♀

MERICAN
EDSTART

♂

♀

OVENBIRD *Seiurus aurocapilla*　　　　　　Uncommon M487
6 in. (15 cm). When breeding, more often heard than seen. Usually seen walking on leafy floor of woods. Suggests a small thrush, but *striped* rather than spotted beneath. *Orangish patch on crown bordered by blackish stripes. White eye-ring.* **VOICE:** Song an emphatic *TEACHer, TEACHer, TEACHer,* etc., in crescendo. In some areas, monosyllabic, *TEACH, TEACH, TEACH,* etc. Call a loud, sharp *tshuk.* **SIMILAR SPECIES:** Waterthrushes. See also spotted thrushes (p. 290). **HABITAT:** Near or on ground in leafy woods; in migration, also thickets.

NORTHERN WATERTHRUSH　　Uncommon to fairly common M488
Parkesia noveboracensis
5¾ in. (15 cm). Suggests a small thrush. *Walks* along water's edge and *teeters* like a Spotted Sandpiper. Brown-backed, with *striped* underparts, strong eyebrow stripe; both eyebrow and underparts vary from whitish to pale yellow. *Throat striped.* **VOICE:** Call a sharp *chink.* Song a vigorous, rapid *twit twit twit sweet sweet sweet chew chew chew* (*chew*s drop in pitch). **SIMILAR SPECIES:** Louisiana Waterthrush, Ovenbird. **HABITAT:** Swamps, bogs, wet woods with standing water, streamsides, pond shores; in migration, also marsh edges, puddles.

LOUISIANA WATERTHRUSH *Parkesia motacilla*　　Very rare M489
6 in. (15 cm). Similar to Northern Waterthrush, but underparts *white on breast, pinkish buff on flanks and undertail coverts.* Bill slightly larger. *Eyebrow stripe pure white and flares noticeably behind eye.* Throat usually *lacks stripes.* **VOICE:** Song musical and ringing; three clear slurred whistles, followed by a jumble of twittering notes dropping in pitch. **SIMILAR SPECIES:** Some nonbreeding Northern Waterthrushes (particularly western form, *S. n. notabilis*) have whitish eyebrow stripe. Northern has small spots or stripes on throat and ground color of underparts is *even-toned* (yellow to off-white), not bicolored like Louisiana. **RANGE:** Eastern species. Rare in s. AZ in winter; casual west to CA. **HABITAT:** Streams, brooks.

WORM-EATING WARBLER *Helmitheros vermivorum*　　Casual
5¼ in. (13 cm). An unobtrusive forager of woodlands. Often probes dead-leaf clusters. *Dull olive,* with *black stripes on buffy head.* Breast *rich buff.* **VOICE:** Song a series of thin dry notes; resembles trill or rattle of Chipping Sparrow, but thinner, more rapid, and insectlike. Call a flat *chip,* also a high *zeet-zeet* in flight. **SIMILAR SPECIES:** Ovenbird, waterthrushes. **RANGE:** Casual vagrant from East. **HABITAT:** Woodlands, undergrowth.

PROTHONOTARY WARBLER *Protonotaria citrea*　　Casual
5½ in. (14 cm). A golden bird. *Male:* Entire head and breast deep *yellow to orangey.* Wings blue-gray *with no bars. Female:* Duller. **VOICE:** Song *zweet zweet zweet zweet zweet zweet,* on one pitch. Call a loud *seep.* **RANGE:** Casual visitor from East. **SIMILAR SPECIES:** Yellow and Blue-winged warblers. **HABITAT:** Moist woodlands, backwaters, river edges.

WARBLERS

OVENBIRD

NORTHERN
WATERTHRUSH

whitish
variant

typical

LOUISIANA
WATERTHRUSH

WORM-EATING
WARBLER

♀

♂

PROTHONOTARY
WARBLER

KENTUCKY WARBLER *Oporornis formosus*   Casual

5¼ in. (13 cm). Note *broad black sideburns* and *yellow spectacles.*
VOICE: Song a rapid rolling chant, *tory-tory-tory-tory* or *churry-churry-churry-churry,* suggestive of Carolina Wren, but less musical. Call a rich, low *tup.* **SIMILAR SPECIES:** Common Yellowthroat lacks spectacles. See also Hooded Warbler. **RANGE:** Very rare vagrant from East to Southwest and CA. **HABITAT:** Woodland undergrowth.

CONNECTICUT WARBLER *Oporornis agilis*   Scarce M490

5¾–6 in. (15 cm). Shy and skulking. Similar to MacGillivray's and Mourning warblers, but slightly larger; note *walking behavior* — on limbs and ground — and *complete white eye-ring, long undertail coverts* reaching almost to tail tip. *Breeding:* Hood gray in male, gray-brown in female. *Nonbreeding female and immature:* Duller, with brownish hood, paler throat. **VOICE:** Repetitious *chip-chup-ee, chip-chup-ee, chip-chup-ee, chip* or *sugar-tweet, sugar-tweet, sugar-tweet.* **SIMILAR SPECIES:** Breeding Mourning Warbler lacks eye-ring (but immature has slightly broken one). Male has black throat. Also, Connecticut walks, Mourning hops. Nashville Warbler also has eye-ring, but is smaller, has yellow throat, and is a more active feeder. See also MacGillivray's Warbler. **HABITAT:** Poplar bluffs, muskeg, mixed woods; in migration, undergrowth. Feeds mostly on ground. Migrates east of Rockies.

MOURNING WARBLER *Oporornis philadelphia*   Scarce M491

5¼ in. (13 cm). Shy and skulking. Olive above, yellow below, with slate gray hood encircling head and neck. *Male:* Has irregular black bib. *Female and immature:* May have thin, light eye-ring that is barely broken, typically not thicker eye-arcs of MacGillivray's Warbler, but this difference may be minimal. Some breeding females and most nonbreeding birds show yellow wash on throat, sometimes extending through middle breast and resulting in bird *not* appearing "hooded." Yellow undertail coverts of medium length of the three similar *Oporornis* warblers. **VOICE:** Song *chirry, chirry, chorry, chorry* (*chorry* lower). Considerable variation. Call a hard, buzzy, wrenlike *chack.* **SIMILAR SPECIES:** MacGillivray's and Connecticut warblers. **HABITAT:** Thickets, undergrowth. Migrates east of Rockies.

MACGILLIVRAY'S WARBLER *Oporornis tolmiei*   Uncommon M492

5¼ in. (13 cm). *Male:* Olive above, yellow below, with *slate gray hood* (blackish lores and upper breast) completely encircling head and neck. *Partial white eye-ring is broken fore and aft, forming crescent shapes. Female:* Similar, but hood paler, washed out on throat. *Immature:* Like a dull female. **VOICE:** Song a rolling *chiddle-chiddle-chiddle, turtle-turtle,* last notes dropping; or *sweeter-sweeter-sweeter, sugar-sugar.* Call a low, hard *chik,* given often. **SIMILAR SPECIES:** Immature told from young Mourning Warbler in fall by *grayish white,* not yellowish, throat and by complete pale grayish breast-band. Some Orange-crowned Warblers also have grayish head contrasting with olivey yellow body and pale, broken eye-ring; but they are shaped and behave differently, are duller yellow, and have blurry breast streaks. See voice. **HABITAT:** Low dense undergrowth.

WARBLERS

KENTUCKY
WARBLER

Nashville Warbler
(p. 304)
for comparison

♂

♀

CONNECTICUT
WARBLER

mature

♀

MOURNING
WARBLER

♂

immature
♀

♀

MACGILLIVRAY'S
WARBLER

♂

immature
♀

COMMON YELLOWTHROAT *Geothlypis trichas*   Common M493
5 in. (13 cm). Wrenlike. *Male: Black (Lone Ranger) mask,* yellow throat
and upper breast. *Female and immature:* Olive-brown, with rich
yellow throat, duller below, but brighter yellow undertail coverts;
lack or have only a suggestion of black mask. **VOICE:** Bright rapid
chant, *witchity-witchity-witchity-witch;* sometimes *witchy-witchy-witchy-witch.* Call a husky *tchep.* **SIMILAR SPECIES:** Female and immature distinguished from immature *Oporornis* warbler by whitish
belly, smaller size. **HABITAT:** Swamps, marshes, wet thickets, woodland edges.

WILSON'S WARBLER *Wilsonia pusilla*   Common M494
4¾ in. (12 cm). Note longish tail, dark beady eye. *Male:* Golden yellow
with *round black cap. Female:* May show trace of cap (on forecrown).
Immature: Some lack even suggestion of dark cap; they are golden-looking birds with yellow stripe above *beady eye* and *yellow lores.*
Constantly moving and flitting about. **VOICE:** Song a thin, rapid little
chatter, dropping in pitch at end: *chi chi chi chi chi chet chet.* Call a
flat *timp.* **SIMILAR SPECIES:** Yellow Warbler has yellow spots on
shorter tail, yellow edging in wings. See also Orange-crowned Warbler. Vocal differences important. Female Hooded Warbler has white
spots on tail, dark lores. **HABITAT:** Thickets and trees along streams,
moist tangles, low shrubs, willows, alders.

HOODED WARBLER *Wilsonia citrina*   Casual
5¼ in. (13 cm). *Male: Black hood* or cowl encircles yellow face and
forehead. *Female:* Lacks hood, although yellow face may be sharply
outlined (adults); aside from *white tail spots,* may lack other distinctive marks. **VOICE:** Song a loud whistled *weeta wee-tee-o.* Also other
arrangements; slurred *tee-o* is a clue. Call a sharp *chink,* like waterthrushes or California Towhee. **SIMILAR SPECIES:** Female and immature Wilson's Warbler lack tail spots and any suggestion of Hooded's
face pattern. **RANGE:** Rare to casual vagrant from East. **HABITAT:**
Wooded undergrowth.

CANADA WARBLER *Wilsonia canadensis*   Scarce M495
5¼ in. (13 cm). The "necklaced warbler." *Male: Solid gray above;*
bright yellow below, with *necklace of short black stripes;* white vent.
Female and immature: Similar; necklace fainter, upperparts may be
washed with brownish. All have *spectacles of white eye-ring and yellow loral stripe.* No white in wings or tail. **VOICE:** Song a staccato
burst, irregularly arranged. *Chip, chupety swee-ditchety.* Call *tchip.*
SIMILAR SPECIES: Magnolia and Grace's warblers. **HABITAT:** Forest
undergrowth, shady thickets. Migrates east of Rockies.

WARBLERS

COMMON
YELLOWTHROAT

♀

♂

♀

WILSON'S
WARBLER

♂

♀

♀

HOODED
WARBLER

♂

♀

CANADA
WARBLER

♂

321

PAINTED REDSTART *Myioborus pictus*   Uncommon M497
5¾ in. (15 cm). Beautiful; postures with half-spread wings and tail, showing off *large white patches*. Black head and upperparts; *large bright red patch* on lower breast and belly. White crescent under eye. *Juvenile:* Lacks red. **VOICE:** Song a repetitious *weeta weeta weeta wee* or *weeta weeta chilp chilp chilp*. Call *clee-ip*, suggesting a siskin, not warbler. **SIMILAR SPECIES:** Red-faced Warbler, American Redstart. **HABITAT:** Pine-oak canyons and mountains; comes to sugar-water feeders.

RED-FACED WARBLER   Uncommon, local M496
Cardellina rubrifrons
5½ in. (14 cm). The only U.S. warbler with *bright red face*. Has gray back, black patch on head, and white nape. Females and immatures only slightly duller than adult male. **VOICE:** Clear, sweet song, similar to Yellow Warbler. Call a sharp *chip* or *chup*. **SIMILAR SPECIES:** Painted Redstart has overlapping range in Southwest. **HABITAT:** Open fir and pine-oak forests in upper canyons, mountains.

RUFOUS-CAPPED WARBLER *Basileuterus rufifrons*   Casual
5 in. (13 cm). *Rufous cap and cheek* separated by white eyebrow stripe. Throat and upper breast bright yellow, upperparts olive. Long, spindly tail often held cocked up at angle. **VOICE:** Accelerating series of whistled, musical chips and warbles. Call *tick*. **SIMILAR SPECIES:** Common Yellowthroat. **RANGE:** Visitor from Mex. to s. AZ and w. TX. **HABITAT:** Thick brush, oak woodlands near water.

YELLOW-BREASTED CHAT *Icteria virens*   Uncommon M498
7½ in. (19 cm). Our largest warbler with *heavy bill* and *long tail*. Note *white* spectacles, *bright yellow* throat and breast. No wing bars. Habitat and voice suggest a thrasher or mockingbird. **VOICE:** Repeated whistles, alternating with harsh notes and soft *caws*. Suggests Northern Mockingbird, but repertoire more limited; much longer pauses between phrases. Single notes: *whoit, kook, zhairr*, etc. Often sings in short, awkward courtship display flight. **SIMILAR SPECIES:** Common Yellowthroat (much smaller). **HABITAT:** Brushy tangles, briars, stream thickets.

PAINTED REDSTART

adult

juvenile

RED-FACED WARBLER

RUFOUS-CAPPED WARBLER

♂

Common Yellowthroat
(p. 320)
for comparison

YELLOW-BREASTED CHAT

Cardinals, Buntings, and Allies
Family Cardinalidae (see p. 346)

HEPATIC TANAGER *Piranga flava*   Uncommon, local M542
8 in. (20 cm). *Male:* Darker than Summer Tanager; orange-red, *brightest on crown and throat,* with *dark ear patch, dark bill, grayish flanks. Female:* Dull yellowish and gray, but shares male's pattern with dusky gray bill, cheeks, and flanks; yellow on throat may be tinged orange. **VOICE:** Song very similar to Black-headed Grosbeak's. Call a single *chuck.* **SIMILAR SPECIES:** Summer Tanager. **HABITAT:** Nests in open mountain and canyon woodlands with oaks, pines.

SUMMER TANAGER *Piranga rubra*   Uncommon M543
7¾ in. (20 cm). *Male: Rose red,* with *pale* bill. *Female: Mustard yellow* below, sometimes flushed with orange; pale bill. Young males may be patched with red. **VOICE:** Call a staccato *pi-tuk* or *pik-i-tuk-i-tuk.* Song robinlike phrases, richer and less nasal than Western Tanager's. **SIMILAR SPECIES:** Northern Cardinal. Hepatic Tanager has darker bill, grayish cheek, grayish flanks; brightest on crown and throat. **HABITAT:** Riparian woodlands, oaks.

SCARLET TANAGER *Piranga olivacea*   Casual
7 in. (18 cm). *Breeding male: Flaming scarlet,* with *jet-black* wings and tail. *Female and nonbreeding male: Greenish olive* above, *yellowish* below; male has *blackish wings;* young has single faint wing bar. **VOICE:** Song similar to Western's. Call *chip-burr.* **SIMILAR SPECIES:** Summer and Western tanagers, Northern Cardinal, Vermilion Flycatcher. **RANGE:** Casual visitor from East. **HABITAT:** Deciduous and mixed forests, shade trees.

WESTERN TANAGER *Piranga ludoviciana*   Fairly common M544
7¼ in. (18 cm). Our only tanager with *strong wing bars. Male:* Yellow with black back, wings, and tail, and *reddish head. Female and immature:* Variably yellow below, with white belly; dull olive above, dull grayish "saddle" may be apparent on back. **VOICE:** Song is short phrases; similar to American Robin's in form, but less sustained, hoarser. Calls a dry *pr-tee* or *pri-ti-tic* and breathy *whee?* **SIMILAR SPECIES:** Resembles female orioles, but tail shorter, bill stouter. Worn birds in late summer may have very faint wing bars. **HABITAT:** Nests in open coniferous or mixed forests; widespread in migration; a few winter in blooming eucalyptus in CA.

FLAME-COLORED TANAGER *Piranga bidentata*   Casual
7¼ in. (18 cm). *Male: Fire red* with *streaked back, dark ear patch,* white wing bars, white tips on tertials and tail corners. *Female:* Looks like female Western, but note *streaked back, dark cheek patch,* pale tips on tertials and tail, and dark bill. Hybrids are known. **VOICE:** Husky and burry series of phrases, like a slowed-down Western. **RANGE:** Casual spring and summer visitor from Mex. to mountains of se. AZ; accidental to TX. **HABITAT:** Pine-oak forests.

HEPATIC
TANAGER

♂

immature

♀

♂

immature
changing
to adult

♂

♀

SUMMER
TANAGER

♂

♂ changing

nonbreeding
♂

♀

breeding
♂

orange variant
♂

SCARLET TANAGER

WESTERN
TANAGER

♀

♀

♂

nonbreeding
♂

breeding ♂

FLAME-
COLORED
TANAGER

EMBERIZIDS: SPARROWS, OLD WORLD BUNTINGS, AND RELATIVES
Family Emberizidae

This large family of songbirds, whose taxonomic relationships are incompletely understood, comprises species with short conical bills, such as seedeaters, towhees, sparrows, longspurs, and Old World buntings. FOOD: Seeds, insects, fruit, varying seasonally. RANGE: Worldwide.

GREEN-TAILED TOWHEE
Uncommon to fairly common M499

Pipilo chlorurus

7¼ in. (18 cm). A slender finchlike bird, known by its *rufous cap,* conspicuous *white throat,* gray chest, and plain *olive green upperparts.* VOICE: Call a catlike mewing note. Song variable; sweet notes, followed by burry notes: *weet-churr-cheeeeee-churr.* HABITAT: Brushy mountain slopes, open pine woods with brushy understory, sage; in winter, also brushy riparian woods.

EASTERN TOWHEE *Pipilo erythrophthalmus*
Casual M501

8 in. (20–21 cm). Formerly lumped with Spotted Towhee. Distinguished by *white base to primaries* and *lack of white spots on back.* VOICE: Song *drink-your-tea,* last syllable higher, wavering. Call a loud *chewink!* RANGE: Casual visitor from East to western plains and Southwest. HABITAT: Open woods, undergrowth, brushy edges.

SPOTTED TOWHEE *Pipilo maculatus*
Common M500

8 in. (20–21 cm). Smaller than a robin; rummages among leaf litter. Readily recognized by *rufous sides and flash of white in tail, back heavily spotted with white* (amount varying geographically). VOICE: Song a drawn-out, buzzy *chweeeeee.* Sometimes *chup chup chup zeeeeeeee;* variable. Call a catlike *gu-eeee?* or (Southwest mountains) rising and falling *chreeeer.* SIMILAR SPECIES: Eastern Towhee. HABITAT: Open woods, undergrowth, chaparral, brushy edges, gardens.

CANYON TOWHEE *Melozone fusca*
Uncommon M502

8¾ in. (22 cm). Slightly paler and grayer than California Towhee, with rufous crown, faint necklace, and dark spot on breast. VOICE: Call an odd *shed-lp* or *kedlp.* Song an accelerating string of call notes. HABITAT: Brushy areas in canyons and deserts, residential areas.

CALIFORNIA TOWHEE *Melozone crissalis*
Common M503

9 in. (23 cm). This common, ground-loving bird suggests a very plain, overgrown sparrow. Note streaked buffy throat. VOICE: Call a metallic *chink.* Song a rapid *chink-chink-ink-ink-ink-ink-ink-ink* on one pitch; often ends in trill. SIMILAR SPECIES: Canyon and Abert's towhees, California Thrasher. HABITAT: Brushy areas, chaparral, coastal sage scrub, canyons, gardens.

ABERT'S TOWHEE *Melozone aberti*
Fairly common M504

9½ in. (24 cm). A desert species, similar to Canyon Towhee, but note *blackish facial patch.* VOICE: Call a sharp *peek* and high squeal. Song a rapid series of high *peek* and lower *tuk* notes. HABITAT: Riparian scrub, desert brush, mesquite, parks.

TOWHEES

GREEN-TAILED
TOWHEE

EASTERN
TOWHEE

♀

juvenile

♂

♂

juvenile

SPOTTED TOWHEE

♀

NYON
WHEE

CALIFORNIA TOWHEE

ABERT'S
TOWHEE

RUFOUS-WINGED SPARROW
Scarce, local M505

Peucaea carpalis

5¾ in. (15 cm). An AZ specialty. Suggests Chipping Sparrow, but plumper bodied, tail not notched. *Double black "whiskers,"* rufous eye line, gray stripe through rufous crown. *Rufous shoulder* not easily seen. **VOICE:** Song one or two sweet introductory notes and a rapid series of musical chips on one pitch. **SIMILAR SPECIES:** Rufous-crowned Sparrow. **HABITAT:** Desert grasslands, thorn brush, desert hackberry, mesquite.

RUFOUS-CROWNED SPARROW
Uncommon M508

Aimophila ruficeps

6 in. (15 cm). A dark sparrow with plain dusky breast, rufous cap and line behind eye, and rounded tail. Note *black whiskers* bordering throat and *distinct circular whitish eye-ring.* Seen singly or in pairs. **VOICE:** Song stuttering, gurgling, suggesting a thin, weak House Wren song. Call *dear, dear, dear.* **SIMILAR SPECIES:** Chipping Sparrow. **HABITAT:** Grassy or rocky slopes with sparse low bushes.

BOTTERI'S SPARROW *Peucaea botterii*
Uncommon, local M507

6 in. (15 cm). Nondescript. Has buffy breast, plain brown tail lacking white corners. *Best told by voice.* Bill slightly curved on upper edge. **VOICE:** Song a constant tinkling and "pitting," sometimes running into a dry trill on same pitch. Very unlike song of Cassin's Sparrow. **SIMILAR SPECIES:** Cassin's Sparrow, breeding in same habitat, is almost identical, but grayer, has faint dusky streaks on flanks, small white corners to tail, straighter upper edge to bill; upperparts often look spotted (streaked in Botteri's). **HABITAT:** Desert grasslands and bunch grass (particularly sacaton grass).

CASSIN'S SPARROW *Peucaea cassinii*
Fairly common M506

6 in. (15 cm). A large, drab sparrow of open arid country; underparts dingy without markings, or with faint streaking on flanks. Upperparts often appear *more spotted than streaked. Pale or whitish corners* on tail. *Best clue is song.* **VOICE:** Song one or two short notes, a high sweet trill, and two lower notes: *ti ti tseeeeeee tay tay.* Often "skylarks" in air, giving trill at climax; Botteri's Sparrow does not skylark. **SIMILAR SPECIES:** Botteri's and Savannah sparrows. **HABITAT:** Desert grasslands and semiarid prairies, bushes.

SWAMP SPARROW *Melospiza georgiana*
Uncommon M529

5¾ in. (15 cm). A rather plump, dark, *rusty-winged* sparrow with tawny flanks and *broad black back striping.* Adult: Rusty cap, blue-gray neck and breast. Immature: *Blackish* or dark rust crown, *olive-gray neck and breast;* dim flank streaking. **VOICE:** Song a loose trill, similar to Chipping Sparrow's but slower, sweeter, and stronger. Call a hard *cheep,* similar to Black or Eastern phoebe. **SIMILAR SPECIES:** Song and Lincoln's sparrows. Chipping, Field, and American Tree sparrows are longer tailed and have wing bars. **HABITAT:** Nests in freshwater marshes with bushes, cattails, sedges, willows; winters in marshes, pond edges, moist brushy areas, weedy ditches.

SPARROWS

RUFOUS-
WINGED
SPARROW

RUFOUS-
CROWNED
SPARROW

BOTTERI'S
SPARROW

CASSIN'S
SPARROW

SWAMP
SPARROW

immature

adult

329

LARK SPARROW *Chondestes grammacus*   Fairly common M517
6½ in. (17 cm). *Adult:* A large pale sparrow with *quail-like head pattern,* dark *tail with much white at corners,* and dark *central breast spot* on clean grayish white underparts. *Juvenile:* Head pattern duller, a few dusky streaks on breast sides. **VOICE:** A broken song; clear notes and trills with pauses between, characterized by buzzing and churring passages. Call a sharp *tsip.* **SIMILAR SPECIES:** Vesper Sparrow. **HABITAT:** Open country with bushes, trees; pastures, roadsides.

SAGE SPARROW *Artemisiospiza belli*   Uncommon M519
6–6¼ in. (15–16 cm). A gray sparrow of arid brush. Note *breast spot, heavy dark "whiskers,"* and white eye-ring. Gray head contrasts with browner back and wing. Long tail often *flicked and waved* about. Often seen running on ground, with tail held high, like a miniature thrasher. "Bell's" Sparrow, a subspecies resident west of Sierra Nevada in CA, is darker, with heavier black whiskers. **VOICE:** Song four to seven mechanically delivered notes, *tsit-tsoo-tseee-tsay* (third note highest). Or *tsit, tsit, tsi you, tee a-tee.* Twittering call. **SIMILAR SPECIES:** Juvenile Black-throated Sparrow. **HABITAT:** Sage and saltbush flats; in winter, also creosote bush. "Bell's" found in dry brushy foothills, chaparral.

BLACK-THROATED SPARROW   Fairly common M518
Amphispiza bilineata
5½ in. (14 cm). *Adult: White face stripes* and *jet-black throat and chest. Juvenile:* Seen into fall; may be confused with Sage Sparrow but note *bold supercilium* and *blacker tail* with more white at corners. **VOICE:** Song a sweet *cheet cheet cheeeeeeee* (two short, clear opening notes and a fine trill on lower or higher pitch); calls are light tinkling notes. **SIMILAR SPECIES:** Sage Sparrow. **HABITAT:** Arid brush, creosote-bush and cactus deserts, juniper hillsides.

FIVE-STRIPED SPARROW   Very rare, local M509
Amphispiza quinquestriata
6 in. (15 cm). A rare Mexican sparrow. *Dusky,* with *five white stripes* on head (white throat, eyebrow, and jaw line) and single black spot on dark gray breast. **VOICE:** High-pitched, watery phrases, each note repeated several times, like a thrasher does. Call a sharp *tchak!* **SIMILAR SPECIES:** Black-throated and Sage sparrows. **HABITAT:** Dense shrubs on dry canyon slopes, rocky arid hillsides.

BLACK-CHINNED SPARROW *Spizella atrogularis* Uncommon M515
5¾ in. (15 cm). A small, slim, somewhat juncolike sparrow (with no white in tail); has *streaked brown back,* but *head and underparts medium gray. Breeding male: Small pinkish bill* encircled by *black chin* and facial patch. *Female and nonbreeding male:* Lack black face. **VOICE:** Song a sweet series of notes on about same pitch, or descending slightly; starts with several high, thin, clear notes and ends in rough trill, *sweet, sweet, sweet, weet-trrrrrrr.* **SIMILAR SPECIES:** Black-throated Sparrow, juncos. **HABITAT:** Brushy mountain slopes, open chaparral, juniper; winters on rocky, brushy canyon slopes, usually in flocks.

SPARROWS

adult

juvenile

LARK SPARROW

"Bell's" (coastal)

SAGE SPARROW

juvenile

adult

adult

juvenile

FIVE-STRIPED SPARROW

adult

adult

BLACK-THROATED SPARROW

♀

BLACK-CHINNED SPARROW

♂

AMERICAN TREE SPARROW *Spizella arborea*   Uncommon M510
6¼ in. (16 cm). Note *dark "stickpin,"* on breast, and *red-brown cap. Bill dark above, yellow below;* white wing bars; rufous wash on flanks. **VOICE:** Song sweet, variable, opening on one or two high, clear notes. Call *tseet;* feeding call a musical *teelwit.* **SIMILAR SPECIES:** Field and Chipping sparrows. **HABITAT:** Arctic and taiga scrub, willow thickets; in winter, brushy roadsides, weedy edges, freshwater marshes (particularly with cattails).

CHIPPING SPARROW *Spizella passerina*   Common M511
5½ in. (14 cm). *Breeding:* A small, slim, long-tailed, plain-breasted sparrow with bright *rufous cap, black eye line, white eyebrow. Nonbreeding:* Duller; note *dark eyeline, dirty grayish breast, gray rump. Juvenile:* Shows fine streaks on breast, rump not as gray; this plumage may be held until midautumn in western birds. **VOICE:** Song a dry chipping rattle on one pitch. Call a thin *tseet.* **SIMILAR SPECIES:** Clay-colored and Brewer's sparrows. Also Rufous-winged and Swamp sparrows. **HABITAT:** Open woods, especially pine, oak; orchards, farms, towns, lawns, feeders. Often forms flocks in fall and winter.

CLAY-COLORED SPARROW *Spizella pallida*   Uncommon M512
5½ in. (14 cm). Like a pale, nonbreeding Chipping Sparrow, but buffier, with *pale lores, sharply outlined ear patch,* more contrasting gray nape, bolder white mustache, *browner rump,* whiter underparts. **VOICE:** Unbirdlike; three or four low, flat buzzes: *bzzz, bzzz, bzzz.* Call a thin *tseet,* like Chipping's but higher. **SIMILAR SPECIES:** See also Brewer's Sparrow. **HABITAT:** Scrub, brushy prairies, weedy areas.

FIELD SPARROW *Spizella pusilla*   Scarce, local M514
5¾ in. (15 cm). A small, slim, rusty-capped sparrow. Note *pink bill,* white eye-ring, plain buffy breast; rusty upperparts, and weak face striping. *Juvenile:* Has finely streaked breast, but this plumage not held long. **VOICE:** Song opens on deliberate, sweet, slurring notes, speeding into a trill (which ascends, descends, or stays on same pitch). Call *tseew.* **SIMILAR SPECIES:** American Tree, Chipping, and Brewer's sparrows. **HABITAT:** Overgrown fields, pastures, brush.

BREWER'S SPARROW *Spizella breweri*   Fairly common M513
5½ in. (14 cm). A small, slim, pale, *nondescript* sparrow of sagebrush and desert scrub. Resembles Chipping and Clay-colored sparrows. Note pale lores, brownish rump, pale *eye-ring,* and *lack of white central crown stripe.* "Timberline" subspecies has slightly bolder plumage; nests near tree line in n. Rockies of Canada and extreme e. AK. **VOICE:** Song long, musical buzzy trills on different pitches; canary-like. Call a thin *tsee.* **SIMILAR SPECIES:** Chipping and Clay-colored sparrows. **HABITAT:** Nests in sagebrush, saltbush; winters in brushy plains and deserts, weedy fields. "Timberline" Sparrow nests near tree line, mostly in stunted willow.

SPARROWS

breeding

nonbreeding

CHIPPING SPARROW

juvenile

AMERICAN
TREE
SPARROW

breeding

nonbreeding

FIELD
SPARROW

CLAY-COLORED SPARROW

juvenile

adult

BREWER'S SPARROW

333

SAVANNAH SPARROW *Passerculus sandwichensis*   Common M521

5½–5¾ in. (14–15 cm). This streaked, open-country sparrow suggests a small Song Sparrow, but it usually has *yellowish on front of eyebrow (may be lacking or difficult to see in some birds); whitish stripe through crown; short,* notched tail; pinker legs. Noting tail notch and length is an identification aid when flushing sparrows. "Large-billed" Savannah Sparrow is scarce and local post-breeding visitor to Salton Sea and coastal s. CA from w. Mex. Has larger, paler bill and pale but warm-toned brownish body. "Belding's" Savannah Sparrow is one of several dark subspecies that are permanent residents in coastal salt marshes of CA; threatened. **VOICE:** Song a lisping, buzzy *tsit-tsit-tsit, tseeee-tsaaay* (last note lower). Call a light *tsu.* **SIMILAR SPECIES:** Song Sparrow's tail longer, rounded. See also Vesper Sparrow. Song similar to Grasshopper's except for Savannah's lower last note. **HABITAT:** Open fields, farms, meadows, salt marshes, prairies, dunes.

BAIRD'S SPARROW   Scarce, local, secretive M523
Ammodramus bairdii

5½ in. (14 cm). An elusive, skulking prairie sparrow. Light breast crossed by *narrow band* of fine streaks. Key mark is *ocher* median crown stripe and nape. *Juvenile:* Pale edges form scaly pattern above. **VOICE:** Song begins with two or three high musical *zips,* ends with trill on lower pitch; more musical than Savannah Sparrow. **SIMILAR SPECIES:** Savannah Sparrow. **HABITAT:** Native grasslands, scattered bushes used as song perches.

GRASSHOPPER SPARROW   Uncommon M522
Ammodramus savannarum

5 in. (13 cm). A small, compact, flat-headed sparrow of taller grasslands. Crown with pale median stripe; *yellow lores; whitish eye-ring;* note relatively *unstriped buffy breast. Juvenile:* Has dusky streaks on breast. **VOICE:** Very thin, dry, insectlike *pi-tup zeeeeeeeeeeee.* **SIMILAR SPECIES:** Le Conte's Sparrow. Grasshopper's song similar to Savannah Sparrow's. **HABITAT:** Grasslands, hayfields, pastures, prairies.

LE CONTE'S SPARROW *Ammodramus leconteii*   Uncommon M524

5 in. (13 cm). A skulking sparrow of prairie marshes, boggy fields. Note *bright orange* eyebrow and buffy breast (with streaks *confined to sides).* Other points are *purplish chestnut streaks on nape,* white median crown stripe, strong stripes on back. **VOICE:** Song two extremely thin, grasshopper-like hisses. **SIMILAR SPECIES:** Nelson's and Grasshopper sparrows. **HABITAT:** Grassy marshes, tallgrass fields, weedy hayfields.

NELSON'S SPARROW   Scarce M525
Ammodramus nelsoni

5 in. (13 cm). A shy marshland skulker. Note bright *orange on face,* surrounding gray ear patch. *Breast warm buff with blurry streaks.* Gray central crown and *unmarked gray nape.* **VOICE:** Song a buzzy, two-part *shleeee-tup.* **SIMILAR SPECIES:** Le Conte's Sparrow. **HABITAT:** In summer, prairie marshes, muskeg; in winter, coastal marshes.

SAVANNAH SPARROW

"Belding's"

typical

"Large-billed"

ault

juvenile

GRASSHOPPER
SPARROW

BAIRD'S
SPARROW

NELSON'S
SPARROW

LE CONTE'S
SPARROW

FOX SPARROW *Passerella iliaca*   Uncommon M526
7 in. (18 cm). A large, plump sparrow; most subspecies have *rusty rump and tail.* Action towhee-like, kicking among dead leaves. *Breast heavily streaked* with triangular spots. Many subspecies; can be roughly divided into four groups: (1) "Red" group: bright rusty with rusty back stripes (northern); (2) "Sooty" group: dusky or sooty head, back (unstreaked), and upper breast (Northwest coast); (3) "Slate-colored" group: gray-headed and gray-backed (unstreaked), yellowish-based bill (Rockies, Great Basin); and (4) "Thick-billed" group: similar to 3 but large-billed (southern Cascades, CA mountains). In fall and winter, some of these types intermingle. **VOICE:** Song brilliant and musical; a varied arrangement of short clear notes and sliding whistles. Call varies by type, a sharp *chink* (type 4) to flatter *chup.* **SIMILAR SPECIES:** Hermit Thrush. **HABITAT:** Wooded undergrowth, montane chaparral, tundra thickets, other brush, feeders.

SONG SPARROW *Melospiza melodia*   Common M527
5¾–6½ in. (15–17 cm). This common midsized sparrow has a *long rounded tail* and *heavy breast streaks* that merge into a *large central spot. Juvenile:* More finely streaked, often lacks central spot. Song Sparrows vary widely in color and size, as shown opposite. Many subspecies are recognized. **VOICE:** Song a variable series of notes, some musical, some buzzy; usually starts with three or four bright repetitious notes, *sweet sweet sweet,* etc. Call a low, nasal *tchep.* **SIMILAR SPECIES:** Savannah, Lincoln's, and Swamp sparrows. **HABITAT:** Thickets, brush, marshes, roadsides, gardens, feeders; avoids open fields.

LINCOLN'S SPARROW *Melospiza lincolnii*   Fairly common M528
5¾ in. (15 cm). A somewhat skulking species, prefers to be near cover. Similar to Song Sparrow, but smaller and trimmer, side of face grayer, sharp breast streaks *much finer* and overlay band of *creamy buff* that contrasts with whitish belly and throat; also has narrow whitish eye-ring and buffy mustache. **VOICE:** Song sweet and gurgling; suggests both House Wren and Purple Finch; starts with low passages, rises abruptly, drops. Calls a hard *tik* and buzzy *zzzeeet.* **SIMILAR SPECIES:** Song and Swamp sparrows. **HABITAT:** Nests in willow and alder thickets, muskeg, brushy bogs; in winter, thickets, bushes, gardens, sometimes feeders.

VESPER SPARROW *Pooecetes gramineus*   Uncommon M516
6¼ in. (16 cm). *White outer tail feathers* are conspicuous when bird flies. Otherwise suggests largish Savannah or pale Song Sparrow, but has *whitish eye-ring.* Bend of wing *chestnut (difficult to see).* Note *white malar stripe* and lack of central crown stripe. **VOICE:** Song throatier than Song Sparrow's; usually begins with two clear minor notes, followed by two higher ones. **SIMILAR SPECIES:** Savannah Sparrow has shorter tail without white; lacks distinct eye-ring; has white central crown stripe. Other sparrowlike field birds with white tail-sides or corners include pipits, longspurs, and Lark Sparrow. **HABITAT:** Meadows and prairies with scattered trees or bushes (such as sage), roadsides, farm fields.

STREAKED SPARROWS

"Red" (North and East)

"Slate-colored" (Rockies and Great Basin)

"Thick-billed" (OR, CA)

"Sooty" (Northwest Coast)

FOX SPARROW

Southwest

AK

East

(typical)

SONG SPARROW

LINCOLN'S SPARROW

VESPER SPARROW

WHITE-THROATED SPARROW   Uncommon M530
Zonotrichia albicollis

6¾ in. (17 cm). *Adult:* A gray-breasted sparrow with white throat and yellow above the lores. Polymorphic; some adults have black and white head stripes, others brown and tan. *Immature:* May be somewhat streaked on breast. **VOICE:** Song several clear pensive whistles, easily imitated; one or two clear notes, followed by three quavering notes on a different pitch. Call a thin, slurred *tseet;* also a hard *chink.* **SIMILAR SPECIES:** White-crowned Sparrow. **HABITAT:** Thickets, brush, undergrowth of coniferous and mixed woodlands. In winter, also visits feeders, preferring to stay on ground, often with White-crowned or Golden-crowned sparrows.

WHITE-CROWNED SPARROW   Common M532
Zonotrichia leucophrys

7 in. (18 cm). This species comprises multiple subspecies, which exhibit variation in color of lores (whitish or black) and bill (orangey, pinkish, or yellowish). "Gambel's" subspecies nests on western tundra. They have orange bills and pale lores. *Adult:* Clear grayish breast, puffy crown *striped with black and white. Immature:* Head stripes dark red-brown and light buff. **VOICE:** Song one or more clear, plaintive whistles (similar to White-throated Sparrow), followed by husky trilled whistles. Variable; many local dialects. Call a sharp *pink.* **SIMILAR SPECIES:** White-throated Sparrow. Immature Golden-crowned Sparrow slightly larger, has *duskier bill and underparts,* more muted head pattern, *dull yellowish forehead.* **HABITAT:** Brush, forest edges, thickets, coastal sage scrub, gardens, parks; in winter, also farms, desert washes, chaparral, feeders.

HARRIS'S SPARROW *Zonotrichia querula*   Uncommon M531

7½ in. (19 cm). Large. *Adult: Black face encircling pink bill. Immature:* Has buffy brown head, pink bill, and blotch of black on breast. **VOICE:** Song has quavering quality of White-throated Sparrow: clear whistles on same pitch, or one or two at one pitch, the rest slightly lower; general effect *minor.* Alarm call *wink.* **HABITAT:** Stunted boreal forests; in winter, brush, hedgerows, open woods. May mix with White-crowned Sparrows in nonbreeding season.

GOLDEN-CROWNED SPARROW   Fairly common M533
Zonotrichia atricapilla

7¼ in. (18 cm). Similar to White-crowned Sparrow, but without white head stripes; instead, adult has *dull yellow central crown stripe,* bordered broadly with black. Dusky bill. Immature birds and some nonbreeding adults may look like large female House Sparrows but are longer tailed and darker, usually with dull yellow suffusion on forehead. **VOICE:** Song three to five high whistled notes of plaintive minor quality, coming down scale, *oh-dear-me.* Sometimes a faint trill. Call a sharp *tsew.* **SIMILAR SPECIES:** White-crowned Sparrow. **HABITAT:** Nests in boreal, subalpine, and tundra scrub, willow thickets, stunted spruces; in winter, similar to that of White-crowned (with which it is often found in mixed flocks), but Golden-crowned favors denser shrubs, particularly chaparral.

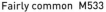

SPARROWS

tan-striped morph

immature

white-striped morph

WHITE-THROATED SPARROW

adult

immature

"Gambel's"

WHITE-ROWNED PARROW

adult

immature

GOLDEN-CROWNED SPARROW

breeding adult

immature

HARRIS'S SPARROW

DARK-EYED JUNCO *Junco hyemalis*　　　　　　**Common M534**
6–6½ in. (15–16 cm). This hooded sparrow is characterized by *white outer tail feathers* that flash conspicuously as it flies away. Bill and belly usually whitish. Male may have dark hood; female and immature duller. Juvenile in summer finely streaked on breast, hence its white outer tail feathers might even suggest Vesper Sparrow. *Note:* Until 1970s this species was divided into four full species in N. America. Some have gray sides, others rusty or pinkish. They are now lumped as one highly complex species. Intergrades are known. Treated separately, the main subspecies groups are known as follows.
　　"Oregon" Junco is generally the most widespread subspecies in West. Male has *rusty brown back* with *blackish hood* and *buffy or rusty sides.* Female duller, but note contrast between paler gray hood and brown back, convex shape to lower border of hood.
　　"Pink-sided" Junco is found from the Rockies westward, south of AK. Has a pale gray hood, pink flanks, and black lores.
　　"Gray-headed" Junco occurs in Great Basin and s. Rockies. Rufous patch on back of otherwise pale to medium gray plumage, with *gray sides* and *gray head, dark lores.* Breeders in Southwest have bicolored bill.
　　"Slate-colored" Junco is most northern and eastern form, wintering mainly east of Rockies, sparingly westward. A gray junco with *gray back*, white belly. Female and immature duller gray tinged brownish. The more uniform coloration, lacking rusty areas, is distinctive. Some particularly brownish young birds may be confused with "Oregon" Junco.
　　"White-winged" Junco breeds in Black Hills region. A large, pale form with gray back; usually has *two whitish wing bars* and exhibits considerably more white in tail (four outer feathers on each side). *Note:* Some "Slate-colored" Juncos can show thin, weak wing bars.
　　VOICE: Song a loose trill, suggestive of Chipping Sparrow but more musical. Call a light *smack;* also clicking or twittering notes. **HABITAT:** Nests in coniferous and mixed woods. In nonbreeding season, open woods, undergrowth, roadsides, brush, parks, gardens, feeders; usually in flocks, regularly containing multiple subspecies.

YELLOW-EYED JUNCO *Junco phaeonotus*　　**Uncommon, local M535**
6¼ in. (16 cm). Our only junco with *yellow eyes,* which give it a somewhat fierce look. Otherwise like "Gray-headed" Junco except that rufous on back *extends onto wing.* Walks rather than hops. **VOICE:** Song musical, unjunco-like; more complicated, three-part: *chip chip chip, wheedle wheedle, che che che che che.* **HABITAT:** Coniferous forests, pine-oak woods; in winter, some come down to slightly lower elevations in canyons, including at feeders.

♀

♂

juvenile

"Oregon"

DARK-EYED JUNCO

Rockies/Great Basin

"Gray-headed"

♂

"Pink-sided"

♂

Southwest

♀

"Slate-colored"

♂

"White-winged"

♂

♂

YELLOW-EYED JUNCO

LAPLAND LONGSPUR
Uncommon to fairly common M537

Calcarius lapponicus

6¼ in. (16 cm). Lapland Longspurs — like Horned Larks, pipits, and other longspurs — are birds of open country; in flight, they appear to have shorter tail. In nonbreeding season, longspurs are often found in flocks of larks. *Breeding male: Black face outlined with white* is distinctive. Rusty collar. *Female and nonbreeding male:* Sparse black streaks on sides, dull rusty nape, and smudge across breast. Note *dark frame to rear cheek, rufous brown wing coverts,* tail pattern. **VOICE:** In flight, a dry rattle, also a musical *teew;* when perched, a soft *pee-dle.* Song in display flight is vigorous, musical. **SIMILAR SPECIES:** Smith's Longspur buffier below; note face pattern. Other longspurs have more white in tail. American Pipit and Horned Lark have thin bill, different plumage. **HABITAT:** In summer, tundra; in winter, fields, prairies, shores.

CHESTNUT-COLLARED LONGSPUR
Uncommon M539

Calcarius ornatus

6 in. (15 cm). *Breeding male:* Solid *black* below, except on throat and lower belly; nape *chestnut. Female and nonbreeding:* Adult males show dull black belly, but otherwise all are sparrowlike; best field mark is tail pattern — dark triangle on white tail — and flight call. **VOICE:** Song short, feeble, but musical; suggests Western Meadowlark. Call a finchlike *ji-jiv* or *kittle-kittle,* unique among longspurs. **SIMILAR SPECIES:** McCown's Longspur. **HABITAT:** Plains, native-grass prairies; generally prefers some cover, and winter flocks may disappear in grass until flushed.

MCCOWN'S LONGSPUR
Uncommon, local M536

Rhynchophanes mccownii

6 in. (15 cm). *Breeding male:* Crown and breast patch black, tail largely white. Hindneck *gray. Female and nonbreeding male:* Rather plain; note tail pattern and *swollen-looking, fleshy bill.* **VOICE:** Song in display flight is clear sweet warbles, suggestive of Lark Bunting. Call a dry rattle, softer than Lapland Longspur's. Also a soft *pink.* **SIMILAR SPECIES:** Nonbreeding Chestnut-collared Longspur darker, more heavily marked below, have slightly smaller, darker bill, different call. **HABITAT:** Plains, prairies, short-grass and dirt fields.

SMITH'S LONGSPUR *Calcarius pictus*
Scarce, local M538

6¼ in. (16 cm). This secretive longspur prefers enough grassy cover to disappear in. It is *warm buff on entire underparts.* Tail edged with white, as in Vesper Sparrow and Lapland Longspur. *Breeding male: Deep buff;* ear patch with *white spot,* strikingly outlined by *black triangle. Female and nonbreeding: Buffy breast* lightly streaked; some males may show white shoulder patch. **VOICE:** Rattling or clicking notes in flight (has been likened to winding of a cheap watch). Song sweet, warblerlike, terminating in *WEchew.* Does not sing in flight. **SIMILAR SPECIES:** Lapland and Chestnut-collared longspurs, Vesper Sparrow, Sprague's Pipit. **HABITAT:** Prairies, fields, airports; in summer, tundra with scattered bushes.

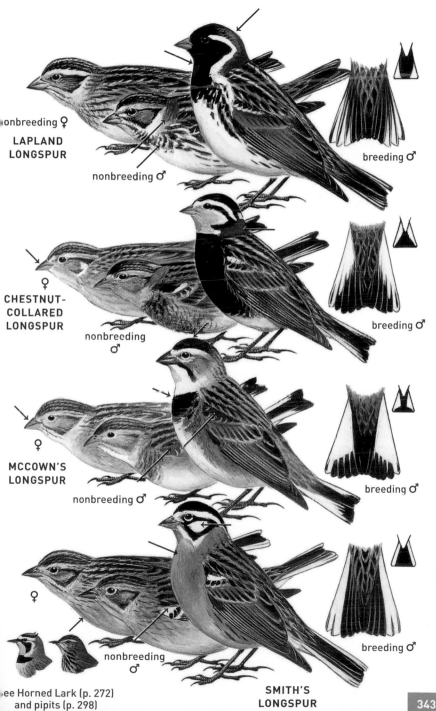

LONGSPURS

nonbreeding ♀
**LAPLAND
LONGSPUR**

nonbreeding ♂

breeding ♂

♀
**CHESTNUT-
COLLARED
LONGSPUR**

nonbreeding
♂

breeding ♂

♀
**MCCOWN'S
LONGSPUR**

nonbreeding ♂

breeding ♂

♀

nonbreeding
♂

breeding ♂

ee Horned Lark (p. 272)
and pipits (p. 298)

**SMITH'S
LONGSPUR**

343

SNOW BUNTING *Plectrophenax nivalis*   Uncommon M540

6¾ in. (17 cm). Snow Buntings often swirl over snowy fields or dunes in flocks, sometimes mixed with Horned Larks or Lapland Longspurs. No other N. American songbird (except McKay's Bunting) shows so much white. In winter some individuals, especially females and immatures, may look quite brown, but when they fly their flashing *white wing patches* identify them. Overhead, Snow Bunting looks almost entirely white, whereas American Pipit and Horned Lark are mostly black-tailed. Breeding male has black back, contrasting with white head and underparts. **VOICE:** Call a sharp, whistled *teer* or *tew;* also a rough, purring *brrt,* both similar to Lapland Longspur's calls. Song a musical *ti-ti-chu-ree,* repeated. **SIMILAR SPECIES:** In w. AK, see McKay's Bunting. Albino landbirds — such as juncos — are sometimes mistaken for Snow Buntings. **HABITAT:** Prairies, fields, dunes, shores; in summer, tundra.

MCKAY'S BUNTING *Plectrophenax hyperboreus*   Scarce, local M541

7 in. (18 cm). A specialty of w. AK, breeding regularly only on St. Matthew and Hall Is. *Breeding male:* Almost pure white, except for ends of primaries and scapulars and near tips of central tail feathers. *Breeding female:* Shows some dark on back. *Nonbreeding:* Both sexes have light touches of warm tan-brown above, but less than in Snow Bunting. Wings and tail show more white. Hybridizes with Snow Bunting. **VOICE:** Song of male said to suggest American Goldfinch. **SIMILAR SPECIES:** Breeding male Snow Bunting has *black* back. Female and winter Snow Buntings browner; note coloration and pattern of tail, rump, and back. **HABITAT:** Tundra, barrens, shores; in nonbreeding season, often in mixed flocks with Snow Buntings, sometimes at feeders.

RUSTIC BUNTING *Emberiza rustica*   Casual

5¾–6 in. (16 cm). A *rusty,* sparrowlike bird with *rusty* breast-band and *dark cheek outlined in white.* Head slightly crested, bill pink. *Breeding male:* Black head markings. *Female and immature:* Light spot on brown cheek patch, rusty brown sides and rump. **VOICE:** Short, musical jumble of notes, ending on down-slurred *chew.* **RANGE:** Regular Asian stray to w. AK islands, casual farther south.

BRAMBLING   Rare, local

Fringilla montifringilla (Family Fringillidae, p. 360)

6¼ in. (16 cm). *Tawny* or *orangey buff* breast and shoulders, *whitish rump distinctive in flight. Breeding male:* Black head and back. *Female and nonbreeding:* Gray cheek (with dark markings in male) bordered by dark, flanks streaked or spotted. **VOICE:** Call a rising, whiny *zweee;* in flight, a distinctive nasal, hollow *eck.* **SIMILAR SPECIES:** This rarely seen species might be confused with more common N. American birds, including Black-headed Grosbeak and Spotted or Eastern towhee. **RANGE:** Eurasian species; regular on w. AK islands, casual but widespread records elsewhere.

BUNTINGS AND BRAMBLING

nonbreeding ♂

nonbreeding ♀

Snow Bunting
breeding ♂

SNOW BUNTING

Snow Bunting

♀

♂

breeding ♂

breeding ♀

McKay's Bunting

♂

MCKAY'S BUNTING

nonbreeding ♂

breeding ♂

RUSTIC BUNTING

♀

breeding ♂

nonbreeding ♂

BRAMBLING

345

CARDINALS, BUNTINGS, AND ALLIES
Family Cardinalidae

Medium-sized colorful songbirds with heavy bills. Songs loud and rich. **FOOD:** Seeds, fruit, insects. **RANGE:** New World.

ROSE-BREASTED GROSBEAK   Scarce M547
Pheucticus ludovicianus
8 in. (20 cm). *Adult male:* Black and white, with large triangle of red on breast and thick pale bill. Wing linings pink. *Immature male:* In first-autumn plumage similar to female, but has touch of red on buffier breast. *Female:* Similar to female Black-headed but breast *heavily streaked,* bill *pale.* **VOICE:** Song similar to Black-headed's. Call a squeaky *kick* or *eek.* **SIMILAR SPECIES:** Female told from female Purple and Cassin's finches by larger size, obvious wing bars, and pink bill. **HABITAT:** Deciduous woods, orchards, groves.

BLACK-HEADED GROSBEAK   Fairly common M548
Pheucticus melanocephalus
8¼ in. (21 cm). *Male:* Breast, collar, and rump *dull orange-brown;* head black; bold black-and-white wing and tail pattern. *Female and immature:* Upperparts brown, streaked; head strongly patterned with light stripes and dark ear patch. Breast strongly *washed with butter-scotch;* dark streaks on sides *fine.* **VOICE:** Song consists of rising and falling passages; resembles American Robin's song, but more fluent and mellow. Call a flat *ik* or *eek.* **SIMILAR SPECIES:** Rose-breasted Grosbeak. **HABITAT:** Deciduous and mixed woods groves; sometimes feeders.

YELLOW GROSBEAK *Pheucticus chrysopeplus*   Casual
9¼ in. (24 cm). Bulkier and heavier-billed than Black-headed Grosbeak. *Male:* Golden yellow and black. *Female:* Duller, with streaked back and crown. **VOICE:** *Cheer-reah, churr-weoh.* **SIMILAR SPECIES:** Evening and Black-headed grosbeaks. **RANGE:** Mexican; casual visitor to Southwest. Some may be escapees. **HABITAT:** Deciduous woods.

NORTHERN CARDINAL   Uncommon to fairly common M545
Cardinalis cardinalis
8¾ in. (22 cm). *Male: All-red* with *crest,* black face, and *triangular red-dish bill. Female:* Buff brown, with some red on wings and tail, crest, and *heavy reddish bill.* **VOICE:** Song is clear, slurred whistles, repeated. Several variations: *what-cheer cheer cheer* or *birdy birdy birdy,* etc. Call a short, sharp *tik.* **SIMILAR SPECIES:** Pyrrhuloxia. Male Summer and Hepatic tanagers. **HABITAT:** Woodland edges, thickets, deserts, gardens, feeders.

PYRRHULOXIA   Uncommon to fairly common M546
Cardinalis sinuatus
8¾ in. (22 cm). Similar to Northern Cardinal but grayer with longer crest and *pale yellowish bill with curved upper mandible.* **VOICE:** Song similar to Northern Cardinal's but usually not two-part. **SIMILAR SPECIES:** Best told from Northern Cardinal by bill color and shape. **HABITAT:** Mesquite, thorn scrub, deserts, feeders.

GROSBEAKS AND FINCHES

ROSE-BREASTED GROSBEAK

breeding ♂

eeding ♂

♀

breeding ♂

BLACK-HEADED GROSBEAK

♀

♂

♀

YELLOW GROSBEAK

NORTHERN CARDINAL

♂

♀

juvenile

♂

PYRRHULOXIA

♀

BLUE GROSBEAK *Passerina caerulea* Uncommon M549

6¾ in. (17 cm). About size of Brown-headed Cowbird; *thick bill,* often *flips or twitches tail. Adult male:* Deep *dull blue* with *broad chestnut wing bars. Immature male:* A mixture of brown and blue. *Female:* Warm brown, with two *rusty buff wing bars;* rump or tail may be tinged with blue. **VOICE:** Warbling song, phrases rising and falling; suggests Purple or House finch, but slower, more guttural. Call a sharp *chink,* in flight a flat *bzzzt.* **SIMILAR SPECIES:** Female Indigo Bunting smaller with smaller bill and weaker wing bars. **HABITAT:** Thickets, hedgerows, riparian undergrowth, brushy hillsides, weedy ditches.

INDIGO BUNTING *Passerina cyanea* Uncommon to scarce M551

5½ in. (14 cm). *Male:* A small deep blue finch. In early spring, blue is blotchy. Nonbreeding male like female, but with some blue in wings and tail. *Female and immature:* Very similar to female Lazuli but *wing bars weaker,* breast duller with *faint streaks,* upperparts warmer. Like Blue Grosbeak, may flick or jerk tail sideways. **VOICE:** Song similar to Lazuli but slower with phrases more paired. Calls similar. **SIMILAR SPECIES:** Blue Grosbeak (larger) has rusty wing bars. See Lazuli Bunting. **HABITAT:** Overgrown brushy fields, riparian thickets, bushy wood edges.

LAZULI BUNTING *Passerina amoena* Fairly common M550

5½ in. (14 cm). *Breeding male:* Turquoise blue with burnt orangey breast and white belly, suggesting a bluebird, but with *white wing bars. Nonbreeding male:* Brownish tips to feathers mute some of blue. *Female and immature:* A plain brown finch with *buffy wing bars* and *warm buffy unstreaked breast.* Juvenile may retain fine, sharp streaks into fall. Hybrids with Indigo Bunting are regular. **VOICE:** Song a lively, ringing warble, often ending in a quick sputter. Call a sharp *spit* and a dry buzz. **SIMILAR SPECIES:** Indigo Bunting. **HABITAT:** Open brush, grassy hillsides with scattered bushes, riparian shrubs, grassy patches in chaparral, weedy fields and ditches; sometimes feeders.

PAINTED BUNTING *Passerina ciris* Rare M553

5½ in. (14 cm). *Male:* A striking patchwork of *blue-violet, green, and red. Female and immature:* Electric green above, paling to lemon yellow below; *no other small finch is so green. Juvenile:* Grayer above with only tinge of green, duller below. **VOICE:** Song a wiry warble; suggests Warbling Vireo. Call a sharp *chip.* **HABITAT:** Riparian undergrowth, brushy hedgerows, woodland edges, stands of weedy grass. Escapees may occur.

VARIED BUNTING *Passerina versicolor* Scarce, local M552

5½ in. (14 cm). *Male:* A small dark finch with plum purple body (looks black at a distance). Crown, face, and rump blue; nape *bright red;* "colored like an Easter egg." *Female:* Similar to female Indigo but *lacks wing bars and breast streaks.* **VOICE:** Song thin, bright, more distinctly phrased, less warbled than Painted Bunting's; notes not as paired as Indigo Bunting's. **HABITAT:** Riparian thickets, mesquite and other scrub in washes and lower canyons.

BLUE FINCHES, ETC.

adult ♂

♀

breeding ♂

molting ♂

BLUE GROSBEAK

INDIGO BUNTING

♀

breeding ♂

LAZULI BUNTING

♂

PAINTED BUNTING

♀

VARIED BUNTING

♂

DICKCISSEL *Spiza americana*　　　　　　Uncommon **M554**
6¼ in. (16 cm). A grass- and farmland bird. *Male:* Suggests a miniature meadowlark (black bib, yellow chest). Has chestnut shoulder
patch. In fall, bib obscure. *Female and immature:* Much like female
House Sparrow, but with bolder stripe over eye (often tinged yellowish), touch of yellow on breast, and blue-gray bill. **VOICE:** Song a staccato *dick-ciss-ciss-ciss*. Call a short, hard buzz. **HABITAT:** Alfalfa and
other fields, meadows, prairies, weedy patches.

LARK BUNTING　　　　　　　　　　Fairly common **M520**
Calamospiza melanocorys (Family Emberizidae)
7 in. (18 cm). A plump, short-tailed prairie bird. Gregarious in nonbreeding season. Note rather *heavy, blue-gray bill. Breeding male:*
Black, with *large white wing patches. Female, immature, and nonbreeding male:* Brown, streaked. Adult males retain some black. All show
whitish or *buffy white wing patches* and *tail corners.* **VOICE:** Song, given
in display flight, composed of cardinal-like slurs, unmusical chatlike
*chug*s, piping whistles and trills; each note repeated 3 to 11 times.
Call a flat, mellow *heew.* **SIMILAR SPECIES:** Bobolink. **HABITAT:** Plains,
prairies; in winter, also weedy desert lowlands and farm fields.

BLACKBIRDS AND ORIOLES Family Icteridae

Varied color patterns; sharp bills. Some black and iridescent; orioles are highly
colored. Sexes unlike. **FOOD:** Insects, fruit, seeds, waste grain, small aquatic
life. **RANGE:** New World; most in Tropics.

WESTERN MEADOWLARK *Sturnella neglecta*　Fairly common **M559**
9½ in. (24 cm). A chunky, brown, starling-shaped bird of grasslands.
When flushed, shows conspicuous *white sides on short tail.* When
perched on a post or wire shows *bright yellow breast crossed by black
V.* **VOICE:** Song variable; 7 to 10 flutelike notes, gurgling and double-
note, unlike clear whistles of Eastern Meadowlark. Calls *chupp* or
chuck and a dry rattle. **SIMILAR SPECIES:** See Eastern Meadowlark.
HABITAT: Grasslands, cultivated fields and pastures, meadows, prairies, marsh edges, roadsides.

EASTERN MEADOWLARK *Sturnella magna*　　Uncommon **M558**
9½ in. (24 cm). Very similar to Western Meadowlark but yellow on
throat *does not invade malar; crown stripes darker* (less streaked with
buff); wingbeats stiffer, snappier — like a Spotted Sandpiper (more
starlinglike in Western). Subspecies found in e. N. America more
richly colored above than Western, with buffier flanks. Southwestern
subspecies — "Lilian's" Meadowlark — paler overall, with *more white
in tail* (much more white than Western); best identified by voice.
VOICE: Song composed of two clear, slurred whistles, *tee-yah, tee-
yair* (last note slurred and descending). Call a rasping or buzzy *dzrrt;*
also a guttural chatter. **SIMILAR SPECIES:** Western Meadowlark. **HABI-
TAT:** Open fields and pastures, meadows, prairies, marsh edges;
"Lilian's" partial to grasslands.

OPEN FIELD BIRDS

DICKCISSEL

breeding
♂

♀

nonbreeding

**Bobolink
(p. 352)**
for comparison

breeding ♂

♀

(nonbreeding ♂
similar)

LARK BUNTING

**EASTERN
MEADOWLARK**

**WESTERN
MEADOWLARK**

RED-WINGED BLACKBIRD *Agelaius phoeniceus*   Common **M556**
8½–8¾ in. (22 cm). *Adult male:* Black, with *bright red or orange-red epaulets,* most conspicuous in breeding display. Often red is concealed and only yellowish margin shows. *Immature male:* Sooty brown, mottled (like female), but with red shoulders. *Female:* Brownish, with sharply pointed bill and *well-defined dark streaking* below; may have pinkish tinge to throat. Gregarious, traveling and roosting in flocks during nonbreeding season. "Bicolored" subspecies in cen. CA. **VOICE:** Calls a loud *check* and a high, slurred *tee-err.* Song a liquid, gurgling *konk-la-ree.* **SIMILAR SPECIES:** Tricolored Blackbird. **HABITAT:** Breeds in marshes, brushy swamps, fields, pastures, roadsides; forages also in cultivated land, feedlots, towns, feeders, etc.

TRICOLORED BLACKBIRD *Agelaius tricolor* Uncommon, local **M557**
8½–8¾ in. (22 cm). *Male:* Similar to Red-winged Blackbird, but shoulder patch darker red, with conspicuous *white margin.* (*Note:* Some male Red-wingeds have whitish margins as well.) Overall plumage slightly glossier. *Female:* Darker than most races of Red-winged, particularly on belly, and never shows pinkish on throat, but difficult to identify. See voice. Highly gregarious. Nests in dense colonies, whereas Red-winged is territorial. In nonbreeding season, may segregate by sex. **VOICE:** More nasal than Red-winged: *on-ke-kaangh.* A nasal *kemp.* **SIMILAR SPECIES:** Red-winged Blackbird. **HABITAT:** Nests in cattail or tule marshes, sometimes farm fields; forages in fields, farms, feedlots, park lawns.

YELLOW-HEADED BLACKBIRD   Fairly common **M560**
Xanthocephalus xanthocephalus
9–9¾ in. (23–25 cm). Gregarious. *Adult male:* A robin-sized blackbird, with *yellow head and breast;* in flight, shows *white wing patch. Female and immature male:* Smaller (female) and browner; most of yellow confined to throat and chest; lower breast streaked with white; white wing patch restricted or lacking. **VOICE:** Song consists of low, hoarse rasping notes produced with much effort; suggests rusty hinges. Call a low *kruck* or *kack.* **HABITAT:** Nests in freshwater marshes. Forages in farm fields, open country, feedlots. Often associates with other blackbirds in fall and winter.

BOBOLINK *Dolichonyx oryzivorus*   Uncommon, local **M555**
7 in. (18 cm). *Breeding male:* Our only songbird that is *solid black below and largely white above,* suggesting a dress suit on backward. Has buff-yellow nape. Birds in fresh plumage in spring show extensive brownish tips to dark feathering. *Female and nonbreeding male:* A bit larger than House Sparrow; rich buff-yellow, with dark striping on crown and back. Bill more like a sparrow's than a blackbird's. Note pointed tail feathers. **VOICE:** Song, in hovering flight and quivering descent, ecstatic and bubbling: starts with low, reedy notes and rollicks upward. Flight call a clear *ink.* **SIMILAR SPECIES:** Male Lark Bunting has white confined to wings. Female Red-winged Blackbird heavily striped below; longer bill, less buff-yellow overall. **HABITAT:** Hayfields, moist meadows.

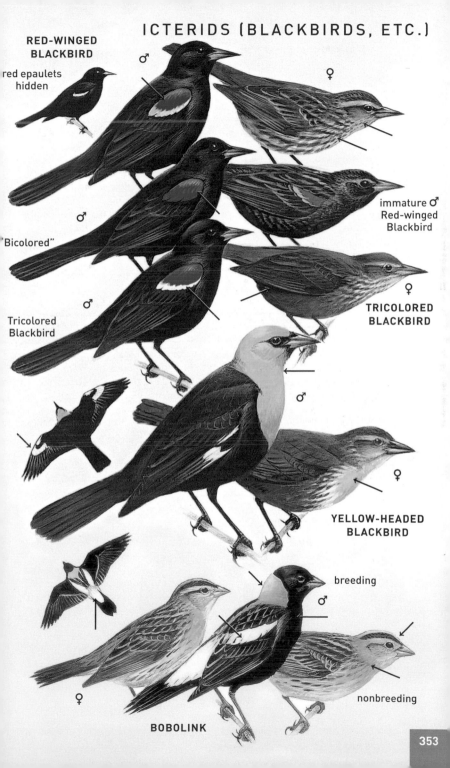

ICTERIDS (BLACKBIRDS, ETC.)

**RED-WINGED
BLACKBIRD**

red epaulets
hidden

♂

♀

♂

"Bicolored"

immature ♂
Red-winged
Blackbird

♂

Tricolored
Blackbird

♀

**TRICOLORED
BLACKBIRD**

♂

♀

**YELLOW-HEADED
BLACKBIRD**

breeding

♂

♀

nonbreeding

BOBOLINK

RUSTY BLACKBIRD
Euphagus carolinus

Uncommon to scarce M561

9 in. (23 cm). Rusty only in fall and winter; otherwise suggests Brewer's Blackbird. *Breeding male:* A medium-sized blackbird with pale yellow eye. Black head may show faint *greenish* gloss (not purplish). *Breeding female:* Slate colored, with *light eye. Nonbreeding and immature:* Variably *washed with rusty,* including *rusty edgings to flight feathers, buffy eyebrow, narrow dark patch through eye;* males *barred* below, have pale gray rump. **VOICE:** Call *chack.* "Song" a split creak, like a rusty hinge: *kush-a-lee,* alternating with *ksh-lay.* **SIMILAR SPECIES:** Brewer's Blackbird, Common Grackle. **HABITAT:** River groves, wooded swamps, muskeg, pond edges, sometimes livestock pens. May associate with other blackbirds in mixed-species flocks during fall and winter.

BREWER'S BLACKBIRD *Euphagus cyanocephalus*   Common M562

9 in. (23 cm). A common and familiar blackbird. *Male:* All black, with whitish eye; in good light, *purplish* reflections may be seen on head and neck, with some greenish reflections on body. *Female:* Brownish gray, with *dark* eye. **VOICE:** Song a harsh, wheezy, creaking *ksh-eee.* Call *chack.* **SIMILAR SPECIES:** Breeding male Rusty Blackbird flatter black with dull *greenish* head reflections (hard to see); bill slightly longer. Female Rusty has *light* eye. Unlike Rusty (both sexes), adult Brewer's remain in same plumage year-round and do not acquire a rusty look in fall and winter. See also Brown-headed Cowbird. **HABITAT:** Fields, mountain meadows, prairies, farms, feedlots, towns, parks, lawns, shopping malls, parking lots.

COMMON GRACKLE *Quiscalus quiscula*   Uncommon M563

12½ in. (32 cm). *Male:* A large, *iridescent,* yellow-eyed blackbird, larger than a robin, with long, wedge-shaped or *keel-shaped (when breeding)* tail. In good light, iridescent purple-blue on head. *Female:* Somewhat smaller and duller, with less wedge-shaped tail. *Juvenile:* Sooty, with dark eyes. **VOICE:** Call *chuck* or *chack.* "Song" a split rasping note. **SIMILAR SPECIES:** Great-tailed Grackle, Brewer's Blackbird. **HABITAT:** Cropland, towns, parks, feeders, groves; swampy woods; often nests in conifers.

GREAT-TAILED GRACKLE *Quiscalus mexicanus*   Common M564

Male 18 in. (46 cm); female 15 in. (38 cm). Like several other blackbirds, often found in large flocks. *Male:* A very large, purple-glossed blackbird, distinctly larger than Common Grackle and with longer, more ample tail. *Female:* Smaller than male; dark gray-brown above, warm brown below. Adults of both sexes have yellow eyes. **VOICE:** Harsh *check check check;* also a high *kee-kee-kee-kee.* Shrill, discordant notes, whistles, and clucks. A rapid, upward-slurring *ma-ree.* **SIMILAR SPECIES:** Common Grackle (smaller). **HABITAT:** Groves, farms, feedlots, towns, city parks, parking lots.

BLACKBIRDS AND GRACKLES

RUSTY BLACKBIRD

breeding ♂

breeding ♀

nonbreeding ♂

♀

BREWER'S BLACKBIRD

variant immature ♂

♂

COMMON GRACKLE

♀

♂

♂

GREAT-TAILED GRACKLE

♀

355

BROWN-HEADED COWBIRD *Molothrus ater*   Common M566

7½ in. (19 cm). A rather small blackbird. *Male:* Black with *brown head.* *Female:* Gray-brown with lighter throat; note short *finchlike bill.* *Juvenile:* Paler than female. Buffy gray, with soft breast streaking and pale scaling (edges) above; this plumage held into early fall. Often seen being fed by smaller birds whose nests have been parasitized. When flocking with other blackbirds, cowbirds look smaller and feed on ground with tails lifted high. **VOICE:** Flight call *weee-titi* (high whistle, two lower notes). Song a bubbly and creaky *glug-glug-gleeee.* **SIMILAR SPECIES:** Female told from female Brewer's Blackbird by its *stubby bill* and smaller size. Juvenile starling has longer bill, shorter tail. **HABITAT:** In nesting season, where passerine nest-hosts are numerous, a variety of forests and woodlands; also farms, fields, feedlots, lawns, feeders. Parasitizes a wide variety of smaller bird nests. Never builds its own nest.

BRONZED COWBIRD *Molothrus aeneus*   Uncommon M565

8½–8¾ in. (21–22 cm). Red eye often conspicuous. Bill longer than Brown-headed Cowbird's. *Male:* Slightly larger and more *bull-headed* than Brown-headed Cowbird. Does *not* have brown head. *Ruff* on nape. *Female:* Smaller nape ruff; darker than female Brown-headed. **VOICE:** High-pitched mechanical creakings. Male's display very animated. **HABITAT:** Cropland, brush, semiopen country, feedlots. Parasitizes a variety of smaller bird nests. Never builds its own nest.

ORCHARD ORIOLE *Icterus spurius*   Uncommon, local M567

7–7¼ in. (18 cm). A small, short-billed oriole. Often flicks tail sideways. *Male:* All dark; rump and underparts *deep chestnut. Female and immature:* Olive above, yellowish below; two white wing bars. First-spring male has black bib down to chest. **VOICE:** Song a fast-moving outburst interspersed with piping whistles and guttural notes. Suggests Purple or House finch. A strident slurred *wheeer!* at or near end is distinctive. Call a soft *chuck.* **SIMILAR SPECIES:** Females and immatures difficult to tell from young Hooded Orioles but note Hooded's more curved bill, longer tail, and weaker wing bars. Some female and immature Baltimore Orioles have black throat (as do immature male Orchards), but are slightly larger and more orange. See voice. **HABITAT:** Wood edges, orchards, shade trees; more likely than other orioles to be seen in brushy areas.

SCOTT'S ORIOLE *Icterus parisorum*   Uncommon M571

8¾–9 in. (22–23 cm). *Adult male:* Solid black head and back and *lemon yellow* pattern distinguish it. *Female:* More greenish yellow below and more olivey gray and streaked above than other female orioles. Many have black on throat and face. **VOICE:** Song composed of rich fluty whistles; suggests Western Meadowlark. Call a harsh *chuck.* **SIMILAR SPECIES:** Female Hooded and Bullock's orioles. **HABITAT:** Dry woods and scrub in desert mountains, yucca forests, Joshua trees, pinyon-juniper, sugar-water feeders. Also eucalyptus and date palms in winter.

COWBIRDS AND ORIOLES

BROWN-HEADED
COWBIRD

♂

♀

molting
immature ♂

juvenile

♀

♂

BRONZED
COWBIRD

♂

ORCHARD
ORIOLE

immature
♂

♀

♀

♂

SCOTT'S
ORIOLE

immature

BALTIMORE ORIOLE *Icterus galbula*   Uncommon, local M570

8¼–8½ in. (21–22 cm). *Adult male:* Flame orange and black, with solid black head, orange sides to tail. *Female and immature:* Olive-brown above, burnt orange-yellow below; two white wing bars. Many adult females have traces of black on head, suggesting hood of male. Some immature females very dull, with grayer back, limited orange (mostly on plain face and breast), and whitish vent; much like female Bullock's Oriole. **VOICE:** Song rich, piping whistles. Call a low, whistled *hewli.* Chatter call not as rough as Bullock's. **SIMILAR SPECIES:** Dull female Baltimore much like female Bullock's, but latter has more distinct dark eye line and yellowish supercilium, plain gray back lacking dark scalloping, and yellowish rather than orange undertail coverts. Female Orchard Oriole greener than female Baltimore. **HABITAT:** Open deciduous woods, elms, shade trees.

BULLOCK'S ORIOLE *Icterus bullockii*   Fairly common M569

8¼–8½ in. (21–22 cm). *Adult male:* Note *orange cheeks* and *dark eye line, large white wing patches, and black-tipped tail. Female:* Dark eye line, yellowish supercilium, plain gray back, *whitish belly. Immature male:* Similar to female, but slightly more orange and has black goatee. May hybridize with Baltimore Oriole. **VOICE:** Accented double notes and one or two piping notes. Calls include a rough chatter and low *churp.* **SIMILAR SPECIES:** Baltimore Oriole; also Hooded and Orchard orioles. **HABITAT:** Deciduous and riparian woods, oaks, shade trees, ranch yards; small numbers winter in blooming eucalyptus in CA.

HOODED ORIOLE *Icterus cucullatus*   Fairly common M568

7½–8 in. (19–20 cm). *Male:* Orange and black, with black throat and *orange crown.* In winter, back obscurely scaled. *Female:* Similar to female Bullock's Oriole, but bill longer, slightly curved; more extensively yellow below; back olive-gray; head and tail more yellowish. Call different. *Immature:* Like female, with slightly shorter bill; much like female Orchard Oriole. **VOICE:** Song consists of rambling, grating notes and piping whistles: *chut chut chut whew whew;* opening notes throaty. Call an up-slurred, whistled *eek* or *wheenk.* **SIMILAR SPECIES:** Orchard and Scott's orioles. **HABITAT:** Open woods, shade trees, towns, gardens, palms, sugar-water feeders.

STREAK-BACKED ORIOLE *Icterus pustulatus*   Casual

8¼ in. (21 cm). Breeding adult has *streaked back.* Much white in wing. Otherwise resembles Hooded Oriole or perhaps immature male Bullock's Oriole. *Male:* Basically yellow-orange, head much deeper orange. *Female:* Duller, back more olivaceous, but streaking still obvious. **VOICE:** Rich warble, similar to Baltimore or Bullock's oriole. **SIMILAR SPECIES:** Adult male Hooded Oriole in winter shows crescent-shaped dark edges to back feathers, not streaks, and bill not as thick at base. **RANGE:** Very rare visitor from Mex., mostly in fall and winter, to se. AZ; casual west to CA and east to TX. **HABITAT:** Arid scrub, woodland edges.

ORIOLES

BALTIMORE
ORIOLE

♂

♀

immature

BULLOCK'S
ORIOLE

♂

♀

immature ♂

HOODED ORIOLE

♂

♀

STREAK-
BACKED
ORIOLE

♂

Fringilline and Cardueline Finches and Allies Family Fringillidae

These birds have a seed-cracking bill, relatively short, notched tail, and somewhat undulating flight. Sexes usually unlike. Tend to be more arboreal than sparrows. FOOD: Seeds, insects, small fruit. RANGE: Worldwide.

BLACK ROSY-FINCH *Leucosticte atrata*   Uncommon, local M573
6–6¼ in. (16 cm). Differs from other rosy-finches by adult male's blackish body color, feathering sometimes edged in gray. Female and immature grayer; the only truly grayish rosy-finch. VOICE: High chirping notes, suggestive of House Sparrow. HABITAT: Similar to other rosy-finches.

BROWN-CAPPED ROSY-FINCH   Uncommon, local M574
Leucosticte australis
6–6¼ in. (16 cm). The plainest rosy-finch. Like Gray-crowned, but male has more restricted gray on head, darker crown. Female and immature much drabber than male. VOICE: High chirping notes, suggestive of House Sparrow. HABITAT: Similar to other rosy-finches.

GRAY-CROWNED ROSY-FINCH   Uncommon M572
Leucosticte tephrocotis
6–8 in. (16–20 cm). A large, *dark brown finch,* with *pinkish wash* on belly, wings, and rump. *Light gray patch* on back of head (reduced on female and immature). Subspecies vary in size and amount of gray on head. "Hepburn's" subspecies breeds in western mountains. Widespread in winter. VOICE: High chirping notes, suggestive of House Sparrow. SIMILAR SPECIES: Black and Brown-capped rosy-finches. HABITAT: Rocky summits, alpine cirques and snowfields; also rocky islands; winters in open country at mid and lower elevations, regular at feeders in mountain towns and ski areas.

WHITE-WINGED CROSSBILL   Uncommon, irregular M580
Loxia leucoptera
6½ in. (17 cm). All plumages show *crossed mandibles, bold white wing bars,* and white tertial tips. VOICE: Calls a liquid *peet-peet* and a dry *chi-dit.* Song a succession of loud trills on different pitches. SIMILAR SPECIES: Red Crossbill may show a single weak wing bar. HABITAT: Spruce and fir forests, hemlocks. Erratic and irruptive wanderings, especially in winter.

RED CROSSBILL *Loxia curvirostra*   Uncommon, irregular M579
5¾–7 in. (14–17 cm). Has a heavy head and short tail. Note *crossed mandibles* and *plain wings.* The sound when it cracks cones of evergreens often betrays its presence. Usually found in *flocks.* Many subspecies vary slightly in bill size, body size, and color; most readily distinguished by flight call. VOICE: Call a hard *jip-jip* or *kip-kip-kip* (in some populations, *kwit-kwit* or *kewp-kewp*). Song consists of finchlike warbled passages, *jip-jip-jip-jeeaa-jeeaa;* trills, *chips.* SIMILAR SPECIES: White-winged Crossbill. HABITAT: Variety of conifers; rarely at feeders. Erratic and irruptive wanderings, especially in winter.

ROSY-FINCHES AND
CROSSBILLS

BLACK ROSY-FINCH

BROWN-CAPPED
ROSY-FINCH

♀

immature

♂

♂

GRAY-CROWNED
ROSY-FINCH

♂

"pburn's"
y-crowned
y-Finch

Pribilofs

♂

♂

♀

WHITE-WINGED
CROSSBILL

RED
CROSSBILL

♀

♂

juvenile

361

COMMON REDPOLL   Uncommon, irregular M581
Acanthis flammea

5¼ in. (13 cm). Note *bright red forehead* and *black chin* of this little winter finch. Male has *pink breast.* Usually found in flocks. **VOICE:** In flight, a rattling *chet-chet-chet.* Song a varied mix of trills and other calls. **SIMILAR SPECIES:** Hoary Redpoll, Pine Siskin. **HABITAT:** Birches, tundra scrub. In winter, weeds, brush, thistle feeders.

HOARY REDPOLL *Acanthis hornemanni*   Scarce, irregular M582

5¼–5½ in. (13–14 cm). In nonbreeding season, often found in flocks of Common Redpolls. *Very similar.* Look for a "frostier" bird, with whiter rump containing *little or no streaking.* Also note *stubbier bill* and lighter streaking on flanks and undertail coverts. Some individuals *very difficult to identify.* **VOICE:** Similar to Common Redpoll. **HABITAT:** Birches, tundra scrub. In winter, weeds, brush, feeders.

HOUSE FINCH *Haemorhous mexicanus*   Common M578

5¾–6 in. (14–15 cm). Slimmer than Purple or Cassin's finch. *Male:* Breast, forehead, stripe over eye, and rump vary from *red to orange to almost deep yellow* (diet related). Note *dark streaks* on sides. *Female:* Separated from female Purple and Cassin's finches by shape, and *bland face.* **VOICE:** Song bright and disjointed; often ends in nasal *wheer.* Call suggests a House Sparrow's *chirp,* but more musical. **HABITAT:** Cities, suburbs, feeders, farms.

PURPLE FINCH *Haemorhous purpureus*   Uncommon M576

6 in. (15 cm). Like a sparrow dipped in raspberry juice. *Adult male:* Dull rose red, brightest on head, chest, and rump. *Flanks unstreaked. Female and immature:* Heavily streaked, brown; note bold head pattern, deeply notched tail, undertail coverts with few or no streaks. Juvenile is darker, more heavily streaked, and lacks red forehead. **VOICE:** Song a fast lively warble; call a dull, flat, metallic *pik* or *tick.* **SIMILAR SPECIES:** Cassin's and House finches. **HABITAT:** Woods, groves, suburbs, feeders.

CASSIN'S FINCH *Haemorhous cassinii*   Fairly common M577

6¼ in. (16 cm). *Adult male:* Very similar to Purple Finch, but red of breast paler; *red crown contrasts abruptly* with brown nape; bill has straighter ridge. *Female and immature:* Sharper streaking above and below, streaked undertail coverts, pale eye-ring, and bill shape distinguish it from Purple Finch. **VOICE:** Song flutier and more varied than Purple's. Call a musical *chidiup.* **HABITAT:** Conifers in mountains, at feeders; some move to lower elevations in winter.

PINE GROSBEAK *Pinicola enucleator*   Scarce M575

8¾–9 in. (23 cm). A tame, robin-sized finch with stubby bill, longish tail and white wing bars. Flight undulating. May be seen on dirt roads. *Adult male:* Dull rose red. *Female:* Gray; head and rump tinged with dull mustard yellow. *Immature male:* Similar to female, but with touch of russet on head and rump. **VOICE:** Song a rich, rapid warbling. Call a musical *chee-vli* in Rockies and Cascades; *pe-pew-pew* in the north. **SIMILAR SPECIES:** Crossbills, Purple and Cassin's finches. **HABITAT:** Conifers, particularly lodgepole pines, larches.

RED FINCHES, ETC.

COMMON
REDPOLL

orange
variant

♂

♀

♂

HOUSE
FINCH

♀

♂

PURPLE
FINCH

♂

HOARY
REDPOLL

♀

♀

♂

♀

CASSIN'S
FINCH

♂

PINE GROSBEAK

EVENING GROSBEAK　　　　　　Uncommon, irregular M587
Coccothraustes vespertinus
8 in. (20 cm). A *chunky, starling-sized, short-tailed* finch with *very large, pale, conical bill* (sometimes tinged greenish). *Male:* Dull yellow, with darker head, *yellow eyebrow,* and black-and-white wings. *Female:* Silver gray, with white wing patches. Gregarious. **VOICE:** Song a short, uneven warble. Also a ringing, finchlike *clee-ip;* a high, clear *thew.* **SIMILAR SPECIES:** American Goldfinch (much smaller). **HABITAT:** Coniferous and mixed forests; in winter, also fruiting shrubs, feeders.

AMERICAN GOLDFINCH *Spinus tristis*　　　Fairly common M586
5 in. (13 cm). Goldfinches are distinguished from other small, olive-yellow birds (warblers, etc.) by their short, conical bill and behavior. *Breeding male: Yellow with black forehead and wings. Breeding female:* Dull yellow-olive; with blackish wings and conspicuous wing bars. *Nonbreeding:* Much like breeding female, but brownish; yellow on throat, bill dark. **VOICE:** Song clear, light, canary-like. In undulating flight, each dip is punctuated by *ti-DEE-di-di* or *po-ta-to-chip.* **SIMILAR SPECIES:** Other goldfinches, Yellow Warbler. **HABITAT:** Patches of thistles and weeds, dandelions on lawns, sweet-gum balls, open woods, edges; in winter, also feeders, where often in flocks.

LESSER GOLDFINCH *Spinus psaltria*　　　Fairly common M584
4½ in. (11 cm). *Male:* Dark above, yellow below, white on wings. Males of subspecies *psaltria* (s. Rockies) have *black* back; males of western subspecies *hesperophilus* have *greenish* back. Some birds intermediate. *Female:* Similar to nonbreeding American Goldfinch, but yellower below, *less contrasting wing bars, yellowish* (not white) *undertail coverts,* and *dark rump.* Calls differ. **VOICE:** Sweet, plaintive, whiny notes, *tee-yee* (rising) and *tee-yer* (dropping). Song more phrased than American Goldfinch's; will imitate other bird calls. **HABITAT:** Open brushy and weedy country, open woods, wooded streams, towns, parks, gardens, feeders.

LAWRENCE'S GOLDFINCH　　　　Uncommon, irregular M585
Spinus lawrencei
4¾ in. (12 cm). Known in all plumages by *large amount of yellow in wings. Male: Black face. Female and immature:* Very *plain and gray.* **VOICE:** Song similar to Lesser Goldfinch's, but with high tinkling notes and even more mimicry. Call distinctive: *tink-oo,* syllables emphasized equally. **SIMILAR SPECIES:** Other goldfinches. **HABITAT:** Oak-pine and riparian woodland edges, chaparral, ranch yards, parks; often found near isolated water sources.

PINE SISKIN *Spinus pinus*　　　Fairly common, irregular M583
5 in. (13 cm). Goldfinch-like but *heavily streaked* with *a touch of yellow in wings.* Often first detected by voice, flying over. **VOICE:** Call a loud *chlee-ip;* also a light *tit-i-tit;* a buzzy *shreeeee.* Song suggests goldfinch, but coarser, wheezy. **SIMILAR SPECIES:** Goldfinches, House Finch, Common Redpoll. **HABITAT:** Conifers, mixed woods, alders, sweet-gum balls, weedy areas, feeders.

♂

♀

EVENING GROSBEAK

nonbreeding ♂

breeding ♂

♀

AMERICAN GOLDFINCH

♂

♀

LESSER GOLDFINCH

black-backed

green-backed

♂

PINE SISKIN

♀

♂

LAWRENCE'S GOLDFINCH

♀

OLD WORLD SPARROWS Family Passeridae

Old World sparrows differ from our native sparrows (which are in the Emberizidae family) in several subtle ways, including having a more curved culmen (ridge on bill). The introduced and widespread House Sparrow is the best-known species. **FOOD:** Mainly insects, seeds. **RANGE:** Widespread in Old World, two species introduced in New World.

HOUSE SPARROW *Passer domesticus*   Common M588
6¼ in. (16 cm). Introduced from Europe in 1840. Familiar to many people. Sooty city birds often bear little resemblance to clean country males with *black throat, white cheeks, chestnut nape.* Much plainer female and young lack black throat, have dingy breast, and dull eye stripe *behind eye only;* note *single bold wing bar.* **VOICE:** Hoarse *chirp* and *shillip* notes, also a rising *sweep.* **SIMILAR SPECIES:** Female Dickcissel, buntings, sparrows. **HABITAT:** Cities, towns, farms, feeders.

WEAVERS Family Ploceidae

Old World family including weavers and bishops. Escaped captives established locally in s. CA and possibly very locally elsewhere. **FOOD:** Seeds, insects. **RANGE:** Native to Old World. Several species introduced.

ORANGE BISHOP *Euplectes franciscanus*   Uncommon, local
4¼ in. (10 cm). This small member of the weaver finch family is native to Africa but escaped cage birds have become established in CA. There is a local population in Los Angeles area. Short tail, large head, large bill. *Breeding male: Bright reddish body; black face, bill, belly. Female and nonbreeding male:* Similar to female House Sparrow or Grasshopper Sparrow, but with larger, *paler bill, short tail.*

ESTRILDID FINCHES Family Estrildidae

Old World family represented in N. America by escaped cage birds, including Nutmeg Mannikin.

NUTMEG MANNIKIN *Lonchura punctulata*   Uncommon, local
4½ in. (11 cm). A small, dark finch, native to se. Asia but escaped cage birds have become established in CA. Established very locally in moderate numbers in s. CA. *Adult:* Dark, *cocoa brown* body, large dark bill, brown *belly checked with white.* Sexes similar. *Juvenile:* Pale brown overall, bill dark.

INTRODUCED FINCHLIKE BIRDS

HOUSE
SPARROW

♂

♀

juvenile

Brown-headed
Cowbird
(p. 356)
for comparison

♀

breeding ♂

♀

ORANGE
BISHOP

NUTMEG
MANNIKIN

adult

MAPS

LIFE LIST

INDEX

RANGE MAPS

The maps on the following pages are approximate, giving the general outlines of the range of each species. Within these broad outlines may be many gaps—areas ecologically unsuitable for the species. A Marsh Wren must have a marsh, a Ruffed Grouse a woodland or a forest. Certain species may be extremely local or sporadic for reasons that may or may not be clear. Some birds are extending their ranges, a few explosively. Others are declining or even disappearing from large areas where they were formerly found. Winter ranges are often not as definite as breeding ranges. A species may exist at a very low density near the northern limits of its winter range, surviving through December in mild seasons but often succumbing to the bitter conditions of January and February. Varying weather conditions and food supplies from year to year may result in substantial variations in winter bird populations.

The maps are specific only for the area covered by this field guide. The Mallard, for example, is found over a large part of the globe. The map shows only its range in western North America.

The maps are based on data culled from many publications (particularly from monographs detailing the status and distribution of a state or province's avifauna, as well as from breeding bird atlases), from such journals as *North American Birds* (formerly *American Birds* and *Audubon Field Notes*), and from communication with many state and provincial experts from throughout North America. The following people provided additional help for this edition: Jim Arterburn (Oklahoma), Richard Erickson (Baja), Mark Lockwood (Texas), Jeff Marks (Montana), and Steve Mlodinow (Washington).

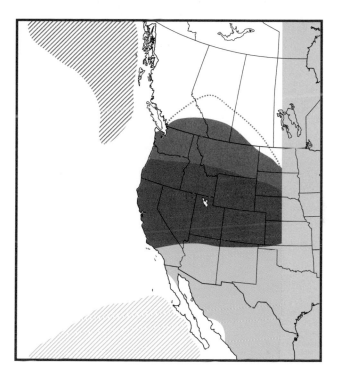

Many maps include comments on population increases and declines, extralimital occurrences, and regular winter or summer ranges outside North America. Migration routes are not depicted in these maps, but side notes sometimes include information on migration. Maps are likewise not filled in with solid color if the species is considered rare, very rare, casual, accidental, and/or a vagrant. Migrants can often be found in suitable habitat in those areas that lie between summering/ breeding areas and wintering/nonbreeding areas.

Key to Range Maps

Red: summer range
Blue: winter range
Purple: year-round range
Red dash line: approximate limits of irregular summer range and/or post-breeding dispersal
Blue dash line: approximate limits of irregular winter range
Purple dash line: approximate limits of irregular year-round range
Striped area: pelagic range

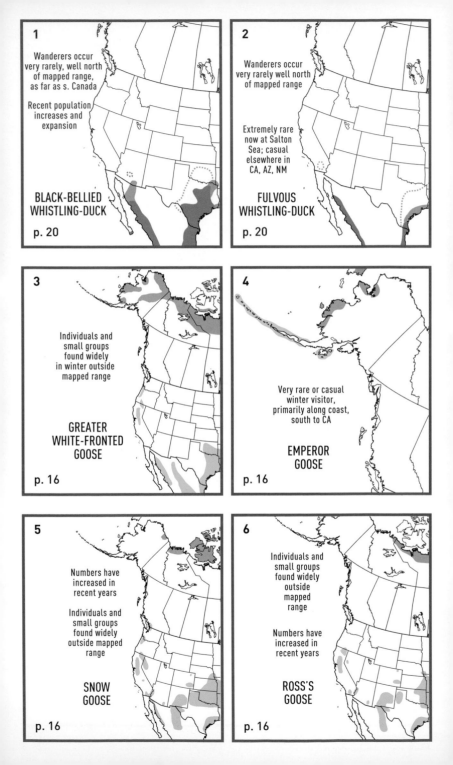

1
Wanderers occur very rarely, well north of mapped range, as far as s. Canada

Recent population increases and expansion

BLACK-BELLIED WHISTLING-DUCK

p. 20

2
Wanderers occur very rarely well north of mapped range

Extremely rare now at Salton Sea; casual elsewhere in CA, AZ, NM

FULVOUS WHISTLING-DUCK

p. 20

3
Individuals and small groups found widely in winter outside mapped range

GREATER WHITE-FRONTED GOOSE

p. 16

4
Very rare or casual winter visitor, primarily along coast, south to CA

EMPEROR GOOSE

p. 16

5
Numbers have increased in recent years

Individuals and small groups found widely outside mapped range

SNOW GOOSE

p. 16

6
Individuals and small groups found widely outside mapped range

Numbers have increased in recent years

ROSS'S GOOSE

p. 16

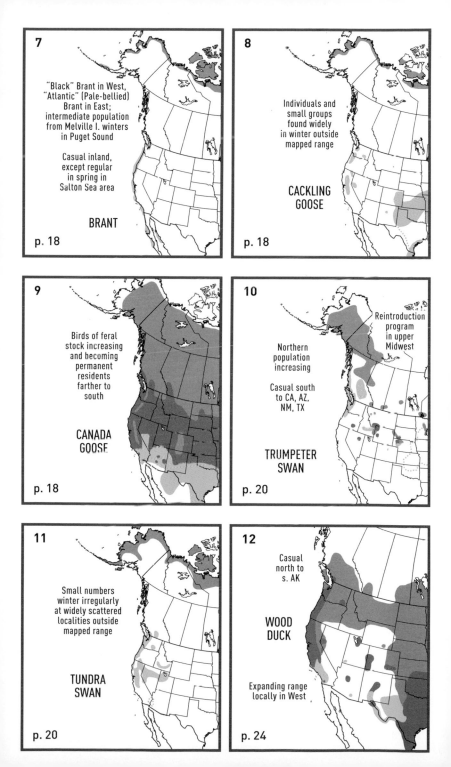

7

"Black" Brant in West, "Atlantic" (Pale-bellied) Brant in East; intermediate population from Melville I. winters in Puget Sound

Casual inland, except regular in spring in Salton Sea area

BRANT

p. 18

8

Individuals and small groups found widely in winter outside mapped range

CACKLING GOOSE

p. 18

9

Birds of feral stock increasing and becoming permanent residents farther to south

CANADA GOOSE

p. 18

10

Reintroduction program in upper Midwest

Northern population increasing

Casual south to CA, AZ, NM, TX

TRUMPETER SWAN

p. 20

11

Small numbers winter irregularly at widely scattered localities outside mapped range

TUNDRA SWAN

p. 20

12

Casual north to s. AK

WOOD DUCK

Expanding range locally in West

p. 24

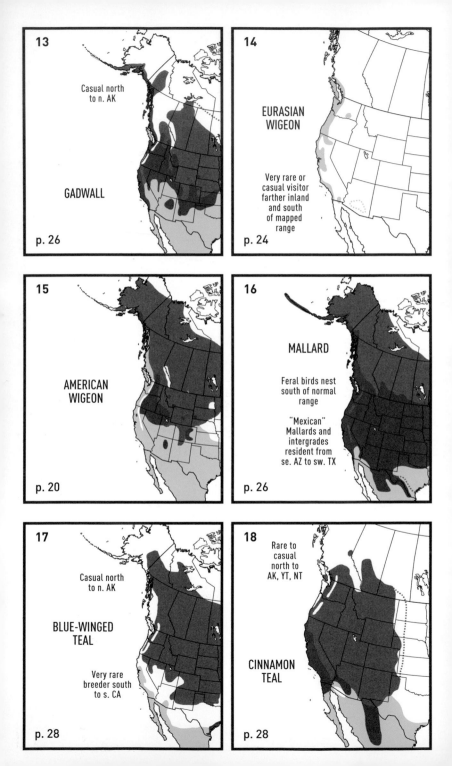

13

Casual north to n. AK

GADWALL

p. 26

14

EURASIAN WIGEON

Very rare or casual visitor farther inland and south of mapped range

p. 24

15

AMERICAN WIGEON

p. 20

16

MALLARD

Feral birds nest south of normal range

"Mexican" Mallards and intergrades resident from se. AZ to sw. TX

p. 26

17

Casual north to n. AK

BLUE-WINGED TEAL

Very rare breeder south to s. CA

p. 28

18

Rare to casual north to AK, YT, NT

CINNAMON TEAL

p. 28

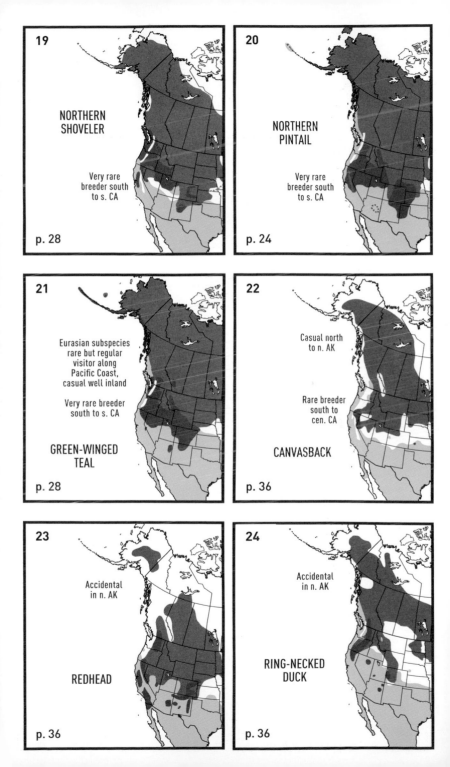

19 NORTHERN SHOVELER

Very rare breeder south to s. CA

p. 28

20 NORTHERN PINTAIL

Very rare breeder south to s. CA

p. 24

21 GREEN-WINGED TEAL

Eurasian subspecies rare but regular visitor along Pacific Coast, casual well inland

Very rare breeder south to s. CA

p. 28

22 CANVASBACK

Casual north to n. AK

Rare breeder south to cen. CA

p. 36

23 REDHEAD

Accidental in n. AK

p. 36

24 RING-NECKED DUCK

Accidental in n. AK

p. 36

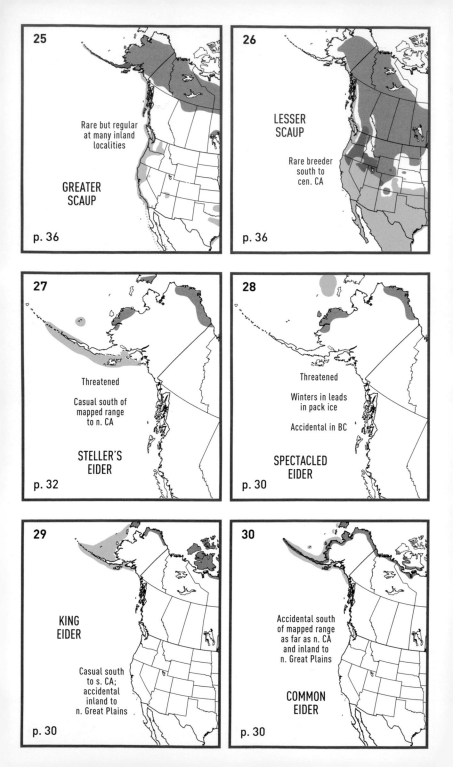

25

Rare but regular
at many inland
localities

GREATER
SCAUP

p. 36

26

LESSER
SCAUP

Rare breeder
south to
cen. CA

p. 36

27

Threatened

Casual south of
mapped range
to n. CA

STELLER'S
EIDER

p. 32

28

Threatened

Winters in leads
in pack ice

Accidental in BC

SPECTACLED
EIDER

p. 30

29

KING
EIDER

Casual south
to s. CA;
accidental inland to
n. Great Plains

p. 30

30

Accidental south
of mapped range
as far as n. CA
and inland to
n. Great Plains

COMMON
EIDER

p. 30

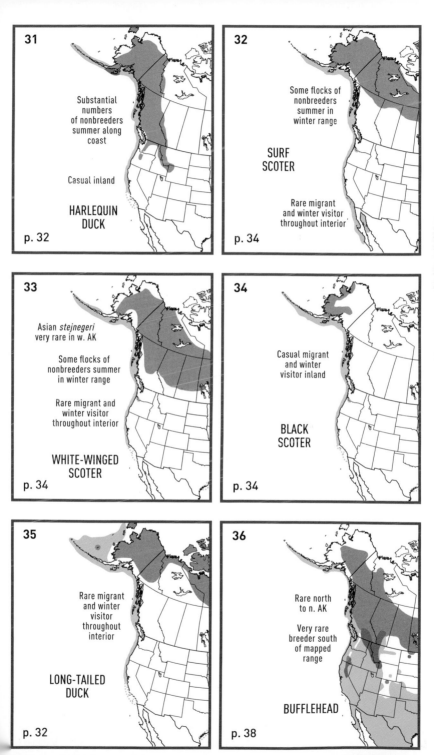

31

Substantial
numbers
of nonbreeders
summer along
coast

Casual inland

**HARLEQUIN
DUCK**

p. 32

32

Some flocks of
nonbreeders
summer in
winter range

**SURF
SCOTER**

Rare migrant
and winter visitor
throughout interior

p. 34

33

Asian *stejnegeri*
very rare in w. AK

Some flocks of
nonbreeders summer
in winter range

Rare migrant and
winter visitor
throughout interior

**WHITE-WINGED
SCOTER**

p. 34

34

Casual migrant
and winter
visitor inland

**BLACK
SCOTER**

p. 34

35

Rare migrant
and winter
visitor
throughout
interior

**LONG-TAILED
DUCK**

p. 32

36

Rare north
to n. AK

Very rare
breeder south
of mapped
range

BUFFLEHEAD

p. 38

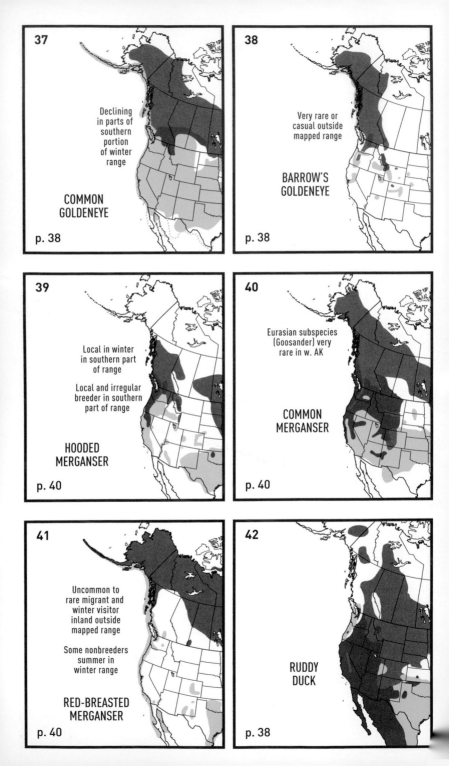

37

Declining in parts of southern portion of winter range

COMMON GOLDENEYE

p. 38

38

Very rare or casual outside mapped range

BARROW'S GOLDENEYE

p. 38

39

Local in winter in southern part of range

Local and irregular breeder in southern part of range

HOODED MERGANSER

p. 40

40

Eurasian subspecies (Goosander) very rare in w. AK

COMMON MERGANSER

p. 40

41

Uncommon to rare migrant and winter visitor inland outside mapped range

Some nonbreeders summer in winter range

RED-BREASTED MERGANSER

p. 40

42

RUDDY DUCK

p. 38

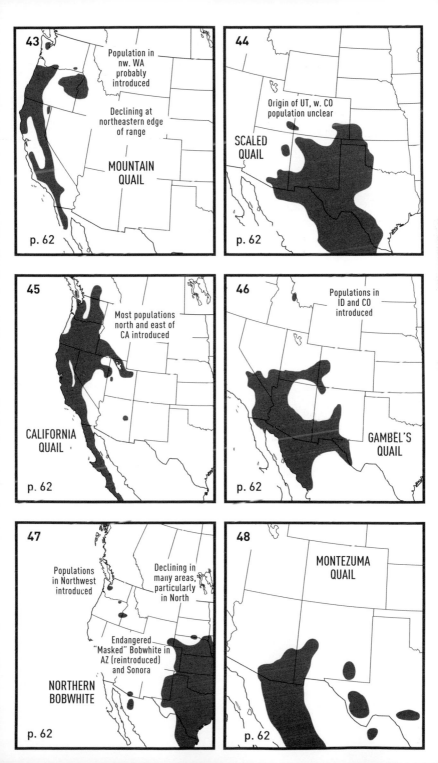

43 MOUNTAIN QUAIL

Population in nw. WA probably introduced

Declining at northeastern edge of range

p. 62

44 SCALED QUAIL

Origin of UT, w. CO population unclear

p. 62

45 CALIFORNIA QUAIL

Most populations north and east of CA introduced

p. 62

46 GAMBEL'S QUAIL

Populations in ID and CO introduced

p. 62

47 NORTHERN BOBWHITE

Populations in Northwest introduced

Declining in many areas, particularly in North

Endangered "Masked" Bobwhite in AZ (reintroduced) and Sonora

p. 62

48 MONTEZUMA QUAIL

p. 62

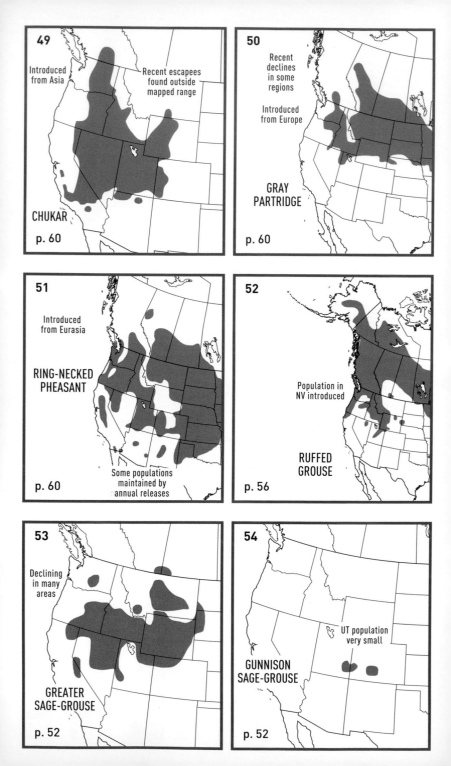

49
Introduced from Asia

Recent escapees found outside mapped range

CHUKAR

p. 60

50
Recent declines in some regions

Introduced from Europe

GRAY PARTRIDGE

p. 60

51
Introduced from Eurasia

RING-NECKED PHEASANT

Some populations maintained by annual releases

p. 60

52
Population in NV introduced

RUFFED GROUSE

p. 56

53
Declining in many areas

GREATER SAGE-GROUSE

p. 52

54
UT population very small

GUNNISON SAGE-GROUSE

p. 52

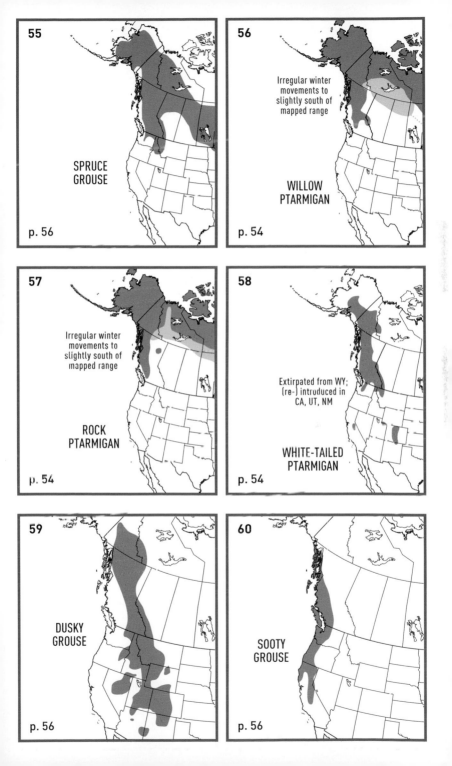

55 SPRUCE GROUSE
p. 56

56 WILLOW PTARMIGAN
Irregular winter movements to slightly south of mapped range
p. 54

57 ROCK PTARMIGAN
Irregular winter movements to slightly south of mapped range
p. 54

58 WHITE-TAILED PTARMIGAN
Extirpated from WY; (re-) introduced in CA, UT, NM
p. 54

59 DUSKY GROUSE
p. 56

60 SOOTY GROUSE
p. 56

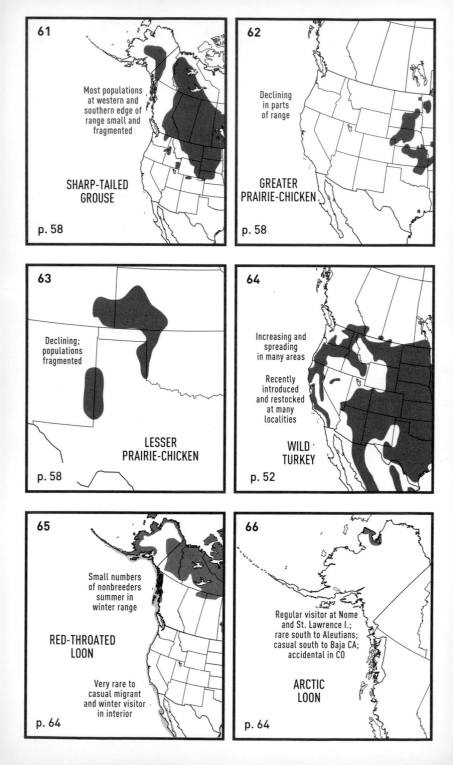

61

Most populations at western and southern edge of range small and fragmented

SHARP-TAILED GROUSE

p. 58

62

Declining in parts of range

GREATER PRAIRIE-CHICKEN

p. 58

63

Declining; populations fragmented

LESSER PRAIRIE-CHICKEN

p. 58

64

Increasing and spreading in many areas

Recently introduced and restocked at many localities

WILD TURKEY

p. 52

65

Small numbers of nonbreeders summer in winter range

RED-THROATED LOON

Very rare to casual migrant and winter visitor in interior

p. 64

66

Regular visitor at Nome and St. Lawrence I.; rare south to Aleutians; casual south to Baja CA; accidental in CO

ARCTIC LOON

p. 64

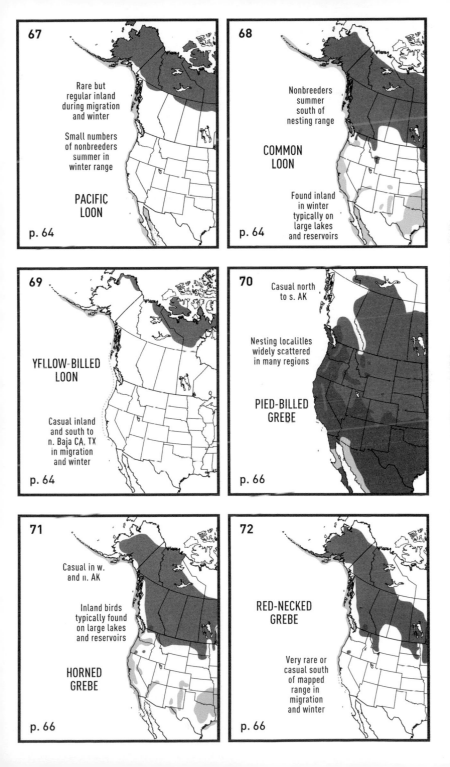

67

Rare but regular inland during migration and winter

Small numbers of nonbreeders summer in winter range

PACIFIC LOON

p. 64

68

Nonbreeders summer south of nesting range

COMMON LOON

Found inland in winter typically on large lakes and reservoirs

p. 64

69

YFLLOW-BILLED LOON

Casual inland and south to n. Baja CA, TX in migration and winter

p. 64

70

Casual north to s. AK

Nesting localities widely scattered in many regions

PIED-BILLED GREBE

p. 66

71

Casual in w. and n. AK

Inland birds typically found on large lakes and reservoirs

HORNED GREBE

p. 66

72

RED-NECKED GREBE

Very rare or casual south of mapped range in migration and winter

p. 66

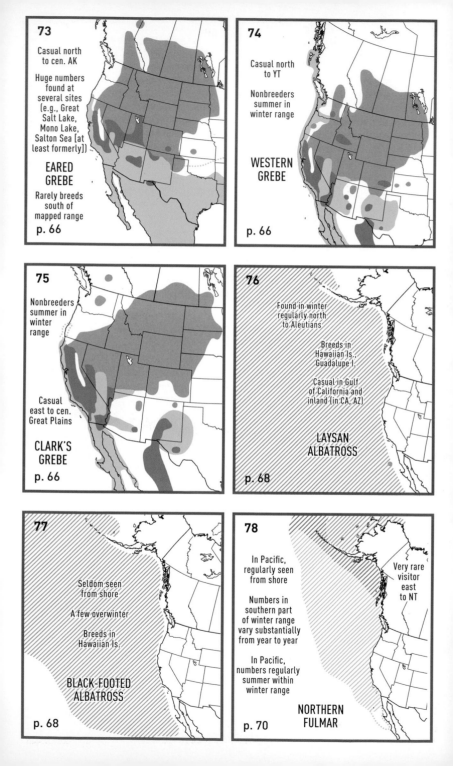

73

Casual north to cen. AK

Huge numbers found at several sites (e.g., Great Salt Lake, Mono Lake, Salton Sea [at least formerly])

EARED GREBE

Rarely breeds south of mapped range

p. 66

74

Casual north to YT

Nonbreeders summer in winter range

WESTERN GREBE

p. 66

75

Nonbreeders summer in winter range

Casual east to cen. Great Plains

CLARK'S GREBE

p. 66

76

Found in winter regularly north to Aleutians

Breeds in Hawaiian Is., Guadalupe I.

Casual in Gulf of California and inland (in CA, AZ)

LAYSAN ALBATROSS

p. 68

77

Seldom seen from shore

A few overwinter

Breeds in Hawaiian Is.

BLACK-FOOTED ALBATROSS

p. 68

78

In Pacific, regularly seen from shore

Numbers in southern part of winter range vary substantially from year to year

In Pacific, numbers regularly summer within winter range

Very rare visitor east to NT

NORTHERN FULMAR

p. 70

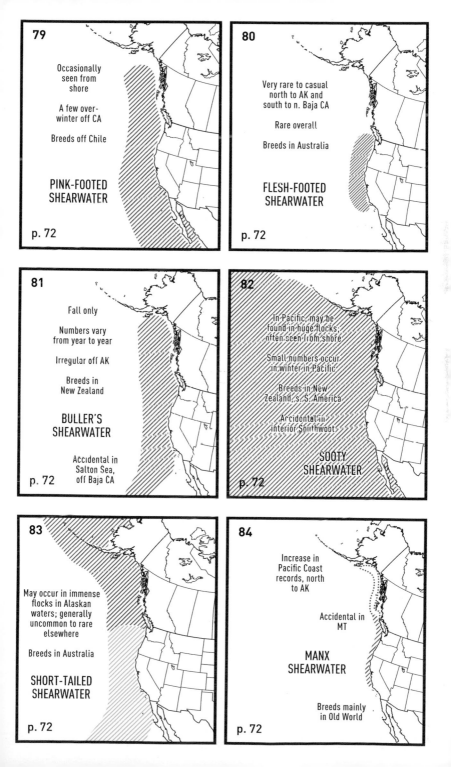

79

Occasionally seen from shore

A few over-winter off CA

Breeds off Chile

PINK-FOOTED SHEARWATER

p. 72

80

Very rare to casual north to AK and south to n. Baja CA

Rare overall

Breeds in Australia

FLESH-FOOTED SHEARWATER

p. 72

81

Fall only

Numbers vary from year to year

Irregular off AK

Breeds in New Zealand

BULLER'S SHEARWATER

Accidental in Salton Sea, off Baja CA

p. 72

82

In Pacific, may be found in huge flocks, often seen from shore

Small numbers occur in winter in Pacific

Breeds in New Zealand, s. S. America

Accidental in interior Southwest

SOOTY SHEARWATER

p. 72

83

May occur in immense flocks in Alaskan waters; generally uncommon to rare elsewhere

Breeds in Australia

SHORT-TAILED SHEARWATER

p. 72

84

Increase in Pacific Coast records, north to AK

Accidental in MT

MANX SHEARWATER

Breeds mainly in Old World

p. 72

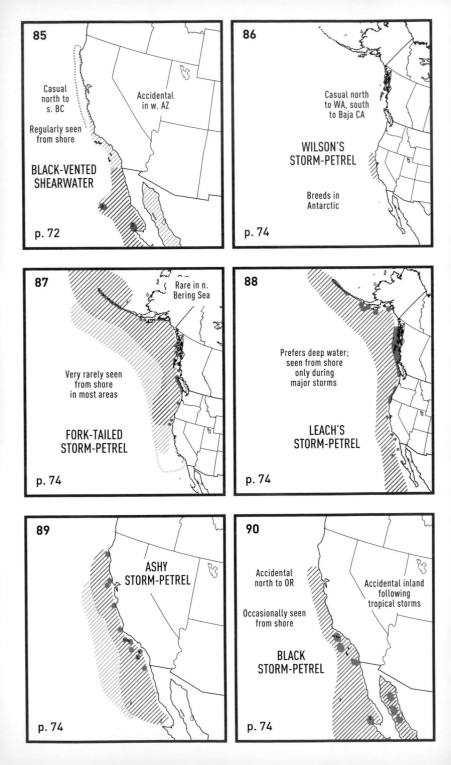

85

Casual north to s. BC

Regularly seen from shore

Accidental in w. AZ

BLACK-VENTED SHEARWATER

p. 72

86

Casual north to WA, south to Baja CA

WILSON'S STORM-PETREL

Breeds in Antarctic

p. 74

87

Rare in n. Bering Sea

Very rarely seen from shore in most areas

FORK-TAILED STORM-PETREL

p. 74

88

Prefers deep water; seen from shore only during major storms

LEACH'S STORM-PETREL

p. 74

89

ASHY STORM-PETREL

p. 74

90

Accidental north to OR

Occasionally seen from shore

Accidental inland following tropical storms

BLACK STORM-PETREL

p. 74

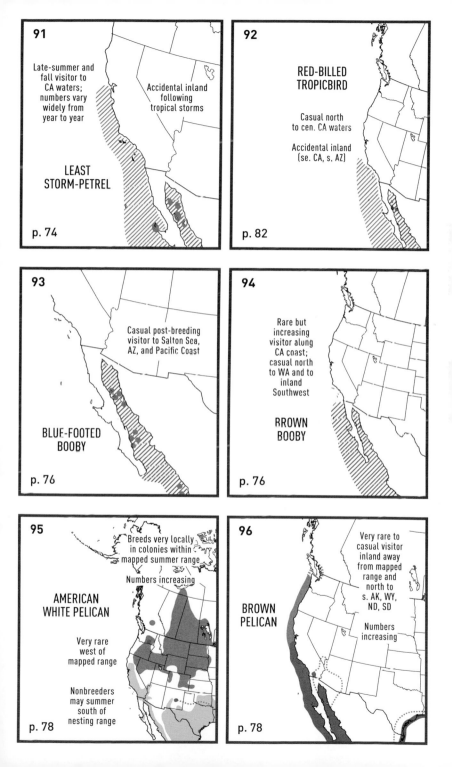

91

Late-summer and fall visitor to CA waters; numbers vary widely from year to year

Accidental inland following tropical storms

LEAST STORM-PETREL

p. 74

92

RED-BILLED TROPICBIRD

Casual north to cen. CA waters

Accidental inland (se. CA, s. AZ)

p. 82

93

Casual post-breeding visitor to Salton Sea, AZ, and Pacific Coast

BLUE-FOOTED BOOBY

p. 76

94

Rare but increasing visitor along CA coast; casual north to WA and to inland Southwest

BROWN BOOBY

p. 76

95

Breeds very locally in colonies within mapped summer range

Numbers increasing

AMERICAN WHITE PELICAN

Very rare west of mapped range

Nonbreeders may summer south of nesting range

p. 78

96

Very rare to casual visitor inland away from mapped range and north to s. AK, WY, ND, SD

Numbers increasing

BROWN PELICAN

p. 78

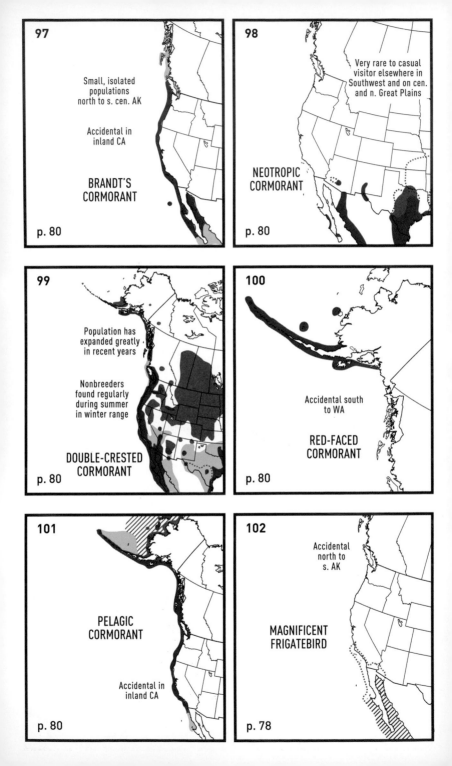

97

Small, isolated populations north to s. cen. AK

Accidental in inland CA

BRANDT'S CORMORANT

p. 80

98

Very rare to casual visitor elsewhere in Southwest and on cen. and n. Great Plains

NEOTROPIC CORMORANT

p. 80

99

Population has expanded greatly in recent years

Nonbreeders found regularly during summer in winter range

DOUBLE-CRESTED CORMORANT

p. 80

100

Accidental south to WA

RED-FACED CORMORANT

p. 80

101

PELAGIC CORMORANT

Accidental in inland CA

p. 80

102

Accidental north to s. AK

MAGNIFICENT FRIGATEBIRD

p. 78

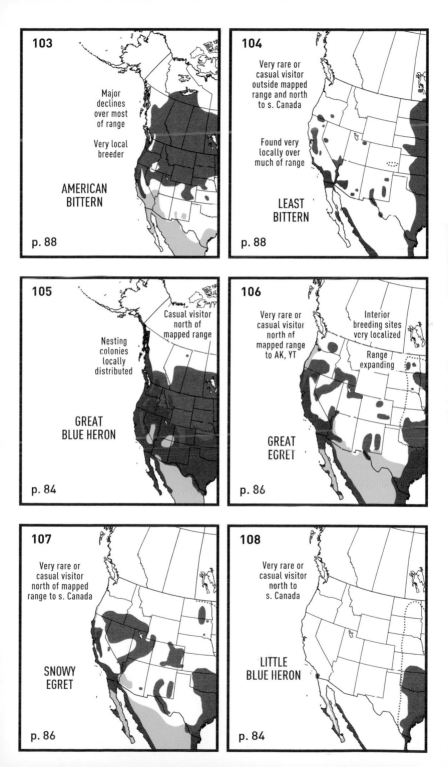

103
Major declines over most of range

Very local breeder

AMERICAN BITTERN

p. 88

104
Very rare or casual visitor outside mapped range and north to s. Canada

Found very locally over much of range

LEAST BITTERN

p. 88

105
Casual visitor north of mapped range

Nesting colonies locally distributed

GREAT BLUE HERON

p. 84

106
Very rare or casual visitor north of mapped range to AK, YT

Interior breeding sites very localized

Range expanding

GREAT EGRET

p. 86

107
Very rare or casual visitor north of mapped range to s. Canada

SNOWY EGRET

p. 86

108
Very rare or casual visitor north to s. Canada

LITTLE BLUE HERON

p. 84

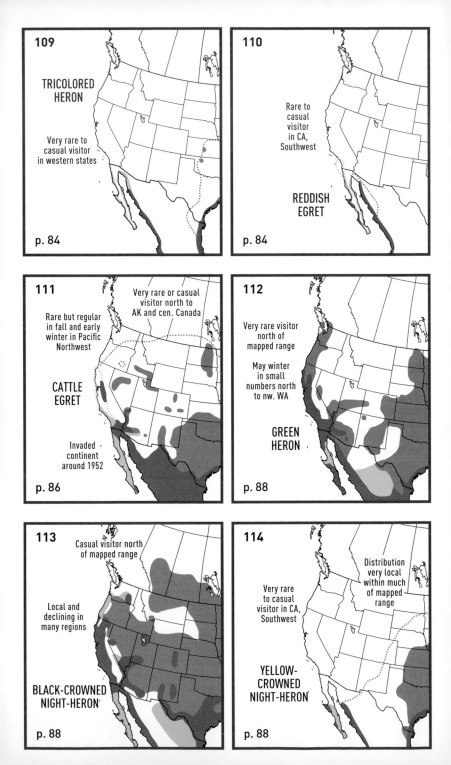

109

TRICOLORED HERON

Very rare to casual visitor in western states

p. 84

110

Rare to casual visitor in CA, Southwest

REDDISH EGRET

p. 84

111

Very rare or casual visitor north to AK and cen. Canada

Rare but regular in fall and early winter in Pacific Northwest

CATTLE EGRET

Invaded continent around 1952

p. 86

112

Very rare visitor north of mapped range

May winter in small numbers north to nw. WA

GREEN HERON

p. 88

113

Casual visitor north of mapped range

Local and declining in many regions

BLACK-CROWNED NIGHT-HERON

p. 88

114

Distribution very local within much of mapped range

Very rare to casual visitor in CA, Southwest

YELLOW-CROWNED NIGHT-HERON

p. 88

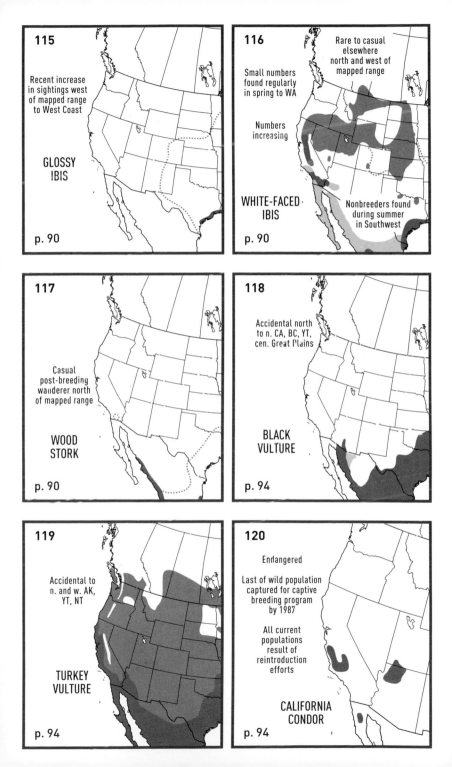

115 GLOSSY IBIS

Recent increase in sightings west of mapped range to West Coast

p. 90

116 WHITE-FACED IBIS

Rare to casual elsewhere north and west of mapped range

Small numbers found regularly in spring to WA

Numbers increasing

Nonbreeders found during summer in Southwest

p. 90

117 WOOD STORK

Casual post-breeding wanderer north of mapped range

p. 90

118 BLACK VULTURE

Accidental north to n. CA, BC, YT, cen. Great Plains

p. 94

119 TURKEY VULTURE

Accidental to n. and w. AK, YT, NT

p. 94

120 CALIFORNIA CONDOR

Endangered

Last of wild population captured for captive breeding program by 1987

All current populations result of reintroduction efforts

p. 94

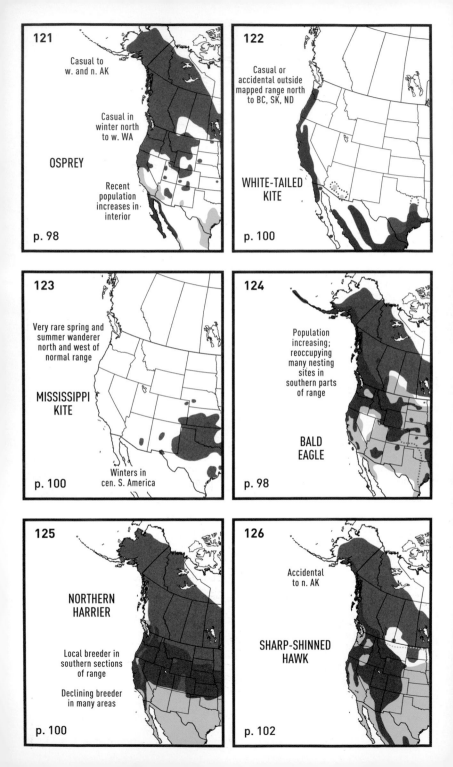

121

Casual to w. and n. AK

Casual in winter north to w. WA

OSPREY

Recent population increases in interior

p. 98

122

Casual or accidental outside mapped range north to BC, SK, ND

WHITE-TAILED KITE

p. 100

123

Very rare spring and summer wanderer north and west of normal range

MISSISSIPPI KITE

Winters in cen. S. America

p. 100

124

Population increasing; reoccupying many nesting sites in southern parts of range

BALD EAGLE

p. 98

125

NORTHERN HARRIER

Local breeder in southern sections of range

Declining breeder in many areas

p. 100

126

Accidental to n. AK

SHARP-SHINNED HAWK

p. 102

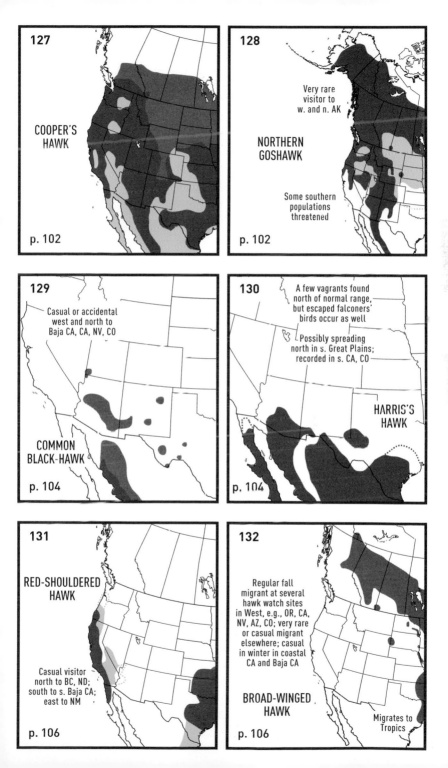

127

COOPER'S
HAWK

p. 102

128

Very rare
visitor to
w. and n. AK

NORTHERN
GOSHAWK

Some southern
populations
threatened

p. 102

129

Casual or accidental
west and north to
Baja CA, CA, NV, CO

COMMON
BLACK-HAWK

p. 104

130

A few vagrants found
north of normal range,
but escaped falconers'
birds occur as well

Possibly spreading
north in s. Great Plains;
recorded in s. CA, CO

HARRIS'S
HAWK

p. 104

131

RED-SHOULDERED
HAWK

Casual visitor
north to BC, ND;
south to s. Baja CA;
east to NM

p. 106

132

Regular fall
migrant at several
hawk watch sites
in West, e.g., OR, CA,
NV, AZ, CO; very rare
or casual migrant
elsewhere; casual
in winter in coastal
CA and Baja CA

BROAD-WINGED
HAWK

Migrates to
Tropics

p. 106

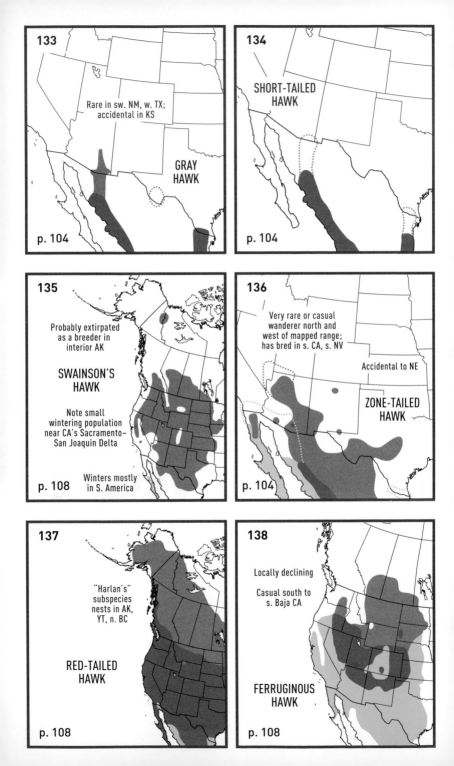

133 Rare in sw. NM, w. TX; accidental in KS

GRAY HAWK

p. 104

134 SHORT-TAILED HAWK

p. 104

135 Probably extirpated as a breeder in interior AK

SWAINSON'S HAWK

Note small wintering population near CA's Sacramento–San Joaquin Delta

Winters mostly in S. America

p. 108

136 Very rare or casual wanderer north and west of mapped range; has bred in s. CA, s. NV

Accidental to NE

ZONE-TAILED HAWK

p. 104

137 "Harlan's" subspecies nests in AK, YT, n. BC

RED-TAILED HAWK

p. 108

138 Locally declining

Casual south to s. Baja CA

FERRUGINOUS HAWK

p. 108

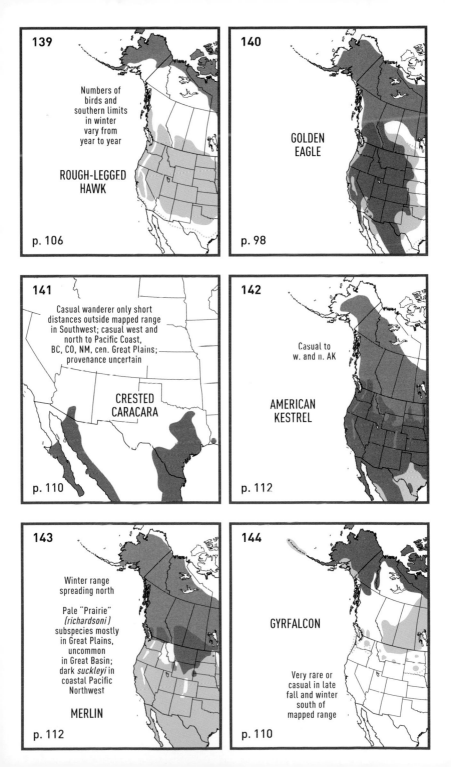

139

Numbers of birds and southern limits in winter vary from year to year

ROUGH-LEGGED HAWK

p. 106

140

GOLDEN EAGLE

p. 98

141

Casual wanderer only short distances outside mapped range in Southwest; casual west and north to Pacific Coast, BC, CO, NM, cen. Great Plains; provenance uncertain

CRESTED CARACARA

p. 110

142

Casual to w. and n. AK

AMERICAN KESTREL

p. 112

143

Winter range spreading north

Pale "Prairie" *(richardsoni)* subspecies mostly in Great Plains, uncommon in Great Basin; dark *suckleyi* in coastal Pacific Northwest

MERLIN

p. 112

144

GYRFALCON

Very rare or casual in late fall and winter south of mapped range

p. 110

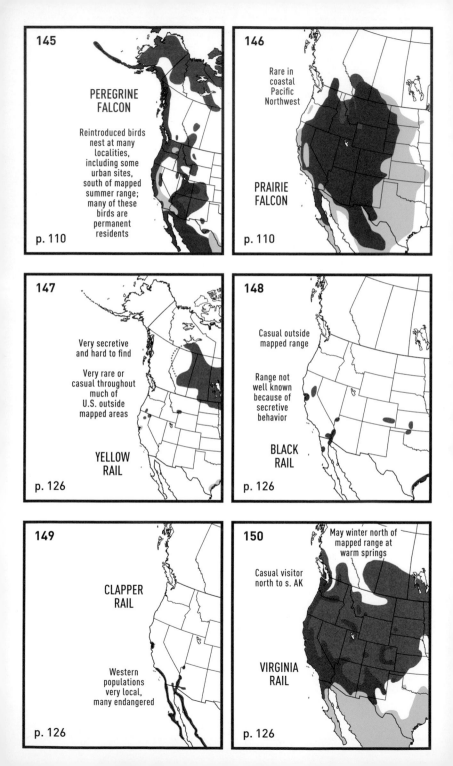

145

PEREGRINE FALCON

Reintroduced birds nest at many localities, including some urban sites, south of mapped summer range; many of these birds are permanent residents

p. 110

146

Rare in coastal Pacific Northwest

PRAIRIE FALCON

p. 110

147

Very secretive and hard to find

Very rare or casual throughout much of U.S. outside mapped areas

YELLOW RAIL

p. 126

148

Casual outside mapped range

Range not well known because of secretive behavior

BLACK RAIL

p. 126

149

CLAPPER RAIL

Western populations very local, many endangered

p. 126

150

May winter north of mapped range at warm springs

Casual visitor north to s. AK

VIRGINIA RAIL

p. 126

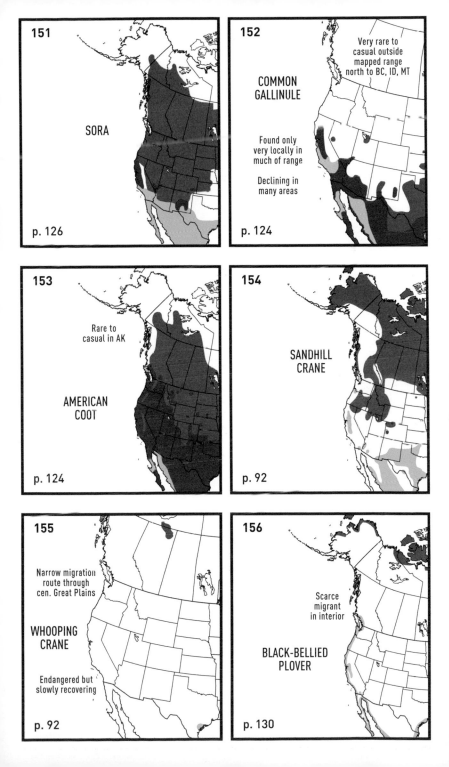

151 SORA
p. 126

152 COMMON GALLINULE
Very rare to casual outside mapped range north to BC, ID, MT
Found only very locally in much of range
Declining in many areas
p. 124

153 AMERICAN COOT
Rare to casual in AK
p. 124

154 SANDHILL CRANE
p. 92

155 WHOOPING CRANE
Narrow migration route through cen. Great Plains
Endangered but slowly recovering
p. 92

156 BLACK-BELLIED PLOVER
Scarce migrant in interior
p. 130

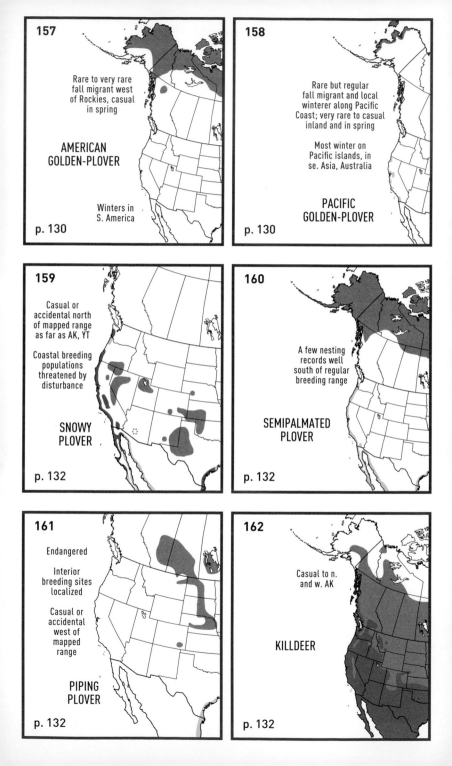

157

Rare to very rare
fall migrant west
of Rockies, casual
in spring

**AMERICAN
GOLDEN-PLOVER**

Winters in
S. America

p. 130

158

Rare but regular
fall migrant and local
winterer along Pacific
Coast; very rare to casual
inland and in spring

Most winter on
Pacific islands, in
se. Asia, Australia

**PACIFIC
GOLDEN-PLOVER**

p. 130

159

Casual or
accidental north
of mapped range
as far as AK, YT

Coastal breeding
populations
threatened by
disturbance

**SNOWY
PLOVER**

p. 132

160

A few nesting
records well
south of regular
breeding range

**SEMIPALMATED
PLOVER**

p. 132

161

Endangered

Interior
breeding sites
localized

Casual or
accidental
west of
mapped
range

**PIPING
PLOVER**

p. 132

162

Casual to n.
and w. AK

KILLDEER

p. 132

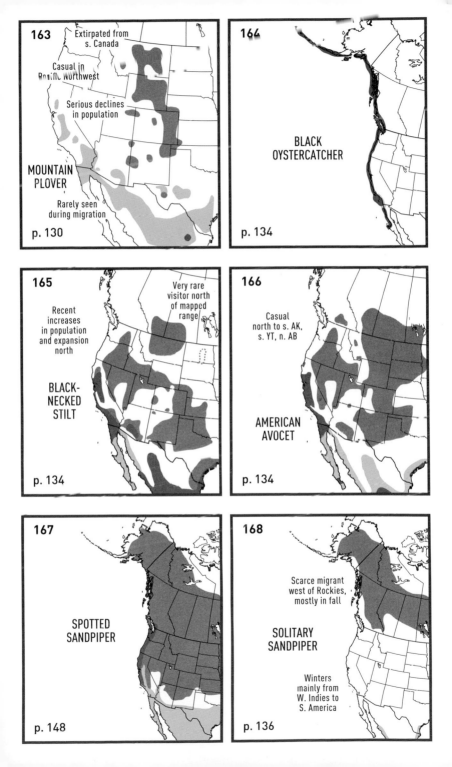

163
Extirpated from s. Canada
Casual in Pacific Northwest
Serious declines in population
MOUNTAIN PLOVER
Rarely seen during migration
p. 130

164
BLACK OYSTERCATCHER
p. 134

165
Recent increases in population and expansion north
Very rare visitor north of mapped range
BLACK-NECKED STILT
p. 134

166
Casual north to s. AK, s. YT, n. AB
AMERICAN AVOCET
p. 134

167
SPOTTED SANDPIPER
p. 148

168
Scarce migrant west of Rockies, mostly in fall
SOLITARY SANDPIPER
Winters mainly from W. Indies to S. America
p. 136

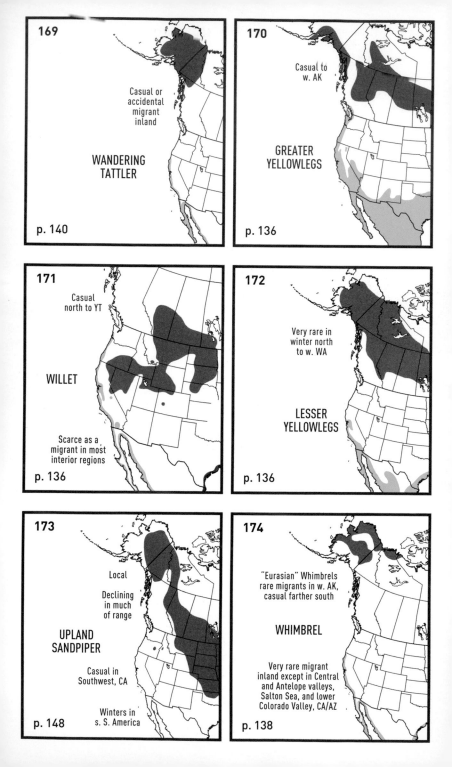

169

Casual or accidental migrant inland

WANDERING TATTLER

p. 140

170

Casual to w. AK

GREATER YELLOWLEGS

p. 136

171

Casual north to YT

WILLET

Scarce as a migrant in most interior regions

p. 136

172

Very rare in winter north to w. WA

LESSER YELLOWLEGS

p. 136

173

Local

Declining in much of range

UPLAND SANDPIPER

Casual in Southwest, CA

Winters in s. S. America

p. 148

174

"Eurasian" Whimbrels rare migrants in w. AK, casual farther south

WHIMBREL

Very rare migrant inland except in Central and Antelope valleys, Salton Sea, and lower Colorado Valley, CA/AZ

p. 138

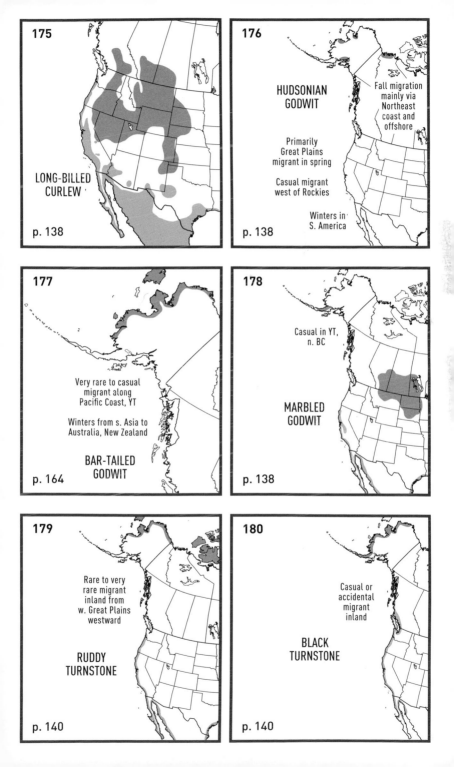

175

LONG-BILLED
CURLEW

p. 138

176

HUDSONIAN
GODWIT

Primarily
Great Plains
migrant in spring

Casual migrant
west of Rockies

Winters in
S. America

Fall migration
mainly via
Northeast
coast and
offshore

p. 138

177

Very rare to casual
migrant along
Pacific Coast, YT

Winters from s. Asia to
Australia, New Zealand

BAR-TAILED
GODWIT

p. 164

178

Casual in YT,
n. BC

MARBLED
GODWIT

p. 138

179

Rare to very
rare migrant
inland from
w. Great Plains
westward

RUDDY
TURNSTONE

p. 140

180

Casual or
accidental
migrant
inland

BLACK
TURNSTONE

p. 140

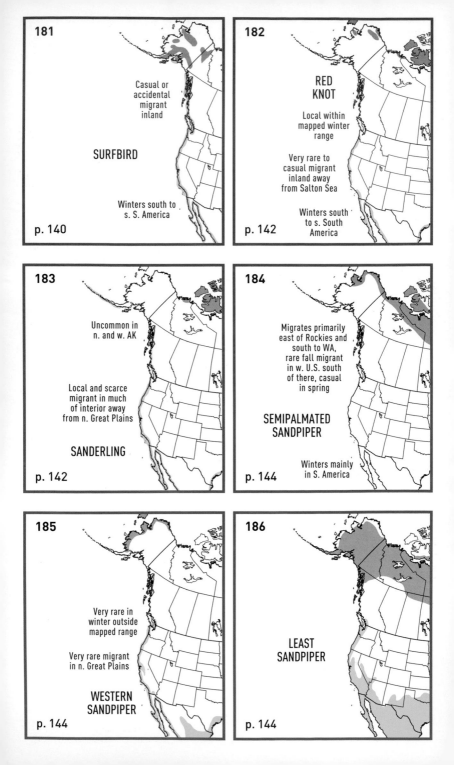

181

Casual or accidental migrant inland

SURFBIRD

Winters south to s. S. America

p. 140

182

RED KNOT

Local within mapped winter range

Very rare to casual migrant inland away from Salton Sea

Winters south to s. South America

p. 142

183

Uncommon in n. and w. AK

Local and scarce migrant in much of interior away from n. Great Plains

SANDERLING

p. 142

184

Migrates primarily east of Rockies and south to WA, rare fall migrant in w. U.S. south of there, casual in spring

SEMIPALMATED SANDPIPER

Winters mainly in S. America

p. 144

185

Very rare in winter outside mapped range

Very rare migrant in n. Great Plains

WESTERN SANDPIPER

p. 144

186

LEAST SANDPIPER

p. 144

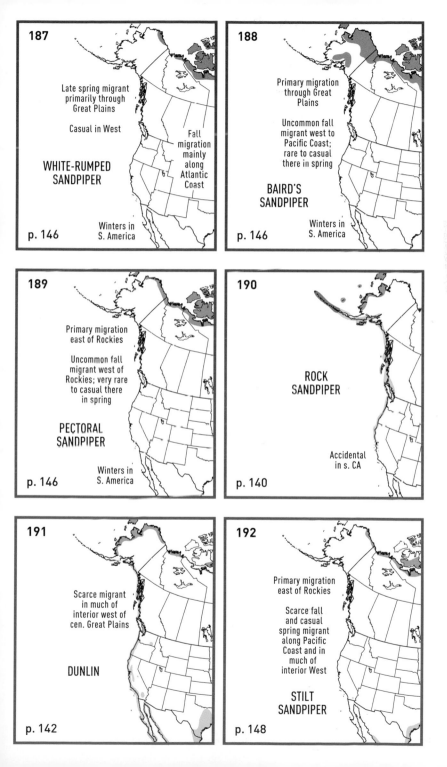

187

Late spring migrant primarily through Great Plains

Casual in West

Fall migration mainly along Atlantic Coast

WHITE-RUMPED SANDPIPER

p. 146

Winters in S. America

188

Primary migration through Great Plains

Uncommon fall migrant west to Pacific Coast; rare to casual there in spring

BAIRD'S SANDPIPER

p. 146

Winters in S. America

189

Primary migration east of Rockies

Uncommon fall migrant west of Rockies; very rare to casual there in spring

PECTORAL SANDPIPER

p. 146

Winters in S. America

190

ROCK SANDPIPER

Accidental in s. CA

p. 140

191

Scarce migrant in much of interior west of cen. Great Plains

DUNLIN

p. 142

192

Primary migration east of Rockies

Scarce fall and casual spring migrant along Pacific Coast and in much of interior West

STILT SANDPIPER

p. 148

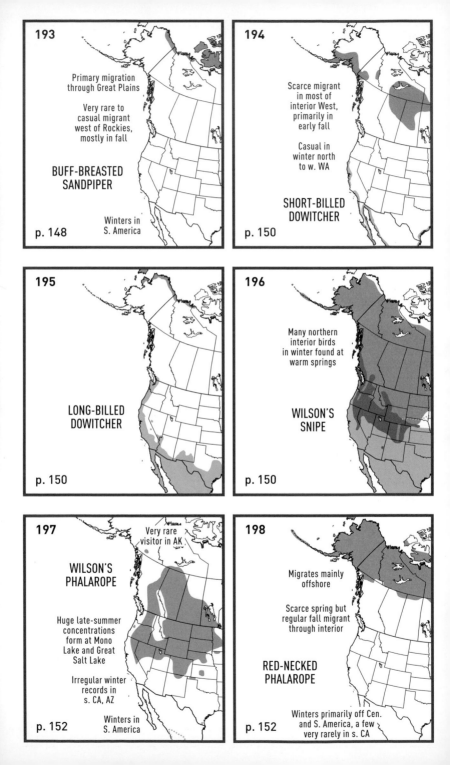

193

Primary migration
through Great Plains

Very rare to
casual migrant
west of Rockies,
mostly in fall

**BUFF-BREASTED
SANDPIPER**

Winters in
S. America

p. 148

194

Scarce migrant
in most of
interior West,
primarily in
early fall

Casual in
winter north
to w. WA

**SHORT-BILLED
DOWITCHER**

p. 150

195

**LONG-BILLED
DOWITCHER**

p. 150

196

Many northern
interior birds
in winter found at
warm springs

**WILSON'S
SNIPE**

p. 150

197

Very rare
visitor in AK

**WILSON'S
PHALAROPE**

Huge late-summer
concentrations
form at Mono
Lake and Great
Salt Lake

Irregular winter
records in
s. CA, AZ

Winters in
S. America

p. 152

198

Migrates mainly
offshore

Scarce spring but
regular fall migrant
through interior

**RED-NECKED
PHALAROPE**

Winters primarily off Cen.
and S. America, a few
very rarely in s. CA

p. 152

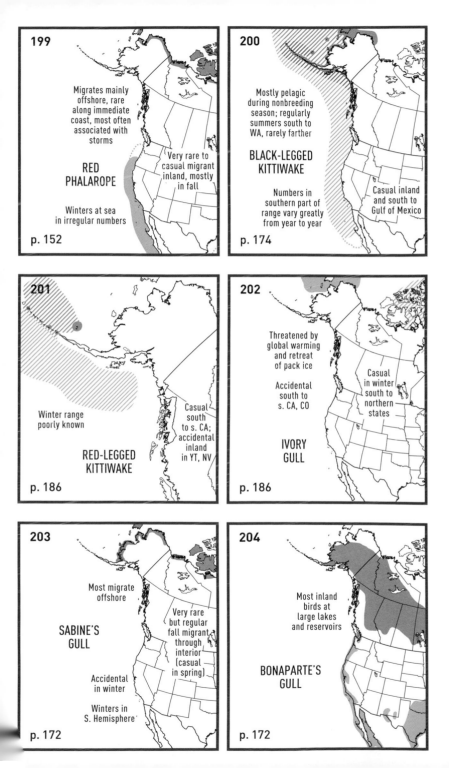

199

Migrates mainly offshore, rare along immediate coast, most often associated with storms

RED PHALAROPE

Very rare to casual migrant inland, mostly in fall

Winters at sea in irregular numbers

p. 152

200

Mostly pelagic during nonbreeding season; regularly summers south to WA, rarely farther

BLACK-LEGGED KITTIWAKE

Numbers in southern part of range vary greatly from year to year

Casual inland and south to Gulf of Mexico

p. 174

201

Winter range poorly known

RED-LEGGED KITTIWAKE

Casual south to s. CA; accidental inland in YT, NV

p. 186

202

Threatened by global warming and retreat of pack ice

Accidental south to s. CA, CO

IVORY GULL

Casual in winter south to northern states

p. 186

203

Most migrate offshore

SABINE'S GULL

Very rare but regular fall migrant through interior (casual in spring)

Accidental in winter

Winters in S. Hemisphere

p. 172

204

Most inland birds at large lakes and reservoirs

BONAPARTE'S GULL

p. 172

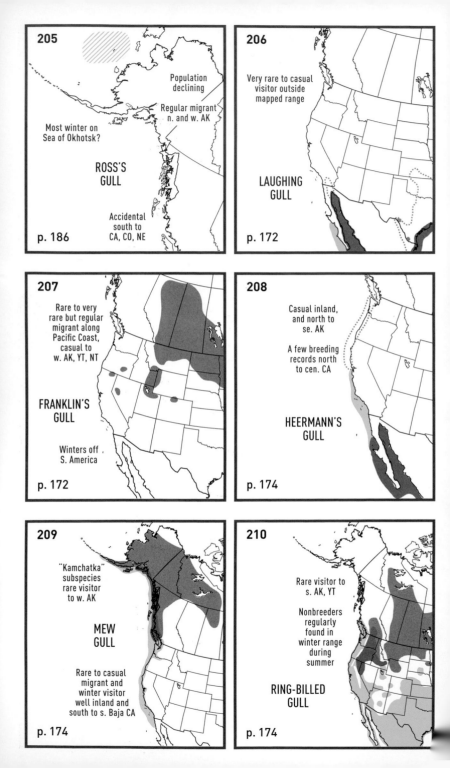

205

Population declining

Regular migrant n. and w. AK

Most winter on Sea of Okhotsk?

ROSS'S GULL

Accidental south to CA, CO, NE

p. 186

206

Very rare to casual visitor outside mapped range

LAUGHING GULL

p. 172

207

Rare to very rare but regular migrant along Pacific Coast, casual to w. AK, YT, NT

FRANKLIN'S GULL

Winters off S. America

p. 172

208

Casual inland, and north to se. AK

A few breeding records north to cen. CA

HEERMANN'S GULL

p. 174

209

"Kamchatka" subspecies rare visitor to w. AK

MEW GULL

Rare to casual migrant and winter visitor well inland and south to s. Baja CA

p. 174

210

Rare visitor to s. AK, YT

Nonbreeders regularly found in winter range during summer

RING-BILLED GULL

p. 174

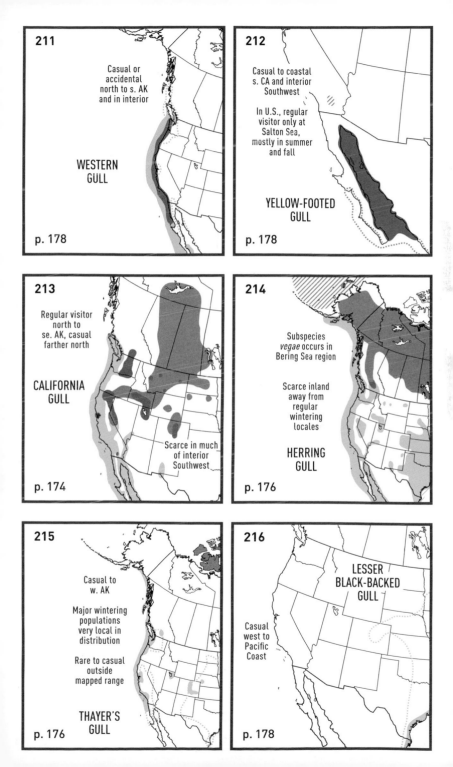

211

Casual or accidental north to s. AK and in interior

WESTERN GULL

p. 178

212

Casual to coastal s. CA and interior Southwest

In U.S., regular visitor only at Salton Sea, mostly in summer and fall

YELLOW-FOOTED GULL

p. 178

213

Regular visitor north to se. AK, casual farther north

CALIFORNIA GULL

Scarce in much of interior Southwest

p. 174

214

Subspecies *vegae* occurs in Bering Sea region

Scarce inland away from regular wintering locales

HERRING GULL

p. 176

215

Casual to w. AK

Major wintering populations very local in distribution

Rare to casual outside mapped range

THAYER'S GULL

p. 176

216

LESSER BLACK-BACKED GULL

Casual west to Pacific Coast

p. 178

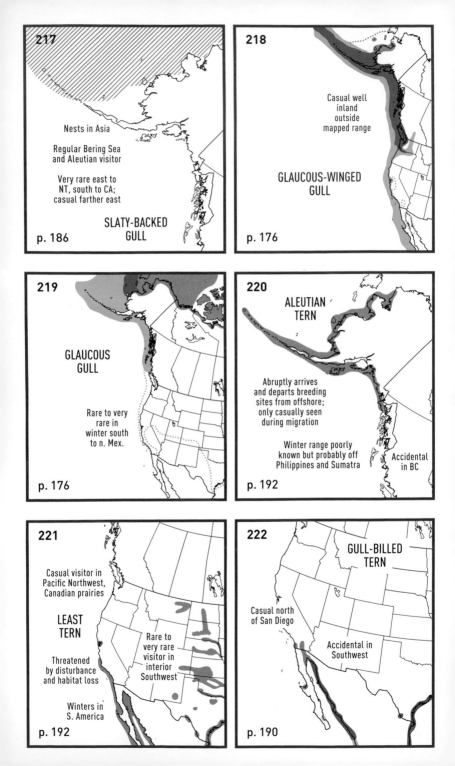

217

Nests in Asia

Regular Bering Sea
and Aleutian visitor

Very rare east to
NT, south to CA;
casual farther east

SLATY-BACKED
GULL

p. 186

218

Casual well
inland
outside
mapped range

GLAUCOUS-WINGED
GULL

p. 176

219

GLAUCOUS
GULL

Rare to very
rare in
winter south
to n. Mex.

p. 176

220

ALEUTIAN
TERN

Abruptly arrives
and departs breeding
sites from offshore;
only casually seen
during migration

Winter range poorly
known but probably off
Philippines and Sumatra

Accidental
in BC

p. 192

221

Casual visitor in
Pacific Northwest,
Canadian prairies

LEAST
TERN

Threatened
by disturbance
and habitat loss

Winters in
S. America

Rare to
very rare
visitor in
interior
Southwest

p. 192

222

GULL-BILLED
TERN

Casual north
of San Diego

Accidental in
Southwest

p. 190

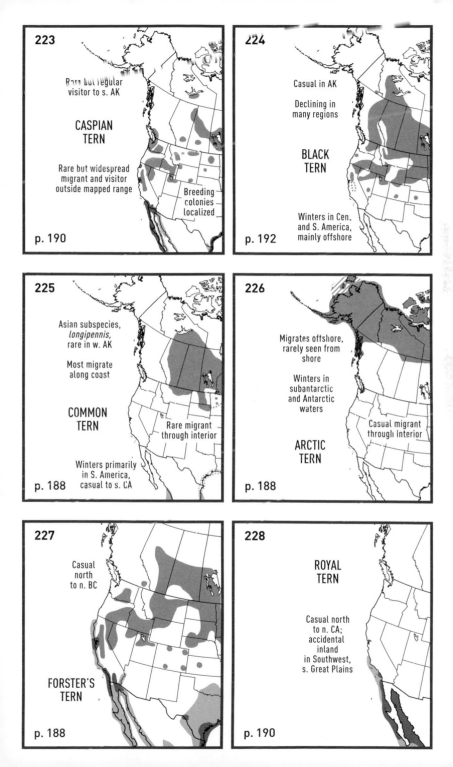

223

Rare but regular visitor to s. AK

CASPIAN TERN

Rare but widespread migrant and visitor outside mapped range

Breeding colonies localized

p. 190

224

Casual in AK

Declining in many regions

BLACK TERN

Winters in Cen. and S. America, mainly offshore

p. 192

225

Asian subspecies, *longipennis*, rare in w. AK

Most migrate along coast

COMMON TERN

Rare migrant through interior

Winters primarily in S. America, casual to s. CA

p. 188

226

Migrates offshore, rarely seen from shore

Winters in subantarctic and Antarctic waters

Casual migrant through Interior

ARCTIC TERN

p. 188

227

Casual north to n. BC

FORSTER'S TERN

p. 188

228

ROYAL TERN

Casual north to n. CA; accidental inland in Southwest, s. Great Plains

p. 190

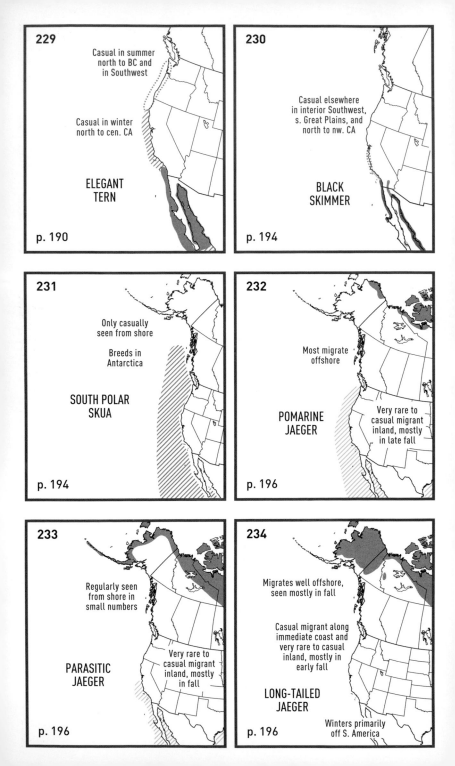

229

Casual in summer
north to BC and
in Southwest

Casual in winter
north to cen. CA

ELEGANT
TERN

p. 190

230

Casual elsewhere
in interior Southwest,
s. Great Plains, and
north to nw. CA

BLACK
SKIMMER

p. 194

231

Only casually
seen from shore

Breeds in
Antarctica

SOUTH POLAR
SKUA

p. 194

232

Most migrate
offshore

Very rare to
casual migrant
inland, mostly
in late fall

POMARINE
JAEGER

p. 196

233

Regularly seen
from shore in
small numbers

Very rare to
casual migrant
inland, mostly
in fall

PARASITIC
JAEGER

p. 196

234

Migrates well offshore,
seen mostly in fall

Casual migrant along
immediate coast and
very rare to casual
inland, mostly in
early fall

LONG-TAILED
JAEGER

p. 196

Winters primarily
off S. America

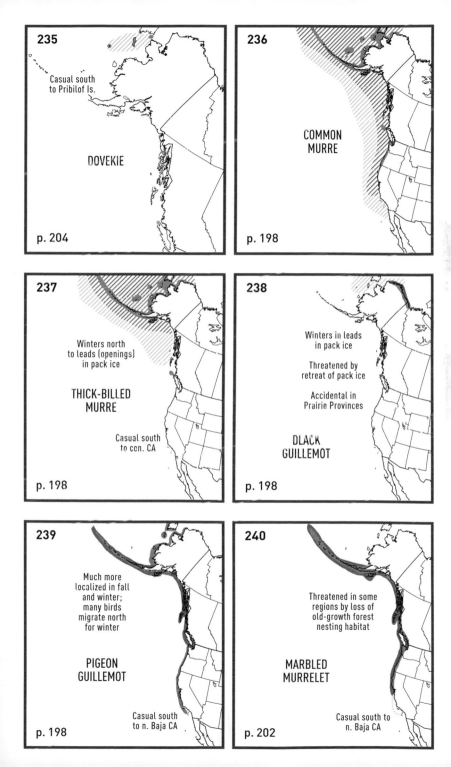

235

Casual south to Pribilof Is.

DOVEKIE

p. 204

236

COMMON MURRE

p. 198

237

Winters north to leads (openings) in pack ice

THICK-BILLED MURRE

Casual south to cen. CA

p. 198

238

Winters in leads in pack ice

Threatened by retreat of pack ice

Accidental in Prairie Provinces

BLACK GUILLEMOT

p. 198

239

Much more localized in fall and winter; many birds migrate north for winter

PIGEON GUILLEMOT

Casual south to n. Baja CA

p. 198

240

Threatened in some regions by loss of old-growth forest nesting habitat

MARBLED MURRELET

Casual south to n. Baja CA

p. 202

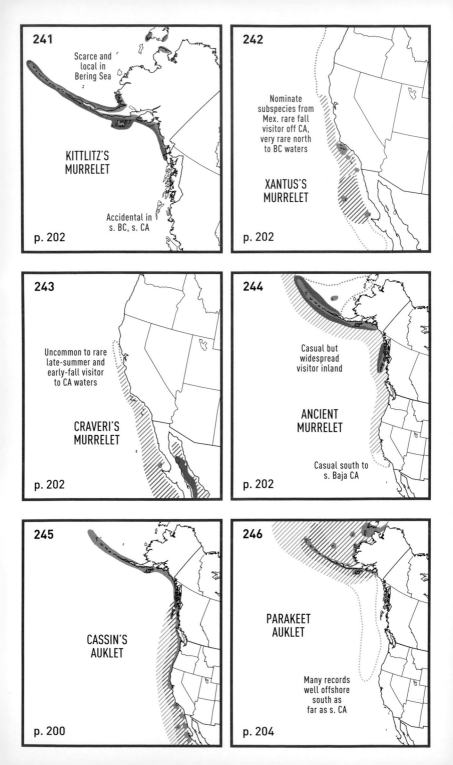

241

Scarce and local in Bering Sea

KITTLITZ'S MURRELET

Accidental in s. BC, s. CA

p. 202

242

Nominate subspecies from Mex. rare fall visitor off CA, very rare north to BC waters

XANTUS'S MURRELET

p. 202

243

Uncommon to rare late-summer and early-fall visitor to CA waters

CRAVERI'S MURRELET

p. 202

244

Casual but widespread visitor inland

ANCIENT MURRELET

Casual south to s. Baja CA

p. 202

245

CASSIN'S AUKLET

p. 200

246

PARAKEET AUKLET

Many records well offshore south as far as s. CA

p. 204

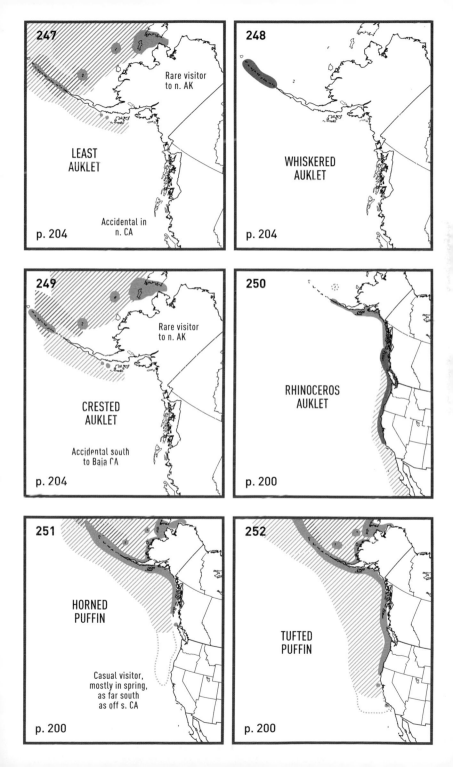

247

Rare visitor
to n. AK

LEAST
AUKLET

Accidental in
n. CA

p. 204

248

WHISKERED
AUKLET

p. 204

249

Rare visitor
to n. AK

CRESTED
AUKLET

Accidental south
to Baja CA

p. 204

250

RHINOCEROS
AUKLET

p. 200

251

HORNED
PUFFIN

Casual visitor,
mostly in spring,
as far south
as off s. CA

p. 200

252

TUFTED
PUFFIN

p. 200

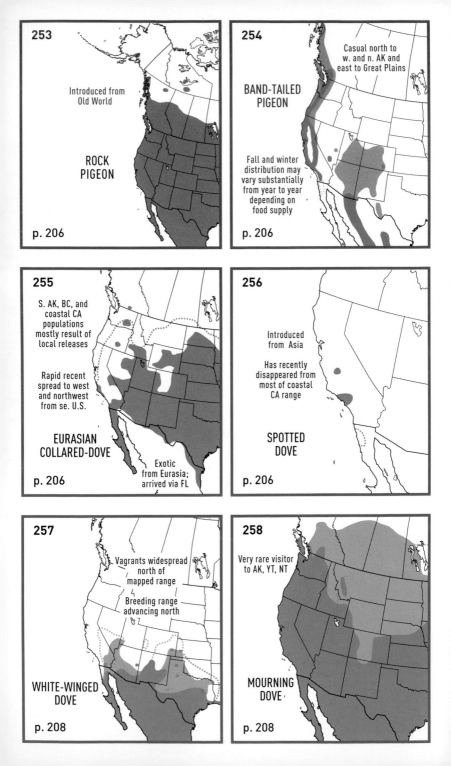

253

Introduced from Old World

ROCK PIGEON

p. 206

254

Casual north to w. and n. AK and east to Great Plains

BAND-TAILED PIGEON

Fall and winter distribution may vary substantially from year to year depending on food supply

p. 206

255

S. AK, BC, and coastal CA populations mostly result of local releases

Rapid recent spread to west and northwest from se. U.S.

EURASIAN COLLARED-DOVE

Exotic from Eurasia; arrived via FL

p. 206

256

Introduced from Asia

Has recently disappeared from most of coastal CA range

SPOTTED DOVE

p. 206

257

Vagrants widespread north of mapped range

Breeding range advancing north

WHITE-WINGED DOVE

p. 208

258

Very rare visitor to AK, YT, NT

MOURNING DOVE

p. 208

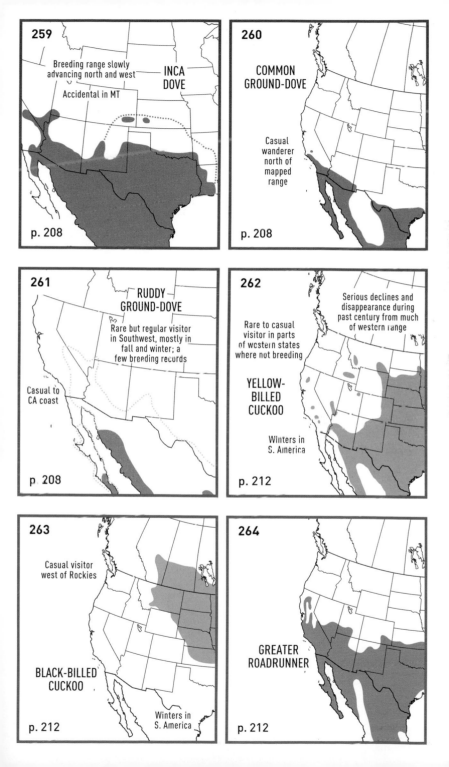

259 INCA DOVE
Breeding range slowly advancing north and west
Accidental in MT
p. 208

260 COMMON GROUND-DOVE
Casual wanderer north of mapped range
p. 208

261 RUDDY GROUND-DOVE
Rare but regular visitor in Southwest, mostly in fall and winter; a few breeding records
Casual to CA coast
p. 208

262 YELLOW-BILLED CUCKOO
Serious declines and disappearance during past century from much of western range
Rare to casual visitor in parts of western states where not breeding
Winters in S. America
p. 212

263 BLACK-BILLED CUCKOO
Casual visitor west of Rockies
Winters in S. America
p. 212

264 GREATER ROADRUNNER
p. 212

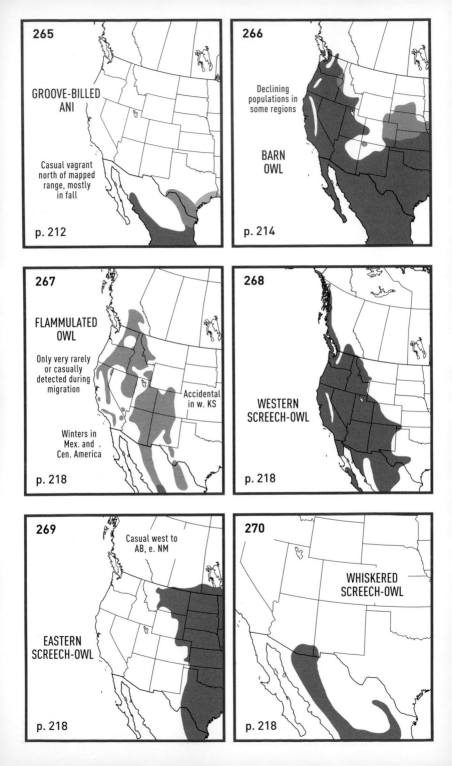

265
GROOVE-BILLED
ANI

Casual vagrant
north of mapped
range, mostly
in fall

p. 212

266
Declining
populations in
some regions

BARN
OWL

p. 214

267
FLAMMULATED
OWL

Only very rarely
or casually
detected during
migration

Accidental
in w. KS

Winters in
Mex. and
Cen. America

p. 218

268
WESTERN
SCREECH-OWL

p. 218

269
Casual west to
AB, e. NM

EASTERN
SCREECH-OWL

p. 218

270
WHISKERED
SCREECH-OWL

p. 218

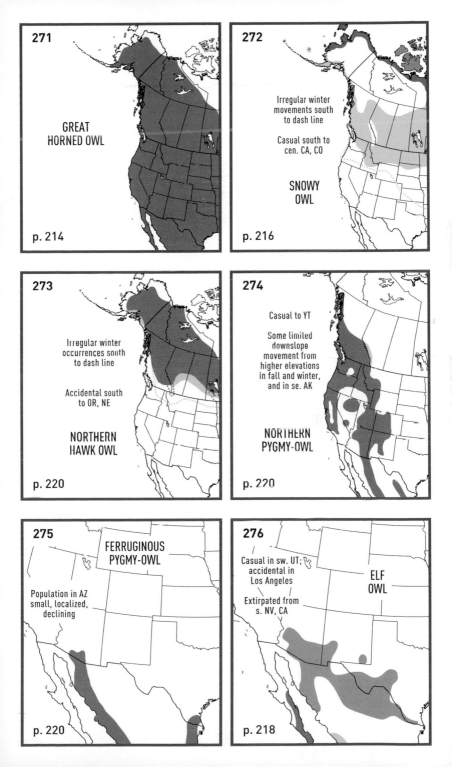

271

GREAT
HORNED OWL

p. 214

272

Irregular winter
movements south
to dash line

Casual south to
cen. CA, CO

SNOWY
OWL

p. 216

273

Irregular winter
occurrences south
to dash line

Accidental south
to OR, NE

NORTHERN
HAWK OWL

p. 220

274

Casual to YT

Some limited
downslope
movement from
higher elevations
in fall and winter,
and in se. AK

NORTHERN
PYGMY-OWL

p. 220

275

FERRUGINOUS
PYGMY-OWL

Population in AZ
small, localized,
declining

p. 220

276

Casual in sw. UT;
accidental in
Los Angeles

Extirpated from
s. NV, CA

ELF
OWL

p. 218

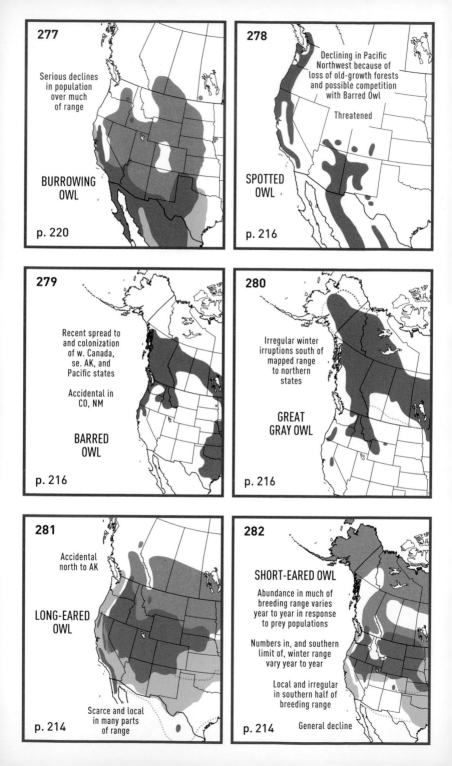

277

Serious declines in population over much of range

BURROWING OWL

p. 220

278

Declining in Pacific Northwest because of loss of old-growth forests and possible competition with Barred Owl

Threatened

SPOTTED OWL

p. 216

279

Recent spread to and colonization of w. Canada, se. AK, and Pacific states

Accidental in CO, NM

BARRED OWL

p. 216

280

Irregular winter irruptions south of mapped range to northern states

GREAT GRAY OWL

p. 216

281

Accidental north to AK

LONG-EARED OWL

Scarce and local in many parts of range

p. 214

282

SHORT-EARED OWL

Abundance in much of breeding range varies year to year in response to prey populations

Numbers in, and southern limit of, winter range vary year to year

Local and irregular in southern half of breeding range

General decline

p. 214

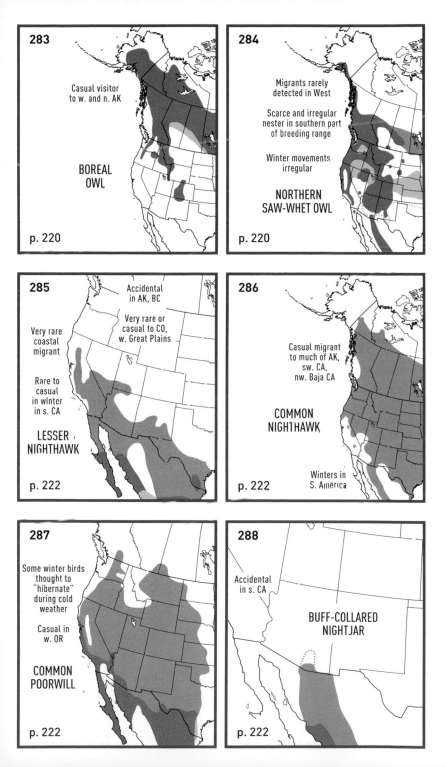

283 Casual visitor to w. and n. AK

BOREAL OWL

p. 220

284 Migrants rarely detected in West

Scarce and irregular nester in southern part of breeding range

Winter movements irregular

NORTHERN SAW-WHET OWL

p. 220

285 Accidental in AK, BC

Very rare or casual to CO, w. Great Plains

Very rare coastal migrant

Rare to casual in winter in s. CA

LESSER NIGHTHAWK

p. 222

286 Casual migrant to much of AK, sw. CA, nw. Baja CA

COMMON NIGHTHAWK

Winters in S. America

p. 222

287 Some winter birds thought to "hibernate" during cold weather

Casual in w. OR

COMMON POORWILL

p. 222

288 Accidental in s. CA

BUFF-COLLARED NIGHTJAR

p. 222

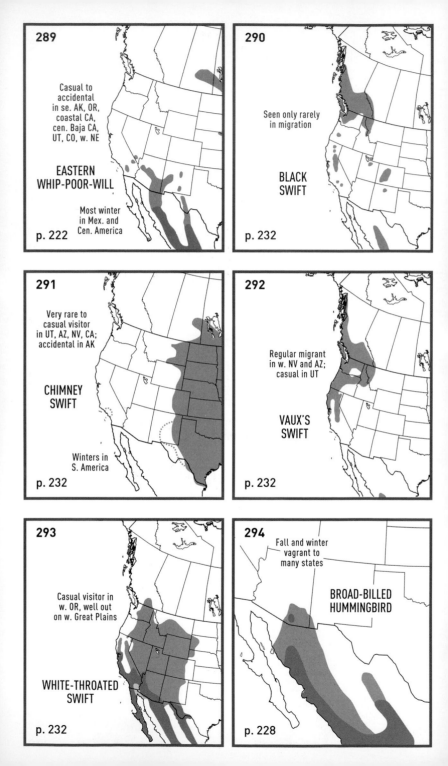

289

Casual to
accidental
in se. AK, OR,
coastal CA,
cen. Baja CA,
UT, CO, w. NE

EASTERN
WHIP-POOR-WILL

Most winter
in Mex. and
Cen. America

p. 222

290

Seen only rarely
in migration

BLACK
SWIFT

p. 232

291

Very rare to
casual visitor
in UT, AZ, NV, CA;
accidental in AK

CHIMNEY
SWIFT

Winters in
S. America

p. 232

292

Regular migrant
in w. NV and AZ;
casual in UT

VAUX'S
SWIFT

p. 232

293

Casual visitor in
w. OR, well out
on w. Great Plains

WHITE-THROATED
SWIFT

p. 232

294

Fall and winter
vagrant to
many states

BROAD-BILLED
HUMMINGBIRD

p. 228

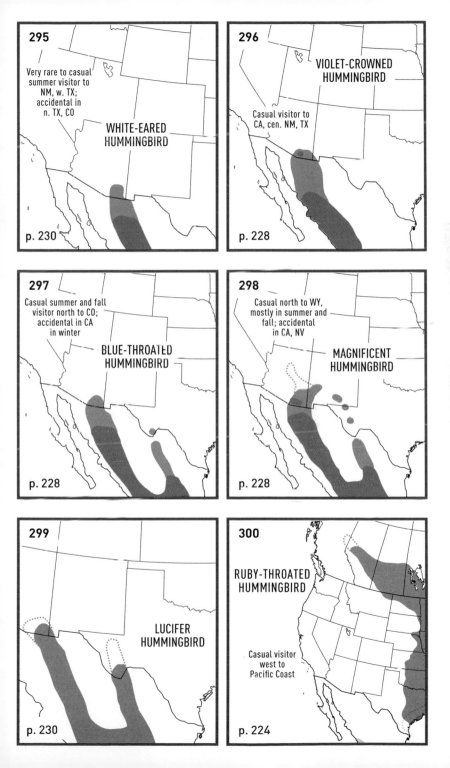

295

Very rare to casual summer visitor to NM, w. TX; accidental in n. TX, CO

WHITE-EARED HUMMINGBIRD

p. 230

296

VIOLET-CROWNED HUMMINGBIRD

Casual visitor to CA, cen. NM, TX

p. 228

297

Casual summer and fall visitor north to CO; accidental in CA in winter

BLUE-THROATED HUMMINGBIRD

p. 228

298

Casual north to WY, mostly in summer and fall; accidental in CA, NV

MAGNIFICENT HUMMINGBIRD

p. 228

299

LUCIFER HUMMINGBIRD

p. 230

300

RUBY-THROATED HUMMINGBIRD

Casual visitor west to Pacific Coast

p. 224

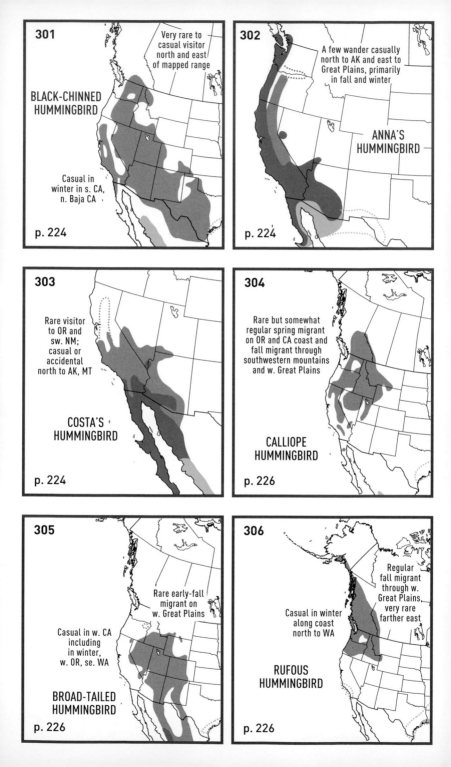

301

Very rare to casual visitor north and east of mapped range

BLACK-CHINNED HUMMINGBIRD

Casual in winter in s. CA, n. Baja CA

p. 224

302

A few wander casually north to AK and east to Great Plains, primarily in fall and winter

ANNA'S HUMMINGBIRD

p. 224

303

Rare visitor to OR and sw. NM; casual or accidental north to AK, MT

COSTA'S HUMMINGBIRD

p. 224

304

Rare but somewhat regular spring migrant on OR and CA coast and fall migrant through southwestern mountains and w. Great Plains

CALLIOPE HUMMINGBIRD

p. 226

305

Rare early-fall migrant on w. Great Plains

Casual in w. CA including in winter, w. OR, se. WA

BROAD-TAILED HUMMINGBIRD

p. 226

306

Regular fall migrant through w. Great Plains, very rare farther east

Casual in winter along coast north to WA

RUFOUS HUMMINGBIRD

p. 226

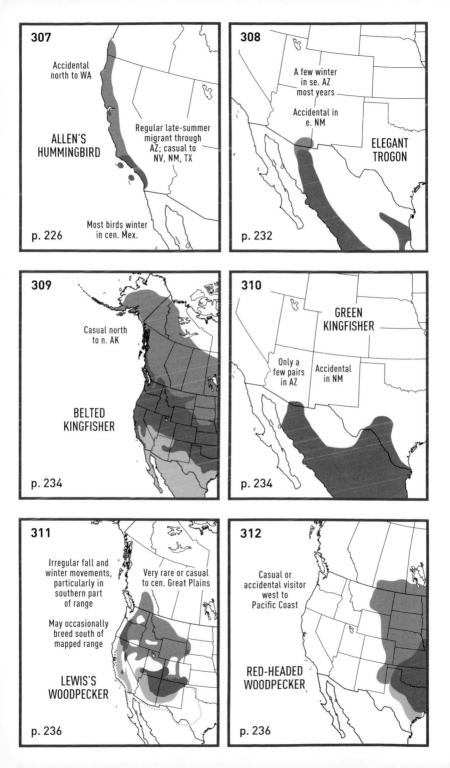

307

Accidental north to WA

ALLEN'S HUMMINGBIRD

Regular late-summer migrant through AZ; casual to NV, NM, TX

Most birds winter in cen. Mex.

p. 226

308

A few winter in se. AZ most years

Accidental in e. NM

ELEGANT TROGON

p. 232

309

Casual north to n. AK

BELTED KINGFISHER

p. 234

310

GREEN KINGFISHER

Only a few pairs in AZ

Accidental in NM

p. 234

311

Irregular fall and winter movements, particularly in southern part of range

May occasionally breed south of mapped range

Very rare or casual to cen. Great Plains

LEWIS'S WOODPECKER

p. 236

312

Casual or accidental visitor west to Pacific Coast

RED-HEADED WOODPECKER

p. 236

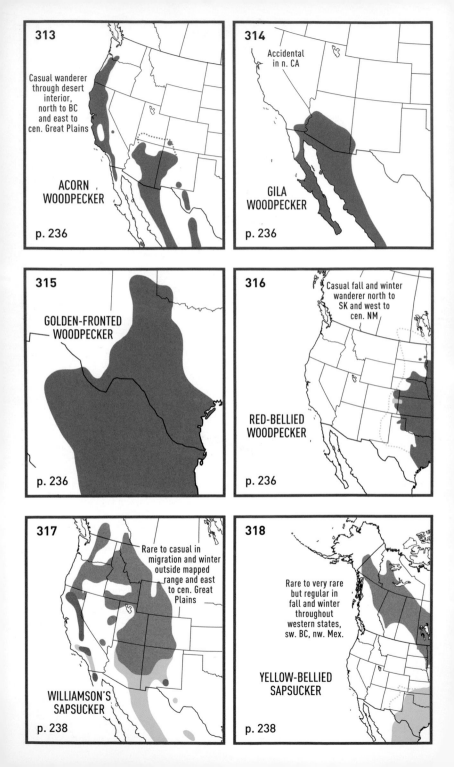

313

Casual wanderer through desert interior, north to BC and east to cen. Great Plains

ACORN WOODPECKER

p. 236

314

Accidental in n. CA

GILA WOODPECKER

p. 236

315

GOLDEN-FRONTED WOODPECKER

p. 236

316

Casual fall and winter wanderer north to SK and west to cen. NM

RED-BELLIED WOODPECKER

p. 236

317

Rare to casual in migration and winter outside mapped range and east to cen. Great Plains

WILLIAMSON'S SAPSUCKER

p. 238

318

Rare to very rare but regular in fall and winter throughout western states, sw. BC, nw. Mex.

YELLOW-BELLIED SAPSUCKER

p. 238

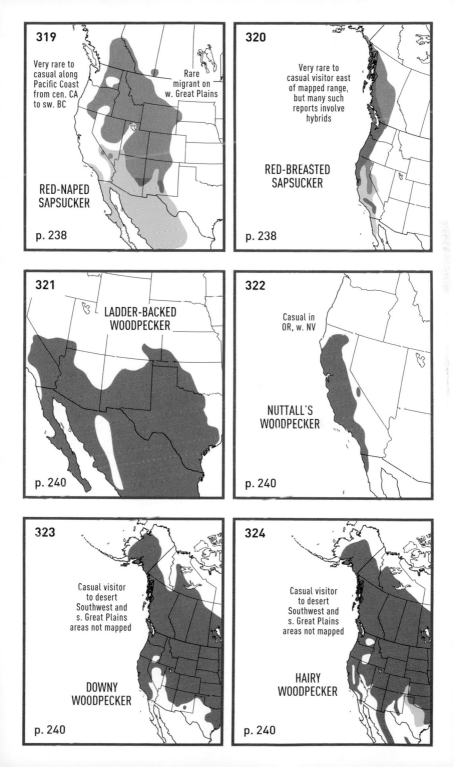

319

Very rare to casual along Pacific Coast from cen. CA to sw. BC

Rare migrant on w. Great Plains

RED-NAPED SAPSUCKER

p. 238

320

Very rare to casual visitor east of mapped range, but many such reports involve hybrids

RED-BREASTED SAPSUCKER

p. 238

321

LADDER-BACKED WOODPECKER

p. 240

322

Casual in OR, w. NV

NUTTALL'S WOODPECKER

p. 240

323

Casual visitor to desert Southwest and s. Great Plains areas not mapped

DOWNY WOODPECKER

p. 240

324

Casual visitor to desert Southwest and s. Great Plains areas not mapped

HAIRY WOODPECKER

p. 240

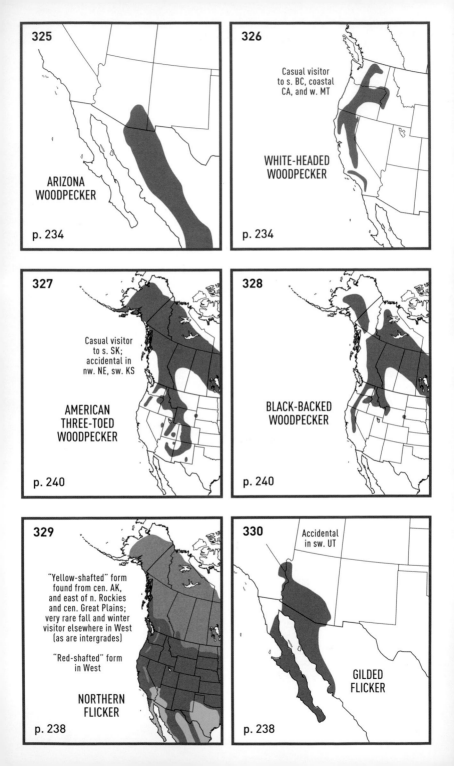

325 ARIZONA WOODPECKER p. 234

326 WHITE-HEADED WOODPECKER
Casual visitor to s. BC, coastal CA, and w. MT
p. 234

327 AMERICAN THREE-TOED WOODPECKER
Casual visitor to s. SK; accidental in nw. NE, sw. KS
p. 240

328 BLACK-BACKED WOODPECKER p. 240

329 NORTHERN FLICKER
"Yellow-shafted" form found from cen. AK, and east of n. Rockies and cen. Great Plains; very rare fall and winter visitor elsewhere in West (as are intergrades)

"Red-shafted" form in West
p. 238

330 GILDED FLICKER
Accidental in sw. UT
p. 238

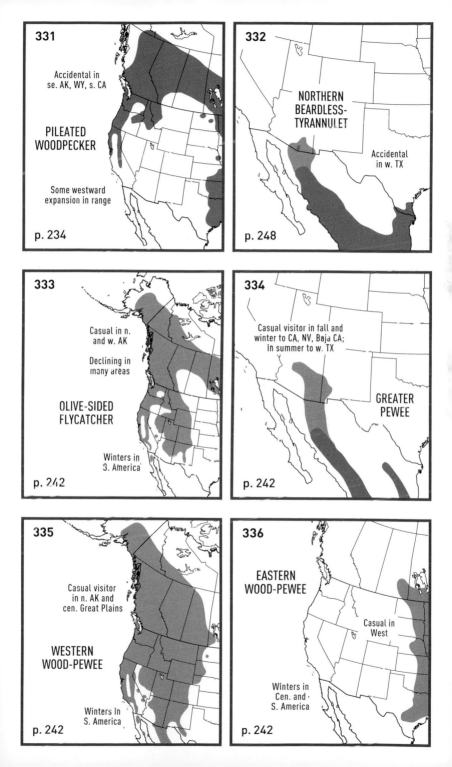

331

Accidental in se. AK, WY, s. CA

PILEATED
WOODPECKER

Some westward
expansion in range

p. 234

332

NORTHERN
BEARDLESS-
TYRANNULET

Accidental
in w. TX

p. 248

333

Casual in n.
and w. AK

Declining in
many areas

OLIVE-SIDED
FLYCATCHER

Winters in
S. America

p. 242

334

Casual visitor in fall and
winter to CA, NV, Baja CA;
In summer to w. TX

GREATER
PEWEE

p. 242

335

Casual visitor
in n. AK and
cen. Great Plains

WESTERN
WOOD-PEWEE

Winters In
S. America

p. 242

336

EASTERN
WOOD-PEWEE

Casual in
West

Winters in
Cen. and
S. America

p. 242

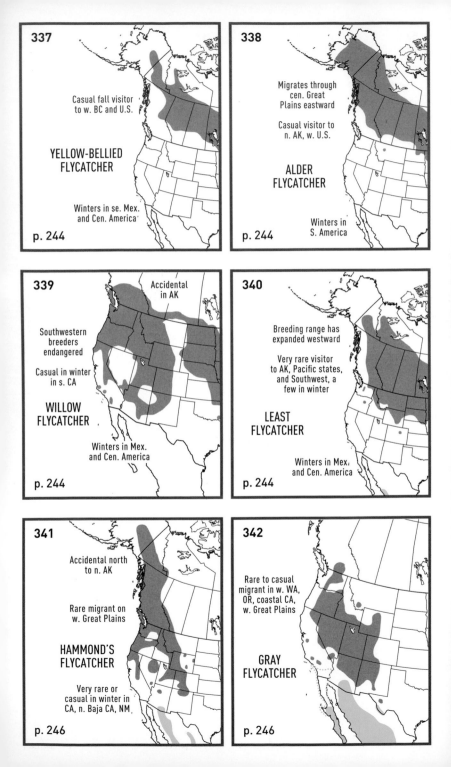

337

Casual fall visitor
to w. BC and U.S.

**YELLOW-BELLIED
FLYCATCHER**

Winters in se. Mex.
and Cen. America

p. 244

338

Migrates through
cen. Great
Plains eastward

Casual visitor to
n. AK, w. U.S.

**ALDER
FLYCATCHER**

Winters in
S. America

p. 244

339

Accidental
in AK

Southwestern
breeders
endangered

Casual in winter
in s. CA

**WILLOW
FLYCATCHER**

Winters in Mex.
and Cen. America

p. 244

340

Breeding range has
expanded westward

Very rare visitor
to AK, Pacific states,
and Southwest, a
few in winter

**LEAST
FLYCATCHER**

Winters in Mex.
and Cen. America

p. 244

341

Accidental north
to n. AK

Rare migrant on
w. Great Plains

**HAMMOND'S
FLYCATCHER**

Very rare or
casual in winter in
CA, n. Baja CA, NM

p. 246

342

Rare to casual
migrant in w. WA,
OR, coastal CA,
w. Great Plains

**GRAY
FLYCATCHER**

p. 246

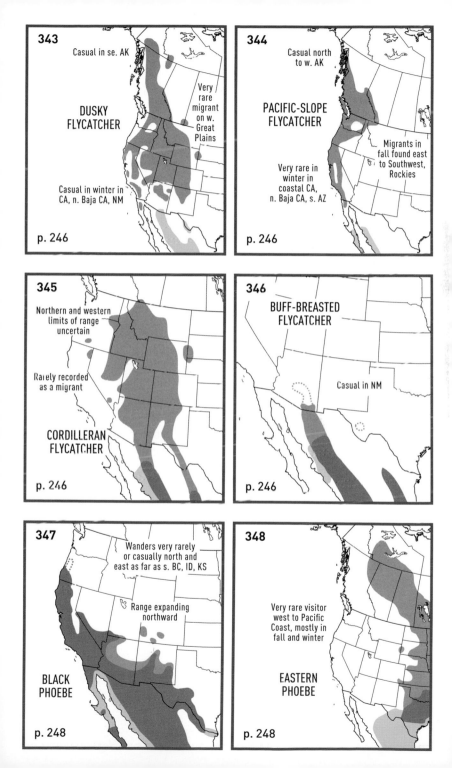

343

Casual in se. AK

Very rare migrant on w. Great Plains

DUSKY FLYCATCHER

Casual in winter in CA, n. Baja CA, NM

p. 246

344

Casual north to w. AK

PACIFIC-SLOPE FLYCATCHER

Migrants in fall found east to Southwest, Rockies

Very rare in winter in coastal CA, n. Baja CA, s. AZ

p. 246

345

Northern and western limits of range uncertain

Rarely recorded as a migrant

CORDILLERAN FLYCATCHER

p. 246

346

BUFF-BREASTED FLYCATCHER

Casual in NM

p. 246

347

Wanders very rarely or casually north and east as far as s. BC, ID, KS

Range expanding northward

BLACK PHOEBE

p. 248

348

Very rare visitor west to Pacific Coast, mostly in fall and winter

EASTERN PHOEBE

p. 248

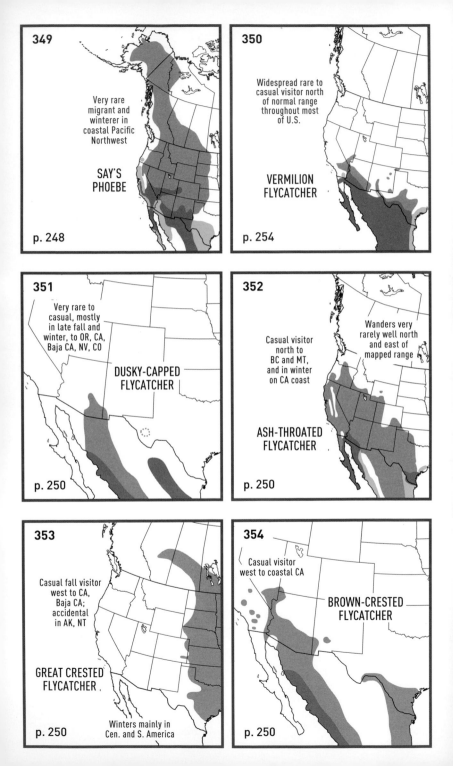

349

Very rare migrant and winterer in coastal Pacific Northwest

SAY'S PHOEBE

p. 248

350

Widespread rare to casual visitor north of normal range throughout most of U.S.

VERMILION FLYCATCHER

p. 254

351

Very rare to casual, mostly in late fall and winter, to OR, CA, Baja CA, NV, CO

DUSKY-CAPPED FLYCATCHER

p. 250

352

Wanders very rarely well north and east of mapped range

Casual visitor north to BC and MT, and in winter on CA coast

ASH-THROATED FLYCATCHER

p. 250

353

Casual fall visitor west to CA, Baja CA; accidental in AK, NT

GREAT CRESTED FLYCATCHER

Winters mainly in Cen. and S. America

p. 250

354

Casual visitor west to coastal CA

BROWN-CRESTED FLYCATCHER

p. 250

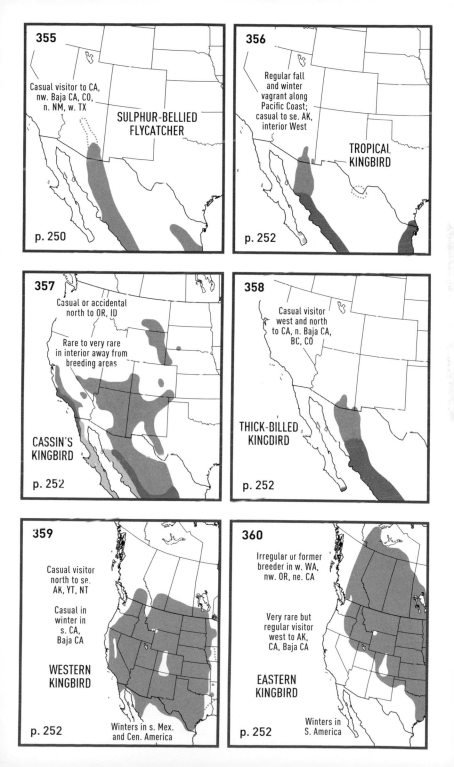

355

Casual visitor to CA, nw. Baja CA, CO, n. NM, w. TX

SULPHUR-BELLIED FLYCATCHER

p. 250

356

Regular fall and winter vagrant along Pacific Coast; casual to se. AK, interior West

TROPICAL KINGBIRD

p. 252

357

Casual or accidental north to OR, ID

Rare to very rare in interior away from breeding areas

CASSIN'S KINGBIRD

p. 252

358

Casual visitor west and north to CA, n. Baja CA, BC, CO

THICK-BILLED KINGBIRD

p. 252

359

Casual visitor north to se. AK, YT, NT

Casual in winter in s. CA, Baja CA

WESTERN KINGBIRD

Winters in s. Mex. and Cen. America

p. 252

360

Irregular or former breeder in w. WA, nw. OR, ne. CA

Very rare but regular visitor west to AK, CA, Baja CA

EASTERN KINGBIRD

Winters in S. America

p. 252

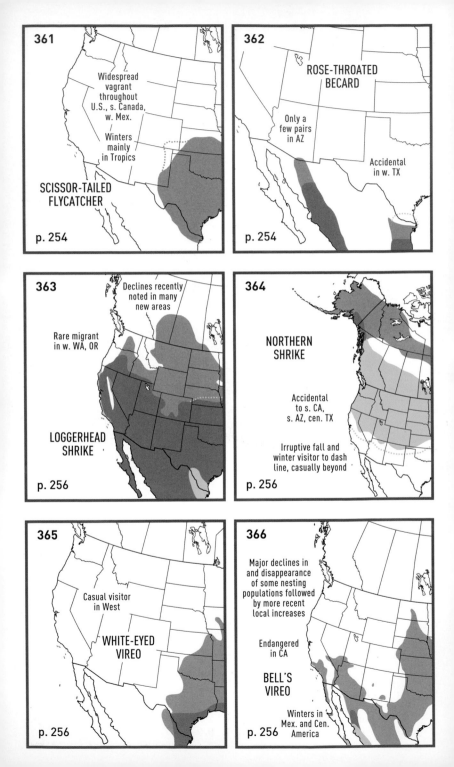

361
Widespread vagrant throughout U.S., s. Canada, w. Mex.

Winters mainly in Tropics

SCISSOR-TAILED FLYCATCHER

p. 254

362
ROSE-THROATED BECARD

Only a few pairs in AZ

Accidental in w. TX

p. 254

363
Declines recently noted in many new areas

Rare migrant in w. WA, OR

LOGGERHEAD SHRIKE

p. 256

364
NORTHERN SHRIKE

Accidental to s. CA, s. AZ, cen. TX

Irruptive fall and winter visitor to dash line, casually beyond

p. 256

365
Casual visitor in West

WHITE-EYED VIREO

p. 256

366
Major declines in and disappearance of some nesting populations followed by more recent local increases

Endangered in CA

BELL'S VIREO

Winters in Mex. and Cen. America

p. 256

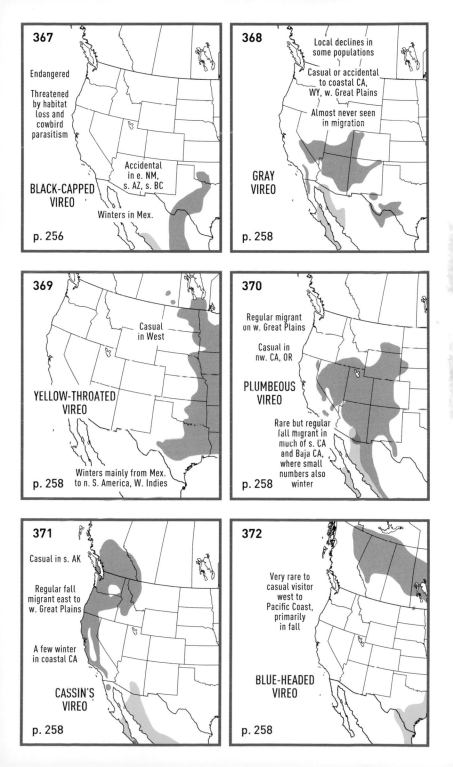

367

Endangered

Threatened by habitat loss and cowbird parasitism

Accidental in e. NM, s. AZ, s. BC

BLACK-CAPPED VIREO

Winters in Mex.

p. 256

368

Local declines in some populations

Casual or accidental to coastal CA, WY, w. Great Plains

Almost never seen in migration

GRAY VIREO

p. 258

369

Casual in West

YELLOW-THROATED VIREO

Winters mainly from Mex. to n. S. America, W. Indies

p. 258

370

Regular migrant on w. Great Plains

Casual in nw. CA, OR

PLUMBEOUS VIREO

Rare but regular fall migrant in much of s. CA and Baja CA, where small numbers also winter

p. 258

371

Casual in s. AK

Regular fall migrant east to w. Great Plains

A few winter in coastal CA

CASSIN'S VIREO

p. 258

372

Very rare to casual visitor west to Pacific Coast, primarily in fall

BLUE-HEADED VIREO

p. 258

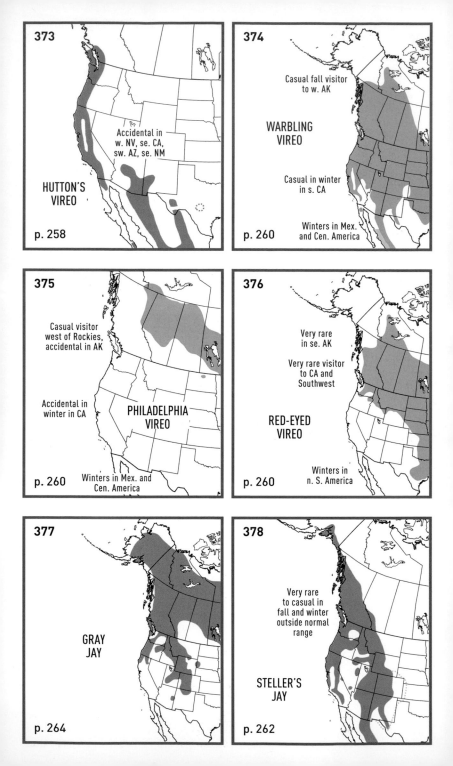

373

Accidental in
w. NV, se. CA,
sw. AZ, se. NM

HUTTON'S
VIREO

p. 258

374

Casual fall visitor
to w. AK

WARBLING
VIREO

Casual in winter
in s. CA

Winters in Mex.
and Cen. America

p. 260

375

Casual visitor
west of Rockies,
accidental in AK

Accidental in
winter in CA

PHILADELPHIA
VIREO

Winters in Mex.
and Cen. America

p. 260

376

Very rare
in se. AK

Very rare visitor
to CA and
Southwest

RED-EYED
VIREO

Winters in
n. S. America

p. 260

377

GRAY
JAY

p. 264

378

Very rare
to casual in
fall and winter
outside normal
range

STELLER'S
JAY

p. 262

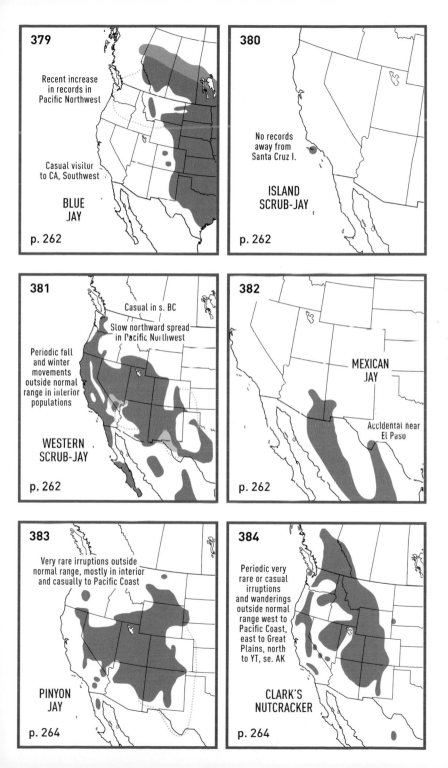

379

Recent increase in records in Pacific Northwest

Casual visitor to CA, Southwest

BLUE JAY

p. 262

380

No records away from Santa Cruz I.

ISLAND SCRUB-JAY

p. 262

381

Casual in s. BC

Slow northward spread in Pacific Northwest

Periodic fall and winter movements outside normal range in interior populations

WESTERN SCRUB-JAY

p. 262

382

MEXICAN JAY

Accidental near El Paso

p. 262

383

Very rare irruptions outside normal range, mostly in interior and casually to Pacific Coast

PINYON JAY

p. 264

384

Periodic very rare or casual irruptions and wanderings outside normal range west to Pacific Coast, east to Great Plains, north to YT, se. AK

CLARK'S NUTCRACKER

p. 264

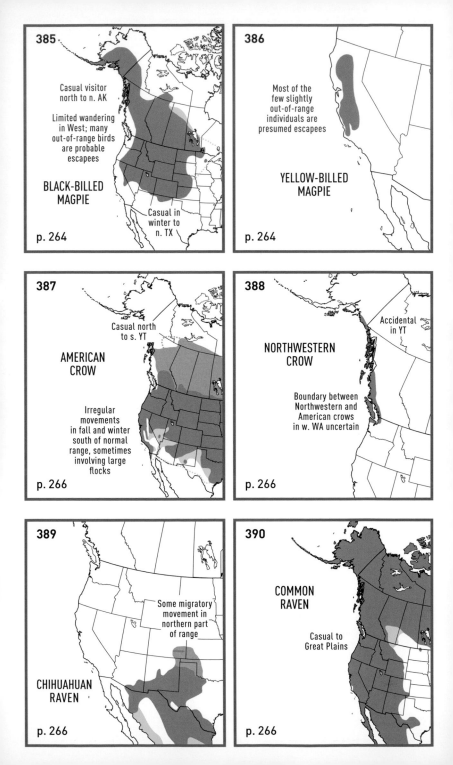

385

Casual visitor north to n. AK

Limited wandering in West; many out-of-range birds are probable escapees

BLACK-BILLED MAGPIE

Casual in winter to n. TX

p. 264

386

Most of the few slightly out-of-range individuals are presumed escapees

YELLOW-BILLED MAGPIE

p. 264

387

Casual north to s. YT

AMERICAN CROW

Irregular movements in fall and winter south of normal range, sometimes involving large flocks

p. 266

388

Accidental in YT

NORTHWESTERN CROW

Boundary between Northwestern and American crows in w. WA uncertain

p. 266

389

Some migratory movement in northern part of range

CHIHUAHUAN RAVEN

p. 266

390

COMMON RAVEN

Casual to Great Plains

p. 266

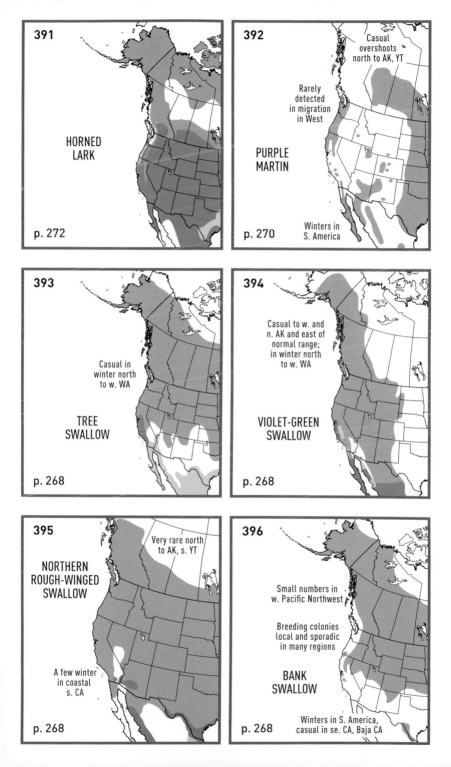

391

HORNED
LARK

p. 272

392

Casual
overshoots
north to AK, YT

Rarely
detected
in migration
in West

PURPLE
MARTIN

p. 270

Winters in
S. America

393

Casual in
winter north
to w. WA

TREE
SWALLOW

p. 268

394

Casual to w. and
n. AK and east of
normal range;
in winter north
to w. WA

VIOLET-GREEN
SWALLOW

p. 268

395

Very rare north
to AK, s. YT

NORTHERN
ROUGH-WINGED
SWALLOW

A few winter
in coastal
s. CA

p. 268

396

Small numbers in
w. Pacific Northwest

Breeding colonies
local and sporadic
in many regions

BANK
SWALLOW

Winters in S. America,
casual in se. CA, Baja CA

p. 268

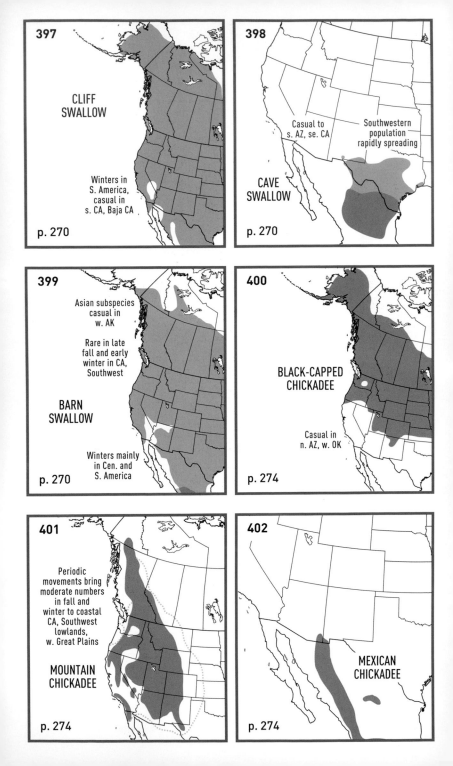

397

CLIFF
SWALLOW

Winters in
S. America,
casual in
s. CA, Baja CA

p. 270

398

Casual to
s. AZ, se. CA

Southwestern
population
rapidly spreading

CAVE
SWALLOW

p. 270

399

Asian subspecies
casual in
w. AK

Rare in late
fall and early
winter in CA,
Southwest

BARN
SWALLOW

Winters mainly
in Cen. and
S. America

p. 270

400

BLACK-CAPPED
CHICKADEE

Casual in
n. AZ, w. OK

p. 274

401

Periodic
movements bring
moderate numbers
in fall and
winter to coastal
CA, Southwest
lowlands,
w. Great Plains

MOUNTAIN
CHICKADEE

p. 274

402

MEXICAN
CHICKADEE

p. 274

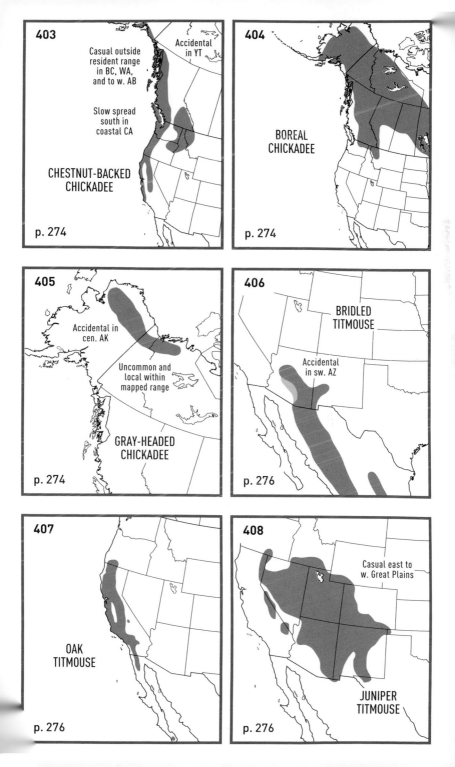

403

Casual outside resident range in BC, WA, and to w. AB

Accidental in YT

Slow spread south in coastal CA

CHESTNUT-BACKED CHICKADEE

p. 274

404

BOREAL CHICKADEE

p. 274

405

Accidental in cen. AK

Uncommon and local within mapped range

GRAY-HEADED CHICKADEE

p. 274

406

BRIDLED TITMOUSE

Accidental in sw. AZ

p. 276

407

OAK TITMOUSE

p. 276

408

Casual east to w. Great Plains

JUNIPER TITMOUSE

p. 276

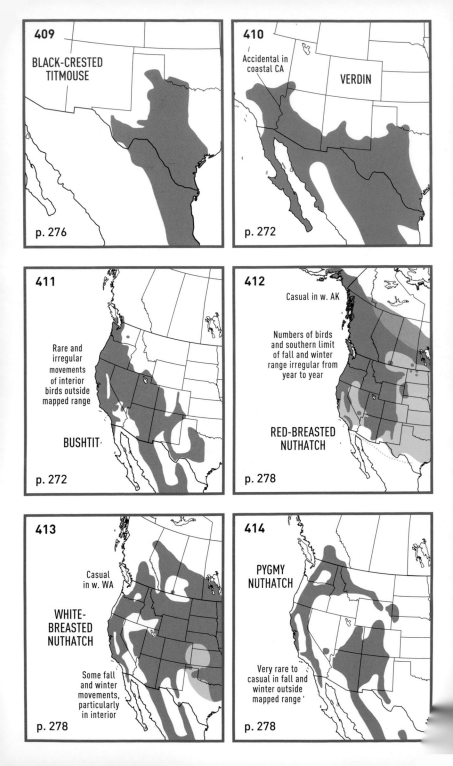

409

BLACK-CRESTED
TITMOUSE

p. 276

410

Accidental in
coastal CA

VERDIN

p. 272

411

Rare and
irregular
movements
of interior
birds outside
mapped range

BUSHTIT

p. 272

412

Casual in w. AK

Numbers of birds
and southern limit
of fall and winter
range irregular from
year to year

RED-BREASTED
NUTHATCH

p. 278

413

Casual
in w. WA

WHITE-
BREASTED
NUTHATCH

Some fall
and winter
movements,
particularly
in interior

p. 278

414

PYGMY
NUTHATCH

Very rare to
casual in fall and
winter outside
mapped range

p. 278

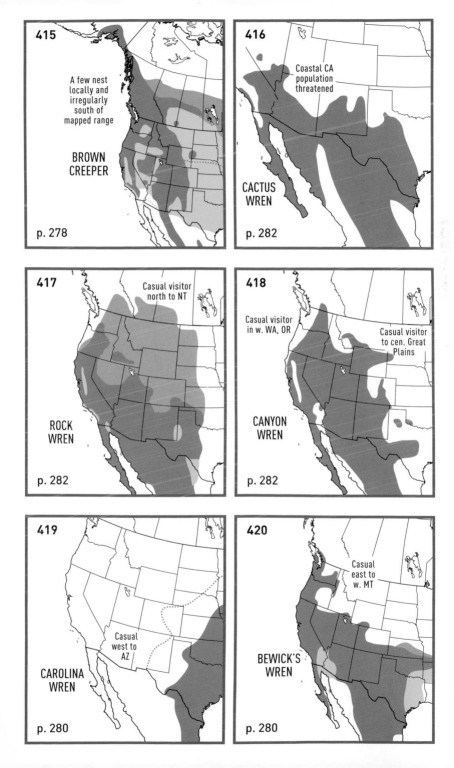

415

A few nest locally and irregularly south of mapped range

BROWN CREEPER

p. 278

416

Coastal CA population threatened

CACTUS WREN

p. 282

417

Casual visitor north to NT

ROCK WREN

p. 282

418

Casual visitor in w. WA, OR

Casual visitor to cen. Great Plains

CANYON WREN

p. 282

419

Casual west to AZ

CAROLINA WREN

p. 280

420

Casual east to w. MT

BEWICK'S WREN

p. 280

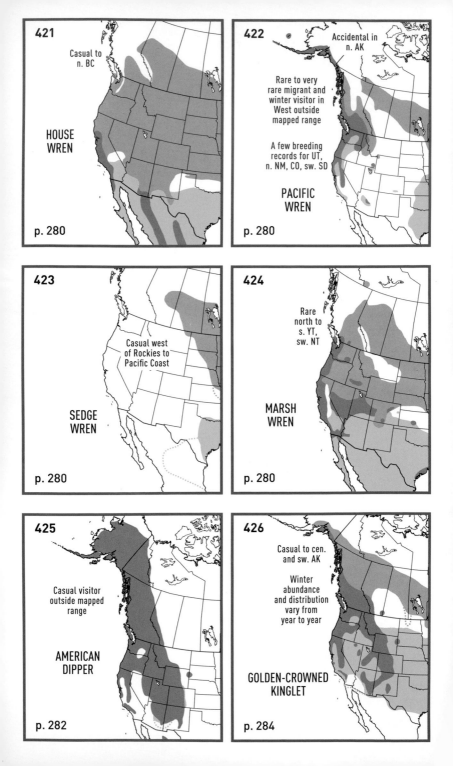

421
Casual to n. BC

HOUSE
WREN

p. 280

422
Accidental in n. AK

Rare to very rare migrant and winter visitor in West outside mapped range

A few breeding records for UT, n. NM, CO, sw. SD

PACIFIC
WREN

p. 280

423
Casual west of Rockies to Pacific Coast

SEDGE
WREN

p. 280

424
Rare north to s. YT, sw. NT

MARSH
WREN

p. 280

425
Casual visitor outside mapped range

AMERICAN
DIPPER

p. 282

426
Casual to cen. and sw. AK

Winter abundance and distribution vary from year to year

GOLDEN-CROWNED
KINGLET

p. 284

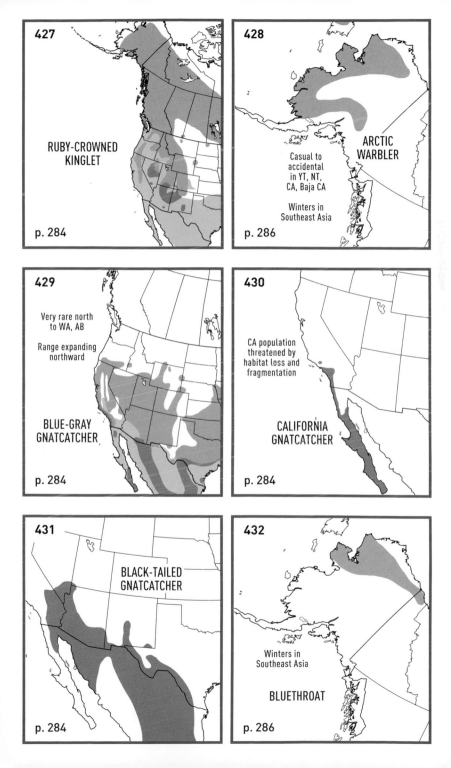

427
RUBY-CROWNED
KINGLET
p. 284

428
ARCTIC
WARBLER
Casual to
accidental
in YT, NT,
CA, Baja CA

Winters in
Southeast Asia
p. 286

429
Very rare north
to WA, AB

Range expanding
northward

BLUE-GRAY
GNATCATCHER
p. 284

430
CA population
threatened by
habitat loss and
fragmentation

CALIFORNIA
GNATCATCHER
p. 284

431
BLACK-TAILED
GNATCATCHER
p. 284

432
Winters in
Southeast Asia

BLUETHROAT
p. 286

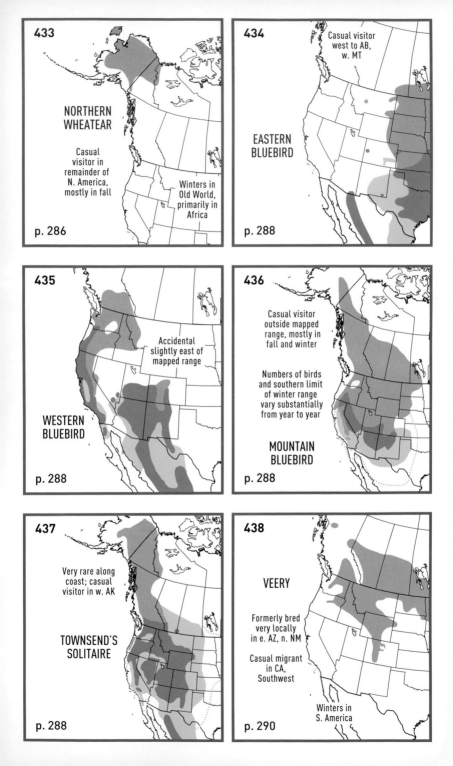

433

NORTHERN
WHEATEAR

Casual
visitor in
remainder of
N. America,
mostly in fall

Winters in
Old World,
primarily in
Africa

p. 286

434

Casual visitor
west to AB,
w. MT

EASTERN
BLUEBIRD

p. 288

435

Accidental
slightly east of
mapped range

WESTERN
BLUEBIRD

p. 288

436

Casual visitor
outside mapped
range, mostly in
fall and winter

Numbers of birds
and southern limit
of winter range
vary substantially
from year to year

MOUNTAIN
BLUEBIRD

p. 288

437

Very rare along
coast; casual
visitor in w. AK

TOWNSEND'S
SOLITAIRE

p. 288

438

VEERY

Formerly bred
very locally
in e. AZ, n. NM

Casual migrant
in CA,
Southwest

Winters in
S. America

p. 290

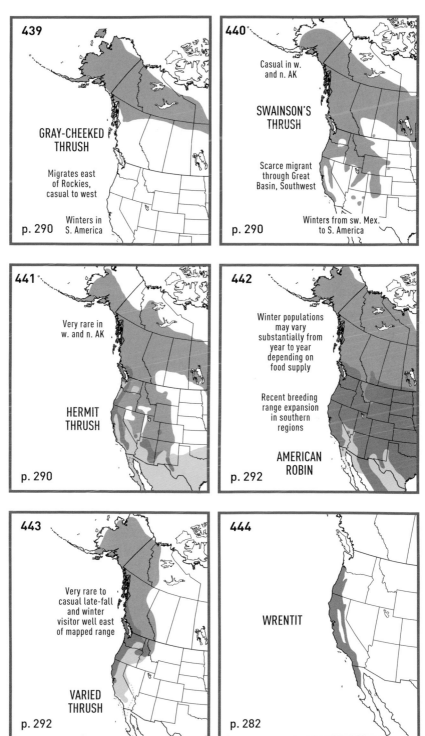

439

GRAY-CHEEKED THRUSH

Migrates east of Rockies, casual to west

Winters in S. America

p. 290

440

Casual in w. and n. AK

SWAINSON'S THRUSH

Scarce migrant through Great Basin, Southwest

Winters from sw. Mex. to S. America

p. 290

441

Very rare in w. and n. AK

HERMIT THRUSH

p. 290

442

Winter populations may vary substantially from year to year depending on food supply

Recent breeding range expansion in southern regions

AMERICAN ROBIN

p. 292

443

Very rare to casual late-fall and winter visitor well east of mapped range

VARIED THRUSH

p. 292

444

WRENTIT

p. 282

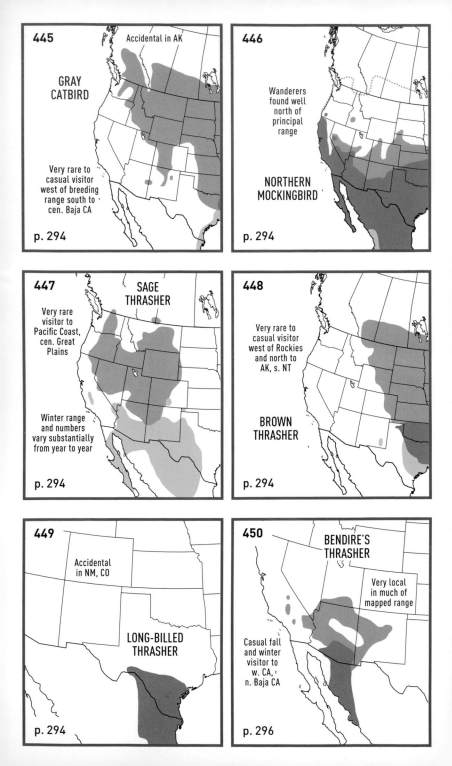

445
Accidental in AK

GRAY CATBIRD

Very rare to casual visitor west of breeding range south to cen. Baja CA

p. 294

446
Wanderers found well north of principal range

NORTHERN MOCKINGBIRD

p. 294

447
SAGE THRASHER

Very rare visitor to Pacific Coast, cen. Great Plains

Winter range and numbers vary substantially from year to year

p. 294

448
Very rare to casual visitor west of Rockies and north to AK, s. NT

BROWN THRASHER

p. 294

449
Accidental in NM, CO

LONG-BILLED THRASHER

p. 294

450
BENDIRE'S THRASHER

Very local in much of mapped range

Casual fall and winter visitor to w. CA, n. Baja CA

p. 296

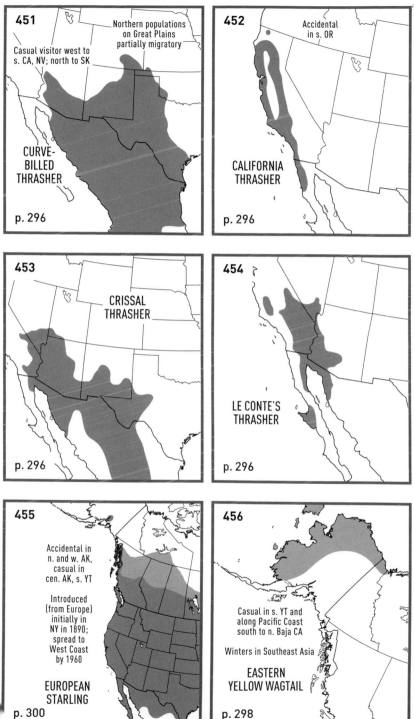

451

Casual visitor west to s. CA, NV; north to SK

Northern populations on Great Plains partially migratory

CURVE-BILLED THRASHER

p. 296

452

Accidental in s. OR

CALIFORNIA THRASHER

p. 296

453

CRISSAL THRASHER

p. 296

454

LE CONTE'S THRASHER

p. 296

455

Accidental in n. and w. AK, casual in cen. AK, s. YT

Introduced (from Europe) initially in NY in 1890; spread to West Coast by 1960

EUROPEAN STARLING

p. 300

456

Casual in s. YT and along Pacific Coast south to n. Baja CA

Winters in Southeast Asia

EASTERN YELLOW WAGTAIL

p. 298

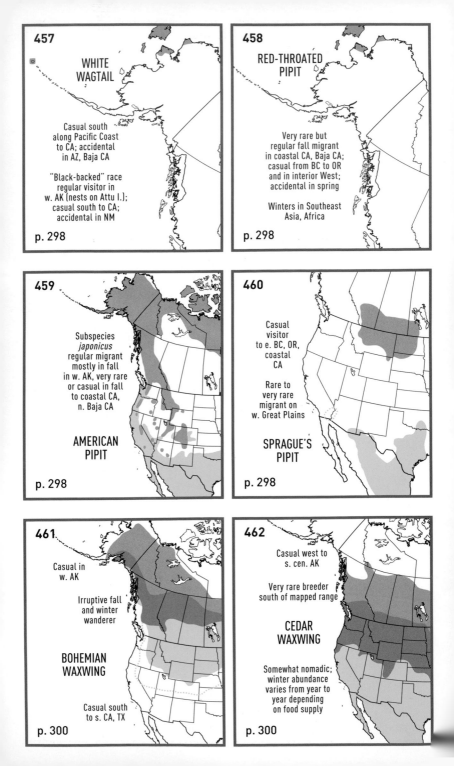

457

WHITE
WAGTAIL

Casual south
along Pacific Coast
to CA; accidental
in AZ, Baja CA

"Black-backed" race
regular visitor in
w. AK (nests on Attu I.);
casual south to CA;
accidental in NM

p. 298

458

RED-THROATED
PIPIT

Very rare but
regular fall migrant
in coastal CA, Baja CA;
casual from BC to OR
and in interior West;
accidental in spring

Winters in Southeast
Asia, Africa

p. 298

459

Subspecies
japonicus
regular migrant
mostly in fall
in w. AK, very rare
or casual in fall
to coastal CA,
n. Baja CA

AMERICAN
PIPIT

p. 298

460

Casual
visitor
to e. BC, OR,
coastal
CA

Rare to
very rare
migrant on
w. Great Plains

SPRAGUE'S
PIPIT

p. 298

461

Casual in
w. AK

Irruptive fall
and winter
wanderer

BOHEMIAN
WAXWING

Casual south
to s. CA, TX

p. 300

462

Casual west to
s. cen. AK

Very rare breeder
south of mapped range

CEDAR
WAXWING

Somewhat nomadic;
winter abundance
varies from year to
year depending
on food supply

p. 300

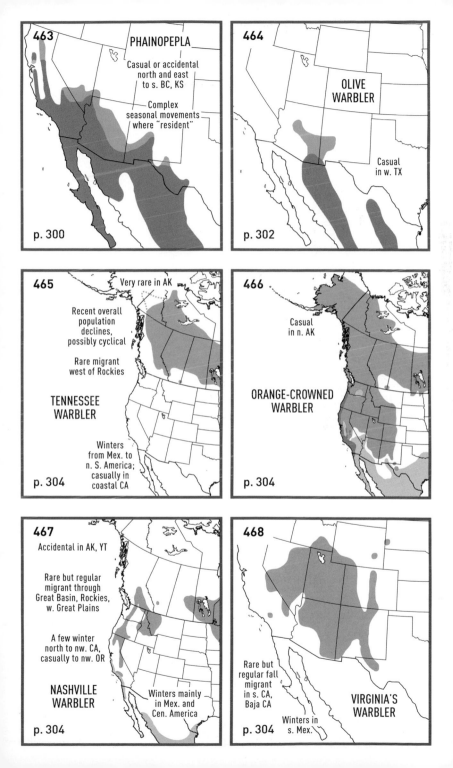

463 PHAINOPEPLA

Casual or accidental north and east to s. BC, KS

Complex seasonal movements where "resident"

p. 300

464 OLIVE WARBLER

Casual in w. TX

p. 302

465

Very rare in AK

Recent overall population declines, possibly cyclical

Rare migrant west of Rockies

TENNESSEE WARBLER

Winters from Mex. to n. S. America; casually in coastal CA

p. 304

466

Casual in n. AK

ORANGE-CROWNED WARBLER

p. 304

467

Accidental in AK, YT

Rare but regular migrant through Great Basin, Rockies, w. Great Plains

A few winter north to nw. CA, casually to nw. OR

NASHVILLE WARBLER

Winters mainly in Mex. and Cen. America

p. 304

468

Rare but regular fall migrant in s. CA, Baja CA

Winters in s. Mex.

VIRGINIA'S WARBLER

p. 304

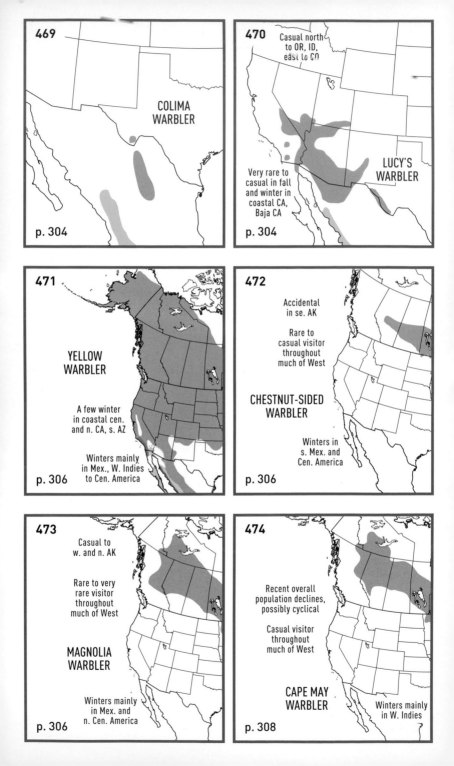

469 COLIMA WARBLER
p. 304

470 Casual north to OR, ID, east to CO
Very rare to casual in fall and winter in coastal CA, Baja CA
LUCY'S WARBLER
p. 304

471 YELLOW WARBLER
A few winter in coastal cen. and n. CA, s. AZ
Winters mainly in Mex., W. Indies to Cen. America
p. 306

472 Accidental in se. AK
Rare to casual visitor throughout much of West
CHESTNUT-SIDED WARBLER
Winters in s. Mex. and Cen. America
p. 306

473 Casual to w. and n. AK
Rare to very rare visitor throughout much of West
MAGNOLIA WARBLER
Winters mainly in Mex. and n. Cen. America
p. 306

474 Recent overall population declines, possibly cyclical
Casual visitor throughout much of West
CAPE MAY WARBLER
Winters mainly in W. Indies
p. 308

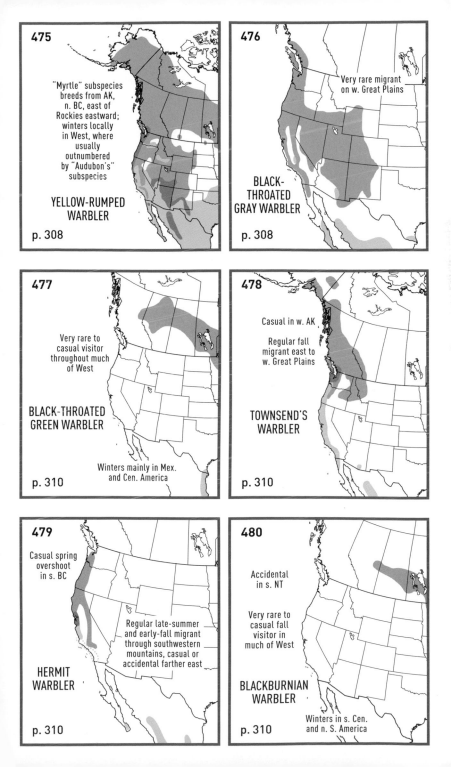

475

"Myrtle" subspecies breeds from AK, n. BC, east of Rockies eastward; winters locally in West, where usually outnumbered by "Audubon's" subspecies

YELLOW-RUMPED WARBLER

p. 308

476

Very rare migrant on w. Great Plains

BLACK-THROATED GRAY WARBLER

p. 308

477

Very rare to casual visitor throughout much of West

BLACK-THROATED GREEN WARBLER

Winters mainly in Mex. and Cen. America

p. 310

478

Casual in w. AK

Regular fall migrant east to w. Great Plains

TOWNSEND'S WARBLER

p. 310

479

Casual spring overshoot in s. BC

Regular late-summer and early-fall migrant through southwestern mountains, casual or accidental farther east

HERMIT WARBLER

p. 310

480

Accidental in s. NT

Very rare to casual fall visitor in much of West

BLACKBURNIAN WARBLER

p. 310

Winters in s. Cen. and n. S. America

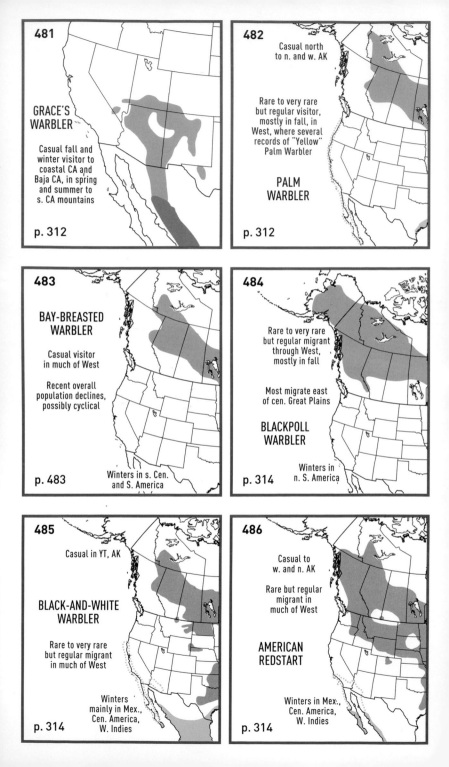

481

GRACE'S
WARBLER

Casual fall and
winter visitor to
coastal CA and
Baja CA, in spring
and summer to
s. CA mountains

p. 312

482

Casual north
to n. and w. AK

Rare to very rare
but regular visitor,
mostly in fall, in
West, where several
records of "Yellow"
Palm Warbler

PALM
WARBLER

p. 312

483

BAY-BREASTED
WARBLER

Casual visitor
in much of West

Recent overall
population declines,
possibly cyclical

Winters in s. Cen.
and S. America

p. 483

484

Rare to very rare
but regular migrant
through West,
mostly in fall

Most migrate east
of cen. Great Plains

BLACKPOLL
WARBLER

Winters in
n. S. America

p. 314

485

Casual in YT, AK

BLACK-AND-WHITE
WARBLER

Rare to very rare
but regular migrant
in much of West

Winters
mainly in Mex.,
Cen. America,
W. Indies

p. 314

486

Casual to
w. and n. AK

Rare but regular
migrant in
much of West

AMERICAN
REDSTART

Winters in Mex.,
Cen. America,
W. Indies

p. 314

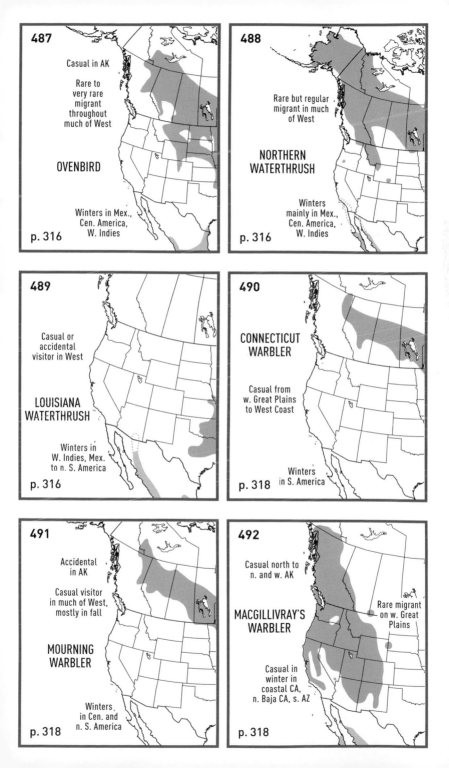

487

Casual in AK

Rare to
very rare
migrant
throughout
the West

OVENBIRD

Winters in Mex.,
Cen. America,
W. Indies

p. 316

488

Rare but regular
migrant in much
of West

NORTHERN
WATERTHRUSH

Winters
mainly in Mex.,
Cen. America,
W. Indies

p. 316

489

Casual or
accidental
visitor in West

LOUISIANA
WATERTHRUSH

Winters in
W. Indies, Mex.
to n. S. America

p. 316

490

CONNECTICUT
WARBLER

Casual from
w. Great Plains
to West Coast

Winters
in S. America

p. 318

491

Accidental
in AK

Casual visitor
in much of West,
mostly in fall

MOURNING
WARBLER

Winters
in Cen. and
n. S. America

p. 318

492

Casual north to
n. and w. AK

MACGILLIVRAY'S
WARBLER

Rare migrant
on w. Great
Plains

Casual in
winter in
coastal CA,
n. Baja CA, s. AZ

p. 318

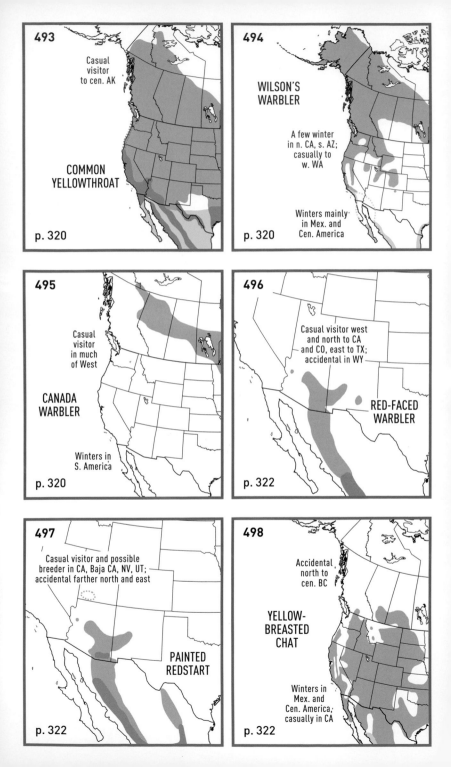

493
Casual visitor to cen. AK

COMMON YELLOWTHROAT

p. 320

494
WILSON'S WARBLER

A few winter in n. CA, s. AZ; casually to w. WA

Winters mainly in Mex. and Cen. America

p. 320

495
Casual visitor in much of West

CANADA WARBLER

Winters in S. America

p. 320

496
Casual visitor west and north to CA and CO, east to TX; accidental in WY

RED-FACED WARBLER

p. 322

497
Casual visitor and possible breeder in CA, Baja CA, NV, UT; accidental farther north and east

PAINTED REDSTART

p. 322

498
Accidental north to cen. BC

YELLOW-BREASTED CHAT

Winters in Mex. and Cen. America; casually in CA

p. 322

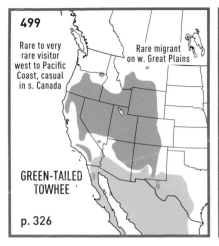

499

Rare to very rare visitor west to Pacific Coast, casual in s. Canada

Rare migrant on w. Great Plains

GREEN-TAILED TOWHEE

p. 326

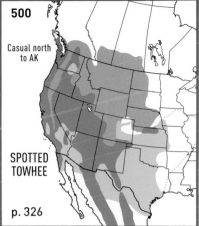

500

Casual north to AK

SPOTTED TOWHEE

p. 326

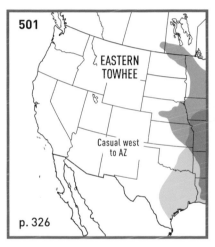

501

EASTERN TOWHEE

Casual west to AZ

p. 326

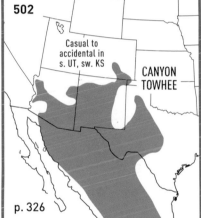

502

Casual to accidental in s. UT, sw. KS

CANYON TOWHEE

p. 326

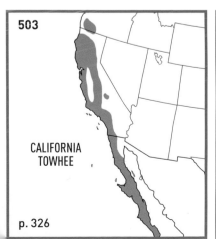

503

CALIFORNIA TOWHEE

p. 326

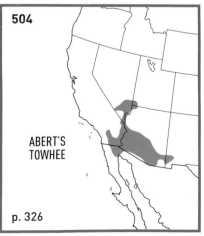

504

ABERT'S TOWHEE

p. 326

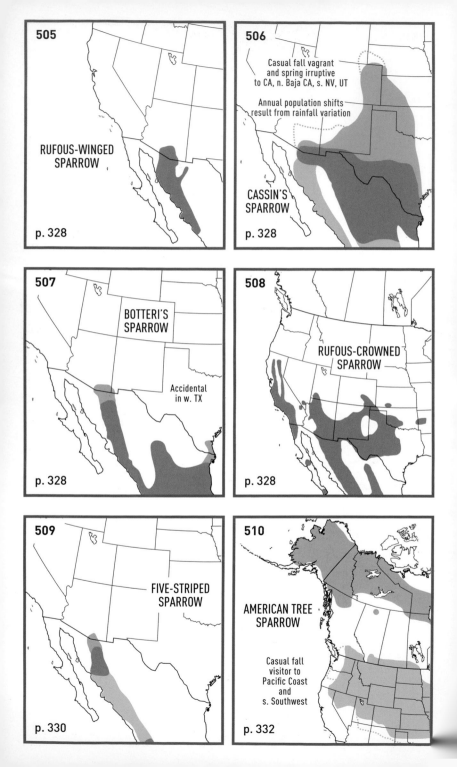

505
RUFOUS-WINGED
SPARROW
p. 328

506
Casual fall vagrant
and spring irruptive
to CA, n. Baja CA, s. NV, UT
Annual population shifts
result from rainfall variation
CASSIN'S
SPARROW
p. 328

507
BOTTERI'S
SPARROW
Accidental
in w. TX
p. 328

508
RUFOUS-CROWNED
SPARROW
p. 328

509
FIVE-STRIPED
SPARROW
p. 330

510
AMERICAN TREE
SPARROW
Casual fall
visitor to
Pacific Coast
and
s. Southwest
p. 332

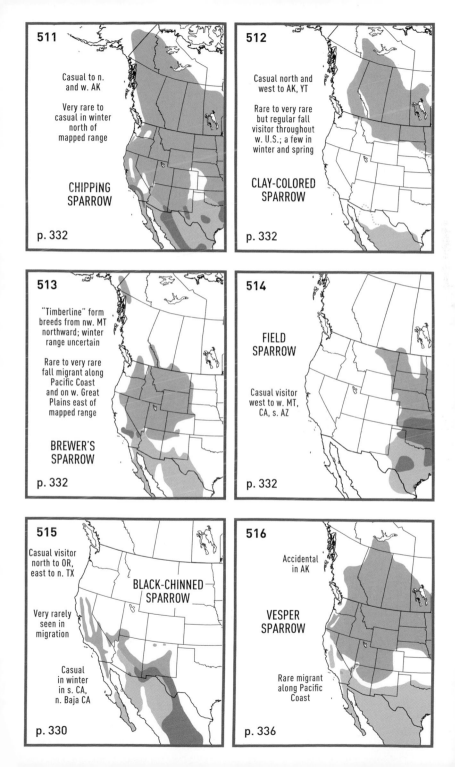

511

Casual to n. and w. AK

Very rare to casual in winter north of mapped range

CHIPPING SPARROW

p. 332

512

Casual north and west to AK, YT

Rare to very rare but regular fall visitor throughout w. U.S.; a few in winter and spring

CLAY-COLORED SPARROW

p. 332

513

"Timberline" form breeds from nw. MT northward; winter range uncertain

Rare to very rare fall migrant along Pacific Coast and on w. Great Plains east of mapped range

BREWER'S SPARROW

p. 332

514

FIELD SPARROW

Casual visitor west to w. MT, CA, s. AZ

p. 332

515

Casual visitor north to OR, east to n. TX

BLACK-CHINNED SPARROW

Very rarely seen in migration

Casual in winter in s. CA, n. Baja CA

p. 330

516

Accidental in AK

VESPER SPARROW

Rare migrant along Pacific Coast

p. 336

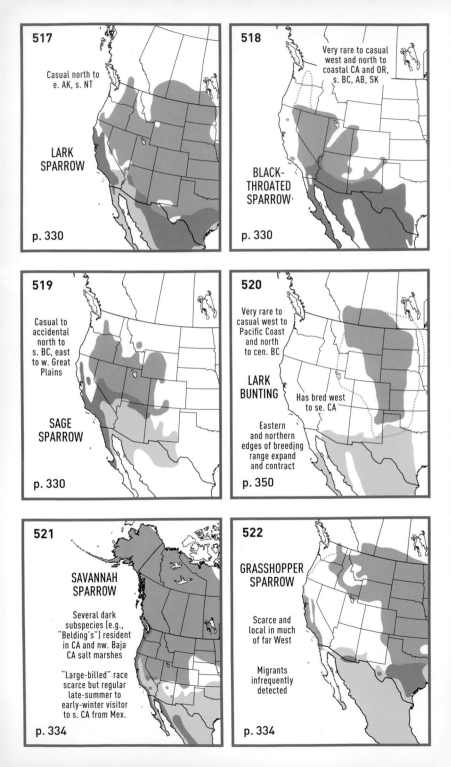

517

Casual north to
e. AK, s. NT

LARK
SPARROW

p. 330

518

Very rare to casual
west and north to
coastal CA and OR,
s. BC, AB, SK

BLACK-
THROATED
SPARROW

p. 330

519

Casual to
accidental
north to
s. BC, east
to w. Great
Plains

SAGE
SPARROW

p. 330

520

Very rare to
casual west to
Pacific Coast
and north
to cen. BC

LARK
BUNTING

Has bred west
to se. CA

Eastern
and northern
edges of breeding
range expand
and contract

p. 350

521

SAVANNAH
SPARROW

Several dark
subspecies (e.g.,
"Belding's") resident
in CA and nw. Baja
CA salt marshes

"Large-billed" race
scarce but regular
late-summer to
early-winter visitor
to s. CA from Mex.

p. 334

522

GRASSHOPPER
SPARROW

Scarce and
local in much
of far West

Migrants
infrequently
detected

p. 334

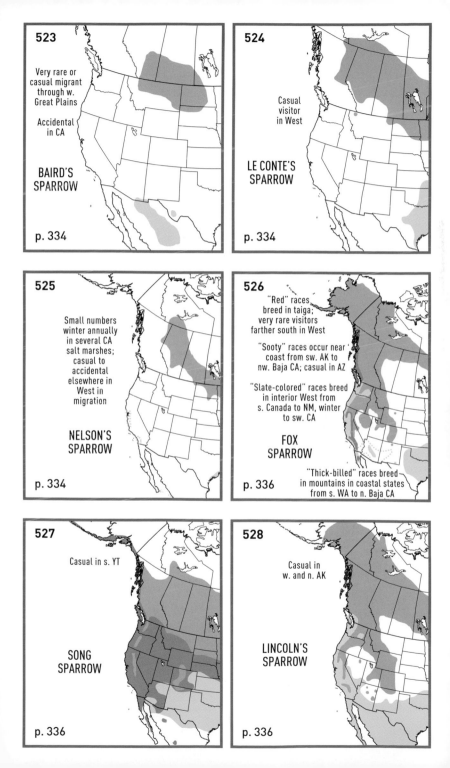

523 Very rare or casual migrant through w. Great Plains

Accidental in CA

BAIRD'S SPARROW

p. 334

524 Casual visitor in West

LE CONTE'S SPARROW

p. 334

525 Small numbers winter annually in several CA salt marshes; casual to accidental elsewhere in West in migration

NELSON'S SPARROW

p. 334

526 "Red" races breed in taiga; very rare visitors farther south in West

"Sooty" races occur near coast from sw. AK to nw. Baja CA; casual in AZ

"Slate-colored" races breed in interior West from s. Canada to NM, winter to sw. CA

FOX SPARROW

p. 336

"Thick-billed" races breed in mountains in coastal states from s. WA to n. Baja CA

527 Casual in s. YT

SONG SPARROW

p. 336

528 Casual in w. and n. AK

LINCOLN'S SPARROW

p. 336

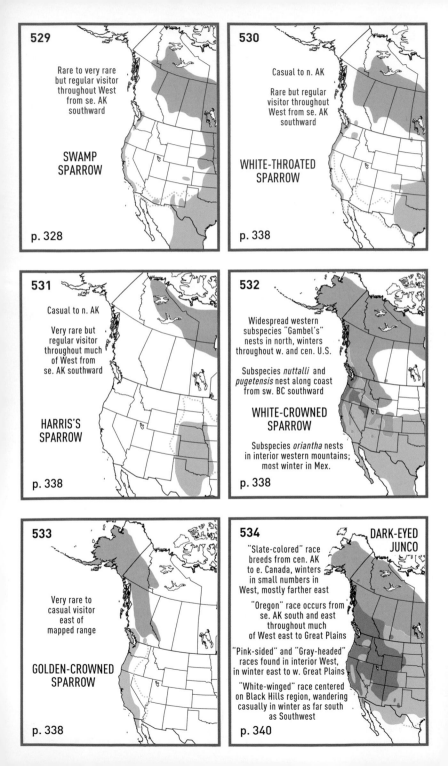

529

Rare to very rare but regular visitor throughout West from se. AK southward

SWAMP SPARROW

p. 328

530

Casual to n. AK

Rare but regular visitor throughout West from se. AK southward

WHITE-THROATED SPARROW

p. 338

531

Casual to n. AK

Very rare but regular visitor throughout much of West from se. AK southward

HARRIS'S SPARROW

p. 338

532

Widespread western subspecies "Gambel's" nests in north, winters throughout w. and cen. U.S.

Subspecies *nuttalli* and *pugetensis* nest along coast from sw. BC southward

WHITE-CROWNED SPARROW

Subspecies *oriantha* nests in interior western mountains; most winter in Mex.

p. 338

533

Very rare to casual visitor east of mapped range

GOLDEN-CROWNED SPARROW

p. 338

534

DARK-EYED JUNCO

"Slate-colored" race breeds from cen. AK to e. Canada, winters in small numbers in West, mostly farther east

"Oregon" race occurs from se. AK south and east throughout much of West east to Great Plains

"Pink-sided" and "Gray-headed" races found in interior West, in winter east to w. Great Plains

"White-winged" race centered on Black Hills region, wandering casually in winter as far south as Southwest

p. 340

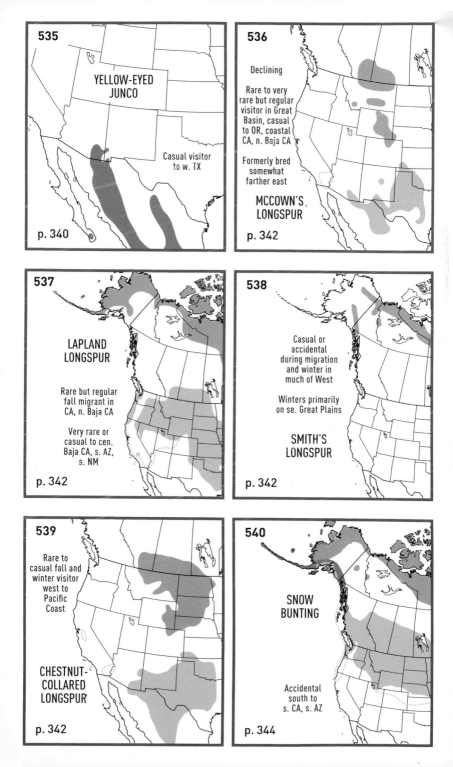

535

YELLOW-EYED
JUNCO

Casual visitor
to w. TX

p. 340

536

Declining

Rare to very
rare but regular
visitor in Great
Basin, casual
to OR, coastal
CA, n. Baja CA

Formerly bred
somewhat
farther east

MCCOWN'S
LONGSPUR

p. 342

537

LAPLAND
LONGSPUR

Rare but regular
fall migrant in
CA, n. Baja CA

Very rare or
casual to cen.
Baja CA, s. AZ,
s. NM

p. 342

538

Casual or
accidental
during migration
and winter in
much of West

Winters primarily
on se. Great Plains

SMITH'S
LONGSPUR

p. 342

539

Rare to
casual fall and
winter visitor
west to
Pacific
Coast

CHESTNUT-
COLLARED
LONGSPUR

p. 342

540

SNOW
BUNTING

Accidental
south to
s. CA, s. AZ

p. 344

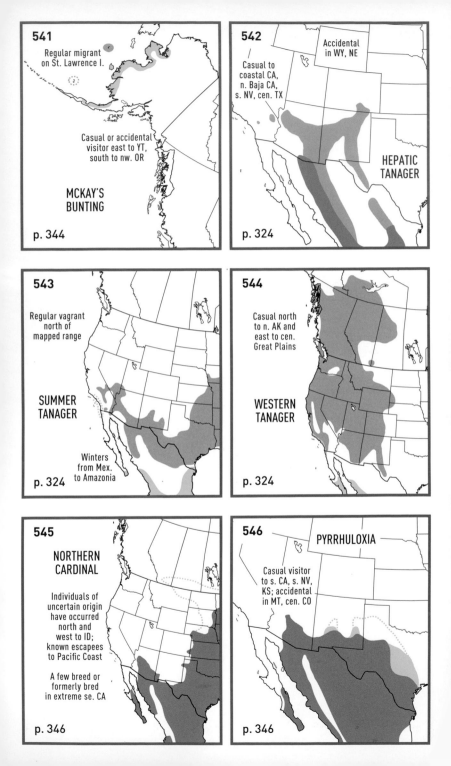

541

Regular migrant on St. Lawrence I.

Casual or accidental visitor east to YT, south to nw. OR

MCKAY'S BUNTING

p. 344

542

Accidental in WY, NE

Casual to coastal CA, n. Baja CA, s. NV, cen. TX

HEPATIC TANAGER

p. 324

543

Regular vagrant north of mapped range

SUMMER TANAGER

Winters from Mex. to Amazonia

p. 324

544

Casual north to n. AK and east to cen. Great Plains

WESTERN TANAGER

p. 324

545

NORTHERN CARDINAL

Individuals of uncertain origin have occurred north and west to ID; known escapees to Pacific Coast

A few breed or formerly bred in extreme se. CA

p. 346

546

PYRRHULOXIA

Casual visitor to s. CA, s. NV, KS; accidental in MT, cen. CO

p. 346

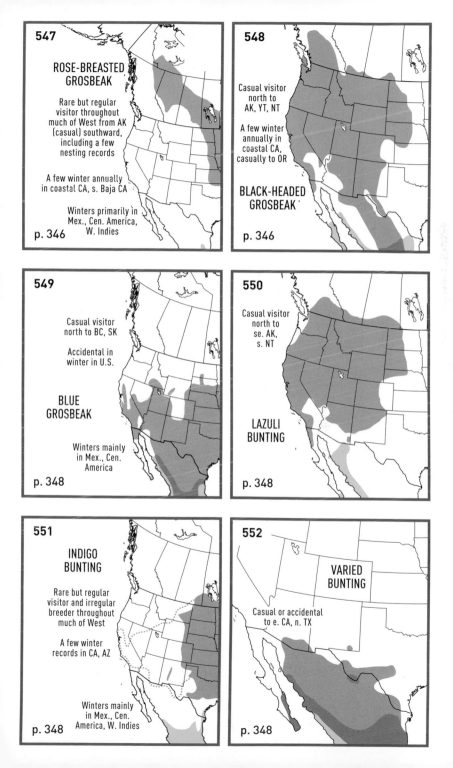

547

ROSE-BREASTED GROSBEAK

Rare but regular visitor throughout much of West from AK (casual) southward, including a few nesting records

A few winter annually in coastal CA, s. Baja CA

Winters primarily in Mex., Cen. America, W. Indies

p. 346

548

Casual visitor north to AK, YT, NT

A few winter annually in coastal CA, casually to OR

BLACK-HEADED GROSBEAK

p. 346

549

Casual visitor north to BC, SK

Accidental in winter in U.S.

BLUE GROSBEAK

Winters mainly in Mex., Cen. America

p. 348

550

Casual visitor north to se. AK, s. NT

LAZULI BUNTING

p. 348

551

INDIGO BUNTING

Rare but regular visitor and irregular breeder throughout much of West

A few winter records in CA, AZ

Winters mainly in Mex., Cen. America, W. Indies

p. 348

552

VARIED BUNTING

Casual or accidental to e. CA, n. TX

p. 348

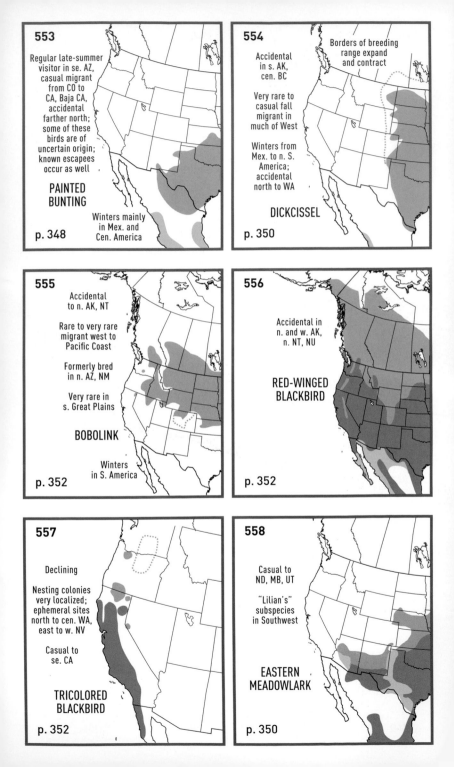

553

Regular late-summer visitor in se. AZ, casual migrant from CO to CA, Baja CA, accidental farther north; some of these birds are of uncertain origin; known escapees occur as well

PAINTED BUNTING

Winters mainly in Mex. and Cen. America

p. 348

554

Borders of breeding range expand and contract

Accidental in s. AK, cen. BC

Very rare to casual fall migrant in much of West

Winters from Mex. to n. S. America; accidental north to WA

DICKCISSEL

p. 350

555

Accidental to n. AK, NT

Rare to very rare migrant west to Pacific Coast

Formerly bred in n. AZ, NM

Very rare in s. Great Plains

BOBOLINK

Winters in S. America

p. 352

556

Accidental in n. and w. AK, n. NT, NU

RED-WINGED BLACKBIRD

p. 352

557

Declining

Nesting colonies very localized; ephemeral sites north to cen. WA, east to w. NV

Casual to se. CA

TRICOLORED BLACKBIRD

p. 352

558

Casual to ND, MB, UT

"Lilian's" subspecies in Southwest

EASTERN MEADOWLARK

p. 350

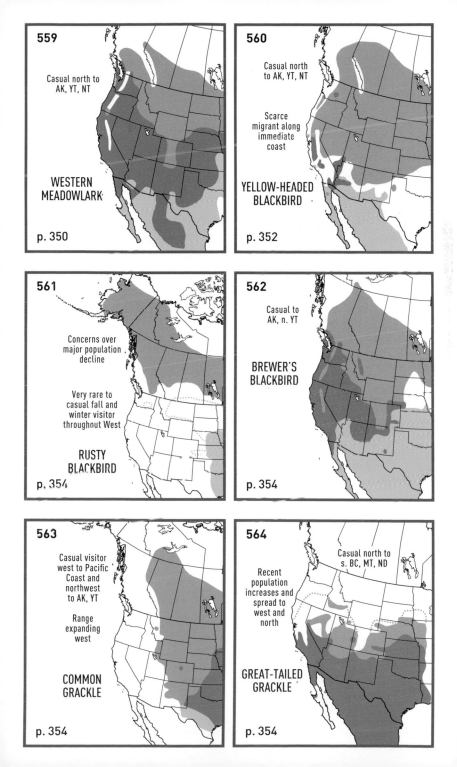

559

Casual north to
AK, YT, NT

WESTERN
MEADOWLARK

p. 350

560

Casual north
to AK, YT, NT

Scarce
migrant along
immediate
coast

YELLOW-HEADED
BLACKBIRD

p. 352

561

Concerns over
major population
decline

Very rare to
casual fall and
winter visitor
throughout West

RUSTY
BLACKBIRD

p. 354

562

Casual to
AK, n. YT

BREWER'S
BLACKBIRD

p. 354

563

Casual visitor
west to Pacific
Coast and
northwest to AK, YT

Range
expanding
west

COMMON
GRACKLE

p. 354

564

Casual north to
s. BC, MT, ND

Recent
population
increases and
spread to
west and
north

GREAT-TAILED
GRACKLE

p. 354

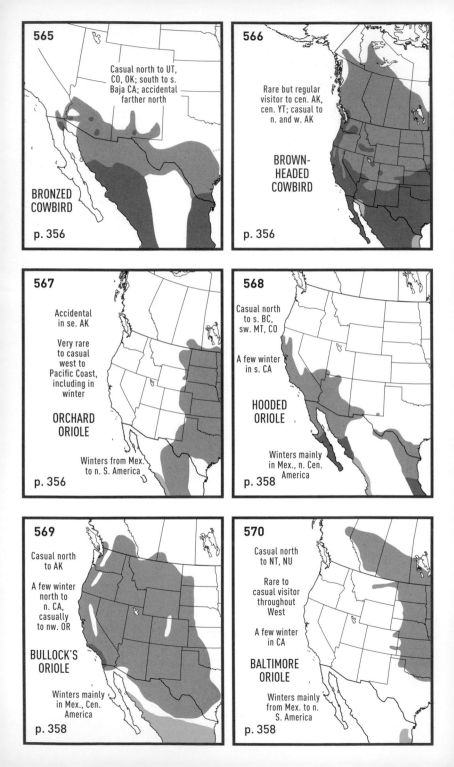

565

Casual north to UT, CO, OK; south to s. Baja CA; accidental farther north

BRONZED COWBIRD

p. 356

566

Rare but regular visitor to cen. AK, cen. YT; casual to n. and w. AK

BROWN-HEADED COWBIRD

p. 356

567

Accidental in se. AK

Very rare to casual west to Pacific Coast, including in winter

ORCHARD ORIOLE

Winters from Mex. to n. S. America

p. 356

568

Casual north to s. BC, sw. MT, CO

A few winter in s. CA

HOODED ORIOLE

Winters mainly in Mex., n. Cen. America

p. 358

569

Casual north to AK

A few winter north to n. CA, casually to nw. OR

BULLOCK'S ORIOLE

Winters mainly in Mex., Cen. America

p. 358

570

Casual north to NT, NU

Rare to casual visitor throughout West

A few winter in CA

BALTIMORE ORIOLE

Winters mainly from Mex. to n. S. America

p. 358

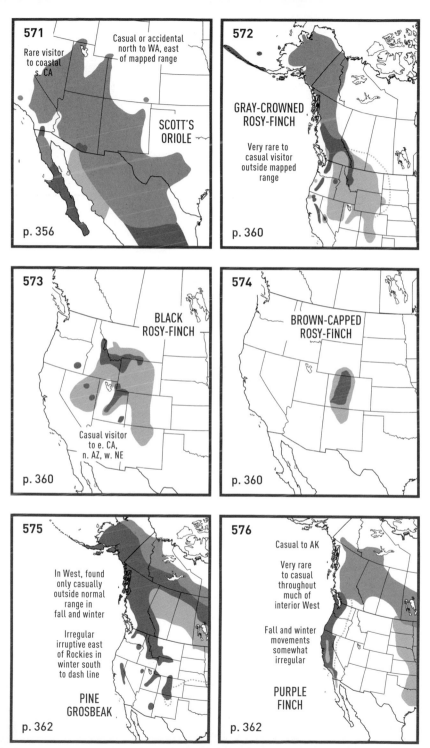

571
Rare visitor to coastal s. CA

Casual or accidental north to WA, east of mapped range

SCOTT'S ORIOLE

p. 356

572
GRAY-CROWNED ROSY-FINCH

Very rare to casual visitor outside mapped range

p. 360

573
BLACK ROSY-FINCH

Casual visitor to e. CA, n. AZ, w. NE

p. 360

574
BROWN-CAPPED ROSY-FINCH

p. 360

575
In West, found only casually outside normal range in fall and winter

Irregular irruptive east of Rockies in winter south to dash line

PINE GROSBEAK

p. 362

576
Casual to AK

Very rare to casual throughout much of interior West

Fall and winter movements somewhat irregular

PURPLE FINCH

p. 362

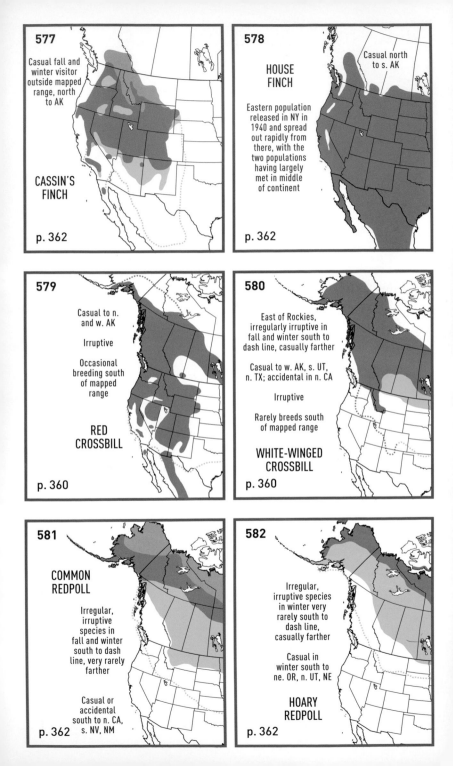

577

Casual fall and winter visitor outside mapped range, north to AK

CASSIN'S FINCH

p. 362

578

Casual north to s. AK

HOUSE FINCH

Eastern population released in NY in 1940 and spread out rapidly from there, with the two populations having largely met in middle of continent

p. 362

579

Casual to n. and w. AK

Irruptive

Occasional breeding south of mapped range

RED CROSSBILL

p. 360

580

East of Rockies, irregularly irruptive in fall and winter south to dash line, casually farther

Casual to w. AK, s. UT, n. TX; accidental in n. CA

Irruptive

Rarely breeds south of mapped range

WHITE-WINGED CROSSBILL

p. 360

581

COMMON REDPOLL

Irregular, irruptive species in fall and winter south to dash line, very rarely farther

Casual or accidental south to n. CA, s. NV, NM

p. 362

582

Irregular, irruptive species in winter very rarely south to dash line, casually farther

Casual in winter south to ne. OR, n. UT, NE

HOARY REDPOLL

p. 362

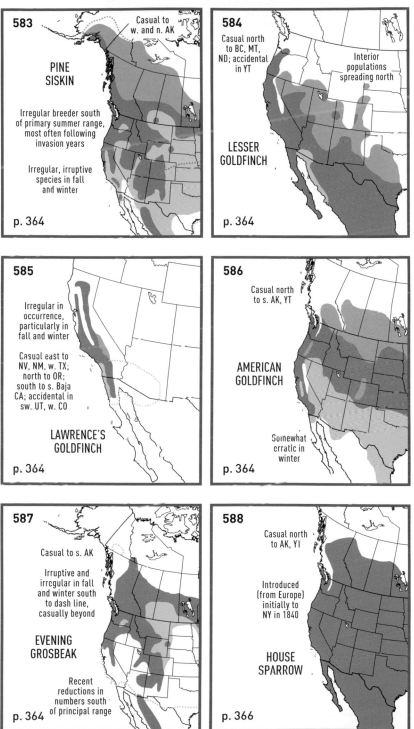

583

Casual to w. and n. AK

PINE SISKIN

Irregular breeder south of primary summer range, most often following invasion years

Irregular, irruptive species in fall and winter

p. 364

584

Casual north to BC, MT, ND; accidental in YT

Interior populations spreading north

LESSER GOLDFINCH

p. 364

585

Irregular in occurrence, particularly in fall and winter

Casual east to NV, NM, w. TX; north to OR; south to s. Baja CA; accidental in sw. UT, w. CO

LAWRENCE'S GOLDFINCH

p. 364

586

Casual north to s. AK, YT

AMERICAN GOLDFINCH

Somewhat erratic in winter

p. 364

587

Casual to s. AK

Irruptive and irregular in fall and winter south to dash line, casually beyond

EVENING GROSBEAK

Recent reductions in numbers south of principal range

p. 364

588

Casual north to AK, YT

Introduced (from Europe) initially to NY in 1840

HOUSE SPARROW

p. 366

LIFE LIST

Keep a Life List. Check off the birds you have seen.

The list on the following pages includes all of the birds shown on the plates, except for some of the accidentals that have not been verified.

For a checklist of all the birds of North America, see the *ABA Checklist: Birds of the Continental United States and Canada,* compiled by the Checklist Committee of the American Birding Association, 4945 North 30th Street, Suite 200, Colorado Springs, CO 80919-3151 (www.aba.org/checklist). It lists every species that has occurred north of the Mexican border.

In the following list, birds are grouped first under orders (identified by the Latin ending *-formes*), followed by families (*-dae* ending), and then species. Sequencing of orders and families follows the American Ornithologists' Union's Check-list of North American Birds (1998 through the 50th supplement, from 2009), as do the scientific names for genus and species. Scientific names are not given below but can be found in the species accounts throughout the book.

Species marked with an asterisk are exotic and unestablished. Though not countable on official ABA lists, they are included here because birders may encounter them and wish to record their sightings.

ORDER ANSERIFORMES

Ducks, Geese, and Swans (Anatidae)
_____ Black-bellied Whistling-Duck
_____ Fulvous Whistling-Duck
_____ Greater White-fronted Goose
_____ Emperor Goose
_____ Snow Goose
_____ Ross's Goose
_____ Brant
_____ Cackling Goose
_____ Canada Goose
_____ Mute Swan
_____ Trumpeter Swan
_____ Tundra Swan
_____ Wood Duck

_____Gadwall
_____Eurasian Wigeon
_____American Wigeon
_____Mallard
_____Blue-winged Teal
_____Cinnamon Teal
_____Northern Shoveler
_____White-cheeked Pintail
_____Northern Pintail
_____Garganey
_____Green-winged Teal
_____Canvasback
_____Redhead
_____Ring-necked Duck
_____Tufted Duck
_____Greater Scaup
_____Lesser Scaup
_____Steller's Eider
_____Spectacled Eider
_____King Eider
_____Common Eider
_____Harlequin Duck
_____Surf Scoter
_____White-winged Scoter
_____Black Scoter
_____Long-tailed Duck
_____Bufflehead
_____Common Goldeneye
_____Barrow's Goldeneye
_____Smew
_____Hooded Merganser
_____Common Merganser
_____Red-breasted Merganser
_____Ruddy Duck

ORDER GALLIFORMES

New World Quail (Odontophoridae)
_____Mountain Quail
_____Scaled Quail
_____California Quail
_____Gambel's Quail
_____Northern Bobwhite
_____Montezuma Quail

Partridges, Grouse, Turkeys, and Old World Quail (Phasianidae)
_____Chukar
_____Himalayan Snowcock
_____Gray Partridge
_____Ring-necked Pheasant

_____Ruffed Grouse
_____Greater Sage-Grouse
_____Gunnison Sage-Grouse
_____Spruce Grouse
_____Willow Ptarmigan
_____Rock Ptarmigan
_____White-tailed Ptarmigan
_____Dusky Grouse
_____Sooty Grouse
_____Sharp-tailed Grouse
_____Greater Prairie-Chicken
_____Lesser Prairie-Chicken
_____Wild Turkey

ORDER GAVIIFORMES

Loons (Gaviidae)
_____Red-throated Loon
_____Arctic Loon
_____Pacific Loon
_____Common Loon
_____Yellow-billed Loon

ORDER PODICIPEDIFORMES

Grebes (Podicipedidae)
_____Least Grebe
_____Pied-billed Grebe
_____Horned Grebe
_____Red-necked Grebe
_____Eared Grebe
_____Western Grebe
_____Clark's Grebe

ORDER PROCELLARIIFORMES

Albatrosses (Diomedeidae)
_____Laysan Albatross
_____Black-footed Albatross
_____Short-tailed Albatross

Shearwaters and Petrels (Procellariidae)
_____Northern Fulmar
_____Murphy's Petrel
_____Mottled Petrel
_____Cook's Petrel
_____Pink-footed Shearwater
_____Flesh-footed Shearwater
_____Buller's Shearwater
_____Sooty Shearwater

_____Short-tailed Shearwater
_____Manx Shearwater
_____Black-vented Shearwater
Storm-Petrels (Hydrobatidae)
_____Wilson's Storm-Petrel
_____Fork-tailed Storm-Petrel
_____Leach's Storm-Petrel
_____Ashy Storm-Petrel
_____Black Storm-Petrel
_____Least Storm-Petrel

ORDER PELECANIFORMES

Tropicbirds (Phaethontidae)
_____Red-billed Tropicbird
_____Red-tailed Tropicbird
Boobies and Gannets (Sulidae)
_____Masked Booby
_____Blue-footed Booby
_____Brown Booby
_____Red-footed Booby
Pelicans (Pelecanidae)
_____American White Pelican
_____Brown Pelican
Cormorants (Phalacrocoracidae)
_____Brandt's Cormorant
_____Neotropic Cormorant
_____Double-crested Cormorant
_____Red-faced Cormorant
_____Pelagic Cormorant
Frigatebirds (Fregatidae)
_____Magnificent Frigatebird

ORDER CICONIIFORMES

Bitterns, Herons, and Allies (Ardeidae)
_____American Bittern
_____Least Bittern
_____Great Blue Heron
_____Great Egret
_____Snowy Egret
_____Little Blue Heron
_____Tricolored Heron
_____Reddish Egret
_____Cattle Egret
_____Green Heron
_____Black-crowned Night-Heron

_____Yellow-crowned Night-Heron
Ibises and Spoonbills (Threskiornithidae)
_____White Ibis
_____Glossy Ibis
_____White-faced Ibis
_____Roseate Spoonbill
Storks (Ciconiidae)
_____Wood Stork
New World Vultures (Cathartidae)
_____Black Vulture
_____Turkey Vulture
_____California Condor

ORDER FALCONIFORMES

Hawks, Kites, Eagles, and Allies (Accipitridae)
_____Osprey
_____Mississippi Kite
_____Bald Eagle
_____White-tailed Eagle
_____Northern Harrier
_____Sharp-shinned Hawk
_____Cooper's Hawk
_____Northern Goshawk
_____Common Black-Hawk
_____Harris's Hawk
_____Red-shouldered Hawk
_____Broad-winged Hawk
_____Gray Hawk
_____Short-tailed Hawk
_____Swainson's Hawk
_____Zone-tailed Hawk
_____Red-tailed Hawk
_____Ferruginous Hawk
_____Rough-legged Hawk
_____Golden Eagle
Caracaras and Falcons (Falconidae)
_____Crested Caracara
_____Eurasian Kestrel
_____American Kestrel
_____Merlin
_____Eurasian Hobby
_____Aplomado Falcon
_____Gyrfalcon
_____Peregrine Falcon
_____Prairie Falcon

ORDER GRUIFORMES

Rails, Gallinules, and Coots (Rallidae)

_____Yellow Rail
_____Black Rail
_____Clapper Rail
_____Virginia Rail
_____Sora
_____Purple Gallinule
_____Common Moorhen
_____American Coot

Cranes (Gruidae)

_____Sandhill Crane
_____Common Crane
_____Whooping Crane

ORDER CHARADRIIFORMES

Lapwings and Plovers (Charadriidae)

_____Black-bellied Plover
_____American Golden-Plover
_____Pacific Golden-Plover
_____Lesser Sand-Plover
_____Snowy Plover
_____Wilson's Plover
_____Common Ringed Plover
_____Semipalmated Plover
_____Piping Plover
_____Killdeer
_____Mountain Plover
_____Eurasian Dotterel

Oystercatchers (Haematopodidae)

_____Black Oystercatcher

Stilts and Avocets (Recurvirostridae)

_____Black-necked Stilt
_____American Avocet

Sandpipers, Phalaropes, and Allies (Scolopacidae)

_____Terek Sandpiper
_____Common Sandpiper
_____Spotted Sandpiper
_____Solitary Sandpiper
_____Gray-tailed Tattler
_____Wandering Tattler
_____Spotted Redshank
_____Greater Yellowlegs
_____Common Greenshank
_____Willet
_____Lesser Yellowlegs
_____Wood Sandpiper
_____Upland Sandpiper
_____Little Curlew
_____Eskimo Curlew
_____Whimbrel
_____Bristle-thighed Curlew
_____Long-billed Curlew
_____Black-tailed Godwit
_____Hudsonian Godwit
_____Bar-tailed Godwit
_____Marbled Godwit
_____Ruddy Turnstone
_____Black Turnstone
_____Surfbird
_____Red Knot
_____Sanderling
_____Semipalmated Sandpiper
_____Western Sandpiper
_____Red-necked Stint
_____Little Stint
_____Temminck's Stint
_____Long-toed Stint
_____Least Sandpiper
_____White-rumped Sandpiper
_____Baird's Sandpiper
_____Pectoral Sandpiper
_____Sharp-tailed Sandpiper
_____Rock Sandpiper
_____Dunlin
_____Curlew Sandpiper
_____Stilt Sandpiper
_____Buff-breasted Sandpiper
_____Ruff
_____Short-billed Dowitcher
_____Long-billed Dowitcher
_____Wilson's Snipe
_____Common Snipe
_____Wilson's Phalarope
_____Red-necked Phalarope
_____Red Phalarope

Gulls, Terns, and Skimmers (Laridae)

_____Black-legged Kittiwake
_____Red-legged Kittiwake
_____Ivory Gull
_____Sabine's Gull

_____Bonaparte's Gull
_____Black-headed Gull
_____Little Gull
_____Ross's Gull
_____Laughing Gull
_____Franklin's Gull
_____Black-tailed Gull
_____Heermann's Gull
_____Mew Gull
_____Ring-billed Gull
_____Western Gull
_____Yellow-footed Gull
_____California Gull
_____Herring Gull
_____Thayer's Gull
_____Iceland Gull
_____Lesser Black-backed Gull
_____Slaty-backed Gull
_____Glaucous-winged Gull
_____Glaucous Gull
_____Great Black-backed Gull
_____Sooty Tern
_____Bridled Tern
_____Aleutian Tern
_____Least Tern
_____Gull-billed Tern
_____Caspian Tern
_____Black Tern
_____White-winged Tern
_____Common Tern
_____Arctic Tern
_____Forster's Tern
_____Royal Tern
_____Elegant Tern
_____Black Skimmer

Skuas and Jaegers (Stercorariidae)
_____South Polar Skua
_____Pomarine Jaeger
_____Parasitic Jaeger
_____Long-tailed Jaeger

Auks, Murres, and Puffins (Alcidae)
_____Dovekie
_____Common Murre
_____Thick-billed Murre
_____Black Guillemot
_____Pigeon Guillemot
_____Long-billed Murrelet
_____Marbled Murrelet
_____Kittlitz's Murrelet

_____Xantus's Murrelet
_____Craveri's Murrelet
_____Ancient Murrelet
_____Cassin's Auklet
_____Parakeet Auklet
_____Least Auklet
_____Whiskered Auklet
_____Crested Auklet
_____Rhinoceros Auklet
_____Horned Puffin
_____Tufted Puffin

ORDER COLUMBIFORMES

Pigeons and Doves (Columbidae)
_____Rock Pigeon
_____Band-tailed Pigeon
_____Eurasian Collared-Dove
_____African Collared-Dove*
_____Spotted Dove
_____White-winged Dove
_____Mourning Dove
_____Inca Dove
_____Common Ground-Dove
_____Ruddy Ground-Dove

ORDER PSITTACIFORMES

Lories, Parakeets, Macaws, and Parrots (Psittacidae)
_____Mitred Parakeet*
_____White-fronted Parrot*
_____Yellow-chevroned Parakeet*
_____Red-crowned Parrot
_____Lilac-crowned Parrot*
_____Yellow-headed Parrot*
_____Red-lored Parrot*

ORDER CUCULIFORMES

Cuckoos, Roadrunners, and Anis (Cuculidae)
_____Yellow-billed Cuckoo
_____Black-billed Cuckoo
_____Greater Roadrunner
_____Groove-billed Ani

ORDER STRIGIFORMES

Barn Owls (Tytonidae)
_____Barn Owl
Typical Owls (Strigidae)
_____Flammulated Owl

_____Western Screech-Owl
_____Eastern Screech-Owl
_____Whiskered Screech-Owl
_____Great Horned Owl
_____Snowy Owl
_____Northern Hawk Owl
_____Northern Pygmy-Owl
_____Ferruginous Pygmy-Owl
_____Elf Owl
_____Burrowing Owl
_____Spotted Owl
_____Barred Owl
_____Great Gray Owl
_____Long-eared Owl
_____Short-eared Owl
_____Boreal Owl
_____Northern Saw-whet Owl

ORDER CAPRIMULGIFORMES

Goatsuckers (Caprimulgidae)
_____Lesser Nighthawk
_____Common Nighthawk
_____Common Poorwill
_____Buff-collared Nightjar
_____Whip-poor-will

ORDER APODIFORMES

Swifts (Apodidae)
_____Black Swift
_____Chimney Swift
_____Vaux's Swift
_____White-throated Swift

Hummingbirds (Trochilidae)
_____Broad-billed Hummingbird
_____White-eared Hummingbird
_____Berylline Hummingbird
_____Violet-crowned Hummingbird
_____Blue-throated Hummingbird
_____Magnificent Hummingbird
_____Plain-capped Starthroat
_____Lucifer Hummingbird
_____Ruby-throated Hummingbird
_____Black-chinned Hummingbird
_____Anna's Hummingbird
_____Costa's Hummingbird
_____Calliope Hummingbird
_____Broad-tailed Hummingbird

_____Rufous Hummingbird
_____Allen's Hummingbird

ORDER TROGONIFORMES

Trogons (Trogonidae)
_____Elegant Trogon
_____Eared Quetzal

ORDER CORACIIFORMES

Kingfishers (Alcedinidae)
_____Belted Kingfisher
_____Green Kingfisher

ORDER PICIFORMES

Woodpeckers and Allies (Picidae)
_____Lewis's Woodpecker
_____Red-headed Woodpecker
_____Acorn Woodpecker
_____Gila Woodpecker
_____Golden-fronted Woodpecker
_____Red-bellied Woodpecker
_____Williamson's Sapsucker
_____Yellow-bellied Sapsucker
_____Red-naped Sapsucker
_____Red-breasted Sapsucker
_____Ladder-backed Woodpecker
_____Nuttall's Woodpecker
_____Downy Woodpecker
_____Hairy Woodpecker
_____Arizona Woodpecker
_____White-headed Woodpecker
_____American Three-toed Woodpecker
_____Black-backed Woodpecker
_____Northern Flicker
_____Gilded Flicker
_____Pileated Woodpecker

ORDER PASSERIFORMES

Tyrant Flycatchers (Tyrannidae)
_____Northern Beardless-Tyrannulet
_____Olive-sided Flycatcher
_____Greater Pewee
_____Western Wood-Pewee
_____Eastern Wood-Pewee
_____Yellow-bellied Flycatcher
_____Alder Flycatcher

_____Willow Flycatcher
_____Least Flycatcher
_____Hammond's Flycatcher
_____Gray Flycatcher
_____Dusky Flycatcher
_____Pacific-slope Flycatcher
_____Cordilleran Flycatcher
_____Buff-breasted Flycatcher
_____Black Phoebe
_____Eastern Phoebe
_____Say's Phoebe
_____Vermilion Flycatcher
_____Dusky-capped Flycatcher
_____Ash-throated Flycatcher
_____Great Crested Flycatcher
_____Brown-crested Flycatcher
_____Sulphur-bellied Flycatcher
_____Tropical Kingbird
_____Cassin's Kingbird
_____Thick-billed Kingbird
_____Western Kingbird
_____Eastern Kingbird
_____Scissor-tailed Flycatcher
_____Rose-throated Becard

Shrikes (Laniidae)
_____Loggerhead Shrike
_____Northern Shrike

Vireos (Vireonidae)
_____White-eyed Vireo
_____Bell's Vireo
_____Black-capped Vireo
_____Gray Vireo
_____Yellow-throated Vireo
_____Plumbeous Vireo
_____Cassin's Vireo
_____Blue-headed Vireo
_____Hutton's Vireo
_____Warbling Vireo
_____Philadelphia Vireo
_____Red-eyed Vireo
_____Yellow-green Vireo

Jays and Crows (Corvidae)
_____Gray Jay
_____Steller's Jay
_____Blue Jay
_____Island Scrub-Jay
_____Western Scrub-Jay
_____Mexican Jay
_____Pinyon Jay

_____Clark's Nutcracker
_____Black-billed Magpie
_____Yellow-billed Magpie
_____American Crow
_____Northwestern Crow
_____Chihuahuan Raven
_____Common Raven

Larks (Alaudidae)
_____Sky Lark
_____Horned Lark

Swallows (Hirundinidae)
_____Purple Martin
_____Tree Swallow
_____Violet-green Swallow
_____Northern Rough-winged
        Swallow
_____Bank Swallow
_____Cliff Swallow
_____Cave Swallow
_____Barn Swallow

Chickadees and Titmice (Paridae)
_____Black-capped Chickadee
_____Mountain Chickadee
_____Mexican Chickadee
_____Chestnut-backed Chickadee
_____Boreal Chickadee
_____Gray-headed Chickadee
_____Bridled Titmouse
_____Oak Titmouse
_____Juniper Titmouse
_____Black-crested Titmouse

Verdin (Remizidae)
_____Verdin

Bushtits (Aegithalidae)
_____Bushtit

Nuthatches (Sittidae)
_____Red-breasted Nuthatch
_____White-breasted Nuthatch
_____Pygmy Nuthatch

Creepers (Certhiidae)
_____Brown Creeper

Wrens (Troglodytidae)
_____Cactus Wren
_____Rock Wren
_____Canyon Wren
_____Carolina Wren
_____Bewick's Wren
_____House Wren
_____Winter Wren

_____Sedge Wren
_____Marsh Wren
Dippers (Cinclidae)
_____American Dipper
Kinglets (Regulidae)
_____Golden-crowned Kinglet
_____Ruby-crowned Kinglet
**Old World Warblers and
    Gnatcatchers (Sylviidae)**
_____Dusky Warbler
_____Arctic Warbler
_____Blue-gray Gnatcatcher
_____California Gnatcatcher
_____Black-tailed Gnatcatcher
_____Black-capped Gnatcatcher
Thrushes (Turdidae)
_____Siberian Rubythroat
_____Bluethroat
_____Northern Wheatear
_____Eastern Bluebird
_____Western Bluebird
_____Mountain Bluebird
_____Townsend's Solitaire
_____Veery
_____Gray-cheeked Thrush
_____Swainson's Thrush
_____Hermit Thrush
_____Rufous-backed Robin
_____American Robin
_____Varied Thrush
_____Aztec Thrush
Babblers (Timaliidae)
_____Wrentit
**Mockingbirds and Thrashers
    (Mimidae)**
_____Gray Catbird
_____Northern Mockingbird
_____Sage Thrasher
_____Brown Thrasher
_____Long-billed Thrasher
_____Bendire's Thrasher
_____Curve-billed Thrasher
_____California Thrasher
_____Crissal Thrasher
_____Le Conte's Thrasher
Starlings (Sturnidae)
_____European Starling
Accentors (Prunellidae)
_____Siberian Accentor

Wagtails and Pipits (Motacillidae)
_____Eastern Yellow Wagtail
_____White Wagtail
_____Red-throated Pipit
_____American Pipit
_____Sprague's Pipit
Waxwings (Bombycillidae)
_____Bohemian Waxwing
_____Cedar Waxwing
Silky-flycatchers (Ptilogonatidae)
_____Phainopepla
Olive Warbler (Peucedramidae)
_____Olive Warbler
Wood-Warblers (Parulidae)
_____Blue-winged Warbler
_____Golden-winged Warbler
_____Tennessee Warbler
_____Orange-crowned Warbler
_____Nashville Warbler
_____Virginia's Warbler
_____Colima Warbler
_____Lucy's Warbler
_____Northern Parula
_____Tropical Parula
_____Yellow Warbler
_____Chestnut-sided Warbler
_____Magnolia Warbler
_____Cape May Warbler
_____Black-throated Blue Warbler
_____Yellow-rumped Warbler
_____Black-throated Gray Warbler
_____Golden-cheeked Warbler
_____Black-throated Green
    Warbler
_____Townsend's Warbler
_____Hermit Warbler
_____Blackburnian Warbler
_____Yellow-throated Warbler
_____Grace's Warbler
_____Pine Warbler
_____Prairie Warbler
_____Palm Warbler
_____Bay-breasted Warbler
_____Blackpoll Warbler
_____Black-and-white Warbler
_____American Redstart
_____Prothonotary Warbler
_____Worm-eating Warbler
_____Ovenbird

_____Northern Waterthrush
_____Louisiana Waterthrush
_____Kentucky Warbler
_____Connecticut Warbler
_____Mourning Warbler
_____MacGillivray's Warbler
_____Common Yellowthroat
_____Hooded Warbler
_____Wilson's Warbler
_____Canada Warbler
_____Red-faced Warbler
_____Painted Redstart
_____Rufous-capped Warbler
_____Yellow-breasted Chat

Emberizids (Emberizidae)
_____Green-tailed Towhee
_____Spotted Towhee
_____Eastern Towhee
_____Canyon Towhee
_____California Towhee
_____Abert's Towhee
_____Rufous-winged Sparrow
_____Cassin's Sparrow
_____Botteri's Sparrow
_____Rufous-crowned Sparrow
_____Five-striped Sparrow
_____American Tree Sparrow
_____Chipping Sparrow
_____Clay-colored Sparrow
_____Brewer's Sparrow
_____Field Sparrow
_____Black-chinned Sparrow
_____Vesper Sparrow
_____Lark Sparrow
_____Black-throated Sparrow
_____Sage Sparrow
_____Lark Bunting
_____Savannah Sparrow
_____Grasshopper Sparrow
_____Baird's Sparrow
_____Le Conte's Sparrow
_____Nelson's Sparrow
_____Fox Sparrow
_____Song Sparrow
_____Lincoln's Sparrow
_____Swamp Sparrow
_____White-throated Sparrow
_____Harris's Sparrow
_____White-crowned Sparrow

_____Golden-crowned Sparrow
_____Dark-eyed Junco
_____Yellow-eyed Junco
_____McCown's Longspur
_____Lapland Longspur
_____Smith's Longspur
_____Chestnut-collared Longspur
_____Rustic Bunting
_____Snow Bunting
_____McKay's Bunting

Cardinals, Saltators, and Allies (Cardinalidae)
_____Hepatic Tanager
_____Summer Tanager
_____Scarlet Tanager
_____Western Tanager
_____Flame-colored Tanager
_____Northern Cardinal
_____Pyrrhuloxia
_____Yellow Grosbeak
_____Rose-breasted Grosbeak
_____Black-headed Grosbeak
_____Blue Grosbeak
_____Lazuli Bunting
_____Indigo Bunting
_____Varied Bunting
_____Painted Bunting
_____Dickcissel

Blackbirds (Icteridae)
_____Bobolink
_____Red-winged Blackbird
_____Tricolored Blackbird
_____Eastern Meadowlark
_____Western Meadowlark
_____Yellow-headed Blackbird
_____Rusty Blackbird
_____Brewer's Blackbird
_____Common Grackle
_____Great-tailed Grackle
_____Bronzed Cowbird
_____Brown-headed Cowbird
_____Orchard Oriole
_____Hooded Oriole
_____Streak-backed Oriole
_____Bullock's Oriole
_____Baltimore Oriole
_____Scott's Oriole

**Fringilline and Cardueline Finches
and Allies (Fringillidae)**
_____Brambling
_____Gray-crowned Rosy-Finch
_____Black Rosy-Finch
_____Brown-capped Rosy-Finch
_____Pine Grosbeak
_____Purple Finch
_____Cassin's Finch
_____House Finch
_____Red Crossbill

_____White-Winged Crossbill
_____Common Redpoll
_____Hoary Redpoll
_____Pine Siskin
_____Lesser Goldfinch
_____Lawrence's Goldfinch
_____American Goldfinch
_____Evening Grosbeak

Old World Sparrows (Passeridae)
_____House Sparrow

INDEX

SHORE SILHOUETTES

1 Forster's Tern
2 Black Tern
3 Herring Gull
4 Cormorant
5 Loon
6 Great Blue Heron
7 Mallard
8 Pied-billed Grebe
9 Marbled Godwit
10 Greater Yellowlegs
11 Dowitcher
12 Clapper Rail
13 Whimbrel
14 Black-bellied Plover
15 Turnstone
16 Night-Heron
17 Phalarope
18 Least Sandpiper
19 Semipalmated Plover
20 Sanderling
21 Spotted Sandpiper
22 Killdeer
23 Coot
24 Green Heron

FLIGHT SILHOUETTES

1 Barn Swallow
2 Cliff Swallow
3 Purple Martin
4 Vaux's Swift
5 Starling
6 Common Grackle
7 Blackbird
8 Bluebird
9 Robin
10 Goldfinch
11 House Sparrow
12 Belted Kingfisher
13 Steller's Jay
14 Flicker
15 Mourning Dove
16 Meadowlark
17 Bobwhite
18 Ruffed Grouse
19 Pheasant
20 Nighthawk
21 Crow
22 Sharp-shinned Hawk
23 Kestrel
24 Killdeer
25 Wilson's Snipe